MARY ELIZABETH BRADDON

MARY ELIZABETH BRADDON (1835-1915) was born in Frith
Street, London, the daughter of a solicitor. In about 1840 her parents
separated and she and her mother Fanny moved to St. Leonards-On-Sea
for a short time, after which she spent the rest of her childhood in
London. In the 1850s she took to the stage under the name of Mary
Seyton, her mother accompanying her throughout as 'Mrs. Seyton.' She
performed in numerous provincial towns and cities, and also acted at the
Surrey Theatre, London for one season. During her career as an actress
she wrote poetry and plays in her spare time, and it was during these
years that her first works were published. She left the stage in February
1860 to become a full time writer and her first novel, *Three Times
Dead*, was published by a local publisher in Beverley. In September of
1860 she moved to London, and the following year the novels which
were to make her famous, *Lady Audley's Secret* and *Aurora Floyd*,
began to be serialised in two magazines belonging to the publisher John
Maxwell. Braddon also wrote a number of anonymous novels for lower
class journals, of which *The Black Band; or, The Mysteries of Midnight*
(1861-1862) is the most well known. At this time she set up home with
her publisher, becoming stepmother to his six children, and having six
children of her own. Maxwell was separated from his first wife, due to
her mental instability after the birth of their last child, and Braddon and
Maxwell were not able to marry until after her death in 1874. In 1866
Braddon became editor of Maxwell's magazine *Belgravia*, and this
became the vehicle for most of her novels in the following ten years. In
total Braddon was the author of ninety novels (several were
unacknowledged), numerous short stories, essays and several plays.
From controversial beginnings as a purveyor of immoral sensation
fiction, she became a respected writer. Her last novel, *Mary* (1916), was
published posthumously.

THE LITERARY LIVES OF
MARY ELIZABETH BRADDON
A STUDY OF HER LIFE AND WORK

JENNIFER CARNELL

HASTINGS
THE SENSATION PRESS
2000

This edition published in the United Kingdom in 2000
The Sensation Press
116 Sedlescombe Road North
Hastings
East Sussex TN37 7EN
United Kingdom
Tel/Fax 01424 423780
e-mail: sensationbooks@hotmail.com

A CIP catalogue record for this book is available from the British Library

ISBN 1-902580-02-8

Printed and bound in Great Britain by Biddles Ltd, www.biddles.co.uk

Contents

ILLUSTRATIONS

Theatre Royal Winchester playbill, 14 September 1853, reproduced courtesy of
Winchester City Museum.
'Miss Braddon in Her Daring Flight', Braddon and Maxwell in *The Mask*, 1868
'Miss M.E. Braddon', *Home Journal*, 1874.
Annesley Bank as it is today
M.E. Braddon, *Bookman*, 1912.
'Miss Braddon' by Yoshio Markino, c.1914

Acknowledgements

I would especially like to thank Mary Elizabeth Braddon's grandson, the late Henry Maxwell, for his friendship and encouragement. Thanks are also due to the staff of Brighton Reference Library, Hertfordshire County Records Office, the Harry Ransom Humanities Research Center at the University of Texas at Austin, Richmond Local Studies Collection, Mrs. Brisbane and the Winchester City Museum, June Carnell, Edwin Cole, Vanessa Dinning, Ian and Mildred Karten, Professor Graham Law, my tutor Dr. Sally Ledger, Judy Mckenzie, Professor Michael Slater, Dr. Nicholas Salmon and Chris Willis. I received a travel grant to visit the Harry Ransom Center at the University of Texas from the University of London Central Research Fund and a further contribution from the English Department of Birkbeck College.

In memory of Henry Maxwell.

Introduction

Mary Elizabeth Braddon (1835-1915), the author of approximately ninety books written between 1860 and 1915, was one of the most popular and prolific novelists of her age. As well as being an editor of two magazines, *Belgravia* and the Christmas annual *Mistletoe Bough*, her vast output also included poetry, plays and essays. In the 1860s she was one of the most successful and controversial novelists of her generation, rated alongside Wilkie Collins as the inventor of the sensation genre. These novels were characterised by mystery, strong passions and opinions, and intricate plotting. After the publication of the two novels which made her famous, *Lady Audley's Secret* (1862) and *Aurora Floyd* (1863), Braddon was criticised as a purveyor of immoral fiction.

Novel after novel flowed from her pen, often at the rate of two per year. Braddon also wrote novels influenced by French realism, working class fiction, detective novels, historical novels and 'straight' novels. Her use of, and contribution to, popular culture over many decades provides an excellent insight into the development of genre fiction.

Loved by the subscribers to circulating libraries, and condemned by critics, Braddon was one of the best selling novelists of the nineteenth century. Yet after her death Braddon's work was seen as old fashioned and her novels were gradually forgotten, except as a byword for ridiculous situations and melodrama. Her son Edward failed to interest Cassell in a plan to reprint *Lady Audley's Secret* and *Henry Dunbar* in 1930, and another son, the novelist W.B. Maxwell, wrote in his autobiography, 'Nowadays I am sometimes wounded by the tone of references publicly made to my mother as a writer. The words are not unkind, but they imply a sort of amused tolerance.'[1] A tribute paid by Sir Arthur Quiller-Couch at the time of Braddon's death would have seemed most unlikely:

> Miss Braddon and Wilkie Collins will be studied some day as respectfully as people now study the more sensational Elizabethans.[2]

After decades of neglect, and following the rise of feminist criticism since the 1970s, and the work of people such as Elaine Showalter and Lyn Pykett, critics responded to Braddon and the subversive heroines of two of her earliest novels, *Lady Audley's Secret* (1862) and *Aurora Floyd* (1863), and their place in the sensation fiction of the early 1860s.[3] However, anyone writing about Braddon owes a great debt to her biographer, Robert Lee Wolff, since it was he who did so much to bring about the current revival of interest in Braddon's life and work.[4] At first it seemed as if it would not be possible to add anything new to his carefully researched book, with its wealth of original source material, but as I began to research Braddon's years as an actress and her earliest years as a writer, it became clear to me that there remained much to be discovered and discussed. The biographical chapters are mainly concerned with these early years of Braddon's career, because it seemed to me that this period is less known about and yet of great interest. It is also these years, during which she defied the conventional path of life for a middle class girl by becoming an actress and eventually deciding to live as the common law wife of the publisher John Maxwell, that have attracted the interest of commentators on her fiction. It certainly singles her out as one of the most remarkable and talented women of her generation. This work has only been possible by using newspapers of the period, and I have also made use of Wolff's own considerable collection of Braddon manuscript material.

The first two chapters are almost completely biographical; chapters three to five follow Braddon's development as a successful writer, taking into account contemporary cultural influences. Biographical details are interjected into these later chapters when relevant, but the need for biography covering the later years of Braddon's life was lessened for me because Wolff has already covered them so well in his book. Inevitably one book cannot hope to cover every novel and every year of Braddon's life, but I hope that my work provides much which is new and interesting.

This book is an extended version of my PhD thesis, and is very much a hybrid in that it is both biographical and literary critical, the latter with an emphasis on the bibliographical and cultural-historical. The reason for this is that I aimed to focus as much as possible on the new biographical material, and it is Braddon's early life and career which seemed to especially warrant new research.

Footnotes

1. W.B. Maxwell, *Time Gathered*, p.283.
2. 'Death of Miss Braddon. Great Victorian Novelist. Tributes by Novelists of To-Day', *Daily Mail*, 5 February 1915, p.3.
3. Elaine Showalter, *A Literature of Their Own: British Women Novelists from Bronte to Lessing* (1977: revised London: Virago, 1982); Lyn Pykett, *The Improper Feminine: The Women's Sensation Novel and the New Woman Writing* (London: Routledge, 1992).
4. Robert Lee Wolff, *Sensational Victorian: The Life and Fiction of Mary Elizabeth Braddon* (New York: Garland, 1979).

The Early Years

One of Braddon's regrets was that she had not been born at Skisdon, the home of her grandmother, at St. Kew in Cornwall.[1] Had she been born two days earlier she would have been, but her mother, Fanny, gave birth in London on 4 October 1835 after an uncomfortable stage coach journey of two days. Instead she was born at 2 Frith Street, Soho, the youngest and last child of Henry and Fanny Braddon.[2]

Henry Braddon had been born at Skisdon, as had his brothers and sisters, and he had been educated at a school in nearby Liskeard. He was a solicitor, listed in the law guides as a 'London attorney', and at the time his daughter was born was working from home. This was a respectable enough profession, but Henry Braddon did not conduct himself respectably and was a sore disappointment to his family. After university his mother had bought him a partnership in a well known firm of solicitors, but after only one year the firm preferred to return her money rather than keep him.

Despite this initial setback he had continued with his profession, and in his early twenties he married a nineteen year old Irish girl, Fanny White, the daughter of Anne Babington, a Protestant from Limerick who converted to Catholicism after her marriage to Patrick White. Fanny's uncle was Colonel Babington of County Cavan, who had been a well known cavalry officer in the 14th Light Dragoons during the Peninsular War. The marriage of Anne and Patrick White was not a happy one; Patrick White was not a 'satisfactory person', and Braddon wrote that her grandmother was financially provided for by kind and wealthy friends. The four children of the marriage, three daughters and a son, were brought up as Protestants, and the son later became a vicar in Lincolnshire.

Fanny was educated at various English boarding schools, in Battersea, Newbury and Hereford, and when her sister Mary Anne married William Frederick Delane she went to live with her sister and brother-in-law in Bracknell, Berkshire. At this time William Frederick Delane was a barrister, who had suffered financial losses after an unwise business investment, when he was offered the position of business editor of *The Times*. The connection with *The Times* continued into the next generation, and Fanny's nephew, John Thadeus Delane (1817-1879), became the editor of *The Times* at the age of twenty three in 1841.

At nineteen Fanny White married Henry Braddon. Braddon wrote that her mother later told her that on her part it was not a love match (she had loved another who was now dead), and, although considered handsome by others, was scathing about her husband's appearance – his brown eyes reminded her of those of oxen. He mislead William Delane, who acted as trustee, when a marriage settlement of three hundred pounds a year to be made on Fanny, never brought in more than forty. The marriage started as it was to continue when a financial crisis soon after the wedding meant that all of the new furniture at their home in Alfred Place, as well as Fanny's wedding presents, had to be given up. Braddon observed:

> Mama's life after Alfred Place was acquainted with such trouble as a wife endowed by nature with a delicate and scrupulous honesty, must needs suffer when linked to a careless and happy-go-lucky gentleman who is nobody's enemy but his own. (p.29)

The first of their children, Margaret Eleanor, known as Maggie (1824-1868), was eleven years Mary Braddon's senior and Edward Nicholas Coventry (1829-1904) was eight years older and at a prep school on the Fulham Road when Braddon was a little girl. Presumably because Henry Braddon could not afford to support all of his children, Maggie lived with her grandmother and aunts at Skisdon, and the two sisters were not formally introduced until Maggie was fifteen and Mary four. Despite being the only child in the house Braddon never felt lonely. Her father worked downstairs, and his cousin lived with them at this time while he trained to be a solicitor.

Entertainment at this period for Mary was provided by being taken by their maid to have lunch at her mother's house, and a first trip to the theatre. Braddon's nurse was called Sarah Allen, and she had previously been employed by the Delanes during the time Fanny had lived with them. Sarah Allen said she was part American Indian, but Fanny believed the Norfolk farmer's daughter was of African descent. Mrs. Allen took Mary for frequent walks around the streets of Soho, and to St. James's Park where there were cake stalls and cows still grazed. Braddon's memoirs for this period are full of nostalgia for a way of life which no longer existed, for a London which was simpler and slower compared to the city of 1914 which was changed beyond recognition. Other treats Braddon remembered were being taken to the Soho Bazaar, and being allowed to have a little girl to tea for her fourth birthday. Soon after she and her mother were to leave Frith Street, as all was not well in the Braddon home.

Braddon remembered her whiskered father as being proud of his appearance, particularly of his small feet, with a fondness for filing his nails when he should have been working, and that he was always smart and well dressed. Although he was popular and seemed kind to Braddon when he presented her with sixpence each Sunday, years later she was

told and often said herself, 'Papa was nobody's enemy but his own.'
Henry Braddon's business practices were to set a pattern for the many
dishonest and disreputable father's in Braddon's fiction, and it was not
to be wondered that Fanny Braddon soon came to regret her marriage.
In these early years in Frith Street, Henry Braddon worked from home,
and it was not uncommon for him to omit to pay his clerks their wages
and to get Fanny to tell them that he was not at home. In later life
Braddon found herself looking at the successful solicitors among her
acquaintance, and wishing her father could have been like them.

When Braddon was four years old, Fanny discovered compromising
letters, and, realising her husband was having an affair, initiated a
separation. Divorce was out of the question and, even if it had been
financially possible, a husband's adultery was not sufficient grounds for
obtaining one. Fanny never condemned her husband to her daughter,
and Braddon only discovered the cause of the separation when she
found the letters among her mother's papers after her death. Although
husband and wife only met occasionally after this, Braddon said they
managed to do so without rancour. Fanny Braddon sounds as if she was
a remarkable woman in her own right: unusually for a woman of the
time she had refused to ignore her husband's adultery, she was to
condone and live with her daughter during her years on the stage, and
after she had left the stage and set up home with John Maxwell, even
editing at least one of John Maxwell's magazines. When Mrs. Braddon
died in 1868 her daughter's grief was so immense that she had a
complete mental breakdown and wrote nothing for over a year.

After their separation in February 1840, Henry Braddon moved to
chambers in Covent Garden and Fanny moved with a Mrs. Walden,
who had also left her husband, to live in a house on Maize Hill in St.
Leonards-On-Sea in East Sussex. At this time St. Leonards was a
relatively new and genteel seaside resort, much of it designed by James
Burton (who had hoped to make it another Bath). It was Mrs. Walden
who decided the little girl should learn to read, and lessons began
immediately. Braddon's principal memory from this period was being
taken to the chemist shop under the colonnades on the sea front to be
dosed with medicine. Possibly their new home proved too expensive, as
this was only the first of many moves in the next few years, and while
in St. Leonards they lived briefly in two other houses.

They then returned to London, to a house in Half Moon Street in
Mayfair, where Braddon suffered with a bad chest, and for which Mrs.
Allen, with whom they were reunited after St. Leonards, was blamed
and dismissed. Then they lived in a house near the Strand, and soon
there was another move, this time to Kensington. Here they were joined
by Maggie who had been to a school in Bodmin, where apparently she

learnt little, but where her aunts had been educated. She was to be 'finished' at Scarsdale School, and Braddon accompanied her for six months as the youngest pupil at the school.

Braddon went on her first visit to Skisdon, where her grandmother was now nearly ninety years old. Skisdon was an exciting place for a young child, and Braddon admired the gardens, dairy and brewery. Her uncle, John Braddon, was a solicitor and a keen angler, and through fishing he became a friend of Douglas Cook of the *Saturday Review*; one day the friendship ensured at least one good review in that most critical of journals. At Skisdon Braddon met and admired her cousins Annie and Maria, the daughters of William Braddon who had been a judge for thirty years in Bengal, and whose son William was now working for a commercial company in Calcutta. Braddon never saw her grandmother again, but the house continued to exert an emotional hold on her as the home of the Braddons. Many years later, in 1866, Braddon was to own Skisdon before selling it to her cousin. She was always proud of her Cornish ancestry, often mentioning that it was a Braddon who had represented Cornwall in the first parliament of Elizabeth I, and many of her novels use Cornish settings, and numerous characters bear Cornish surnames.

Fanny and her daughter then moved to the Vale of Heath, Hampstead, where they rented a furnished house for a year from Mr. Greene. Here the six year old Braddon had a governess, Miss Parrot who had taught English at Scarsdale. Next Braddon and her mother moved to 10 Hammersmith Terrace, an attractive street on the waterfront.[3] The area was still relatively rural, Hammersmith was still in Middlesex and Chiswick was a village. This was their home for the next five years and she was to have her first real friends, two little girls who lived next door, Charley and Polly Cayne. Edward and Maggie came for Christmas, and Edward was much admired by all who met him. There were occasional visits to the Delanes in Chatham Place, Blackfriars, their only relatives close enough to visit on foot, but hampers still came from Cornwall with hams and cream, and muslin and other Indian treasures arrived from William Braddon.

Edward was clever, designing his own home-made magazines, and winning competitions in the *Family Herald*, where his only prize was the printing of his initials 'E.N.C.B.' He spent his school holidays divided between his two parents, and Braddon felt much closer to him than her grownup sister. At seven she was so close to her mother that she still shared her bed. She was always relieved that no man '*living*' ever came between them, and as she grew older her mother confided in her about her loveless marriage. Braddon later revealed that from an early age:

> I was my mother's constant companion and confidante, and she
> told me much that is not generally told to a girl before her
> Kenwigg's pigtails are exchanged for a coil of plaits in a
> tortoiseshell comb. (p.30)

Braddon frequently tore her frocks (attempting to mend them in secret), and admitted she was careless with her clothes even in her late teens. For the moment one of her greatest friends was her mother's cook, Sarah Hobbs, a singer of ballads, who kept a tame rat in the kitchen, introduced her to the novels of Edward Bulwer Lytton in the form of an abridged copy of *The Last Days of Pompeii*, and told the eight year old child gory stories of the fourteen inquests she had attended. Sarah Hobbs also took her to see a non conformist preacher, Mr. Miller, and to the Chiswick Fair where they saw peep shows and a performance of *Maria Marten and the Red Barn*.

At the age of eight Braddon attended a day school, run by two young women, the Roslyn sisters, in a house in Black Lion Lane, and where her mother took singing lessons from the elder of the proprietors. Fanny taught her daughter French, and then, perhaps to save money, she decided to educate her entirely at home. In this way Braddon was learning Shakespearean speeches before she was ten years old, and her mother ensured she became a proficient pianist.

Braddon was still exceptionally close to her mother, and she was soon to berate herself for initiating a separation. An elderly friend of her mother's, an upholsterer called Miss Godfrey, had done some work for the Misses Barnet who ran a boarding school called Dartmouth Lodge just off the Old Brompton Road. Enthralled by Miss Godfrey's descriptions of how lovely the school was, the wonderful parties and delicious meals, Braddon asked her mother if she might go. Fanny thought it would teach her to be more ordered and not to lose things so often, and it was agreed that Braddon, now aged nine, would begin there in January 1845.[4]

After school Edward spent a brief time at University College London and then went to work in India in 1847, first for his cousin William the merchant in Calcutta, and then as an estate manager, before working for the East India Railway.[5] Fanny Braddon and her daughters moved to a villa in Camberwell, and in 1848 Fanny decided she would have to take a lodger. It is not known what type of schooling Braddon received in her early teens, but an article in the *Mask* stated Braddon received some of her education in France.[6] If so it was probably not for long, and it may have been under her mother's guidance rather than an actual school.

The girls saw their father sometimes, but others saw him more frequently. A distant cousin, Jane Dayman, often saw Henry Braddon during these years, when he was a guest of her drawing mistress and her mother at a house in St. John's Wood, and she remembered he often spoke of his children, and was especially proud of Edward.[7] When Mary and Maggie did see him, he would ask after the family in Cornwall, but Braddon did not think he returned there 'after his self-enmity developed in fatal ways.' (p.26) Later Braddon and her mother were to be alone once more, as Maggie was to marry an Italian called Antonio Cartighoni.[8] Of these years the nearest to a first hand account is to be found in the early chapters of *The Story of Barbara* (1880) and *A Lost Eden* (1904). In the former her mother appears as Flora Trevornock, 'Irish by birth, English by culture', separated from her solicitor husband, who is deemed 'nobody's enemy but his own'[9] by his friends, but more harmful when he has exploited the trust of his relatives as the 'black sheep of his highly respectable family.' (p.14) The phrases are almost identical in novel and memoirs when describing her father.

Probably, like the Trevornocks of South Lane, Camberwell in the early 1850s, the Camberwell Braddons worried about bills and rates, made trips to the local shops on the Walworth Road and:

> were those social pariahs, poor relations. They belonged to a good old Cornish family, and were very proud of their ancient and eminently respectable lineage. They had uncles and cousins in both services, uncles and cousins well planted in the garden of the Church; but of all these well-placed kindred it was their destiny to see but little. The rich Trevornocks were not unkind or unfeeling. If they had been, the poor Trevornocks could hardly have gone on existing, for it was partly to periodical remittances from her well-to-do relations that Mrs. Trevornock owed her means of living. (p.13)

The Trevornocks receive about £150 a year from relatives, but remain well dressed through the boxes of clothes which arrive regularly from an aunt. The sisters are occasional visitors to their father's chambers at No. 2 St. Alban's Court, Gray's Inn, which resemble those of Braddon's father's down to the japanned boxes with the names of Cornish clients, and where Flossie, like Maggie Braddon, tries to get money out of him for the water rates and badgers him for little things like pens and paper. Like Braddon's father he sits filing his nails and, other than for trifles, Mr. Trevornock has contributed nothing to their home and upkeep. In common with Fanny Braddon, Mrs. Trevornock was humiliated by her husband's debts, executions on their house, the loss of her wedding presents to creditors, and left to face the wageless staff while "Pa used to go to his club, and to races and gambling-houses, and enjoy himself, leaving his clerks without their salaries.' (p.32) Eventually Mrs. Trevornock packed her bags and left with her daughters. Braddon was frank in her novel about Mr. Trevornock's dissolute habits:

> His family had been full of forbearance and long-suffering; they had propped him up when he lurched, and had picked him up and set him on his feet when he fell. But there was an unconquerable downward inclination in Thomas Trevornock. He had vices of which his daughters knew nothing. He had been a drunkard and a gambler. He had squandered his money amidst the lowest surroundings; he had wallowed in the gutter. He had been engaged in so many doubtful transactions that it was a marvel that he had escaped being struck off the rolls. (p.43)

Assuming this part of the novel matches the life of the Braddon family at this time, and, like Mr. Trevornock, Henry Braddon also had chambers at Gray's Inn in the early 1850s,[10] he was actually making some money, and able to 'maintain a reputable appearance in his neatly furnished office' (p.43). So much so that his family thought it was a pity he and his wife did not get back together.

Despite the separation of her parents, Braddon's life was not so very different from many middle class families without ample means. Yet far from waiting to get married, Braddon's path was to be very different. Tall with curly auburn hair, she was musical, and later described as having a very fine speaking voice, and she decided to become an actress.

FOOTNOTES

1. M.E. Braddon, *Before the Knowledge of Evil*, c.1914, unpublished typescript in the Robert Lee Wolff Collection of Victorian Fiction, Harry Ransom Humanities Research Center, The University of Texas at Austin, hereafter referred to as the Wolff Collection. Most of the information here is taken from this account, which consists of Braddon's memoirs of her life from birth until the age of eight. For some reason Braddon gave made-up names to some of the places – for instance, Frith Street is called Fourth Street.

2. The Family Record Center lists from their microfilms of parish registers, a daughter born a year before Braddon: Frances, christened, like Mary at St. Anne's in Soho, on 15 October 1834, the daughter of Henry and Fanny Braddon. She must have died shortly after, and Braddon makes no mention of this sister in her memoirs.

3. In *Before the Knowledge of Evil*, Braddon called Hammersmith Terrace 'Loutherburg Terrace', after the painter J. De Loutherburg who had once lived there.

4. In 'My First Book', Braddon refers to 'My brief experience of boarding school' (p.22) In this account she called the school Cresswell Lodge, which was almost certainly not the real name.

5. 'Death of Sir Edward Braddon', *Tasmanian Mail*, 6 February 1904, p.32.

6. 'Miss Braddon', *The Mask*, vol. I, June 1868, p.137.

7. Letter from K.G. Burns, 12 December 1909, Wolff collection. Burns was Jane Dayman's nephew, and was researching the family tree.

8. The marriage between Maggie and Antonio Cartighoni may have taken place as late as 1860, as a letter from one of the Sawyers in the Wolff collection makes the event sound recent. Maggie had a son called Nicolino.

9. Mary Elizabeth Braddon, *The Story of Barbara* (London: Maxwell, 1880; repr. London: Maxwell, c.1881), p.43.

10. Henry Braddon, according to *Walford's County Families* (1901) died in 1873. I have not located a death certificate, obituary or will for this date, which may mean the year is an error or that he died abroad. (The Henry Braddon I referred to in my PhD thesis as dying in Upton in 1852 turned out to be an unrelated baby) Henry Braddon is listed as a solicitor in the *Law List*, *Post Office London Directory* and *Webster's Red Book* at the following addresses: 29 Southampton Street, Covent Garden 1841; 14 Furnival's Inn, Holborn 1842-1844; 8 Gray's Inn 1851-1852; 5 Danes-inn, Strand 1859-1870.

Chapter One
Mary Elizabeth Braddon's Career as an Actress

In the summer of 1876, when Braddon was forty years old and at the height of her fame as a novelist, she acted in two plays for a special gala evening at the Theatre Royal, Gloucester Street on Jersey. Braddon and her husband returned from their holiday in France to stay at the island's Harris's Hotel in Pier Road before the performance. An advert in all of the local newspapers, including the *Jersey Express* on the 5th of August, announced:

Mr. Wybert Rousby has the pleasure to announce that MISS M.E. BRADDON, THE EMINENT NOVELIST, Authoress of 'Lady Audley's Secret', 'Aurora Floyd', 'Henry Dunbar', 'Joshua Haggard's Daughter', & c. c., being on a visit to the island, has kindly consented to repeat her performance of *Pauline* in DANCE'S Comedy of "Delicate Ground". In which Mr. Rousby had the honour to assist her, in an entertainment, given at her private residence Lichfield House, Richmond.[1]

Naturally this unusual announcement was of the greatest of interest to those on the island, and the chance of witnessing a usually reticent celebrity was too good to be missed. For years, almost since the beginning of her literary fame in the early 1860s, Braddon had always attempted to prevent the public circulation and sale of photographs of herself, even refusing them as gifts to acquaintances, and she preferred, in social situations, that the public did not know that Mrs. Maxwell was the novelist M.E. Braddon.[2] It was, therefore, surprising she should have chosen to make such an exhibition of herself. Although much of the notoriety caused by her 1860s fiction had died down by this date it was only two years after the disagreeable publicity caused when John Maxwell tried to hush up the existence and death of his first wife; the resulting disapproval causing them to vacate their home in Richmond for a year while the scandal died down. Now they were married Braddon was not so shy, but doubtless the rumours, as well as the popularity of her fiction, contributed to the curiosity the event provoked. One newspaper observed she:

must have been flattered (if not amused) at the amount of eager interest manifested by the Jersey public to become acquainted with a "live authoress", – rather an unusual phenomenon in our insular home – and the vast concourse of persons assembled to gratify a morbid curiosity, must have struck her very forcibly as a curious trait of human nature.[3]

In the first play, Charles Dance's *Delicate Ground* (1849), Braddon played Pauline and Rousby appeared as Citizen Sangfroid. The play only had one other part. A comedy, lasting one hour, the roles had been originally played by Charles Mathews and Madame Vestris. Set in post revolutionary France, Pauline is the bored wife of the cold politician Citizen Sangfroid, whom she had married to save her father's life. Alphonse de Grandier, the former aristocratic love she thought dead, reappears and urges her to run away with him. However, her jealousy is aroused by the ease with which Sangfroid offers her a divorce, and, becoming convinced he has another woman, realises it is her husband she really cares for. The comedy ensues when Sangfroid insists on addressing his wife as 'Citizen' and at his convincing his rival that he will be getting a bad deal if he takes on Pauline. In *Still Waters Run Deep* (1853) by Tom Taylor, Braddon was supported by other amateurs: Captain Warren of the 81st Regiment, Captain Hall and H.R. Day of the 47th Regiment, and the well known playwright Paul Meritt.[4]

Every local newspaper covered the event, although any praise was grudgingly given, and the *Jersey Express* described a packed and fashionable house:

> Miss Braddon, we believe, has never appeared on a public stage before, but has on one or two occasions taken part in private theatricals at her own residence. The drama, therefore, is not her forte, though she evidently possesses powers not generally observable in lady amateurs. The fame of Miss Braddon and the desire to see her secured such a house as the walls of the old theatre have not seen for many a long day or night. It was crowded in every part and the sight to the managerial vision must have proved unusually dazzling. His Excellency the Lieutenant Governor and family were present, and the boxes, dress stalls, pit, gallery, everywhere was filled.[5]

The *Jersey Weekly Press and Independent* also believed it was Braddon's first public performance, and while claiming to make allowances for her as an amateur, it still believed her performance to be a world apart from that of the experienced professional actress:

> (she) was greeted on Friday week by a crowded and fashionable audience on what, we believe, is her first public appearance as a theatrical amateur. That great expectations should have been

entertained of her performance on stage was natural. But, if they were entertained, they were not reasonable. It is unlikely on the face of it that an accomplished authoress should be at the same time a great actress, and still less likely in the absence of previous experience. In point of fact, Miss Braddon proved to be a very fair amateur; and beyond that nothing is to be said of her performance. Amateurs are by privilege exempt from criticism; and therefore we are precluded from particular remarks. Miss Braddon would, however, bear the ordeal much better than most amateurs; and it may be remarked, generally, that she forms an artistic conception of the parts she has taken, which we can well understand would be well received among a small audience in a bijou theatre. But without the development of experience, it is scarcely possible she should possess the capacity of judicious exaggeration by which the trained actor conveys dramatic expression to a large audience. Her performance was, however, absolutely respectable in point of ability; and this under the circumstances is praise relatively high as it is actually just. (...) As Pauline she seemed to have more congenial scope for her bent, which appears to be rather towards light comedy, than to the severity of emotion which belongs to Mrs. Sternhold. But deficiency in vocal power told against her in both characters; and, as may be inferred from what we have said before, her demeanour and gestures are lacking in the breadth and incisiveness which only the trained actress can command.[6]

The critic claimed leniency because of Braddon's amateur status, yet made clear that her performance was only that of a competent amateur. Perhaps he would have adjusted his judgement accordingly, and not have perceived this alleged lack of breadth in her acting, if he had known that twenty years earlier Braddon had been a professional actress. It was not uncommon for celebrity or very rich amateur actors who took an occasional role with a professional company for fun to be given bad reviews; perhaps because they were bad, but also because there was prejudice against rich dilettantes for robbing legitimate actors of their roles. But Braddon had acted under the name of Mary Seyton in London and at many provincial theatres, and had done so for eight years, from 1852 to 1860.

Moreover, in 1857 her co-star in Beverley and Hull was the aforementioned Wybert Rousby, yet none of this was mentioned in the advertising, nor a correction issued to the mistaken reviewers. Rousby obviously did not speak of Braddon's past, or word would have got round. Had Braddon's appearance taken place in London or in one of the towns where she had acted in her youth, her past would probably have been recalled. Her association with Rousby in amateur theatricals would have been easily accounted for by the fact that he and his wife had starred in the play she wrote in 1873, *Griselda*. Braddon may well have agreed to act on this occasion because Rousby was in financial difficulties after separating from his wife Clara,[7] and the *Jersey Observer* declared that the full house must have been:

> a sight which must have rejoiced the hearts of those hardworked artistes who for the last two months have endeavoured to amuse, instruct and interest our little community, and that with ill success – but only as far, however, as the money question is concerned.[8]

Sadly Braddon never wrote a public account of her experiences as an actress, dying before she completed her memoirs in which she had only reached the age of eight.[9] Nearly the only press references to it are during the height of her fame in the 1860s, and these are usually in the form of snide hints in reviews.[10] In the many obituaries in 1915 only that of the *Daily Telegraph* had any knowledge of her years on the stage;[11] by this date almost everyone who could remember those years in the 1850s was already dead. In fact so adverse was public opinion concerning the moral state of actresses through much of the nineteenth century that Braddon probably preferred not to bring her past to public attention. Despite this reticence she remained fascinated by the stage; and as indicated by the advertisement she clearly continued to give private performances at her own home, and probably at the homes of friends. For a personal account of her career on the stage and thoughts on the theatre one has to look at a few non-fiction articles and to her novels for clues. Using her novels, newspapers of the 1850s and playbills, this chapter attempts to reconstruct chronologically Braddon's years on the stage from 1852 to 1860.

As a former actress Braddon obviously experienced first-hand the life of a provincial actress. The theatre and the lives of actresses frequently appear in her fiction, and there can be little doubt that their experiences are in part autobiographical. Although it would be unwise to mistake fiction for strict autobiography there are enough clues as to the locations where she acted and the parts she played to suggest Braddon enjoyed putting such details in; for example Justina in *A Strange World* (1875) acts in the Doncaster and York area just as Braddon did, Eliza in *Aurora Floyd* (1863) acts in Lancashire, the concert singer in *Lucius Davoren* (1873) performs in some of the towns where Braddon acted: Stillmington (clearly intended to be Coventry), Brighton, Liverpool and York. In *The Green Curtain* (1911) the actor Godwin acts in Southampton and Reading, just as Braddon had. Doubtless some of her theatrical contemporaries would have recognised many disguised names and 'in jokes'.

The "Lost Years": Mary Braddon's Early Career As An Actress

Although Braddon's career as an actress was highlighted by Robert Lee Wolff's biography, and has often been remarked upon since, remarkably little has been known of the actual details of which companies she worked for and what sort of roles she played. Wolff states that Braddon's acting role in Beverley in 1857 was one of her first appearances on the stage, and that her career therefore lasted for just three years.[12] Wolff's belief in a three year career may have stemmed from the *Daily Telegraph* obituary from which he gained most of his information, and although it gives a great deal of information about Braddon's career when other obituary writers had only hinted at it, it is far from infallible. This stated that Braddon's first stage appearance was as Fairy Pineapple in the Brighton pantomime, *The Prince of Happy Land*, but that is impossible because the production of *The Prince of Happy Land* took place *after* her appearance at Beverley. However, it was always unlikely that even this Beverley performance was really one of her first appearances on the stage. A young actress with no previous experience would rarely have plunged straight into major speaking roles, even in the provincial theatre. Moreover, Braddon is supposed to have appeared as Cinderella in a Liverpool pantomime at a date which must be earlier than 1857.[13] It is now clear that rather than a brief theatrical career of three years, Braddon was in fact on the stage at seventeen years old in 1853, therefore pointing at a career of seven years, and probably eight, in length at least. Her career has been described as unsuccessful, partly because Wolff, misunderstanding an advert he saw in the leading theatrical newspaper the *Era*, said 'even after two years on the stage, MEB in Brighton apparently did not often play speaking parts.'[14]

In actual fact by this date, 1859, Braddon had been on the stage for seven years, always had speaking parts, and had even enjoyed a season at the Surrey Theatre in London as a leading lady. I have discovered that Braddon acted in more towns than has previously been known. Doubtless more will gradually emerge, but so far my researches have revealed that they include Bath, Winchester, Southampton, Reading, Aberdeen, Glasgow, Beverley, Hull, Coventry, Leamington Spa, Stamford, Brighton, Lewes, Doncaster, Leeds, and probably Liverpool and York.[15] Her years on the stage must have been arduous with usually three plays a night, of which it appears she often appeared in two. Long runs of just one play did not exist in the 1850s, so there would have been a large repertoire of roles to learn.

Braddon was also fortunate enough to work with some of the biggest names of the period when they left London and guest starred in provincial towns like Brighton. Amongst these famous actors were Charles and Ellen Kean, Alfred and Mrs. Wigan, Charles and Mrs. Mathews, the African American Ira Aldridge, Mr. and Mrs. Calvert, and Madame Celeste.

For a young woman to go on the stage in the early 1850s was both unusual and shocking. In 1909 Braddon wrote a short piece for *The Press Album* called 'The Woman I Remember', in which she contrasted the position of the young woman of fifty years earlier with that of her Edwardian grandaughter. At a time of the women's suffrage movement and increasing educational opportunities, 1909 presented a world of freedom and opportunity which could have been scarcely conceivable in the 1850s. Braddon depicted the girl of the early 1850s as conventional and timid, and who hardly dared to have an opinion or ambition of her own. As to careers in the 1850s she declared that compared to the present there was very little choice, and if a girl chose a career that offended convention, especially as an actress, the girl sacrificed all claim to respectability:

> Of all those gates which are now open to feminine suitors there were but two open to her. She could go out into the world as a governess, like Jane Eyre, in an age when to be a governess in a vulgar family was worse than the treadmill; or she could go upon the stage, a proceeding which convulsed her family, to the most distant cousin, a thing to be spoken of with bated breath, as the lapse of a lost soul, the fall from Porchester Terrace to the bottomless pit.[16]

Yet this was exactly what the young Braddon did. It was an exceptionally brave and unusual decision for one of her class, and at a time when actresses were often considered immoral, not only by the conservative wing of the church which frequently urged its congregation to boycott the theatre, but as Michael Baker writes:

> Her public exposure automatically linked her in the popular imagination with that other class of public women, prostitutes (...and) equated unconventional female conduct with sexual licence.[17]

Braddon's friend from her earliest days on the stage, Mrs. Adelaide Calvert, later wrote of the great intolerance against actors, and that the reason why actors lived so amongst their own community 'was because they were seldom asked to go anywhere else. Like the heretics of old, the ban of the Church was upon them.'[18] Mrs. Calvert could think of many examples of discrimination from those who considered the stage sinful and an association with actors scandalous. Mrs. Calvert attributed the later change in attitude to the increase of actors and actresses from non theatrical backgrounds, and who were usually middle class. But in the 1850s the middle class influx was some decades off, as was the idea of a respectable actress and even actor. For actresses the gentrification took place later, as Henry Irving's knighthood was accepted in 1895, while his female contemporary Ellen Terry did not get her D.B.E. until 1925 nor Braddon's own close friend Madge Kendal until 1926.

In the 1850s it was recognised that not every young woman was bound to get married. The surplus women problem was already being discussed and enumerated.[19] While it was commonplace for working class women to work, it was uncertain if and what work middle class women should be allowed to do. There was at least some recognition that some middle class women might have to, as a consequence of the fearful fate of spinsterhood, find some sort of occupation. The position of actresses was ambiguous because many considered them working class, and even if they were not it was a classless profession where men and women mixed freely with each other and with manual workers such as stage-hands and carpenters. The opportunities and the discussion about female employment was limited compared to the 1880s and 1890s when it was more organised, with colleges and secretarial schools springing up.[20] As Braddon wrote in her article, it seemed as though the only option in the 1850s was to be a governess, which many took, and the actress, which only a few dared. The stage offered many opportunities and benefits which the former did not; an actress was not in the position of being almost a servant in another's home, she retained her independence, and, although the work was uncertain and often strenuous, if successful she could earn almost as much money as her male contemporaries. Apart from literature it was about the only profession where an artistic and talented woman could make a name for herself. However, at least with literature a degree of privacy and anonymity was retained; the work of an actress could not be more public. It was the bodily use she made of herself that was objectionable, as Michael Baker writes:

> But the tools of the actress's trade were her own body and emotions, attributes which she deliberately and regularly exposed to public gaze and public comment.[21]

But to women themselves, if they dared, it was an attractive option because it allowed independence and freedom of expression. Madge Kendal later observed:

> how many educated girls (...) have turned with a sigh of relief from the prospect of the stereotyped position of the companion or governess to the vista that an honourable connection with the stage holds out to them?[22]

It is easy to imagine that, like many of her heroines, Braddon was stage struck from an early age. Unfortunately her memoirs end before she was able to describe regular visits to the theatre. Her first visit, when she was four years old, to the St. James's Theatre (where *Lady Audley's Secret* would one day be memorably acted and produced by Ruth Herbert) probably curtailed any more for the time being:

> I remember my first theatre, the St. James's. I was taken there to see some performances of dogs and monkeys, with Mama, my godfather, and Mrs. Allen. At the music of the band, and the beat of the drums, and the light and wonder of it all, my first theatre was too much for me, and I burst out crying, whereupon Mama thought I was frightened and I was handed over to Mrs. Allen, to be taken home, ignominiously hustled out of that wonderful place (...) There is another theatre that I remember – Miss Kelly's – where I was taken to an amateur performance in which one of my father's clerks was an actor, but of that I can only remember the length and weariness.[23]

The amateur performance at Miss Kelly's was of Edward Bulwer Lytton's *Richelieu*, and despite the treat of wearing her best dress, Braddon was tired and bored. The St. James's Theatre was at that time managed by Edward Hooper, who was a friend of the Braddon family, showing that when the time came for Braddon to enter the profession she already had some contacts. Next came a visit to the Adelphi where the six year old Braddon saw Mrs. Yates (whose son Edmund she later met when working on John Maxwell's magazines) and, 'I was sensible of the pathos and sincerity of her acting'.[24] Despite their lack of money after her parents separated Braddon was fortunate that her mother was able to take her to the best London theatres, where they frequently had a box. This was because Mrs. Braddon's nephew, John Thadeus Delane, was the editor of the *Times* and he received as many tickets as he wanted because of his position. Delane 'provided my mother with as many private boxes and dress-circles as she could comfortably use.'[25]

In 1845 one production made a great impression on her: a production of Planché's *Cinderella* at the Lyceum, with Mrs. Keeley in the title role and Alfred Wigan as the Prince. As an adult Braddon was to act with both of these famous actors, but the glamour and beauty of one of Planché's 'Fairy Extravaganzas' fired the child's imagination:

> Miss Fairbrother and Miss Fortescue as Cinderella's wicked sisters, and Mrs. Keeley as Cinderella, and I know that the book of the words remained for a long time one of my literary treasures, and was read and read again. Miss Fairbrother's grace and beauty as a débardeuse at the Prince's Ball, haunted my memory, and was reproduced by pencil and colours to the best of my ability in many childish attempts at portraiture.[26]

When she was thirteen or fourteen Braddon saw Buckstone in his play *Married Life*, with most of the original cast, and Fanny Stirling (one of her favourite actresses) in *Time Tries All*. Another favourite was Charles Mathews, and she was particularly struck by his performance as the villain in *The Chain of Events* in 1852.

It was not long after this that the decision was made that Braddon herself was going to go on the stage. In this she was fully supported by her mother, Fanny Braddon, who chaperoned her throughout. Despite Henry Braddon's role as black sheep (and Braddon herself clearly never got over the father who had let them down so often), Braddon considered her ancestry to be that of an old and noble Cornish family, and it was probably to protect the feelings of her family that she adopted a stage name.

Braddon chose the stage name 'Mary Seyton'. Quite why she chose that particular surname is unclear and may never be known. Later pseudonyms generally had some sort of connection: Lady Caroline Lascelles (the pseudonym she used when writing *The Black Band* in 1861) was taken from a family name of Frederick Lascelles Wraxall, a fellow contributor and editor of Maxwell's magazines, and Babington White combined the family names of her mother. Where Seyton came from is not known, although it may have been a fashionable name because there was a well known concert singer called Clara Seyton at the time, and also a Mr. and Mrs. Seyton who acted in Leeds in the 1850s; there was a Mary Seaton (and Seyton is sometimes spelt this way in newspapers of the period) in history, who was one of Mary

Queen of Scots's ladies in waiting; or it may be she took the name of a village called Seaton (to which she refers in a short story of the 1880s) near her family home in the West country. The *Telegraph* obituary says she actually called herself Mary-Ann, which must be so as one newspaper of the period describes her as Miss Mary Ann Seyton, as does a later book.[27] As might be expected her change of name was partly to placate scandalised relatives, her son, William Maxwell, recalling:

> It was shocking that a well-brought-up girl should dream of adopting the calling. My mother's relations, probably horror stricken, implored her not to do it, or if she must persist in her rash enterprise to carry it through without using the family name.[28]

The choice of Mary Ann may have been after Fanny Braddon's sister, Mary Anne Delane.

Acting seems to have been Braddon's second attempt at a public career. At the time of the publication of *Lady Audley's Secret* the *Brighton Gazette* revealed that the author was the same Miss M.A. Seyton who had acted in the town two years previously, adding that the *Court Journal* had recently reported:

> It appears that Miss Braddon, the authoress of Lady Audley's Secret, first took a liking for music, tried it and was pronounced a failure.[29]

This may well be the case, since Braddon's mother had been very keen for her to learn music as a child,[30] (she was later rated a 'very good player', and especially fond of Mozart) and her novel *Lucius Davoren* (1873) follows a concert singer on tour from town to town. In *A Lost Eden* (1904) Flora wants at first to be a singer, and despite her distinct lack of ability at the age of fifteen, 'The career of Jenny Lind, who was snubbed by her earliest masters, was a stimulus to girlish dreams.'[31] If indeed Braddon did make an attempt at becoming a professional singer it must have been short lived, for she was still very young when she became an actress. Nevertheless, her singing talents would have stood her in good stead for her roles in pantomimes and burlesques.

Braddon always gave out her date of birth as 1837, noting more than once that it was the same year as Victoria became queen.[32] The accepted date now is 1835.[33] It is surely most unlikely Braddon could have thought herself two years younger than she was. Perhaps when she began her stage career she was worried she was already too old at seventeen to start a profession to which many started as children, and were usually born in to; children such as the Ternan sisters and Ellen and Kate Terry for example.

Having been privately educated, and having her mother as a chaperone wherever she toured, must have marked her out from the other actresses. At this date the middle class, especially women, had hardly entered the theatre. In fact there were not many actresses of any class: the 1851 census showed less than nine hundred described themselves as actresses, a figure which doubled ten years later.[34] Most actresses in the 1850s went into the theatre at a very early age, as the children of actors, like Justina in *A Strange World* (1875) who, because of it, has none of the romantic illusions of the cloistered middle class girl visiting the theatre:

> "I've seen too much of the theatre. If I'd been a young lady, now, shut up in a drawing-room all my life, and brought to the theatre for the first time to see 'Romeo and Juliet', I could fancy myself wanting to play Juliet; but I've seen too much of the ladder Juliet stands on in the balcony scene, and the dirty-looking man that holds it steady for her, and the way she quarrels with Mrs. Wappers the nurse, between the acts. (...) All the poetry has been taken out of it for me, father."[35]

A young woman of eighteen could easily have been on the stage for fifteen years. For someone like Braddon this was a disadvantage, as it is for Lucy in *Dead Sea Fruit* who, when about to play Pauline in *The Lady of Lyons*, says:

> "I love it dearly, and I hope some day to get on, for papa's sake. But I find the life of an actress much harder than I thought, and it is very difficult to get on. (...)You see, most actors and actresses have been a long time in the profession, and they have a kind of prejudice against amateurs and novices, and try to put them down."[36]

It is impossible to know how much family opposition there was to this step. The change of name probably indicates some disapproval, but it can only be a matter for conjecture. For a middle class entrant to change her name to disguise her true identity was not uncommon: a parallel case would be that of Helen Taylor, the step-daughter of John Stuart Mill, who at about the same time changed her name and secretly tried a career on the stage in the provinces where no one would know her.[37] Whatever really happened, Mrs. Braddon certainly came to approve of her daughter's career, for she accompanied her wherever she went and entertained her daughter's new friends. There may well have been objections at first to overcome; in a partly autobiographical story, 'Across the Footlights', vicar's daughter Rosalie Melford becomes Rosalie Morton, once she has persuaded her mother:

> Much pleading and many long discussions were needed before the mother would consent to her child's appearance on the boards. The Vicar's widow had heard terrible stories of theatres; and she had to be reminded again and again of the glorious examples of feminine virtue to be seen on the metropolitan stage; and that if there were some shadows on the dramatic profession, there are also spots upon the sun. And then they were very poor, those two, in their shabby London lodging. They had drunk deep of the cup of genteel penury. And the mother could but own that it would be a nice thing if her darling were earning from twenty to thirty pounds a week at the Haymarket or the Lyceum.[38]

Fanny Braddon had been in financial straits since she had separated from her husband. In a letter in the Wolff collection a Braddon relative, sending ten pounds for Mrs. Braddon's son Edward who was in India, adds 'I hope you may succeed in filling your house to your satisfaction.'[39] That Mrs. Braddon had had to advertise for a lodger must have been a downward step for a family who had an entry in the directory *Walford's County Families*. So, while not poor, mother and daughter did, to an extent, rely on handouts from relatives and needed to look to their own abilities to make money and remain independent. Braddon's son W.B. Maxwell, who believed his mother became an actress at the age of nineteen and for only two years (surely showing that Braddon did not even tell her own children much about her years on the stage), recalled one of her main aims was to support her mother:

> I know that her principal object was to be self-supporting and if possible earn money sufficient to relieve my grandmother's anxieties.[40]

Further clues can be found in one of Braddon's most autobiographical novels, *A Lost Eden* (1904). Set in the 1850s, the two sisters, Flora and Marion, live in Camberwell just as Braddon did with her mother and sister. Flora's ambitions turn to the stage and she gains her first work in non speaking roles in London. If Braddon was indeed like her young heroine Flora at fifteen years old she was already reluctant to accept the passive role that society has allotted her:

She was irrepressible, utterly without reverence for superior age or maternal influence, warm-hearted, impulsive, volatile, a young bird that had lately found the strength of its wings and was impatient of the fate that forbade its flight. There was something in her looks and her movements, bright eyes and parted lips, light step and rapid changes of attitude, that suggested a caged bird beating itself against prison bars. (p.23)

Flora has many autobiographical elements in common with the young Mary Braddon, and certainly much of the background detail suggests similarities. Probably, like Flora, Braddon had appeared successfully in Camberwell amateur dramatics at private houses; Flora has played Mrs. Bounce in *Box and Cox* (Buckstone) at a local housewarming where she is told by her admiring audience, "I was a born actress, and that it would be a sin to deprive me of a great career" (p.136). In another novel, *Strangers and Pilgrims* (1873), the heroine, Elizabeth Luttrell, plays the lead in an amateur production of Charles Reade's *Peg Wolfington* and wishes herself an actress. Perhaps with the rueful experience of time Braddon points out that an inspired performance on one amateur occasion is not grounds for a career, adding that Elizabeth was:

forgetting that this flame which burned so brilliantly tonight might be only a meteoric light, and that although a clever young woman, with an ardent nature, may for once in her life fling herself heart and soul into a stage-play, and by a kind of inspiration dispense with the comprehension and experience that can only come from profession training, it is no reason she should be able to repeat her triumph, and to go on repeating it *ad libitum*.[41]

In *A Lost Eden*, however, Flora's spirits and enthusiasm for acting will not be dampened, and she soon declares herself even more forcibly, in a way that would have seemed unusual for a girl in 1852: "it lies between burying one's self alive or having a career" (p.139). Flora encounters much opposition at first from her sister Marion, but Flora is realistic and knows she will not become a star straight away:

"I know that I shall have to begin at the bottom of the ladder, and that my first salary won't do much more than pay for my omnibus. (...) Even Miss Mandlebert says I ought to be good enough for speaking parts in two or three months." (pp.137-138)

Quite possibly, like Flora, Braddon began performing at a London theatre as a non speaking extra; a London theatre would have been easy for Braddon to get to from their home in Camberwell by omnibus, and would have been a more sensible step than risk failure and expense by going straight into a provincial engagement and have to leave home.

> Flora smiled at her sister's ignorance, and explained that at the Phoenix there were eight extra ladies, who must be young, and ought to be pretty, who adorned the stage, as lights of the harem, in an Oriental burlesque, as guests in an adapted French comedy, as peeresses, peasants, pages, peris – creatures necessary to the brightness of the evening's entertainment, sparkling, fascinating, all grace and movement, but speechless. This kind of engagement Flora declared to be the best education for a future Helen Faucit or Julia Bennet. (p.137)

Flora has an actress friend called Miss Mandlebert and, as Wolff points out, there was a Miss Mandlebert in Hull when Braddon was acting there, and he suggests the character was based on the real actress.[42] Miss Mandlebert is to use her influence with stage manager Mr. Burley to get Flora the job as an extra, a service, she says, for which an agent might have charged her a guinea:

> "And Miss Mandlebert says she will keep on the look-out for me, and the first opening she sees of a small part in a farce, she'll get round the author, and make him give it to me." (p.137)

Marion is reassured by the looks of Miss Mandlebert, as she does not look as she had imagined an actress:

> She looked the pink of respectability (...) She wore neither paint nor powder, and had a commonplace manner which seemed reassuring. (p.140)

Flora's first appearance is as a sixteen year old walk-on in 1853 at the Phoenix theatre on the Strand. Mr. Hooper, the friend of Mrs. Braddon mentioned earlier, was at about this time the manager of the Strand theatre, and it is tempting to think the Strand could have been the theatre where Braddon might have started as an extra at the same age. Certainly Braddon's description of the Phoenix as 'at this time the smallest theatre in London' (p.158) matches the Strand. Michael J.N. Baker writes, that although nothing could help an untalented actor in the long-term: 'Few actor's careers were not founded upon the personal intervention of friends and relatives, and accordingly nepotism was rife.'[43] Flora has a crush on the lead actor at the Phoenix, Willoughby

Tracy, and so did Braddon on the lead actor Mr. Conway at Mr. Hooper's Strand:

> Mr. Conway was acquiline-nosed and handsome, or at any rate I thought him beautiful; and his dashing gait and swinging cloak, worn over one shoulder, his flapping hat and feather, his rapid unexpected entrances, always at a crisis, were imitated by me in many a melodrama of my own composition in the Theatre Royal Back Parlour.[44]

Flora is, of course, completely disillusioned by the reality of her hero once she starts work at the theatre and sees close-up his grey hair and wrinkles, and transfers her affections to a young actor whose brow reminds her of Byron. *A Lost Eden* opens in 1852 with the funeral of the 'iron duke', Wellington.[45] Flora acts under her own name, but most of Braddon's fictional actresses change it. The opening of the novel also coincides with the probable year of her own theatrical debut.

That Braddon did have a little experience as an amateur actress and then as an extra in London before obtaining a provincial engagement seems most likely. Braddon appeared with extremely well respected companies, who frequently had famous guest stars, and they would have had no need to employ a complete novice. Perhaps, like Flora in *A Lost Eden*, this first provincial engagement, with her first prized speaking role, was in Manchester. The fact that she tried to interest the theatre in Manchester in a pantomime she had written in 1860, suggests she knew the management. In any case at some point, perhaps in late 1852, and, certainly by the spring of 1853, Braddon and her mother left London for the provinces, seeming to some of their friends to have disappeared.[46] It was through acting in the provinces that an actor learnt his trade before trying for a debut in London. When Braddon's son Gerald became an actor she thought it would be best if he started in the provinces, but asked Bram Stoker whether it would be best for him to have some lessons first:

> It seems to me that a few months in a travelling company would be the best start for him. Do you think he ought to take lessons in elocution before beginning, or should he learn everything on the boards?[47]

In the 1850s there was no question about it, the provinces were the training ground, but by the 1880s, when Gerald was beginning to act, the days of the stock company were almost over:

In the good old days a perfectly normal system was universally recognised. London had a number of theatres, in each of which was established a stock company or at least a company engaged for the season. When any deficiencies had to be made up, the managers looked for fresh talent among the scores of other stock companies which could be found either stationed in the larger provincial cities or else working the various circuits of smaller towns. It was recognised that, in ordinary circumstances, any young man or woman who intended to follow the profession had to put in a few years training at these provincial schools; only rarely could a genius or a child of good fortune make his debut in London and be accepted into the Drury Lane or Covent Garden companies. (...) Thus the "good stock company was a kind of histrionic nursery, the young actors and actresses of which were literally in a dramatic school."[48]

One worry of her family must have been what sort of women Braddon would come across if she became an actress, and the fear that their loose morals would rub off on her. Perhaps those who had disapproved felt their fears had been justified when Braddon did go to live with a man who was not her husband nine years later in 1861. From her replies to correspondents in the *Halfpenny Journal* Fanny Braddon did not approve of women of loose morals, or of the men who tried to hang around green rooms or stage doors in order to tempt them, so it is easy to imagine she looked after her daughter carefully.[49] In her novels Braddon defended the position of the morally upright actress, at a time when in many novels an actress denoted a villainess as in, for example, *Miss Forrester* (1866) by Annie Edwardes. Even Braddon did this on occasion with the bigamous actress Mrs. Varney in *Lady Lisle* (1862), and her actress/manager villainess Myra in *Hostages to Fortune* (1875) who not only sneaks racy French plays past the censor but plots against the virtue of an innocent young woman, the wife of her own former lover. However, her 'bad' actresses are not from 'good' families and Braddon was keen to show that it was possible for girls to go on the stage and remain virtuous like Flora in *A Lost Eden* and Mary in *Rough Justice*, but she did not deny the truth either and admitted that there were some actresses who were 'black sheep', who were unable to resist the temptation of wealthy admirers, as she does in *A Lost Eden* when Flora assures her sister that she is quite safe on tour, not from men, but from the contaminating influence of immoral actresses:

You are so particular about my acquaintances that you will be pleased to know these is not a single black sheep in this company –

I mean among the ladies. You will understand this all the better when I tell you that, except among the principals, there isn't a silk umbrella in the theatre. Of course, with my present experience, I am able to keep clear of anybody I don't like; but the worst feature about black sheep is that they are so dreadfully good-natured, always offering one chocolate, or to lend one sashes and jewellery for the stage, and one can hardly tell them that one would rather die of starvation than take a single chocolate cream out of their bag. One has to pretend one hates chocolate. (p.293)

Michael J.N. Baker suggests from his examination of middle class actresses who went on the stage in the 1880s that far from finding comrades who were passionate about acting and literature, they found people they could not help but look down on.[50] Three decades earlier, when she was probably the only middle class actress from a non theatrical background in most of the companies she joined, Braddon seems to have made lasting friendships. In later years actresses like Braddon's friends Madge Kendal and Marie Bancroft were only too keen to promote their own image of domesticity and respectability, (particularly through happy marriage to colleagues); in doing so they raised the position of women in their profession, but when Braddon was on the stage prejudice prevailed, and the opinion of many was that expressed by the *Saturday Review*:

> The objection to the theatre which most people make, is, that actors and actresses are not virtuous characters, or rather, although modesty and prudery may forbid them saying so plainly, they do not much care about the men, but they think that the women are bad.[51]

Both Braddon and her mother must have been relieved to find that there were some actresses who were suitable for her to be friends with, and one of these was Adelaide Biddles, whom she met on one of her first engagements.

Mary Seyton in Southampton and Winchester in 1853: Provincial Circuits and a Debut in London 1853-1857

Although theatrical memoirs became common during a later generation of actresses, few actresses penned memoirs who had been on the stage in the 1850s. One who did was Mrs. Adelaide Calvert with *Sixty Eight Years on the Stage* (1911), and this book provides one of the few contemporary eyewitness accounts of Mary Seyton the actress. Mrs.

Calvert's book also gives a fascinating firsthand account of what it was like to be a nineteenth-century actress. Adelaide Biddles, who later married Charles Calvert, was a year younger than Braddon, and was already an experienced actress born into a theatrical family. In August 1853 she and her sister Clara were engaged by Edwin Holmes, the manager of the Theatre Royal at Southampton, for the new season. Here they met a fellow new member of the company, Mary Seyton, who was almost eighteen years old and had already appeared at the Theatre Royal, Bath. Doubtless, as the Bath Theatre Royal, where Mrs. Macready was lessee (after her death, on 8 March 1853, her son-in-law J.H. Chute took over), was a more prestigious theatre, Braddon would have played small parts and been an extra in crowd scenes. She is not mentioned in any of the reviews in Bath newspapers, but she may have begun at this theatre in the autumn of 1852, the season concluding on 24 May 1853. If she joined the company late in the season, it may have been only for a few days, so that she could be billed at her next engagement as from another Theatre Royal – this was common practice. In *A Lost Eden* Braddon recalled this time as a period of political excitement:

> In that summer of '53 the country thrilled with the expectation of war, and the eyes of Palmerston and of Europe were on a small man with a big nose, who held France in the hollow of his hand, and whom the Emperor Nicholas had refused to call cousin. (p.80)

Clara and Adelaide were paid almost two pounds per week, so presumably Braddon who, like them, was a 'walking lady', would have received less than a pound, which would not have been considered a great deal. Walking ladies generally played lesser parts or the young ingenue. Wolff seems to have confused this with 'walk on' and assumed she usually played non speaking parts. The two Biddles sisters were pleased to make this move because it allowed them to leave home and become independent from their father:

> And so we two girls started on our new life. Our combined salaries barely reached £2, but I resolved never to trouble my father for money, if I could possibly avoid it; and during the following ten months I never did, save once, when we had a week's vacation before Christmas. We both felt very proud to think we were earning our own living, and were no longer a burden on our good father, who had a somewhat large family (by his second wife) to feed, clothe and educate.[52]

The girls were well taken care of by the management, in that they were met at the station and taken to recommended lodgings in St. Michael's Square where they found:

> Two comfortable rooms, where the kind-hearted landlady cooked, waited and looked after us, for the small sum of eight shillings a week.[53]

The young leading actress, Miss Suter, had become ill and her parts were immediately reallocated not to Braddon, but to the already well experienced Adelaide. Miss Suter, who was only sixteen years old herself, died of tuberculosis shortly after, and Adelaide made the most of the prominent roles she was given, soon making an excellent impression on the audiences of the town.

As another example of Braddon using her own career to flesh out that of her fictional characters, in her novel *The Green Curtain* (1911) the hero, an actor called Godwin (an amalgam of Edmund Kean and Henry Irving) makes his debut as a young actor at the Theatre Royal in Southampton, his imagination fired by a childhood visit to this theatre:

> Southampton was no doubt a better nurse of the drama in those days than she is now, for counter attractions were not so many, but the theatre of those days – in which great men and women had acted – was a shabby building in an old street leading down to the water, behind the market and the High Street.[54]

Like her fictional manager Mr. Conray, Edwin Holmes was also the lessee of the Theatre Royal, Winchester. After only a week at Southampton the company transferred to Winchester for a month, and where the *Hampshire Advertiser* called them:

> a company which, if the first night's performance may be taken as a criterion, contains an amount of talent far beyond what is usually found in provincial histrionisn.[55]

As there were no major 'star' performers in the company, and most of the actors seem to have been young, perhaps the cast received more direction than was usual at the time. In later companies Braddon worked for, especially Henry Nye Chart's Brighton company, many famous actors guest starred. Michael J.N. Baker writes of the lack of direction and the prominence given to the leading actor:

miscasting was widespread, scenery and costumes were inadequate and inaccurate (...) The 'star system' discouraged the notion of ensemble playing, and supporting casts accordingly received little or no direction beyond what was necessary to heighten the impact of the lead players, a practice which grew rather than lessened as the provincial circuits, threatened by rival attractions in the 1840s and 1850s, began importing performers of national status.[56]

After the stint at Winchester the company then returned to Southampton. The Biddles sisters soon made friends with their fellow company member, who was also their next door neighbour:

In the house next to ours in St. Michael's Square, the apartments were occupied by Miss Mary Seyton and her mother (Seyton was merely a *nom de theatre*, their real name being Braddon). Mrs. Seyton (as we always addressed her) was a refined, intellectual lady of independent means. She was therefore enabled to indulge in the luxury of hospitality, from which, it is needless to say, the rest of us were debarred. And on Sunday afternoons my sister and I, Mr. Calvert and one or two other members of the company were often invited to tea, and by these pleasant informal meetings we came to know more of each other than the ordinary association of a green-room unfolds.[57]

In *The Green Curtain* Braddon wrote of Godwin's landlady in Southampton, and how not all landladies were keen to let to actors:

She had let to "theatricals" for many years, and she liked them; which was more than every landlady in Southampton would own to. (p.49)

From the local newspapers it would appear that it was Adelaide who was fast becoming the favourite of the company: in Winchester as the daughter Mary in *John Bull*, her 'talents and beauty drew down torrents of applause.'[58] Both hers and Charles Calvert's performances were warmly praised when they and Braddon performed in *The False Friend*, while Braddon 'as Olympia, displayed too much affection.'[59] In *The Green Curtain* Braddon described a Southampton audience who were not always polite, when Godwin finds himself laughed at for his skinny legs and the weakness of his inexperienced voice:

Heaven knows why they laughed. Godwin never knew. A provincial audience is pitiless to youth and inexperience. A battered old mummer, who can bellow and swagger, may command the favour of the pit and gallery; but refinement, grace, even beauty cannot save a novice from derision, if his acting fail to satisfy an unlettered audience. (p.67)

In *Dead Sea Fruit* (1868) Braddon, perhaps remembering her own time as an inexperienced teenage actress, defends the position of the actor – not least because of the hard work involved – as one worthy of respect as an artist and as an individual from a society that looks down on them:

> But if Miss St. Albans was not yet an actress, it is to be remembered that she was only nineteen years of age, and had had little more than a twelvemonth's experience or practice of an art which is perhaps amongst the most difficult and exacting of all arts, and which has no formulae whereby the student may arrive at some comprehension of its mysteries. It is an art that is rarely taught well, and very often taught badly; an art which demands from its professors a moral courage, and an expenditure of physical energy, intellectual power, and emotional feeling demanded by no other art; and when a man happens to be endowed with those many gifts necessary to perfection in this art, he is spoken of in a patronizing tone as "only an actor;" and it is somewhat a matter of wonder that he should be "received in society." (p.109)

Even if Braddon had similar problems with her earlier provincial audiences (more than one critic was to suggest her voice was not strong enough) it did not dampen her enthusiasm or love of drama even when off the stage. In *The Doctor's Wife* (1864) Braddon depicted Isabel Sleaford as a girl made unhappy with life by reading and longing, like Braddon, to be a famous actress or poet, or for something, anything, to happen, living in impoverished circumstances in Camberwell just as Braddon had. One of her favourite day dreams is to escape it all by going on the stage and becoming a famous actress:

> Miss Sleaford let down her long black hair before the looking-glass, and acted to herself in a whisper. She saw her pale face, awful in the dusky glass, her lifted arms, her great black eyes, and she fancied herself dominating a terror-sticken pit. Sometimes she thought of leaving friendly Mr. Raymond, and going up to London with a five-pound note in her pocket, and coming out at one of the theatres as a tragic actress. She would go to the manager, and tell him that she wanted to act. There might be a little difficulty

at first, perhaps, and he would be rather inclined to be doubtful of her powers; but then she would take off her bonnet, and let down her hair, and would draw the long tresses wildly through her thin white fingers – so; she stopped to look at herself in the glass as she did it, – and would cry, "I am not mad; this hair I tear is mine!" and the thing would be done. The manager would exclaim, "Indeed, my dear young lady, I was not prepared for such acting as this. Excuse my emotion; but really, since the days of Miss O'Neil, I don't remember to have witnessed anything to equal your delivery of that speech. Come to-morrow evening and play Constance. You don't want a rehearsal? – no of course not; you know every syllable of the part. I shall take the liberty of offering you fifty pounds a night to begin with, and I shall place one of my carriages at your disposal."[60]

Unlike Braddon, Isabel does not have the talent or the initiative to make her dreams happen, and the reality of hard work on a provincial stage, involving few days off, fifteen hour days, and the stress of finding the next job would have disappointed her.[60] Braddon's depiction of Isabel's histrionic performances in front of the mirror uncannily echo the young Mary Seyton, as Mrs Calvert remembered at Southampton:

One night I had gone to the theatre earlier than usual, in order to get dressed leisurely, and run through my part as I did so, when, as I ascended the stairs to my dressing-room door (*our* dressing-room, as four of us occupied it), I heard a female voice in loud wailing tones, together with a word not usually included in a lady's vocabulary. I crept quietly up and peeped over the top stair. There was Mary, *en négligé*, her hair hanging loosely over her shoulders. She was gazing intently into a large looking-glass, and flourishing her hairbrush wildly, as she again repeated –

"The cruel arrow glanced aside,
The damnèd arrow glanced aside
And pierced thy heart, my love, my bride,
        Oriana!"[62]

The Southampton season seems to have been a happy one for the young Braddon and her new friend Adelaide Biddles. Despite her mother's presence it does not seem that Braddon's social life was entirely curtailed. Mrs. Calvert wrote how they each had their first admirers; she of course later married hers, and she and Charles Calvert became one of the most famous acting couples of the period. Mrs. Calvert remembered that on the subject of their admirers Braddon proved her wit in a way that was probably funnier at the time than it is now, but still giving the impression of a funny, light-hearted girl who was good company:

> These were happy times for us two girls. We each had our first sweetheart. Mine was the "leading gentleman," whilst Mary accepted little attentions from Mr. Brandon, and as an instance of her cleverness, when I said one day, "well, Mary, I wouldn't be seen with a brand on," she retorted, "Well, your taste I call *vert*."[63]

Mr. Brandon's speciality within the company was as a performer of comic songs and as a clown in the pantomime. Southampton was a good training ground for both actresses because Holmes put on a wide variety of plays, pantomimes and burlesques, very much the sort of repertoire Braddon had to learn throughout her time in the provinces. Adelaide recalled, 'My work at Southampton embraced every possible kind of entertainment.'[64] She also explained how they managed to cope with the numerous parts they had to learn, a seemingly impossible task when three plays a night were performed, but the most popular plays and Shakespeare were performed in order:

> "to give us a rest" – every member of the company being thoroughly conversant with them, and able to play their respective parts without a rehearsal.[65]

Adelaide gave no indication as to what sort of manager Edwin Holmes was, but one wonders whether Braddon had him in mind in *The Green Curtain* when Godwin watches the frightened looking young girl playing Gertrude in Hamlet at the Theatre Royal, Southampton:

> It was not Gertrude overawed by Hamlet, but Miss Beverley paralysed by fear of her manager, who complimented her after the closet scene by telling her she was the worst queen he had ever met with. (p.19)

At the end of the season Adelaide had a benefit which, after expenses, gave her the 'little fortune' of eight pounds and fifteen shillings. Adelaide and her sister Clara soon went to America where Adelaide enjoyed great success, and where her sister settled and married. Braddon and her mother went to Reading for a short season which began on the fifteenth of May and lasted for about six weeks. Braddon also sent her fictional actor Godwin with his mother from Southampton to Reading for a season of the same length, even arriving in the same month as Braddon. Mrs. Braddon probably hoped as Godwin's mother, that eventually it would lead to a London season:

> It was in the middle of May when they left the quaint old town by Southampton Water, on the top of the coach that was to carry them as far as Basingstoke on their way to Reading. Leading business! At the theatre Royal, Reading, Godwin was to play the lead. No matter that the coach journey was costly, and that Mrs. Merritt had to draw upon her little capital for travelling expenses. He was to play the lead. He might be in London before the end of the year, with a salary of five pounds a week. He was going to make a long stride forward upon the stony road. The goal seemed so near that the stones hardly mattered. (p.80)

If Braddon had better roles at Reading than she had at Southampton, it was probably because the Theatre Royal at Reading did not have a regular company. In *The Green Curtain* Braddon described the theatre:

> The poor old barn that called itself the Theatre Royal was in the hands of an impecunious low comedian, a favourite in the town, who had taken upon himself the responsibilities of management without a sixpence of capital. (p.80)

Business in Reading was 'dull' but the correspondent of the *Era* reported on the talented cast:

> We have had performances under the patronage of the Militia, the Colonel of the Militia, cum multis aliis, but still the exertions of the manager are not duly appreciated. The performers here worthy of mention are Mr. Jackson, Sedgwick, and Fry; Miss G. Doyle, and Miss Seyton, the latter, though a young actress, bids fair for success.[66]

Reading was not renowned for its theatre, but here at least she was out of Adelaide Calvert's shadow and playing leading parts which got her notice. Although business was not good, she was luckier than the company members who acted at Reading later that year, who were never paid their wages and wrote an angry letter to the *Era*. In *The Green Curtain* Braddon has her Reading actors hungry and unpaid, and so unhappy that the actors leave, 'and the Theatre Royal closed its doors for ever under that management.' (p.81) Perhaps Braddon could see the way things were going at Reading. Finding new companies could be a perilous enterprise, as there were many unscrupulous managers who quickly put a company together. Actors were out of pocket straight away if things went wrong, because of the outlay they had to spend on travelling to their new job. An article in the *Era*, 'Provincial Theatres and Unprincipled Managers', described this as a common problem:

> Every week brings us sundry letters from country actors and actresses, complaining of having been duped out of their salaries, and being left penniless in some provincial town; the worthy manager himself is, of course, *non est inventers*, and, by some infelicitous process or error on the part of the treasurer, the receipts of the last week and the accounts thereof are in like condition.[67]

In January 1855 Braddon and her mother were in Scotland, at the Theatre Royal, Aberdeen.[68] On the 14 January she and her mother wrote a joint letter to a Mr. Younge who was ill in bed, which was probably never posted as the incomplete letter is within the file of family letters to Fanny Braddon in Robert Lee Wolff's collection:

> (I) apologise for not answering your most witty & delightful letter by *return* of post as I was in duty bound – my reason for not so doing was that I was anxious my daughter who professes *l'eloquence du billet* in a much greater degree than I do should add a few lines, & you know Sunday is almost the only leisure day an actress has. (...) (I) hope that when we return to Town you will often give us the pleasure of your charming society at our *villa* at Camberwell. I will take care to let you know directly I return. I like Scotland and the Scotch very much but still I pine for the green meadows & the sweet, cultivated scenes only to be met with I believe in our dear country.[69]

The letter is signed F. Seyton, confirming Mrs. Calvert's statement that Mrs. Braddon had also adopted her daughter's stage name. It is also noteworthy that they had retained their Camberwell home as a base, showing that Mrs. Braddon had retained some sort of independent income from her husband's family, as Mrs. Calvert had suggested, and they were not wholly dependent on what her daughter could earn. If they were able to afford to do so this was a sensible thing to do, as there must have been periods at the end of seasons when Braddon was unemployed. Braddon described such a villa in *The Story of Barbara* and in *A Lost Eden*, Chestnut Lodge, in which Flora and Marion live with their mother in the 1850s:

> She walked all the length of Camberwell Grove, and then turned
> into a road where there were only a few houses in gardens, houses
> of a rustic type, with whitewashed walls and slate roofs, which
> arrogance called villas, while proud-humility talked of them as
> cottages. (p.5)

In more than one novel she alludes to this area of Camberwell, where
she lived as a young girl, and the change in it when the speculators and
land developers moved in. The remainder of the letter to Mr. Younge is
taken up with a teasing note from her daughter, which will be quoted in
the next chapter. Unfortunately the letter breaks off before Mary
Braddon gives any details of how the performances are going, her part
of the letter ends tantalisingly, 'Life here is rather monotonous, we do
pretty...' W.B. Maxwell recalled that Braddon later felt some guilt for
the life she had imposed on her mother during these years:

> She was accompanied by Mrs. Braddon throughout the period, and
> I remember that once when talking to me she reproached herself for
> dragging her mother about from place to place, and entailing so
> much trouble and discomfort on her.[70]

W.B. Maxwell tried to reassure his mother that his grandmother had
doubtless enjoyed the experience, which is probable: Fanny Braddon
had entertained her daughter's friends at Southampton and a few years
later her daughter's friends in Brighton, the Sawyers, also sent regular
messages of greeting to her in their letters to Braddon.

In March of 1855 Braddon was at the Theatre Royal in Stamford for
just over a month, the theatre leased by Henry Johnson. The season was
a short one, ending on 27 April, and apart from a successful pantomime:

> The season has not proved a lucrative one; and the lessee informed
> the audience that for the future he should not undertake the trouble
> and anxieties of forming companies himself, but should give all his
> assistance to any manager who might be disposed to bring a
> talented company at the proper seasons.[71]

Next she was back in Scotland, at the Theatre Royal in Glasgow, where
the most noteworthy production was the spectacular *Battle of the
Alma*.[72] Braddon must have answered an advertisement in the *Era* of 22
July for the new season at the Theatre Royal in Southampton:

> The lessee, having placed the whole, of his arrangements for the
> ensuing season in the hands of his Sole Agent, Mr. Arthur Dellon,

14, Little Russell Street, Covent Garden, requests all applications will be forwarded to Mr. Dellon, as no engagements will be made but through him.[73]

Mr. Dellon's agency was established in 1840. It would be interesting to know if and how often Braddon used an agent herself. At the very beginning of her career, unless she had had an influential friend like Flora had in Miss Mandlebert in *A Lost Eden*, she may have needed an agent to secure provincial engagements. Six years later, when she was writing serials for the *Halfpenny Journal*, several stage struck readers wrote in asking for advice on how to go on the stage. As will be discussed later it was Braddon's mother's job to write the replies to the questions of the magazine's many correspondents, and it was probably she who wrote this reply, as she and Braddon were the members of staff uniquely qualified to give such advice:

> Champion – If you are in London, apply to Mr. George Fisher, Theatrical Agent, Broad Court, Bow Street. You will be treated with integrity, liberality, and attention. He will most likely procure you an engagement in a small country theatre, where you will have to accept a low salary for the sake of learning the profession. The life of an actor is not an idle one, the work is hard, and the remuneration uncertain; but, if you have really talent, and have courage and perseverance to surmount all difficulties, you will find pleasant companions, friendly treatment, and many bright spots in the theatrical profession.[74]

At the same time Braddon used the fiction in the *Halfpenny Journal* to give a favourable impression of the stage, both of the people who worked within and of its role in society, which she considered stabilising. In *The Black Band* (1861) Clara Melville is shown working to support her father and younger siblings as a ballet girl. In a description of a pantomime in which Clara is playing Columbine Braddon added an aside to those who considered theatre going immoral:

> Merry children with bright and joyous faces were assembled in the boxes; happy tradespeople, dressed in their best, filled the crowded benches in the pit; stalwart mechanics, in tier after tier, looked down from the immense and noisy gallery. All was noise, bustle, and confusion; but all, too, was good-temper, and hearty, simple-minded enjoyment. It was altogether a pleasant sight to see; and the austere teachers, who cavil at the harmless amusements afforded by a well-conducted theatre, might have learned a lesson

that night. Husbands were there, surrounded by their wives and children; brothers with their sisters. Surely this was better than the gin palace.[75]

The season in Southampton ended in mid February in 1856, and it must have been a little disappointing to be back with Holmes's company, playing the same sort of roles for him as she had three years earlier. Shortly after this Braddon must have felt success was not far off when she made her debut in London as Madeline in *The Sailor of France* (Johnstone) at the Surrey theatre on 3 March. In her novels she shows actors and actresses struggling for years in the provinces and longing for a chance to display their talent in London. In *Dead Sea Fruit*, Lucy's father had imagined it would be easy for her to get an engagement in London:

> "But I find, alas! that in most cases it is only after years of patient and ill-paid drudgery in small provincial towns the dramatic aspirant works his or her way to the metropolis." (p.97)

Braddon must have known this was a make or break chance for her, and if she did not succeed it was unlikely she would get a second chance in London. For the first few days, in newspapers like the *Daily News*, Braddon's name was prominently displayed in adverts for the Surrey. *The Times* recorded, probably with the bias of her family connection to Delane, Braddon's London debut in *The Sailor of France*, where, for once, she got to play the heroine with love interest. The play had a Republican setting, and the Sailor, played by the lessee Mr. Shepherd, after various adventures obtains a pardon from the President:

> allowing him to marry a very pretty young lady whom he (the President) loves himself. This young lady, who is a prominent personage in the story, having a father and a betrothed to love, and a persecutor to hate, is played by Miss Mary Seyton, a debutante from the provinces, with a most attractive stage figure and a thorough command of all those airs and graces that make up the artless beauty of melodrama.[76]

On the 17 March she acted in what was probably the biggest production she was ever a part of, the newest Surrey spectacular. She played Clara in a drama by J.B. Johnstone inspired by Mayhew's letters in the *London Morning Chronicle*, 'London Labour and the London Poor', called *How We Live in the World of London*. Eight years earlier Johnstone had been prompter and Pantaloon at the Surrey, and in this new play be wrote parts for his two daughters as the children.[77] A critic from the *Era* wrote after the crowded first night:

> (the) ingeniously invented plot has succeeded in weaving into a tolerably connected tale many of the facts with which Mr. Mayhew makes us familiar. (...) the chief merit of the play consists rather in the dioramic truthfulness of its scenes than in the story which is evolved. It is, we believe, a faithful daguerreotype of low life in London (...) In the construction of the piece we object to the tremendous amount of "sentiment" – weak and maudlin sentiment – which pervades it.[78]

A review of 13 April pointed out that despite the new contrasting scenes of high life the best of the dialogue was taken directly from Mayhew's accounts, but that the spectacle itself did not disappoint, giving:

> a graphic illustration of every-day life in the metropolis painted in the strongest but in the truest colours. Rarely have scenic artists produced more effective tableaux than we have here exhibited in Covent-garden by sunrise – Whitechapel Workhouse at midnight in a snow storm – the Dark Arches under the Adelphi (...) and that greatest triumph of all, the destruction of the illicit distillery by fire, with the blazing rafters tumbling and crashing down upon the stage, and the appalling horrors of a conflagration pictured to the eye, even to the minutest details of the sound of the pumping of the engines and the tumultuous assemblage of the terror-stricken crowd.[79]

Also in April Braddon played Araminta in *Sarah's Young Man* (Suter), and in May she played Winifred Wood, the love interest, in *Jack Sheppard*; Mary Anne Keeley, who played Jack, was a well known actress from 1825 until her death in 1899.[80] Mrs. Keeley had originated the part of Jack Sheppard in 1839 and it was probably her most famous part. The role was not played as an actress playing a 'principal boy' as 'her dressing and playing of Jack Sheppard was remarkable for its thorough maleness.'[81] Braddon also played the Countess in *Your Life's in Danger* (Maddison Morton), and Charity in *Martin Chuzzlewit*.

Presumably Braddon did not achieve the hoped-for success, despite the flattering review in the *Times*, as rather than continue in London at another theatre or with a new contract at the Surrey when it reopened she returned to the provinces. J.W. Robertson wrote an article in the *Illustrated Times* in 1864 in which he described the enormous importance that a debut in London could mean for a provincial actress:

if successful her salary could rise to twenty pounds per week, and fame and a proper home would be hers at last. But 'when the L.L. (Leading Lady) makes a failure she returns to the provinces.'[82] The job at the Surrey was probably thanks to Charles Calvert, her Southampton colleague, who had taken a position as acting manager at the Surrey. Adelaide Biddles appeared at the end of season benefit, and shortly afterwards she and Calvert married. In *Dead Sea Fruit* Lucy Alford is not kept on after her London debut and must speedily return to the drudgery of a provincial stage 'unless same powerful and friendly hand shall be interposed in her behalf.' (p.97). Lucy, about to play Pauline in *The Lady of Lyons*, confesses:

> "I love it dearly, and I hope some day to get on, for papa's sake. But I find the life of an actress much harder than I thought, and it is very difficult to get on." (p.100)

Whatever the reason, the lack of an influential friend or insufficient appreciation of her skills, Braddon returned to the provincial circuit, that of Hull.

As previously stated, one of Braddon's first recorded stage appearance by Wolff was in Beverley, and at this time she also acted in Hull – not at the Theatre Royal, but at the Queen's Theatre in Paragon Street (the theatre in *The Black Band* is called the Paragon). This theatre was leased by Joseph Henry Wolfenden and Robert Rivers Melbourne, and they had managed it since 1854. It seated three thousand people, and was built in an Italianate style with stuccoed bricks.[83] Braddon must have stayed on friendly terms with her former manager's widow (Wolfenden died in 1861), as the bibliophile Michael Sadleir had in his collection an inscribed presentation copy to Mrs. Wolfenden of *Aurora Floyd*.[84] Wolfenden and Melbourne opened their fifth season on 28 July with:

> a first-rate company, which has been selected from the principal London and Provincial Theatres, with the greatest regard for the respective reputed ability.[85]

Theatre reviews in the Hull newspapers are few, but there was an accident within days when the tragedian Mr. T. Lyon fractured his ribs while playing Quasimodo when some steps gave way. In September there was a production of *How We Live in the World of London*, which Braddon had so recently played at the Surrey. There was a Crimea war spectacular, *The Fall of Sebastopol; or, The Return of Our Heroes*. In November Ira Aldridge played at the theatre for five nights. Braddon acted with Aldridge a number of times. Although almost forgotten now he was the most famous black actor of the age, and was acting at the Surrey as early as 1833 after his arrival from America, when and after he was often billed as the 'African Rosicus.'[86] When the Queen's Theatre began preparations for the Christmas pantomime, *Humpty Dumpty! Crook'd Back Dick and Jane Shore; or, Harlequin Pearl Prince and Grape*, they advertised for children under four years of age and also for 'respectable girls under twenty. None but parties of good character need apply.'[87] The reward for these girls was not financial; the dancing skills they would acquire was the only recompense. It was clearly important to the management that the reputation of their theatre was not damaged by employing morally questionable girls; they would have been anxious not to offend their better class of patron, as well as the courts who regularly renewed their licence. By being so careful about the moral character of their extras, the imputation would have been that the company's actresses were also above reproach. Wolfenden and Melbourne were credited with having rescued the Queen's Theatre from the 'low and degraded state' of earlier managers.[88] When the licence was renewed the theatre had reason to be proud of its record:

> Mr. MacManus reported there had not been a single case of disorder reported against the theatre for twelve months. The magistrates expressed surprise that the managers had been able to preserve such order.[89]

Although Braddon's performance in *Humpty Dumpty* in January 1857 was not singled out by the newspapers, at least one young boy, David Oliver, recalled 'when first I saw and was charmed' by Mary Seyton as she 'struck my juvenile fancy' and 'I gazed on a resplendent figure, clothed in "shining gold." '[90]

In May 1857, Braddon spent six nights performing at the nearby town of Beverley with a number of other members of the Hull company (while the Grand Opera Company was at the Queen's Theatre), guest starring with the up and coming actor Wybert Rousby (1835-1907), who twenty years later was manager of the Theatre Royal on Jersey. The managers of the Hull company, Wolfenden and Melbourne, decided to perform at the Assembly Rooms in Beverley after they had successfully assisted with the amateur dramatics of the Masonic lodge there. Rousby, who had been born Wybert Boothby, was broadly welcomed as a local boy made good. In *Still Waters Run Deep* Braddon played Mrs. Sternhold. This must have been a favourite and successful part for her, since she was later to play it on an important occasion in Brighton; she and Rousby also recreated their roles from this play in

Jersey twenty years later. When she was twenty two, in 1857, Braddon would have been too young for the part of Mrs. Sternhold, quite probably she was younger than Georgina Ross (the sister of Madge Kendal) who played her niece Mrs. Mildmay, but being tall and looking a little older than she was, she was frequently cast in older, stronger, roles. Rousby played Mr. Mildmay, the husband of Mrs. Sternhold's niece, who proves that 'still waters run deep' beneath his own mild character when he exposes the fraudster Captain Hawksley. Hawksley has masterminded an investment fraud, as well as having made love to the young Mrs. Mildmay and her aunt. Hawksley blackmails Mrs. Sternhold with the compromising letters she has written him. Mrs. Sternhold is a strong and witty character, but through the gallantry of her niece's husband has to accept he is the master of the house. The play was only two years old at this time and had been a huge hit for Tom Taylor. This was not the only good part Braddon had in Beverley: she also played Hortense in Charles Dance's *A Wonderful Woman*, as does Flora in *A Lost Eden*:

> I played the *ingénue* in *A Wonderful Woman*, all *fat*, every line a laugh. I had only just to look my nicest, in your white muslin, with a new white satin sash, and my hair in curls all over my head, and just to speak my words quietly. (p.292)

After the week in Beverley she supported Rousby in leading roles for his week in Hull. She played Helen de Montbrun in *The Love Knot* (Stirling Coyne) and Olivia in *Evadne* (Sheil). A few days later the guest star in Hull was Charles Dillon, and about whom Flora in *A Lost Eden* writes to her sister, 'He was starring here last week – a dear man!' (p.293)

Henry Nye Chart's Brighton Company

It must have been while acting at the Queen's Theatre in Hull, or in a nearby town, that Braddon was spotted by the up and coming actor manager of the Theatre Royal, Brighton, Henry Nye Chart. During the summer of 1857 Nye Chart toured the country as a member of a company of established London actors, the Allied Metropolitan Dramatic Company. Also among the company were Mr. A. Younge (the recipient of the letter written by Braddon and her mother when they were in Scotland two years earlier) and her old friends Adelaide and Charles Calvert, although Mrs. Calvert makes no mention in her autobiography of them meeting Braddon again at this point. On the 8 June this company appeared at Hull for two weeks. Chart engaged

Braddon for his own company, and on 1 August she was acting at the Theatre Royal in Brighton. At the commencement of the season the *Brighton Observer* stated that he 'has been performing in the provinces, on a tour, which has given him a rare opportunity of selecting a good stock company.'[91]

Brighton was at this time a fashionable resort, still known to many as 'London-by-the-Sea'. The town was also experiencing a rapid growth in population, it grew by forty one per cent between 1841 and 1851, and there was a flood of visiting tourists as a result of the London to Brighton train link which opened in 1841. During the summer of 1850 the railway brought seventy five thousand visitors to Brighton in a week, and on Easter Monday in 1861 one hundred and thirty two thousand visitors came to Brighton by train.[92]

It was a step up for Braddon when she joined the Brighton company of Henry Nye Chart, for his was a company that was considered the next best thing to a London engagement. It was noted especially for its famous guest stars, for bringing its audiences the latest plays, and for its imaginative sets. Its performances were attended by the aristocratic residents of the town, and by the many distinguished visitors to the resort. There were also to be no periods of unemployment; when the theatre closed at the end of the season, rather than the company break up and go its disparate ways, unusually for those days, the company went on tour leasing other theatres or guest starring for other managers. Braddon was to remain with the company for three years, three years in which she pursued her long term ambition of becoming a writer. Twenty five years later in the short story 'Across the Footlights' Braddon wrote of Brighton in 1857 as Helmstone-by-the-Sea.[93]

Five and twenty years ago, Helmstone-by-the-Sea was almost as gay and as fashionable a resort as it is now. It was the holiday ground – the lungs of London – just as it is now. Of course, it was not so big. (...) the days when 'Pam' was a power and the Indian Mutiny was still fresh in the minds of men, when Macaulay's History and Tennyson's Idylls were the books of the hour. (...) What a pleasant place it was in those days, with its sparkling parade, and narrowest of side streets, its shabby old baths and shabby old pier, and old-fashioned hotels (...) Helmstone had its own duke, its own resident duke, in that corner mansion on the cliff at the east end of the town. (...it was) at the old Theatre Royal – a smaller, shabbier building than the theatre of today – that Miss Rosalie Morton appeared as fairy-queen in the pantomime of 'Gulliver and the Golden Goose, or Harlequin Little Boy Blue, and

Mary, Mary, quite contrary, how does your garden grow?'
(pp.285-286)

The Theatre Royal is, as Braddon wrote in this story, bigger today than
it was in the 1850s, but structurally it is recognisable as the same
building, and retaining the colonnades of the original. Henry Nye Chart
rebuilt it a few years after Braddon left the company, when he had
purchased the freehold of the theatre. Situated in New Road, Braddon
lodged for at least part of the time at number thirty four, and at other
times a few doors away at number twenty six, above a shop called
Snellings. The road itself had been paid for by the Prince of Wales in
1805 to replace another road which he had sequestered for his own use.
In the same road, which is not a long one, under the same colonnade as
the theatre, was a hotel in the 1850s. Gas lighting had been installed in
the theatre as early as 1819, and Henry Nye Chart introduced further
comforts and decoration, and eventually (in 1866) increased the seating
capacity to almost two thousand.

Henry John Chart (1821-1876), like Braddon, was born in Soho
(coincidentally both he and Braddon were christened at St. Anne's
Church) and like her he did not come from a theatrical family,
abandoning his apprenticeship with the piano maker Broadwood to
become a professional actor. He added 'Nye' to his name in tribute to a
friend, an amateur actor called Henry Nye. His family's initial
prejudices were overcome, and his father, John Chart, a tailor and land
surveyor, became his son's company treasurer, and he and his father
lived in the 'Cottage' attached to the theatre. In 1867 he married the
leading lady, Ellen Elizabeth Rollason, and even before his death in
1876 Mrs. Chart helped with the management, and after which she took
over completely as manager until her own death. Chart who, like many
not born into the profession, had been a keen amateur, started acting at
the Theatre Royal in Brighton in 1850, becoming the lessee of the
theatre in 1854. Chart was clearly well liked and respected by his peers,
and he had the support of most of the local press. His own particular
forte was as a comedian. Braddon remained with the Chart company for
the rest of her acting career, writing fondly of him after the death of his
wife in the *World*,[94] and remaining friends with the Chart family until
her death. Her short story 'Across the Footlights', where a number of
places and people in Brighton have been renamed, contained the
following tribute to him:

Mr. de Courtenay was the kindest of men and of managers. His
actors and actresses adored him. He was so thoroughly good, so

friendly, so honourable, so conscientious, that it was impossible to grumble at anything he did. (p.287)

Her portrayal of Mr. de Courtney is in contrast to some of the mean spirited managers who appear in a number of her novels. His obituary in the *Brighton Gazette* also testified to his generosity as a manager:

> Mr. Henry Nye Chart not only achieved fame as a caterer, but his name echoes throughout every theatre in England as one of the best-principled managers, who never allowed a member of his company to know the want of his salary.[95]

At the beginning of the season at the end of July in 1857 an advert in the *Brighton Gazette* declared that the interior and comfort of the theatre was much improved:

> During the recess the Theatre has been entirely re-painted and decorated, also various improvements made to increase the accommodation of numerous patrons and the public in general. The Dress circle and Boxes have been entirely re-painted and improved.[96]

All of the acting company were new to Brighton, except Cicely Nott who was a great favourite in the town, and William Cooper and G.K. Maskell.[97] At the beginning of the season each year much of the company was new, and some members left during the season when they had the opportunity of a debut in London. In the years Braddon was with Chart's company she seems to have stayed longer than any other actor. On the first night, 1 August 1857, Henry Nye Chart gave a comic opening address, written by William Sawyer, on his duel role as both actor and manager, and the National Anthem was sung 'indifferently' by the company. Unfortunately none of the papers mention in their reviews of *The Prince of Happy Land* Braddon's debut at the Brighton theatre as Fairy Pineapple in Planché's 'Fairy Extravaganza'. The pantomime is written in verse and Fairy Pineapple, who does not appear until the very end of the first act, arrives with her troop of good fairies just as Princess Desiderata has been turned into a white fawn by her rival Princess Nigretta and the wicked Fairy Carabossa. Braddon would have ended the first act with the song 'Come with me to Fairy Land' as the fairies began their ballet. In the second act Fairy Pineapple, summoned by the rubbing of a magic ring, manages to restore the Princess by day, and she sings with the Princess and Floretta 'A Life by the Galley Fire'. Pineapple appears again at the end to bring about a happy conclusion after the Prince has shot the fawn not realising her identity. In the first week the *Brighton Gazette* noted of the play *A Cure for the Heartache*:

> The little part of 'Ellen' was played by Miss Seyton, in a very pleasing and natural manner. (...) In conclusion, we fully believe that when the company thoroughly works together, it will be found to be the best seen in Brighton for many years.[98]

Much of the trade at this theatre and the other provincial theatres where Braddon worked was boosted by events which brought strangers to the town. In Brighton this was usually race week. Other towns too had races, as well as fairs and visits to the town by royalty. Such events were often combined with the theatre, and the stewards of the races would act as patrons for a 'Grand Special Night' at the theatre. Just as the theatre was not quite respectable to many people, nor was the race track; The *Brighton Gazette* felt that the presence of the races and the people who frequented them had lowered the tone of the theatre during Race Week:

> The attendance during Race Week was good. It was more numerous than select, which might have been expected from the motley assemblage in the town, but now that there is no longer this excuse, we trust to see a little more regard to propriety of conduct in the dress circle and boxes than we too frequently observed.[99]

It is noteworthy that when Braddon became famous as a writer of sensation fiction she was as much condemned for her knowledge of the race track as she was for her theatricality.

Also at the beginning of the season Braddon played the Duchess in *The Child of the Regiment*, which was the Brighton favourite Cicely Nott's most successful play. For a young actress it must have been galling that Braddon played parts she was far too old for. It seems to have happened often to her. She played Gertrude in *Hamlet*, Widow Melnotte in *The Lady of Lyons*, and she played Lady Capulet in *Romeo and Juliet* in September 1857 when she was only twenty two years old. Her plight was pitied by one of the newspaper critics:

> We were sorry to see a young and prepossessing lady like Miss Seyton saddled with the character of "Lady Capulet", which she did not play well, simply because it is palpably out of her line.[100]

That this was a cause of much annoyance to Braddon herself can be noted from several comments by her in fiction, where a young actress is similarly humiliated. In *A Lost Eden* Miss Mandlebert warns the excited Flora what sort of parts she will be doomed to play when she starts in the provinces:

> "Oh, it would be heaven," said Flora. "And what sort of parts should I have to play?"
>
> "All sorts – Maria in the *School for Scandal*, the Widow Melnotte, Lady Capulet."
>
> Flora made a wry face. "Juliet's mother – an old woman!"
>
> "Lady Capulet is always played by the youngest actress in the theatre," Miss Mandlebert said severely. "Nobody expects you to make up old." (p.277)

Unfortunately for Braddon she played these sort of roles not just for the first couple of years but throughout her acting career. It was only in her fiction that she was able to give her heroines the sort of roles she really coveted, but never played herself, chief of which appears to have been Pauline in Bulwer Lytton's *The Lady of Lyons*. H.C. Porter later wrote of his impressions of Braddon on the stage at Brighton at this time, while remaining reticent about her actual ability:

> As I have seen her upon the stage, her pale stern features, rather protruding large mouth, and statuesque dignity are vividly impressed on my memory.[101]

In September she played Gulnare in the burlesque *Conrad and Medora*, which the *Era* considered to be 'the best burlesque that has been produced here, under the present management.'[102] Braddon soon came in for criticism when she appeared in *The School for Scandal*, 'Miss Seyton's Lady Sneerwell was execrable.'[103]

The esteem in which Henry Nye Chart was held was further increased when he took the unusual risk in the provinces of commissioning two new plays:

> The enterprising manager, is further, so far treading on the heels of his London contemporaries as to have in preparation two entirely new pieces, written expressly for him.[104]

The first of these was *Distinguished Connections*, in which Braddon played Jane Beaufort, and was a farce by Captain Edward Murray. The *Era* was unimpressed by this effort, finding it weak and derivative: 'The text is inferior, and shows more knowledge of other writings than stage business.'[105]

Despite Brighton's reputation as a place of liberally minded entertainment, there was some concern that its theatre was not always putting on the right sort of plays. The *Brighton Gazette* particularly objected to *Jack Sheppard* as a training ground for working class criminality:

> Talk not to us of the fearful warning of Jack's final end, we know that more glory is unfortunately felt by our lower classes in his daring achievements (...) its characters are thieves, murderers, loose characters, and thief takers; and, surely, enough immorality is compelled to be witnessed in reality in our streets, without having it introduced on the boards of our Theatre.[106]

At various times the play was often banned or censored in response to fears about crime, but its performances in Brighton would have been of interest because the author of the novel on which it was based, William Harrison Ainsworth, lived in the town.

Shortly after this Braddon was praised as Fairy Gentilla in *The Invisible Prince*[107] and she also played in Charles Reade's *Masks and Faces*, which she was later to use so effectively in her novel *Strangers and Pilgrims*; unlike her heroine she was not destined to play Peg Woffington, but the production attracted good reviews:

> (It) was played in a style that has not been surpassed in Brighton. Mr. Cooper played Triplet, the poet, painter, and dramatic author in his very best manner; and Miss Bowering's representation of Peg Woffington called forth the most enthusiastic applause (...) Pomander of Dewar, and Kitty Clive of Miss M. Seyton are deserving a word of praise.[108]

At this time Braddon seems to have been mainly in supporting roles, and although these often brought good reviews they still tended to make her sound like a beginner who was improving. For example, the description of her in *The Honeymoon* (Tobin):

> The Zamora of Miss Seyton was about the best performance we have seen by that young lady, who has greatly improved since the commencement of the season.[109]

She had one of the two female roles in *Little Toddlekins* (Charles Mathews) as Annie Babicombe, 'a very trying part, played with much discernment.'[110] This was a farce about a young man whose marital chances are thwarted by the existence of his forty eight year old step daughter. Confusion ensues when he tries to pass her off as his mother, and pretend that his step daughter is really a small child, 'Little Toddlekins'. Braddon played Annie Babicombe, his young fiancée, who refuses to marry him when she finds out the age of her prospective step daughter. All is resolved when Annie's father marries the step daughter. In the second original play that Chart commissioned, Braddon played Aurelia Maggies in *Eight Hours at the Seaside*, a locally set comedy by *Brighton Herald* journalist and poet William Sawyer, a man who was to become an influential friend to Braddon.

Brighton and on Tour in Coventry in 1858

Just after Christmas and in January 1858 the main feature was the pantomime by Mr. C.A. Somerset, *King Blusterbubble and Grummo the Giant*. Yet again, for the third time, Braddon played the fairy queen of the piece, 'Miss E. (sic) Seyton as "Phenora" a fairy queen did much for the success of the piece.'[111] Although it was not considered to be the best written of pantomimes, the spectacle was very impressive:

> But if the text is not quite up to the mark, this is almost counterbalanced by the magnificence of the dressing, the beauty of the scenery, the grotesqueness of the masks, and the cleverness of the mechanical changes. (...) The introduction was well acted by Miss Seyton.[112]

The *Brighton Guardian* took the contrary view and declared it was the worst pantomime ever seen at Brighton, cheaply done with no merit. The drama critic of the *Guardian* seems to have had a vendetta against Henry Nye Chart's management style at this time, and against the *Brighton Herald* which he described as 'a ready mouthpiece of the Manager.'[113] Chart even stopped advertising in the *Guardian* for a while. The *Guardian* claimed that there had been great losses at the beginning of the season, calling the Grand Fashionable Box Nights advertised in the *Herald* 'begging petitions'. It went on to say that the company had been in some trouble:

> The fortunes of the establishment were, however, for a time rescued from assuming a more serious or embarrassing character by a species of windfall in the shape of what is vulgarly termed a "pull", which the Manager got out of a Fashionable Amateur

Performance at the end of November when he is supposed to have netted something like £130 clear.[114]

In the time Braddon was with the company there were several amateur performances. These consisted of three popular plays performed by amateur gentlemen, supported by the ladies of the company. There were never any lady amateurs when Braddon acted on these occasions; doubtless the women they acted with on private occasions were not allowed to perform to a paying audience and had to be replaced by professionals. Perhaps Chart did adopt this strategy in the hopes of recouping losses, but, having been a keen amateur himself, he was also sympathetic to their enjoyment. It was doubtless annoying to the professional actors to lose their parts to amateurs. The situation may have been slightly different in London where the *Theatrical Journal* profiled lady amateurs as well as men, so perhaps the provinces were a little behind the times in this respect. Braddon probably disapproved of the practice, for when in *Dead Sea Fruit* Lucy acts in London she is replaced as Julia in *The Hunchback*:

> "And there is a young lady coming to play the part – at least, she is not very young – an amateur lady, who comes in a brougham with two horses, and whose dresses, they say, cost hundreds of pounds." (p.137)

Her replacement is rich and haughty, and is insulted at the suggestion she may have any ambition to be an actress, for she is rich enough just to amuse her friends. Laurence says angrily:

> "And are you aware that it is you, and ladies of your class, who bring discredit upon the profession which you condescend to take up for the amusement of your idle evenings? It is this – amateur – element which contaminates the atmosphere of our theatres, and the manager who fosters it is an enemy to the interests he is bound to protect." (pp.137-138)

Also in January Braddon played Lady Margaret in *Lord Darnley*, during which George Melville, who played the hero, battled against a very heavy cold. Braddon again played Widow Melnotte in her favourite play *The Lady of Lyons*, this time Miss Bowering played Pauline and Mr. Steele, it was noticed, had rather a limited costume change:

Mr. Steele (is) a good Beaugeant, though we would suggest to him that it is not customary for a gentleman to wear precisely the same dress for two whole years, even though he may be the son of a Marquis. Miss Seyton was well received as Widow Melnotte.[115]

Mr. Steele's limited costume change may well have stemmed from his own limited means, as actors were usually expected to provide their own costumes. As the Brighton company was long established and had a firm base at one theatre the company must have built up a collection of some costumes for pantomimes, but the actors would have had to provide many of their costumes. In smaller companies actors had to provide all of their costumes, and all had to buy their own wigs and make-up. Doubtless extras in the Brighton company would have had to provide all of their own clothes, but since some of the adverts mention new costumes it would have been unfair to expect the main company members to keep on supplying them. In any case, Braddon warned any aspiring actors amongst her readers of *The Black Band* not to forget these additional expenses:

The would-be actor should remember this. The materials of his art are numerous and expensive, and what is more, they have to be purchased out of his own slender salary; and he must often, perhaps, deprive himself of many comforts in order to procure them. There are few arts so difficult as that of the actor, and perhaps none that in a general way, is so badly paid. (p.226)

The nation and the whole of Brighton celebrated the wedding of the Princess Royal, Princess Victoria, to Prince Frederick of Prussia on 25 January. The theatre played its part, and the admission was free for that evening's entertainment:

The Theatre was engaged and opened under the superintendence of a special committee, entrée being obtained by means of tickets which were, in the first place, conferred only on subscribers to the general fund. There was, of course, a good house; but at no time was it full, for many persons passed in and out, dividing their attention between the Soirée and the Theatre. This was to be regretted, as to some extent it defeated the primary object of securing the greatest amount of amusement to the greatest number of persons.[116]

The house was not full to capacity, as some people had booked seats and not turned up. William Sawyer composed some special verses for the occasion which were sung by Ellen Thirwall, but other than that there 'was no special allusion to the great event of the day. The Mayor entered the stage-box soon after ten and was greeted by general applause. The outside of the house was illuminated with a Star in gas.'[117]

As the season drew to a close the *Guardian* had a final swipe at Chart, speculating, 'is it, as is sometimes hinted, that fortune has cast him on a station somewhat incompatible with his breeding?'[118] Part of its argument was that Chart was putting on too many burlesques which denigrated the actors and their art. The last night of the season did not finish until one thirty in the morning, and during Chart's humorous address the audience joined in, hissing at the name of the *Guardian*.

Chart extended his horizons when he took over a second theatre, the Theatre Royal at Coventry, to which he took his Brighton company. When the Mayor of Coventry, Charles Dresser, attended in March, 'the house in *all parts* was well filled for the first time during the present season.'[119] On 17 March the same paper attributed the poor houses the theatre was experiencing to the poor trade in the town. Braddon did not get to play Mrs. Sternhold in *Still Waters Run Deep*, which she had played opposite Wybert Rousby. It was played instead by Chart's current leading lady, Adelaide Bowering.

Audiences, and the critic for the *Era* at Coventry, were clearly far more conservative than those at Brighton. Business was so bad that Nye Chart became the lessee of the nearby Theatre Royal, Leamington Spa, and the company travelled to the second theatre to play for a number of days.

It was not uncommon for actresses to play male roles, but it was often controversial. Braddon played a number of male parts at Coventry during the 1858 season, including Ricardo in *Miseraldi; or The Dying Gift*, Paris in *Romeo and Juliet*, the Earl of Westmoreland in *Henry IV*, and Francois in Bulwer Lytton's *Richlieu*. Perhaps she was required to play them more often on tour because the company was smaller in size, and actresses had to play whatever sex was needed. They do not seem to be the sort of parts where a sort of fetish element was implied, as described by Tracy C. Davis, but more in the line of straight acting like Charlotte Cushman, an American actress, who had played Romeo in a serious manner.[120] Even so it still attracted attention. Summing up the season the *Era* critic of Coventry was reserved in his praise of Braddon for this very reason, feeling that these male roles offended propriety:

We should be inclined to give Miss Seton (sic) a word of praise for her Francois, did not this lady show rather too evident an inclination to appear in male habiliments, at least if we may judge by the frequency of her appearance in such attire. It is a custom we cannot approve of, but whether the lady or her manager is most to blame, we have no opportunity of ascertaining. Miss Seton shows such excellent taste in dressing the characters of her own sex, that we should wish never to see her in any other.[121]

At Brighton such attire had caused no comment, but objections were not uncommon even in later decades. The display of the legs in male clothing was found deeply disturbing by some, even though it was quite common. In *Dead Sea Fruit*, a journalist rescues a young provincial actress from the stage, before he has fallen in love with her, because he cannot bear to think of her being exposed in such a way when she dances as the 'Cat's-meat Man':

> "I would rather see her under the wheels of a Juggernaut than dancing a cellar-flap breakdown." (p.151)

Such qualms are not shared by Braddon's actresses, for whom it is a matter of fact business. In *A Strange World* Justina, who hates being an actress, plays, just as Braddon did at Coventry, the page Francois in *Richelieu* without any reservations, only mentioning "He has a grand speech. One is bound to get a tremendous round of applause." (p.19)

Chart tried to improve business by bringing in guest stars, such as the Americans Mr. and Mrs. Barney Williams. On the 14 June the Queen visited Coventry and the theatre duly put on a special performance:

> In honour of her Majesty's Visit, there will be a Grand Dramatic and Musical Performance (...) First time in Coventry of the Princess's Comedy entitled *The Queen's Visit, or the Peasant's Journey from Village to Court*.[122]

Chart's own end of season benefit was successful, which must have encouraged him to think that they would have done better if the town had not been in recession.

Although Braddon considered Coventry an ugly town, she made friends while there, and considered her intellectual horizons had been expanded. She used Coventry as a setting more than once in her fiction, most notably as Conventford in *The Doctor's Wife* and as Stillmington in *Lucius Davoren*. It has been noted that the character of Charles Raymond in *The Doctor's Wife* was based, like Mr. Brooke in George Eliot's *Middlemarch*, on Charles Bray.[123]

Charles Bray, well known philosopher, phrenology enthusiast, owner of the *Coventry Herald*, and ribbon manufacturer, was one of George Eliot's closest friends. The leader of intellectual society in Coventry, Charles Bray had rejected formal Christianity for secularism, and had published *Philosophy of Necessity* (1841). His wife Cara was an intelligent and talented woman, and her sister, Sara Hennell, had recently published *Christianity and Infidelity* at the time Braddon met them. The young George Eliot, then still the unpublished Mary Ann Evans, came under their influence in the early 1840s and their company opened new intellectual possibilities to her.

Eliot may have considered Braddon's novels to be 'trash', but Braddon admired Eliot enormously, and it is an extraordinary coincidence that the two very different Mary Anns – poles apart as writers, but both to shock Victorian Britain for much the same reason with their private lives – both came under Bray's influence; albeit for only a brief time in Braddon's case.

Braddon revealed the association many years later in a letter to Edmund Yates, published in the *World* when Bray died. Many years earlier, while she was on tour in Coventry, Bray had spotted Mary and Fanny Seyton in Allesley churchyard. Characteristically Braddon did not mention in her published letter that she was an actress at the time:

> I wonder if it would interest any of your readers that I, too, was "amidst Arcadia born," so that I, too, had, for one bright interval in my youth, the happiness of knowing Mr. and Mrs. Charles Bray and Miss Hennell, whose names have now become household words? Mr. Bray had one of the most genial, happy natures possible to imagine, a gracious, liberal soul, full of sympathy with everything living. He had an open, jovial aspect, candid blue eyes, a rosy face framed in a halo of thick grey hair. He had suffered reverses of fortune, with a more than philosophic cheerfulness, since your typical philosopher is generally grumpy. At the time I visited them, Mr. and Mrs. Bray were living in a smaller house next door to the original Rosehill; but it was an ideal home for lives given up to thought and study – a roomy rambling cottage, with a timbered lawn in front of the drawing-room window, and beyond the slope of the lawn intervening meadows, which gave the enchantment of distance to the roofs and spires of Coventry. The house was lined with bookshelves, from the entrance-hall to the garrets; and under its thatched roof Mr. and Mrs. Bray dispensed the kindest, most refined hospitality, receiving Dickens, Thackeray, Gerald Massey, and all men and women of mark who ever came to Coventry. Even the occasion of my acquaintance with Mr. Bray is

characteristic of the man. He had seen my mother and me sitting with our books in a corner of a picturesque churchyard near Coventry, and had told his sub-editor, with whom we were already acquainted, that people who could appreciate the charm of that particular spot were people he should like to know, whereupon the introduction was made. Then came tea-drinkings and much talk, a most delicious little picnic in the grounds of Stoneleigh, long discussions about phrenology and natural religion, conversations which were like the opening of new worlds to me; but not a word was ever said of *Adam Bede*, although the literary world was just at that time alive with criticism and discussion about that great book. The Brays respected the author's *nom de plume*, and there were no hints or head-shakings, no 'we could an if we would' from any member of that happy trio. I remember hearing Beethoven's Moonlight Sonata for the first time in my life, played by Miss Sarah Hennell. I can see the pretty drawing-room, the large bay-window, the flowery lawn, and far off the blue smoke and slated roofs of one of the ugliest towns in England. The Brays made Coventry beautiful to me in that Springtide.[124]

Charles Bray sounds delightful from this, and every bit as kindly as Charles Raymond, but George Eliot's biographer Frederick Karl has labelled him the 'Don Juan of Coventry'.[125] The Bray household was anything but conventional, and Bray had fathered six children with his cook, persuading his wife to adopt one of them into their household. Initially the young actress sitting in a churchyard may have appealed to Bray on a less worthy level than a shared admiration of the picturesque. For their part, as Braddon was already writing for newspapers (more on this in the next chapter), she and her mother probably thought it would be a good idea to meet the proprietor of the *Coventry Herald*.

The company returned to Brighton for the start of the season on the 31 July and, as seems to have been traditional by now, William Sawyer wrote Chart a humorous speech for opening night. Chart reintroduced his company and Braddon reprised her role in *The Lady of Lyons*, which was described by the *Brighton Herald*:

The usual ceremonies were observed. On the ringing up of the curtain the manager, Mr. Nye Chart, was disclosed, surrounded by the whole of his company, – and this was a signal for a burst of hearty cheering from all parts of the house (...) Miss M. Seyton, who, in her laudable efforts to realize the aged widow Melnotte reminded us of the lady in Coleridge's *Christabel*, whose "Face was as a damsel's face,/ And yet her hair was white." (...) Miss

Seyton appeared to great advantage in the little part given to her in this piece.[126]

Braddon played the title role in a musical burlesque, *Lalla Rookh*, which encouraged the *Brighton Guardian* in its anti burlesque campaign:

> it tends to lure the actor from the "legitimate" school and to corrupt his style (...) our views are strengthened rather than weakened by the recent production of Lallah Rookh (...) Miss M. Seyton is somewhat inanimate as Lallah Rookh.[127]

Lalla Rookh was written by Robert Brough, a writer who later edited a volume of Maxwell's magazine the *Welcome Guest*. A few days later there was a revival of *Eight Hours at the Seaside* which did not start till after midnight:

> Mr. Dewar and Miss Seyton played their original characters, but were evidently quite worn out by a long night's play, and the lady was almost inaudible.[128]

It must have been an exhausting evening, and even when not running as late as this the theatre often had a different atmosphere outside as it closed. Despite its many aristocratic patrons the exterior of the theatre presented a less respectable picture when the prostitutes congregated under the theatre's elegant colonnades. In 1860 'a Graduate of the University of London' in his book *Brighton As It Is* described the scenes surrounding the theatre at night:

> There is the Theatre in the New Road, conducted as theatres usually are, and attended with all those evils which experience has proved to be incidental to amusements of this kind. Close by there is a gin-palace with the usual appendages of plate-glass and flaring gas-lights, where prostitutes resort, in order to ply their sinful calling when the Theatre dismisses. The colonnade, after 11 o'clock, presents a very animated appearance, being then used principally as a promenade by the "women of the town", who are either there for the purpose of entrapping the unwary or of keeping some previous appointment. The women for the most part observe the outward rules of propriety, although on some occasions, we have witnessed scenes of drunken lewdness.[129]

It was scenes such as this which helped to associate in the public mind the links between actresses and prostitution. Braddon herself did not entirely disassociate some women of the theatre from this, describing in *The Black Band* at Her Majesty's Theatre, the Haymarket, the stream of ballet girls exiting the theatre and how those that are poorly but respectably dressed shelter from the rain under the colonnade, but those in silk and velvet get into their waiting broughams. Braddon warned the humble readers of *The Black Band* that these girls would find no pleasure:

> Alas for those who wear costly dresses and glittering jewels, but who, to win these, have bartered that purest of all gems – peace of mind! Lovely and brilliant, animated and fascinating, they appear to be joyous and happy. But we know not of the lonely hours of anguish which may wrack the breast of the hapless ballet girl who has exchanged her humble lodgings for the luxuries of a palace; (...) Weep for them; pity; but do not too harshly blame them! Poorly paid at the best, with, perhaps a drunken father or an invalid mother to support – perhaps the only provider for a band of helpless little sisters – sorely tempted by base and cruel men who hold the ballet-girl only as a toy to minister to their amusement, and to be cast aside for some newer fancy. (p.66)

Ballet girls were notoriously exploited and badly paid; one of the few managers who paid his ballet girls well enough not to have to supplement their income was Charles Kean. By reputation Henry Nye Chart was another, but most did not and Braddon argued that it was no wonder that some of these girls were tempted. She has the star ballerina, Lolota Vizzini, say:

> "it is these small and pitiful salaries that drive the ballet-girl to become that which on first entering the profession she little dreamed of ever being. Bad men offer their jewels and wealth to girls who perhaps are almost starving; and the virtuous world, riding by in carriages, wonders that the ballet-girl falls." (pp.188-189)

Like most Victorian towns and cities Brighton provided great social contrasts, with squalor in close proximity to the opulence of its Regency architecture. Not only were the prostitutes and the gin palace close by, but also some of the poorest homes in Brighton. A surgeon called Nathaniel Paine Baker later described such an area near to the theatre in 1860 called Pimlico and Pym's Gardens where the poorest fishing families lived in unsanitary huts, their children unclothed, and everywhere the smelling, putrid carcasses of fish.[130]

The African American actor Ira Aldridge returned to Brighton to a rapturous reception after a twenty year absence, playing Othello opposite Braddon's friend Florence Haydon as Desdemona. His success was a mystery to the critic of the *Guardian*, who seems never to have liked anything:

> It may be that they tolerate in the African what they would not submit to in the European; but then that is indicative of their sympathy for the coloured race rather than significant of a want of artist appreciation.[131]

In this judgement he was untypical as Aldridge was one of the biggest draws in the 1850s, and was feted throughout Europe including by the Czar when he visited Russia. On the 20 October the newspaper published a letter from Ira Aldridge, defending himself vigorously, explaining how for twenty years he had argued against ignorance and intolerance whenever he found it:

> I have struggled hard, encountering almost insurmountable difficulties, to make not only for myself, a name, but to refute the assertions propagated by the enemies of my race and colour, – that we blacks are incapable of mental cultivation. I did not come to Brighton unsolicited. Mr. N. Chart, a friend of long standing, gave me an invitation, which I (sojourning temporarily in the neighbourhood) accepted. (...) I was mortified and pained on perusing, in Prague (...) Sir, I am not one of those who affect to treat with indifference what the newspapers say of them. When such an assertion is made in my presence I unhesitatingly class the speaker as a false-speaking knave or fool.[132]

The *Guardian* critic also disliked the following star attraction, Sir William Don; Don attracted good audiences wherever he went, for as a genuine baronet of exceptional height he was quite a curiosity:

> Deficient almost of the first principles of his newly adopted profession, his impersonations do not evince the remotest indications of art or artifice (...) If we are doomed to "Stars" pray let us have stars that shine.[133]

Don provides a charming example of an aristocrat going to the bad, as he had become an actor in 1850 (making his debut in New York) after running up enormous debts during a career in the army, spending £83,000 in three years, marrying and separating from an actress called Emily Saunders (with whom Braddon had acted at the Surrey), and having to sell all his property to pay his creditors. He was said to have 'ruined himself with drink and dissipation', and accounts rate him as a poor actor who played parts 'in his own character', but the novelty of his title and demeanour which showed 'conscious superiority, as well as good blood and conversance with the best society, to speak that quality of English' proved an irresistible draw on both sides of the Atlantic.[134] A few years later, in 1862, an impoverished Don died at the age of thirty six in Hobart, Tasmania.

Braddon played various other parts at the beginning of the season, which continued to attract praise. In *Married Life* she played the widowed lady's maid Mrs. Crispe to approval: 'Miss Seyton corrected her Hen-er-y in the most approved fashion,'[135] 'Miss Seyton never played better';[136] 'Miss M. Seyton, as Mrs. Crispe, is the very incarnation of an inquisitive and voluble gentlewoman's waiting-woman.'[137] In *Perdita* 'Her Hermione is very well played, the statue scene being particularly effective.'[138] Braddon made a less good impression in King Lear: 'Miss Haydon and Miss M. Seyton, as Goneril and Regan, were anything but imposing.'[139] Around this time bit-part actor Charles Bunton died, and the company clubbed together to give £15 to his widow.[140]

At the time Alfred and Mrs. Wigan guest starred with the company in early November, Charles Dickens was in Brighton to give readings. Alfred Wigan was a good friend of Dickens, and had acted with him. The Wigans were warmly welcomed by those who visited the theatre, but not all of Brighton was so welcoming. Braddon herself never met Dickens, but he did become involved in a case of prejudice against actors in Brighton at this time. Alfred Wigan's son had been asked to leave his Brighton school on discovery of his father's profession, and Dickens urged Wilkie Collins to write an article about the headmaster's conduct.[141] Dickens certainly did know Henry Nye Chart, as to this day there is a framed letter from Dickens to Chart in the theatre.[142]

November was not a good time for the theatre, audiences were small despite the quality of the drama produced:

> Novelty after novelty is produced; pieces are put upon the stage in a manner scarcely inferior to a London house, but all to no purpose. The benches are almost invariably empty, and a gloom is cast on all around.[143]

At the end of the season the company went to nearby Lewes for a couple of performances at the Corn Exchange, where they had large audiences, and the company 'were, throughout, most creditable to themselves as well as to their manager, and developed a considerable amount of dramatic talent.'[144]

The Brighton Company in 1859

During the January pantomime Braddon played yet another fairy queen, Industria in *Little Red Riding Hood and Baron Von Wolf*, in which 'Industria, Miss Mary Seyton, a fairy with an army of juveniles, protects Little Red Riding Hood and the Boy Blue from their machinations.'[145] In February she played Alkalomb in *Ganem, the Slave of Love*, Prudence in *The Lady of the Camelias* at Ellen Thirwall's benefit, and when Ellen Thirwall played Jack Sheppard, Braddon played the contrastingly honest Thames Darrell, the other male lead. The *Brighton Gazette* said of the benefits:

> The "business" has really been great, averaging, we should say, upwards of £60 each benefit night. This is as it should be. The actor's profession involves considerable anxiety and toil.[146]

As Braddon was not a leading lady she did not have a benefit of her own, and she remained a walking lady, even when actresses who had been with the company for less time than she had left. Others, such as Florence Haydon, who became a leading lady after Fanny Maskell left, were promoted from walking lady ahead of her. At times Braddon must have wondered if she was ever going to get on; she must have known that it was highly unlikely that she was going to become a famous actress after seven years in the provinces. Even though Henry Nye Chart was a great personal friend he was clearly not influenced by such considerations, and would not promote an actress if he did not think she was good enough. At the end of the season the *Brighton Gazette* declared after hearing Henry Nye Chart's end of season speech:

> No manager ever conducted the Brighton Theatre more respectably, no Brighton Manager ever exerted himself more, both as actor and manager, than Mr. Henry Nye Chart.[147]

In his speech Chart said that there had been sixty five new plays that season, many of which were previously unknown to the cast, which gives an indication as to how hard the company had to work. Further indication of Braddon's acting not being admired was given in the *Brighton Gazette* review of the whole season, in which it said:

> Miss Mary Seyton's voice is considerably against her as an actress, and too often suggests to us notions of insipidity in her performances, which perhaps we are not justified in feeling.[148]

On the 14 March the company returned to Coventry, confident of success. The previous year they had attributed the lack of buoyant trade to the recession in the textile trade, but by now this had recovered. Braddon had kept in touch with Charles Bray's friends there, one of whom wrote to her a few months earlier, telling her of the latest discussions, and adding 'We shall be heartily glad to see you, and I trust that we shall be enabled to repeat in the course of next Season those excursions wh. you found so pleasant; but if they are repeated we shall miss one prominent feature in them (...) Bray who goes to Switzerland for (the) greater part of the year.'[149]

On the 18 March Braddon played Lady Florence in *The Little Treasure* by A. Harris, a play which had first been performed four years earlier at the Theatre Royal Haymarket when, coincidentally, Braddon's part was played by Louise Swanborough who later produced Braddon's first play *The Loves of Arcadia* (1860). Again Braddon was twenty years too young for the role of Lady Florence, a woman with a grown up daughter. The play was a comedy involving the daughter's attempts to reunite her long separated parents. On 1 April she again played Mrs. Crispe in *Leap Year*, which had been such a success for her in Brighton.

If Chart had hoped things would be better than the previous year in Coventry he was wrong, as the company's takings were worse. With near empty houses the season closed far earlier than planned. Nye Chart blamed the failure directly on the snobbery of the middle and upper classes of the town:

> Had the upper classes of Coventry awarded me their fair share of support, which I had every reason to expect from the class of entertainment I have placed on the Coventry stage, I should not be at the present moment in this unpleasant position. I am not aware of any cause why myself and my company should be so completely deserted by them; (...) The *artistes* I have brought as my Brighton company I can say, without fear of contradiction, are superior to those any other provincial town can boast of, and I think I need only mention Mr. W. Cooper, Mr. Verner, Mr. Melville, Mr. Dewar, Miss Bowering, Mrs. Woollidge and c. to prove the fact. Those ladies and gentlemen could not come to Coventry as stock

actors and actresses unless the manager had some other theatre to enable him to make it worth their consideration, for the Coventry season is very limited, and the salaries usually paid in towns like this are very small, and very inferior to what they can at all times command. (...) the fact is nobody (comparatively speaking) came to see the Brighton company (...) From some unknown cause to me all my anticipated great events have proved failures. Even the strong body of 300 persons, called the Philanthropic Society, who have taken through the theatre during my management nearly £40 towards their funds, besides two guineas subscribed from my private purse, even then philanthropy could only raise £2 2s. 6d. (...) I find on referring to my books, that all the most intellectual evening's entertainments have produced the *worst* receipts; therefore I hope I may be pardoned for playing such dramas as *Jack Sheppard, The Bottle* & C.[150]

As well as the prejudice of the town, Chart pin-pointed three other areas which had precluded success for the company: the high rental they had to pay, thirty 'transferable silver tickets', and a cheap rival attraction in the form of the Corn Exchange being hired out for 'shilling hops', which he said resentfully were 'very intellectual and agreeable amusements, no doubt, for those who can enjoy them.'[151] He also condemned the small town prejudice against theatres and actors, when society people were hypocritically running their own musical and dramatic soirées which, as Chart pointed out, was drama just the same, only in their case church and society sanctioned it:

for musical and even dramatic entertainments for Mr. and Mrs. German Reed's, Mr and Mrs. Henri Drayton, and such like entertainments, are as dramatic in construction as anything I do, and they succeed better than *I can*; for even the saints can support them, and so ease their conscience by *not being within the walls of a theatre*.[152]

It is also noteworthy that the company did not receive the level of newspaper coverage and support that they got in Brighton: reviews were patchy and one of the local papers did not mention their presence at all.

After the disastrous Coventry season and early quitting of that theatre, the company spent two weeks at the Theatre Royal, Doncaster. Only seven months earlier during race week Charles Dickens and Wilkie Collins followed eighteen year old Ellen Ternan to this theatre, where the father of the Ternan girls had once been the lessee. Also appearing with Ellen and Maria was Fanny Addison whose father was the present lessee – as he was when the Brighton company arrived. Dickens mentioned the town in the 'Lazy Tour of Two Idle apprentices', when he and Wilkie Collins went to see Ellen Ternan act. In it he claimed the town was full of drunks, and watching with what were probably possessive eyes, that the race-going men at the theatre had 'A most odious tendency observable in these distinguished gentlemen to put vile constructions on sufficiently innocent phrases in the play, and then to applaud them in a Satyr-like manner.'[153] He felt particularly affronted by one drunken man's so 'horrible' remarks, that he wondered if actresses should be so exposed:

> whether that *is* a wholesome Art, which sets women apart on a high floor before such a thing as this, though as good as its own sisters, or its own mother.[154]

Dickens of course was quite happy to leave his wife for an actress, but would not let his daughter Kate, who was the same age, become one. For Henry Nye Chart the success of the two weeks helped to recover the Company's fortunes. Sensibly their chances of a good audience were increased by it being race week in the first week, and the second saw the assembly of the First West Yorkshire Yeomanry Cavalry. The 25 May saw the officers of the Cavalry and Earl Fitzwilliam act as patrons. In an advert in the *Doncaster Chronicle* on the 6 May the manager placed an advert announcing the company's opening on 16 May:

> Mr. Addison respectfully intimates that the Ladies and Gentlemen of Mr. Nye Chart's Company are all METROPOLITAN ARTISTES, and bring with them a London, as well as a Provincial, Reputation.[155]

All of the touring company were listed, showing that although the company was smaller than that at Brighton – eight women, eight men, one boy, and the band – it was still a respectable size. The advert also mentions they had brought with them all of their costumes from Brighton, as well as the scenery, so there must have been a great deal to transport from town to town. Braddon played a number of parts, including Mrs. Popples in *The Man of Many Friends*, Belinda in *The Prisoner of Rochelle* and Nan in Charles Reade's *Never Too Late to Mend*. The *Doncaster Gazette* hailed Braddon's performance in a strong role, 'Miss M. Seyton, as Nan, was precisely what the author intended – dashing, fearless, and at home in every scene.'[156] In a less appreciative review in the *Doncaster Chronicle* on 20 May, some space was devoted to Braddon's acting:

> As we have not yet noticed Miss Seyton's acting we may here say a word. Her style is polished and only the result of considerable study, and with a tall and elegant figure her appearance is imposing. She, however, assumes a little too much of the majestic and "Tragedy Queen" in her acting, which in comedy mars the effect extremely. By throwing off this and making her figure a little more flexible, she would place herself beyond criticism.[157]

The first race night guaranteed a good house, and on succeeding nights they had noteworthy patrons, and were attended by the 'principal families of the town'.[158] This was in contrast to their reception in Coventry, where the 'principal' families had made a point of staying away. At the end of two weeks it was declared:

> Although Mr. Nye Chart has been honoured with one of the most successful seasons the theatre has enjoyed for many years, yet it is no more than his untiring and assiduous exertions merited, and the only matter of regret is that his stay in Doncaster has been so limited.[159]

At the beginning of June they were in Hull, this time not at the Queen's Theatre where Chart had first seen Braddon act but at the Theatre Royal under the management of John Pritchard (the Theatre Royal was destroyed by fire later in 1859), where she had a good range of parts including Mrs. Sternhold in *Still Waters Run Deep* and Dinah Blowhard in *Slasher and Crasher* (Maddison Morton). The *Hull Packet* perceived 'Miss Seyton performs very creditably, and has much improved since her departure from Hull.'[160]

Two weeks later the company was in Leeds. Business was not good in the first week because the weather was so fine that audiences stayed away.[161] Braddon played the heroine Miami (a role famously created by Madame Celeste), the daughter of a Frenchman and an Indian, who marries Irish rebel leader Connor O'Kennedy in *Green Bushes* (Buckstone). She also played Florizel in *Perdita* and Mrs. Trictrac in *The Married Rake* (Selby) which the *Era* said was 'capitally done by Miss Mary Seyton and Mr. Dewar as Mr. Flighty and Mrs Trictrac.'[162] During Fair Week the best female roles were taken by the guest star Rebecca Isaacs, whom Braddon had admired before she herself was an actress when she saw Isaacs in *Henri Quatre* at the Strand theatre:

Rebecca Isaacs, whom I knew in after years as the wife of the excellent Tom Roberts, acting manager at the Princess's, was then in the zenith of her popularity – a handsome young Jewess, with magnificent eyes, and a fine mezzo-soprano.[163]

It remains noteworthy that in her two essays of reminiscences about plays and actors she had seen, she never mentioned how she had met them and acted with them. In 'Fifty Years of the Lyceum Theatre' she explained her gap in seeing performances at the Lyceum by only saying, 'I was far away in the north of England during these two managements.'[164]

On 30 July the new season began in Brighton, and again other events in the town influenced the programme:

During the race week the manager will adopt a plan similar to the one which answered so well last year. He will play good stock pieces and favourite farces, leaving for the succeeding week the introduction of one of the latest burlesques.[165]

The opening night followed the usual tradition of Chart introducing the whole company after the singing of the National Anthem. Adelaide Calvert guest starred in *Love Chase* and a long humorous poetic address was written by William Sawyer and read by Nye Chart, part of which referred to the disastrous Coventry tour:

I have found out what "going to Coventry" means.
That it means, for the manager, houses are bare
As Lady Godiva with "nothing to wear,"
With this disadvantage that soon, I could see,
Not one Peeping Tom would come peeping at me.
In fact, though more freely than most folks I went there,
I hope never again to go or be sent there;
But returned to the scenes of my natural sway,
Again I am "monarch of all I survey."[166]

The *Brighton Gazette* complained that on this night the theatre was too hot and 'badly ventilated.'[167] At the beginning of August Braddon played Celia in *As You Like It*, in which she 'deserve(ed) a word of commendation',[168] and Mrs. Calvert played Rosalind. Shortly afterwards she played a 'sufficiently spirited'[169] Clementine in *The Marble Heart*, but on the 5 September Madame Celeste arrived to guest star for two weeks which meant she replaced Braddon in parts she played in the stock company, like Miami in *Green Bushes*. Madame

Celeste had originated and indeed played these roles in Brighton twenty five years earlier.[170] Braddon acted with Madame Celeste in *The Sister's Sacrifice*, playing Madame Belan to the disapproval of the *Brighton Gazette*:

> we should hear with much more pleasure if she would pay more attention to pronunciation and the aspirate.[171]

The week following Madame Celeste brought the American Shakespearean actor James Bennett, who seems to have been unpopular with audiences and critics. Braddon played Gertrude in *Hamlet* and Eleanor in *King John*, although, according to the Brighton Observer, with little success:

> The support he received from the *corps dramatique* was discreditable to the establishment, probably arising from the wish of the performers not to take the shine out of the "star" (...) Miss Seyton's "Queen" exhibited a great want of dignity, and she was too young a representative of the mother of the antique young Hamlet.[172]

The *Brighton Gazette* added to this, saying, 'Miss Seyton's "Queen" was insipid.'[173] The following week Ira Aldridge returned as guest star, and his leading lady in *Othello* was ungallantly described: 'Miss Neville pleasing, though somewhat overweight as Desdemona.'[174] Braddon acted opposite him in *The Slave*, when Aldridge played Gambia and Braddon, later to write about an octoroon slave, played the quadroon slave Zelinda. In the same week the child actors Kate and Ellen Terry made their first appearance in Brighton at the town hall; years after both sisters were to become good friends of Braddon. On the 6 October there was another amateur evening, when the women of the company assisted the Officers of the 4th Dragoon Guards. A number of times during Braddon's years in Brighton local militias put on amateur nights, and Braddon must have got to know a good many officers, as her novels often have them as characters and her poems of the period were full of military themes. However interested the officers performing were, their friends who came to watch were somewhat exuberant. The *Brighton Gazette* described the high spirits produced disapprovingly, and acting under these circumstances, as well as with the officers who were described as untalented, must have been difficult:

> the assemblage frequently displayed bad taste, not to say ill manners, by indulging in a buzzing, boisterous tête à tête during the

performances (...) From the high state of the atmosphere and the excessive heat experienced under such circumstances in this ill-ventilated, – we had almost written dangerous, – house, the laxity which prevailed throughout the evening became doubly irksome.[175]

On the 17 October Alfred and Mrs Wigan were the guest stars for two weeks, when they performed Wigan's own play *A Model for a Wife* and a selection of their most successful plays. In *A Bengal Tiger* (Dance), when there was a full house, 'Mr. Wigan was the firey old East Indian, Sir Paul Pagoda, and they were well played up to by Miss Seyton.'[176] Braddon got a big break on the 24 of October when Mrs. Wigan became suddenly ill and Braddon replaced her at an hour's notice, playing Mrs. Sternhold in *Still Waters Run Deep* opposite Alfred Wigan.[177] Despite her efforts, and stepping in at the last moment, the *Brighton Observer* remained unimpressed:

in consequence of the indisposition of Mrs. Wigan, "Still Waters Run Deep" was substituted for "The Jealous Wife", wherein Miss Seyton enacted the part of Mrs. Sternhold. Criticism would be unjust, considering the untimely notice for preparation; but after witnessing the superior performance of Mrs. Wigan in the same piece on Friday, Miss Seyton's defects were painfully apparent.[178]

It was perhaps unfortunate for Braddon to play the part only a couple of days after Mrs. Wigan, a famous actress who had played Mrs. Sternhold during the first season of the play in London; but the complete opposite was expressed by the *Brighton Gazette*, whose critic had rarely been impressed by her acting:

Justice compels us to commend the performance of Miss Mary Seyton, who, at very short notice, undertook the arduous part of "Mrs. Sternhold." We have never seen this young lady in a part to which she did more justice. She displayed an amount of physique truly remarkable, and her representation of the strong-minded woman does her an infinite deal of credit.[179]

Although Braddon had played the part before, it must have been a nerve-wracking occasion. Another replacement took place when Pauline Burette replaced Ellen Thirwall in Wigan's *The First Night*. Wigan had suggested that Ellen should sing her duet like a young girl, not to burlesque it, but she declared she had been 'insulted' to her husband Frank Hall who then refused to let her go on stage with Wigan.[180]

Braddon appeared in *Jessy Brown; or, The Relief of Lucknow* by Dion Boucicault, based on an allegedly true incident of the Indian Mutiny when the young Scottish lass Jessie Brown heard long before anyone else the pipers of General Havelock approaching the besieged Lucknow. Braddon played Mrs. Campbell and 'did her utmost to make the best of a trifling part.'[181] The play must have been quite spectacular with its siege scenes, cannons firing and liberation at the end by General Havelock. After the part of the Scottish girl Jessie Brown, played by new leading lady Margaret Eburne, Braddon had the best part: Mrs. Campbell is a young widow who married the wrong man and hopes to remarry her first love. She becomes the object of the lust of the evil Nana Sahib, Rajah of Bithoor, who says if she will be his he will leave Lucknow alone and make her two young children princes. Mrs. Campbell is brave in the siege, helping to load guns and swearing to kill herself rather than face a fate worse than death, and to kill her children too. Not surprisingly, as it was only two years after the actual event, the subject matter was considered to be in dubious taste and catering to the cheapest ticket holders in the audience. Doubtless, as when the company were in Coventry, when fashionable tourists were no longer in Brighton the local working class audiences had to be wooed with *Jack Sheppard* or recent true life drama:

> We did not stay to witness it, having no taste for siege horrors dressed up as melodramatic dishes to suit the taste of the 'celestials' who, however, mustered strongly, at half-price, prepared for this enjoyment.[182]

In November Madame Celeste returned, and Braddon again supported her as Geraldine in *Green Bushes*; Madame Celeste was so taken with the talents of Miss Neville (the overweight Desdemona) that she took her with her when she left to join her own company in London at the Lyceum.[183] Braddon had admired Madame Celeste since childhood, and although it must have seemed as if she would never get a second chance on the London stage, she had almost certainly decided by this date to abandon her career as an actress. The week after Mr. and Mrs. Charles Kean arrived, performing in a version of *Hamlet* which was too close to the original text for the liking of the *Brighton Chronicle*:

> we cannot see the use of the foul low language at the end of the second act, no respectable newspaper would think of disgracing its columns with such language, and we certainly cannot see why

actors need use it when other words, quite as effective, might be used without injury to the text of the play.[184]

Further disquiet was caused by the raised ticket prices during their visit. Rather than use the stock company the Keans brought with them their own actors for the other leading roles. The *Brighton Gazette* condemned this decision, arguing that Chart's company were more than equal to the occasion:

> Doubtless this is necessary at many small provincial theatres, and relieves Mr. and Mrs. Kean from many rehearsals, but at Brighton we unhesitatingly pronounce that in the stock company would have been found as efficient representatives, and in some cases even more so than the members of the Princess's Company.[185]

Although Braddon probably had very little to do when the Keans arrived, she admired them both greatly. As for so many, one of her greatest memories of going to the theatre was witnessing Charles Kean in his duel roles as the telepathic twins in *The Corsican Brothers* (Boucicault), 'one of the events of my early youth, a thrilling and never-to-be-forgotten experience.'[186] Ellen Kean was generally considered to be more talented than her husband and Braddon especially admired Ellen Kean's acting in *The Wife's Secret*, 'a play which her exquisite acting had made popular, and which has rarely been heard of since her death.'[187]

Chart continued with his policy of a succession of guest stars when Rebecca Isaacs arrived for two weeks in November. On the 4 December Braddon added to her gallery of 'old lady' roles, this time in *Romeo and Juliet*, when:

> Owing to Mrs. Woollidge's sudden illness, Miss Seyton, at short notice, kindly took her place as the nurse.[188]

At the benefit of Frank Hall and Ellen Thirwall they delivered a duologue by William Sawyer and presented an unusual production of Jerrold's *Black Eyed Susan* when the sexes exchanged roles, much to the irritation of the *Era* critic:

> The female characters in the latter piece were represented by gentlemen and some of the male characters by ladies. This is certainly "from the purpose of playing," and we trust we shall not again have to announce such a prostitution of the stage. As might have been expected, the boxes were nearly empty.[189]

Perhaps so near to Christmas and the pantomime season the cast were more interested in having fun. On the 19 December Henry Nye Chart had his benefit, at which the Marquis and Marchioness of Normandy were the patrons, and Braddon played Mrs Floff in *The Rifle and How to Use It* (Bridgeman). After the theatre had closed for a few days to prepare for the pantomime the company performed for two nights at the nearby town of Lewes at the Corn Exchange. On the way back from Lewes on the Tuesday the omnibus they were in was involved in an accident, and the leading actor and sometimes playwright Robert Soutar injured his leg:

> as they approached the hill about a mile on the road, Mr. Soutar got out on the step of the vehicle, holding on by the window of the door, for the purpose of enjoying a cigar. The night was very windy, and he had not been outside long when the coachman's hat blew off. He was in the act of alighting to seek for it – the night being very dark – when the driver turned his horses aside to prevent the omnibus going back on pulling up. This caused him to miss his standing, and his foot slipping between the step and the vehicle he fell and fractured the leg just above the ankle. He was lifted into the carriage and conveyed home to Brighton where he arrived about half-past two o'clock, when Mr. Burrows was sent for, but so swollen is the part injured, that up to last night it had been found impossible to reduce the fracture.[190]

Interestingly Braddon was to set the demise of her villain on this very road from Lewes to Brighton in her early novel *Lady Lisle* (1862), when Major Varney is dragged from his carriage and beaten about the head. The doctor who attended Soutar, John Cordy Burrows, was also to become a good friend of Braddon.

The Brighton Company seems to have been a friendly company, but even in the comparatively relaxed world of the theatre there were still some events from which women were excluded; a theatrical banquet was held for forty guests at the William the Fourth Inn to celebrate Chart's sixth anniversary as lessee, but none of the women of the company were present.

The Departure From Brighton in 1860

At the end of 1859 and beginning of 1860 Braddon did not appear as the fairy queen or anything else in the Christmas and January pantomime *Harlequin House That Jack Built* which, according to the

Brighton Guardian, was the most successful ever. One new play she appeared in was *Quicksands and Whirlpools*, penned by the injured actor Robert Soutar, of which the *Brighton Guardian* observed 'we are inclined to think that Quicksands and Whirlpools is more suited to the Victoria Theatre than to our more aristocratic atmosphere.'[191] It was based on a serial in the *London Journal* by Percy St. John, a magazine for which Braddon was soon to write herself. Braddon's acting commitments seem to have lessened at this time, probably because by now she was concentrating on her writing, and she had already arranged to leave the company. She had been writing during most of her time on the stage, and at some point this had become her main preoccupation, leading to an increasing lack of interest in performing.

On one occasion, as previously mentioned, in late 1859 in Brighton, Braddon was reunited with her old friend Mrs. Adelaide Calvert. However, the difference now was that Mrs. Calvert was a prominent leading lady, a rising star attraction, while Braddon was still playing secondary roles. Mrs. Calvert attributed Braddon's lack of success to her own loss of interest in her acting career, a lack of interest which led, at times, to a lack of professionalism when they appeared together in *As You Like It*:

> In the company at Brighton, I met again the charming companion of my girlish days at Southampton – Mary Seyton. She and her mother again lived near me. She was still playing walking ladies, and, it was evident, had made little progress in her profession. It was easily accounted for – her heart was not in it. She was writing a novel, and her theatrical work was a secondary consideration. I remember one night – when she was the Celia and I the Rosalind – that half her speeches were impromptu (though, somehow, she always managed to alight on the last three or four words correctly), and I exclaimed in tones of grieved remonstrance, "Oh, Mary, how you can go on for an important Shakespearean part, knowing as little as you do, I can't imagine!" She only laughed and said, "My dear, I gave you all your cues!" which she certainly had, but she had arrived at them by a route which was far from Shakespearean.[192]

Braddon must have realised that after almost eight years on the stage she was not likely to progress any further, especially after her engagement at the Surrey led to no further work in London. Although Mrs. Calvert was doing well, life could often be difficult as a married actress, especially if, as Mrs. Calvert found, there was a quick succession of children:

Towards the end of the season I was again compelled to absent myself – and about the time of its close my third little son, Louis, arrived. Knowing that my landlady was no adept in the culinary art, kind-hearted Mary often stepped across with something covered over in a breakfast cup, and the remark, "Mama has been making some good soup, and I feel sure you would like a little," or, "Mama has stewed some sweetbreads for our supper, and we think a little will do you good."[193]

If Braddon had continued as an actress it may have become harder as she got older; it might have been more insecure, and her roles may have become less interesting, rather like the career and prospective fate of Miss Mandlebert in *A Lost Eden*:

She had what theatrical agents called "a fine appearance", but was not beautiful. Her figure was her strong point: and she had played the young wives and dashing widows in one-act farces, of whom it was required to look nice and speak like a human being, for three or four years at various theatres without blame and without distinction; and in this unambitious walk, with occasional ambitious flights in provincial theatres, she was likely to continue till marriage with a man of means removed her from the boards; or until encroaching Time compelled her to take to spinster aunts and termagant mothers-in-law, instead of wives and widows. (p.140)

Justina, in *A Strange World*, also tells James Penwyn that for unsuccessful actresses like herself life is hard:

"those I know are like horses in a mill, and go the same round year after year. When I think that I may have to lead that kind of life till I die of old age, I almost feel that I should like to drown myself, if it wasn't wicked; but then I haven't any talent. I suppose it would all seem different if I were clever." (p.19)

How good an actress Braddon was is difficult to gauge. Reviews that have been quoted in this chapter differ wildly in their opinion, although more than one suggested her voice was not strong enough. Although Braddon was rarely the leading lady she often had large secondary parts, particularly in comedy which seems to have been her forte. When she did have good dramatic parts like Miami in *Green Bushes*, she had to give way if Chart engaged a guest star like Madame Celeste. Chart's preference for stars to bring in the crowds was an increasing trend observed by the *Brighton Guardian*, when it criticised the 'Star System' which during the 1858 season had produced thirty five star nights and in 1859 sixty five 'to the disparagement of his own Company.'[194]

When Braddon left the stage on 29 February 1860 she finally had a benefit night, shared with two other actresses. None of the local newspapers mentioned that this was her last performance, but it was recognised that she was becoming better known as a writer than she was an actress:

> On Wednesday, Miss Seyton, of literary rather than histrionic fame, appealed, and not in vain, to her friends.[195]

At the end of the season the rest of the company went to Cheltenham, while Braddon departed for Beverley to concentrate on writing. Most actresses who left the stage, left on marrying out of the profession, as in the previous September when Miss Castleton retired from the Brighton company on marrying a barrister, so Braddon was unusual in this. When Braddon first went on the stage she must have longed to make a name for herself in London, but instead she spent seven or eight gruelling years touring the provinces. Nor had she succeeded in making the large amount of money she wanted in order to keep her mother in comfort. As she did not manage to retain the status of leading lady after her season at the Surrey Theatre her wages would never have been large, and even when she finally had a benefit the profits had to be split with two other actresses. At the beginning of her career she was seen as a promising beginner, and this view of her work persisted. Perhaps like Justina in *A Strange World* she later felt her failing was a lack of life experience compared to other actresses. Justina is an untalented actress until she has been unlucky in love and had her lover murdered; after these experiences her performances change and when she makes her London debut she is a great success because: 'Her genius seemed to have been called into being by sorrow.' (p.192) In *Rough Justice* (1898) Braddon seems to suggest that far from being a fallen woman, a middle class actress like Mary Freeland can remain ignorant about the seamier side of life, partly because, like Braddon, she has always had a chaperone and the roles she has played have caused her to idealise what she knows nothing about:

> She had acted in *La Dame aux Camélias*, and had the exalted idea which most innocent women cherish about their fallen sisters. She idealized the guilty love, and told herself that such passions last a life-time.[196]

For the rest of Braddon's life she remained interested in the stage and numbered theatrical people amongst her friends, and her stepson Jack married Alice Wyndham, the daughter of Robert and Mrs. Wyndham. The Wyndhams were on the provincial stage at the same time as Braddon, and later owned the Theatre Royal in Edinburgh. Braddon clearly kept in touch with some of her acting colleagues, the Nye Charts remained life long friends (their son became the closest friend of her son William), as did leading lady Florence Haydon. Florence Haydon continued to act after her marriage to Mr. Waugh, in later years as a member of Charles Hawtrey's company, and she played Mrs. Whitefield in the first production of George Bernard Shaw's *Man and Superman* in 1905. Braddon's son, W.B. Maxwell, also remembered William Creswick, who had employed Braddon at the Surrey, as a regular visitor of his parents. After Braddon and John Maxwell bought Lichfield House in Richmond it seems as if amateur theatricals became part of her life, mentioning them on one occasion to Bulwer Lytton, and almost twenty years after she had acted with Wybert Rousby at Beverley she acted with him at her home, and then joined him at his Theatre on the island of Jersey for a special performance. For once it was her own celebrity, as an author, which drew a large and fashionable audience, and not the presence of a famous actor. John Maxwell was clearly very different to the Victorian husbands or fiancés she portrayed in novels like *Strangers and Pilgrims* and *Dead Sea Fruit*, since he had no problem with amateur dramatics at home, or with his wife taking part in this very public performance.

While unashamed of her acting career, Braddon never referred to it in the few interviews she gave later in life. In 1881 her friend, the critic Charles Kent, must have written to her, after misreading the name of Brandon for Braddon on an advert for the theatre. In her reply she said that after encouraging advice from the 'Master' (who must have been Edward Bulwer Lytton) she had never regretted her decision to leave the stage and devote herself to literature.

> No, my kind Sir, I have not tried to astonish the British Public as the great sorceress (...) When, encouraged by the generous advice of that great Master of his Art whom I revere as the first cause of all I have ever done in literature, I put my hand to the plough, there was no looking back at the more fascinating profession wh I surrendered. I really love the drama & there is one particular line of comedy wh had at one time – twenty years ago – an intense charm for me – but those days are long past – & I have no longer any ambition beyond the walls of my study. The Medea whose name deceived you is *Miss Brandon*.[197]

It would be interesting to know if this Miss Brandon was any relation to Braddon's girlhood admirer at Southampton, Mr. Brandon.

When Braddon became a writer there were some who looked down on her for her theatrical past. Many reviews of the 1860s condemned her dialogue for being too close to that of a melodrama, but behind such criticism lay the disapproval of Braddon the former actress. In *Dead Sea Fruit* Laurence warns Lucy that she will never really get on in the theatre because most actors are born into the profession and consequently get the best chances, but that when she changes careers her former life will still be held against her:

> "malicious people will reproach you with your dramatic associations, and discredit the truth and purity of your nature, because you tried to support your father by the patient exercise of your talents and your industry." (p.153)

Braddon herself was to find the truth of this, but such problems were a couple of years away. When she left Brighton and Henry Nye Chart's company she had a new income from a patron who had enabled her to become a writer, and it is this early writing which forms the subject of the next chapter.

Chapter One Footnotes

1. *Jersey Express*, 5 August 1876, p.3.
2. Braddon rarely granted interviews, refusing many including Miss Brooke Alder's request because she had 'made a rule not to be interviewed by the press.' (13 June 1902, Wolff collection) She also prevented publication of photographs whenever possible, although one pose of the session sold by the London Stereoscopic Company in 1863 shows her holding an issue of *Temple Bar*. Thereafter there were no further approved photographs, and Maxwell told Tillotson, 31 January 1885, 'My wife has an extreme objection to the publication of her portrait! therefore, please deny all applications – refuse absolutely – dissuade – and discourage in every way, all desire to invade the privacy of my wife (...) She only wishes to be known in her novels; and to her own circle of chosen friends.' (*Bolton Evening News* Archive, Bolton Central Library, Greater Manchester) Braddon thanked a photographer in a letter of 8 December 1893, Wolff collection, presumably from the *Windsor Magazine*, for duplicate copies of pictures he had taken of Lichfield House, she told him 'Portrait impossible – I have given that nowhere involving anything like publicity. It is such a comfort in moving about the world to be unrecognised.' Clive Holland, 'Miss Braddon: The Writer and Her Work', *Bookman*, vol. XLII, July 1912, p.53, was a favoured exception, writing that she longed to leave hotels if fellow guests realised who she was, and that her refusal to give pictures meant 'We were therefore fortunate in being able to persuade her to grant permission for the publication of the excellent photo, which was taken about twenty years ago.'
3. *Jersey Observer*, 15 August 1876, p.2.
4. *Jersey Observer*, 8 August 1876, p.3.
5. 'Miss Braddon at the Theatre Royal', *Jersey Express*, 12 August 1876, p.2.
6. 'Miss M.E. Braddon at the Theatre Royal', *Jersey Weekly Press and Independent*, 19 August 1876, p.10.
7. Clara, the daughter of a doctor, ran away from home with Rousby when she was only sixteen years old. Rated as a poor actress she was given leading roles on account of the beauty which led to her being a favourite with audiences and society photographers. After a stormy marriage Clara left Rousby in 1874 and continued a reckless life with the hunting set, and rumours of her drinking abounded. When Clara concealed their daughter in an Exeter Convent, Rousby did not see his child for several years, and when he discovered her whereabouts Clara escaped with the child through a convent window. During the ensuing custody battle, husband and wife attacked the other's moral character,

and custody was instead granted to Clara's sister, with occasional access allowed to each parent. Despite this, Rousby was responsible for all of his estranged wife's debts, and when she was taken to court on several occasions he was deemed liable. Clara died at the age of 27 in 1879.

8. *Jersey Observer*, 15 August 1876, p.2.

9. M.E. Braddon, *Before the Knowledge of Evil*, c.1914, unpublished typescript in the Robert Lee Wolff Collection of Victorian Fiction, Harry Ransom Humanities Research Center, The University of Texas at Austin, hereafter referred to as the Wolff Collection.

10. The only reference is in Joseph Hatton, 'Miss Braddon at Home. A Sketch and an interview', *London Society*, January 1888, p.23. 'She acted in several country theatres.' Braddon does not refer to it in the actual interview.

11. 'Death of Miss Braddon', *Daily Telegraph*, 5 February 1915, p.6. The writer, who was probably Porter, wrote an almost identical piece, 'Miss Braddon at Brighton', *Brighton Gazette*, 6 February 1915, p.7.

12. Robert Lee Wolff, *Sensational Victorian: The Life and Fiction of Mary Elizabeth Braddon* (New York: Garland, 1979) p.46 describes it as still her first season.

13. William Tinsley, *Random Recollections of an Old Publisher* 2 vols (London: Simpkin, Marshall & Co. 1900) II, p.92. Tinsley writes that Charles Millward, writing about life in Liverpool, in the *Liverpool Porcupine*, saw 'Miss Braddon as "Cinderella" in a pantomime at the old Amphitheatre, Kossuth in Liverpool.'

14. Wolff, p.49.

15. 'Death of Miss Braddon. The Famous Novelist's Associations With Beverley', *Beverley Guardian*, 6 February 1915, p.2. 'Miss Braddon, before taking up literature, had taken to the stage, and acted both in Hull and York.'

16. M.E. Braddon, 'The Woman I Remember', *The Press Album* (London: John Murray, 1909), p.5.

17. Michael J.N. Baker, *The Rise of the Victorian Actor* (London: Croom Helm, 1978), p.99.

18. Mrs. Adelaide Calvert, *Sixty-Eight Years on the Stage* (London: Mills and Boon, 1911), p.267. Mrs. Calvert, with her husband, was a part of one of the most famous husband and wives teams, particularly known for their Shakespearean revivals. Charles Calvert died in 1879, and Adelaide continued to perform to acclaim well into this century.

19. Martha Vicinus, *Independent Women: Work and Community for Single Women, 1850-1920* (London: Virago, 1985), pp.293-294. The 1851 census showed that there were 1.5 million unmarried women over the age of twenty, and there were 365,000 more women than men.

20. Joan N. Burstyn, *Victorian Education and the Ideal of Womanhood* (London: Croom Helm, 1980), p.130. Braddon later used her son's female secretary and a woman typist, Miss Dickens, on her manuscripts.

21. Baker, p.89.

22. Tracy C. Davis, *Actresses As Working Women* (London: Routledge, 1991), p.17 quotes Madge Kendal, *The Drama: A paper read at the Congress of the National Association for the Promotion of Social Science* (London: David Brogue, 1884).

23. Braddon, *Before the Knowledge of Evil*, pp.18-19. Another account of this evening appears in M.E. Braddon, 'In the Days of My Youth', *Theatre*, vol. XXIV, 24 September 1894, p.120.

24. Braddon, 'In the Days of My Youth', p.121.

25. Ibid. p.123.

26. Ibid.

27. *Brighton Gazette*, 23 October 1862, p.3 describes Braddon as M.A. Seyton. H.C. Porter, *The History of the Theatres of Brighton from 1774 to 1886* (Brighton: King & Thorne, 1886), p.113 confirms the name of Mary Ann.

28. W.B. Maxwell, *Time Gathered* (London: Hutchinson, 1937), p.274.

29. *Brighton Gazette*, 20 November 1862, p.8.

30. Braddon, *Before the Knowledge* of Evil, pp.148-149.

31. M.E. Braddon, *A Lost Eden* (London: Hutchinson, 1904), p.129.

32. Braddon, *Before the Knowledge of Evil*, p.2.

33. Wolff, p.19 supplies the new year from an unidentified newspaper clipping from 1915 owned by W.B. Maxwell. After noticing the varying ages given in obituaries of Braddon, the rector of St. Anne's Church Soho, Rev. G.C. Wilson found the original baptismal entry, 'Mary Elizabeth Braddon, born October 4 1835, daughter of Henry and Fanny Braddon, solicitor of Frith Street, baptised March 21, 1836.' Looking through rate books he identified the Braddon's house as 'on the east side of Frith Street, contiguous to Soho Square, probably no. 2 not now extant, being displaced for the enlargement of the Women's Hospital.' W.B. Maxwell continued to give 1837 as the year of his mother's birth.

34. Baker, p.81.

35. M.E. Braddon, *A Strange World* (London: Maxwell, 1875; repr. London: Ward, Lock & Tyler, c.1877), p.12.

36. M.E. Braddon, *Dead Sea Fruit* (London: Ward, Lock & Tyler, 1868; repr. London: Ward, Lock & Tyler, c.1869), pp.100-101.

37. Davis, p.73.

38. M.E. Braddon, 'Across the Footlights' in *Under the Red Flag* (London: Maxwell, 1886; repr. London: Simpkin, Marshall, 1890), p.289.

39. Letter in the Wolff collection from a Braddon relative to Fanny Braddon dated 8 January 1848,

40. Maxwell, p.274.

41. M.E. Braddon, *Strangers and Pilgrims* (London: Maxwell, 1873; repr. Maxwell, 1885), p.200.

42. Wolff, p.55. According to reports in the *Era* there were in fact two Miss Mandleberts, sisters; Kate Mandlebert also gave lessons.

43. Baker, p.66.

44. M.E. Braddon, 'In the Days of My Youth', p.124. It is possible the anonymous (semi-fictional?) essay 'My First Love', (*Belgravia*, vol. IXX, January 1873, pp.209-15) may have been by Braddon. The writer describes a stage struck childhood, how she longed to play a tragic heroine, her attempts to interest her friends at school in amateur dramatics and her teenage crush on the leading actor at her local theatre.

45. The account in *A Lost Eden* reads like an eye witness account; but when Braddon was acting in Southampton in 1853 there was a diaroma exhibited of the event narrated by Adelaide Biddles, and it would be interesting to know if Braddon really did see the procession, or was recalling the diorama.

46. Two years later, on 18 May 1855, A. Brown wrote to Fanny Braddon: 'I have frequently wondered what became of you and your daughter.' Wolff collection.

47. Undated letter c.1884 from M.E. Braddon to Bram Stoker, Stoker Correspondence, Brotherton Library, University of Leeds. Braddon hoped Stoker might think of Gerald later for Irving's company. Later she wrote to Lady Monckton, 'How I wish, in your benevolence, you could help my dear eldest son, Gerald, to a London engagement. He really deserves better than to be "walking about" – or "resting".' (24 August, ny, Wolff collection.)

48. Allardyce Nicoll, *A History of Late Nineteenth Century Drama 1850-1900* 2 vols (Cambridge: Cambridge University Press, 1946), II p.54. Quote from 'The Stock Company Question', *Era*, 14 December 1889, p.13.

49. The Editor replied to W. Dis, a concert singer, about his fears over the attentions paid by 'Swells' to his fiancée, a fellow concert singer:
' "Swells" who frequent green rooms are dangerous people, being generally idle, dissipated young men, and the less the ladies connected with either theatres or concert halls have to do with them, the better.' *Halfpenny Journal*, vol. I, 23 September 1861, p.104.

50. Baker, p.39.

51. Baker, p.96 quotes from the *Saturday Review*, 22 March 1862, vol. XIII, p.321.

52. Calvert, p.14.

53. Ibid.

54. M.E. Braddon, *The Green Curtain* (London: Hutchinson, 1911), p.18.

55. *Hampshire Advertiser*, 27 August 1853, p.7.

56. Baker, p.37.

57. Calvert, p.15.

58. *Hampshire Advertiser*, 3 September 1853, p.6.

59. *Hampshire Advertiser*, 29 October 1853, p.5.

60. M.E. Braddon, *The Doctor's Wife* (London: Maxwell, 1864; repr. London: Ward, Lock & Tyler, c.1866), p.66. Braddon's selection of 'Sleaford' for her heroine's surname is interesting in itself; the novel is partly set in the Coventry/Warwick area (the town of Coventford is meant for Coventry), where Braddon herself acted, and there was a Theatre Royal at nearby Sleaford in the neighbouring county of Lincolnshire; it would be fascinating to know if she ever acted there.

61. Baker, p.133.

62. Calvert, pp.16-17.

63. Calvert, p.17.

64. Calvert, pp.23-24.

65. Calvert, p.24.

66. *Era*, 18 June 1854, p.11.

67. 'Provincial Theatres and Unprincipled Managers', *Era*, 4 March 1855, p.11.

68. Angus J. Keith, *A Scotch Play-House: being the historical records of the Old Theatre Royal, Marischal Street, Aberdeen* (Aberdeen: D. Wyllie & Son, 1878) p.52: 'Miss Braddon, whose correct description of matters theatrical in her novels shows a close knowledge of stage life, is credited with having played on these boards.' Wolff describes the surviving part of the manuscript of her play *The Revenge of the Dead* as having on the reverse, 'Miss Seyton, at Mrs. Robinson's, 13 Marischal St., Aberdeen'. The climactic scene at the end of *Dead Sea Fruit* (1868) is set in Aberdeen.

69. Letter from Fanny and Mary Braddon to Mr. Younge, 14 January 1855, Wolff collection.

70. Maxwell, p.275.

71. *Era*, 6 May, p.11.

72. When Braddon returned to Southampton for the new season she was billed as 'Miss Mary Seyton, from the Theatre Royal Glasgow', 25 August 1855, *Hampshire Independent*, p.4.

73. *Era*, 22 July 1855, p.1.

74. 'Notes from the Editor', *Halfpenny Journal*, vol. I, 9 September 1861, p.88.

75. M.E. Braddon, *The Black Band; or, The Mysteries of Midnight* (*Halfpenny Journal*, vol. I, 23 September 1861, p.99; repr. Hastings: Sensation Press, 1998), p.193.

76. *The Times*, 5 March 1856, p.12.

77. W.G. Knight, *A Major London 'Minor': the Surrey Theatre 1805-1865* (London: Society for Theatre Research, 1997), p.262.

78. *Era*, 30 March 1856, p.10.

79. *Era*, 13 April 1856, p.10.

80. Knight, p.229. Mrs. Keeley also contributed reminiscences to a book about herself, but unfortunately gave no mention of her performance with Braddon.

81. *Trilby and Other Plays*, ed. by G. Taylor (Oxford: Oxford University Press, 1996), p.xvi.

82. Robertson, p.115.

83. James Joseph Sheahan, *General and Concise History and Description of the Town and Port of Kingston-Upon-Hull* (London: Simpkin Marshall, 1864), p.525.

84. Michael Sadleir, *XIX Century Fiction, a Bibliographical Record Based on His Own Collection* 2 vols (London: Constable, 1951), I, no. 269, p.44.

85. *Hull Packet*, 25 July 1856. p.1.

86. Knight, p.85.

87. *Hull Packet*, 31 October 1856, p.4.

88. Sheahan, p.525.

89. *Hull Packet*, 10 April 1857, p.5.

90. David Oliver, 'The Late Miss Braddon. An Appreciation', *Hull Times*, 13 February 1915, p.3.

91. *Brighton Observer*, 17 July 1857, p.3.

92. Information on Brighton from Eric Underwood, *Brighton* (London: Batsford, 1978) and Timothy Carder, *The Encyclopedia of Brighton* (Lewes: East Sussex County Libraries, 1990).

93. The original name of Brighton was Brighthelmstone. Other famous places in Brighton appear in the story under disguised names, for example the Old Ship Hotel becomes the Old Yacht Hotel.

94. The following letter was published by 'Atlas' (Edmund Yates) the week after the death of Ellen Nye Chart in the *World*, 9 March 1892, p.20. It was almost certainly written by Braddon, as she had written similar letters to the *World* (when the father of Frederick Selous died in 1892, for example), and the same page carried an essay by her, 'From Forest Depths.'

One who knew Henry Nye Chart some years before his marriage, and who knew Mrs. Nye Chart from the beginning of her married life, would like to add a few words to Atlas's kindly paragraph of last week, since only those who knew her beside the domestic hearth, and as nurse and comforter of an invalid husband, can know all her fine qualities. It may be safely asserted that 'Harry Nye' – his own name was only resumed when he became lessee of the Brighton theatre – popular favourite as he was, both on the stage and off it, never knew what home comfort meant till he married. He lived, for the most part, in the 'Cottage' attached to the theatre – a building which with a certain appearance of snugness combined a stony seclusion from light and air. Here, as William Sawyer used gaily to relate, when a friend dropped into tea there was sometimes a question of sending out to buy tea-things before the modest meal could be served, the property-man having taken all the crockery for the stage. Here, with his good old father, he lived as casually as in a gypsy tent, without the charm of gypsy surroundings. His engagement to a cousin had ended sadly in the death of his fiancée; his later experience of the sex had been far from a happy one, and a very sensitive and affectionate nature had been sorely tried in the course of a long and misplaced attachment. Ellen Rollason came into his life like a burst of sunshine, and cared for him, and thought for him, and helped him with her bright intelligence and clear strong brain as men are rarely helped by their wives. And while helping him in everything connected with the conduct of the Brighton Theatre – then heavily burdened with debt – there was not the smallest detail of his home life which her watchful eyes overlooked. The image of my old friend, as I last saw him, remains in my mind to this hour as a picture of domestic comfort. The pleasant room, the cheery fire, the round table drawn up beside it, with the dainty little dinner, as neatly served as at the best club in London, and the invalid in his easy chair, finding enjoyment in the last dregs of life, sweetened by the loving ministrations of the most womanly wife man ever won for himself.

Braddon rarely, if ever, attended funerals and sent W.B. Maxwell as her representative to Mrs. Nye Chart's funeral.

95. *Brighton Gazette*, 22 June 1876, p.5.

96. *Brighton Gazette*, 30 July 1857, p.4.

97. *Brighton Observer*, 31 July 1857, p.2 listed the whole of the company.

98. *Brighton Gazette*, 8 August 1857, p.6.

99. *Brighton Gazette*, 13 August 1857, p.5

100. *Brighton Gazette*, 10 September 1857, p.5.

101. Porter, p.106.

102. *Era*, 20 September 1857, p.11.

103. *Brighton Observer*, 2 October 1857, p.2.

104. *Brighton Observer*, 2 October, p.2.

105. *Era*, 18 October 1857, p.12.

106. *Brighton Gazette*, 22 October 1857, p.5.

107. *Era*, 25 October 1857, p.11.

108. *Era*, 15 November 1857, p.11.

109. *Era*, 22 November 1857, p.11.

110. *Brighton Gazette*, 3 December 1857, p.8.

111. *Brighton Observer*, 1 January 1858, p.2.

112. *Era*, 3 January 1858, p.13.

113. *Brighton Guardian*, 7 February 1858, p.5.

114. Ibid.

115. *Era*, 17 January, p.11.

116. *Brighton Guardian*, 27 January 1858, p.5.

117. Ibid.

118. *Brighton Guardian*, 7 February 1858, p.5.

119. *Coventry Weekly*, 11 March 1858, p.4.

120. Davis, pp.112-115.

121. *Era*, 2 May 1858, p.11.

122. *Coventry Herald*, 11 June 1858, p.1.

123. Lyn Pykett, introduction for *The Doctor's Wife* (Oxford: Oxford University Press, 1998, pp.xxiv-xxv. Pykett mentions an essay by Christopher Heywood, 'A Source for *Middlemarch*: Miss Braddon's *The Doctor's Wife* and *Madame Bovary*', in which Heywood makes a case for Eliot using Braddon's novel as a source.

124. *World*, 11 February 1885, p.16. The letter was reprinted in F.W. Humberstone, 'Miss Braddon and Coventry', *Coventry Herald*, 12 February 1915, p.5. The latter identified the churchyard as that of Allesley, the smaller house as Ivy Cottage, the editor as J.M. Scott, and added that at the time Braddon met the Brays they did not know George Eliot was the author of *Adam Bede*.

125. Frederick Karl, *George Eliot* (1995; repr. London: Flamingo, 1996, pp.67-71.

126. *Brighton Herald*, 7 August 1858, p.2.

127. *Brighton Guardian*, 18 August, p.4.

128. *Brighton Examiner*, 10 August 1858, p.2.

129. 'A Graduate of the University of London', *Brighton As It Is: Its Pleasures, Practices and Pastimes* (1860), quoted by Underwood, pp.109-110.

130. Nathaniel Paine Blaker, *Reminiscences* (1906), quoted by Underwood, p.108.

131. *Brighton Guardian*, 1 September 1858, p.5.

132. *Brighton Guardian*, 20 October 1858, p.5.

133. *Brighton Guardian*, 8 September 1858, p.4.

134. N. Parker Willis, *Hurry-Graphs; or, Sketches of Scenery, Celebrities, and Society, Taken From Life* (London: Ward, Lock, 1851) pp.145-147. Willis and H.C. Porter put Don's height at only six foot two, so other accounts of seven feet may have exaggerated.

135. *Era*, 5 September 1858, p.11.

136. *Brighton Examiner*, 9 October 1858, p.2.

137. *Brighton Observer*, 22 October 1858, p.2.

138. *Era*, 10 October 1858, p.11.

139. *Brighton Guardian*, 27 October 1858, p.5.

140. *Brighton Examiner*, 26 October 1858, p.5.

141. *The Letters of Charles Dickens*, vol. 8 1856-1858, ed. Graham Storey and Kathleen Tillotson (Oxford: Clarendon Press, 1995), p.649. Letter from Dickens to Wilkie Collins, September 1858.

142. Anthony Dale, *The Theatre Royal Brighton* (Stocksfield: Oriel Press, 1980), pp.25-26. The letter is about Dickens's visit to the theatre in March 1863. Although Dale does not mention Braddon, he reproduces photographs of Henry Nye Chart and his wife.

143. *Brighton Observer*, 3 December 1858, p.2.

144. *Brighton Observer*, 24 December 1858, p.3.

145. *Brighton Observer*, 31 December 1858, p.2.

146. *Brighton Gazette*, 23 February 1859, p.4.

147. *Brighton Gazette*, 3 March 1859, p.3.

148. *Brighton Gazette*, 10 March 1859, p.8.

149. Unidentified correspondent to Braddon, 10 November 1858, Wolff collection. The handwriting is difficult to read, and I only realised the significance of the name Bray two years after my visit to Texas and I read Braddon's letter in the *World*. The correspondent went on to describe one 'of the most interesting squabbles you talk about', concerning higher wages, 'Then came the tug of war. You know the sort of thing – tyrants, oppressors, rights of men, rights of labour, freedom, misery, justice, truth, & all the rest of it.' The writer admitted this 'bored me beyond belief', doubting they knew 'what it is to work as you work or as I work occasionally: I rather guess they don't.' The fact that the letter is addressed to 'Miss Seyton' confirms that this was how she was known to the Bray circle – did they realise who she was after *The Doctor's Wife* was published?

150. *Era*, 15 May 1859, p.11.

151. Ibid.

152. *Brighton Guardian*, 18 May 1859, p.2. Another version of the speech printed in the *Era* omitted the names of the offending residents.

153. Charles Dickens and Wilkie Collins, 'The Lazy Tour of Two Idle Apprentices' (1857; repr. in *No Thoroughfare and Other Stories*, Far Thrupp, Stroud: Alan Sutton, 1990), p.218.

154. Ibid.

155. *Doncaster Chronicle*, 6 May 1859, p.1.

156. *Doncaster, Nottingham and Lincoln Gazette*, 27 May 1859, p.5.

157. *Doncaster Chronicle*, 20 May 1859, p.5.

158. *Doncaster Chronicle*, 27 May 1859, p.5.

159. Ibid.

160. *Hull Packet*, 10 June 1859, p.5.

161. *Era*, 3 July 1859, p.12.

162. *Era*, 31 July 1859, p.12.

163. Braddon, 'In the Days of My Youth', p.124.

164. M.E. Braddon, 'Fifty Years at the Lyceum', *Strand Magazine*, vol. XXV, January 1903, p.38.

165. *Era*, 24 July 1859, p.11.

166. *Era*, 7 August 1859. p. 12.

167. *Brighton Gazette*, 10 August, p.12.

168. *Era*, 14 August, p.11.

169. *Brighton Herald*, 27 August 1859, p.2.

170. *Brighton Gazette*, 15 September 1859, p.5.

171. Ibid.

172. *Brighton Observer*, 23 September 1859, p.2.

173. *Brighton Gazette*, 22 September 1859, p.5.

174. *Era*, 2 October 1859, p.11.

175. *Brighton Gazette*, 12 October 1859, p.5.

176. *Era*, 23 October 1859, p.11.

177. *Era*, 30 October 1859, p.11.

178. *Brighton Observer*, 28 October 1859, p.2.

179. *Brighton Gazette*, 27 October 1859, p.5.

180. *Brighton Gazette*, 2 November 1859, p.5.

181. *Brighton Chronicle*, 2 November 1859, p.2.

182. *Brighton Gazette*, 3 November 1859, p.5.

183. *Era*, 20 November 1859, p.11.

184. *Brighton Chronicle*, 16 November 1859, p.2.

185. *Brighton Gazette*, 10 November 1859, p.8.

186. Braddon, 'In the Days of My Youth', p.124.

187. Ibid. p.125.

188. Porter, p.116.

189. *Era*, 18 December 1859, p.11.

190. *Brighton Observer*, 23 December 1859, p.3.

191. *Brighton Guardian*, 1 February 1860, p.5.

192. Calvert, p.56.

193. Calvert, p.57.
194. *Brighton Guardian*, 29 February 1860, p.4.
195. *Sussex Mercury*, 18 February 1860, p.2.
196. M.E. Braddon, *Rough Justice* (London: Simpkin, Marshall, 1898), p.163.
197. Braddon to Charles Kent, 20 May 1880, Wolff collection.

Chapter Two
The Struggle for Fame: Braddon's Earliest Writing

From an early age Braddon displayed a talent for writing. She was only twenty seven years old when she achieved lasting fame with *Lady Audley's Secret* (1862). Before this she had been a full time writer for two years, and even during her eight years on the stage she had spent her spare time struggling to get her work published or performed. Later in life she expressed surprise that more women did not feel the urge to write, saying that the fact that many novelists were women did not surprise her, but:

> What does surprise me is that every girl who is well educated and endowed with imagination does not long to express herself with her pen.[1]

Braddon felt this longing from early childhood, and all through her years on the stage, until her career as a writer became more important to her than that of an actress. In the latter part of the eighteen fifties and early eighteen sixties, three men were instrumental in her career: her patron John Gilby, the journalist and poet William Sawyer, and finally and most importantly the publisher John Maxwell.

Even as a child Braddon was a prolific writer. Encouraged by the present of a little mahogany desk with a red velvet slope from her brother's godfather, with its 'infinite capacities for literary labour', her chief regret at bed-time was having to close it. She later recalled that when she was only eight years old:

> My first story was based on those fairy tales which first opened to me the world of imaginative literature. My first attempt in fiction, and in round-hand, on carefully pencilled double lines, was a story of two sisters, a good sister and a wicked, and I fear adhered more faithfully to the lines of the archetypal story than the writer's pen kept to the double fence which should have ensured neatness.[2]

At about this time Mary Braddon's mother, Fanny, employed a cook called Sarah Hobbs, and she introduced Braddon to the cheaper variety of literature, the sort of 'literature of the kitchen' that the adult Braddon would be accused of bringing into the parlour. She described Sarah Hobbs as:

> a devourer of the Family Heralds and Reynold's Magazine, and she had a good many numbers of a little stunted duo decimo magazine

which published condensed editions of famous novels, and which she lent to me, whereby in this curtailed form I read "The Last Days of Pompeii" and other famous fiction with great enjoyment.[3]

As Braddon grew older her mother provided her with a host of interesting books, of the kind that a child would enjoy rather than the moralistic brand of religious fiction recommended by advice manuals. Braddon later said, "To my mother I owe my introduction to the great world of imaginative literature. She was a woman with a cultivated mind, a keen wit and a natural taste for what was best in the literature of the time, as well as a devoted student of Shakespeare and Scott."[4] When she was eight years old her mother bought her Maria Edgeworth's three volume book of short stories, *The Parent's Assistant*, which Braddon described as:

> surely the most enchanting stories that ever were written for a little girl of eight – better than even the beautifullest fairy tales, because they were all so real, like slices of life.[5]

She became a keen reader, and although not an only child her brother and sister did not always live with her and her mother, and she did not often have the company of other children. So it was perhaps not surprising that she occupied her time reading and writing, and lived much in her imagination. She was soon reading Charles Lamb, *Swiss Family Robinson*, and Sir Walter Scott's *The Betrothed* and *Kenilworth*, with which 'Mama had opened the gates of that wide region of romance and history, chivalry, tragedy and comedy.'[6] Braddon was even more struck by Dickens when she found:

> with Nicholas Nickleby there was not a dry page. (...) The book seemed written for children, so bright and vivid was every page, so full of life (sic.) people who talked, and of objects that one could see.[7]

Another favourite was *The Vicar of Wakefield*.[8] Although such reading sounds very precocious to the modern reader, it was not so very unusual for children at this time to be reading books that these days sound far too difficult for their age. But Braddon was also soon writing on such a prolific basis that it augured well for her later numerous volumes as an adult:

> The interval between the ages of eight and twelve was a prolific period, fertile in unfinished MSS., among which I can now trace a

historical novel on the Siege of Calais – an Eastern story, suggested by a passionate love of Miss Pardoe's Turkish tales, and Byron's "Bride of Abydos," which my mother, a devoted Byron worshipper, allowed me to read aloud to her – and doubtless murder in the reading – a story of the Hartz Mountains, with audacious flights in German diablerie; and lastly very seriously undertaken, and very perseveringly worked upon, a domestic story, the outline of which was suggested by the same dear and sympathetic mother.[9]

These subjects sound very ambitious for a child of that age, but they are also imitative, showing the sort of things her mother was reading. Just before she turned eleven she started a story based on a suggestion of her mother, 'The Old Arm Chair', which was about an impoverished couple, at the mercy of their evil landlord, who are about to have their beloved chair taken from them when the covers are torn to reveal a convenient stash of bank notes hidden by an ancestor:

> My brief experience of boarding school occurred at this time, and I well remember writing "The Old Arm Chair" in a penny account book, in the schoolroom of Cresswell Lodge, and that I was both surprised and offended at the laughter of the kindly music teacher who, coming into the room to summon a pupil, and seeing me gravely occupied, enquired what I was doing, and was intensely amused at my stolid method of composition, plodding on undisturbed by the voices and occupations of the older girls around me.[10]

Her mother always encouraged her in her writing, and Mrs. Braddon herself had ghosted her husband's sporting column many years before their separation for Pitman's *Sporting Magazine* under the pseudonyms of 'Rough Robin' and 'Gilbert Forester'. They had at first done so for fun, but surprised by the size of the cheque which rewarded their labour it was decided they, or rather Fanny Braddon, would continue until 'his own enemy', her husband, ruined yet another enterprise by dishonest dealing:

> Mama remained unhonoured and unknown, the ghost who supplied the flowing paragraphs and lavish quotations from Byron. (...) Papa and Mama collaborated for some years. Papa hunted, and shot, and enjoyed himself immensely, and provided vivid descriptions of clinking runs or tremendous shoots, and Mama developed his crude notes in magazine English, and all went the better in the home for

this additional source of income, till there came an unlucky bill transaction in which his own enemy offended the good lady who was the proprietor of the magazine, and never again appeared in the list of her contributors.[11]

After their separation Mrs. Braddon had written for *Bentley's Miscellany* in the 1840s, and later her literary abilities were to become useful to her daughter and John Maxwell.[12]

At school Braddon 'used to astonish her school fellows by the energy and completeness with which she covered all the sheets of her copy-books, not always, be it remarked, with the moral maxims with which they were headed, but far oftener, indeed, with the beginnings of hair-raising and exciting romances to which her vivid imagination gave birth.'[13] As a child she wrote 'innumerable plays'[14] and in her early teens Braddon was much affected by her reading of Charlotte Bronte, especially Jane Eyre, a one volume reprint of which was borrowed from a circulating library:

> I was laid up with a sick-headache, (...) and the book was given to me for a solace before my mother or elder sister had looked at it. I forgot my headache. The story gripped me from the first page. (...) I was enough of a schoolgirl to be thrilled by the moving scenes at the cruel school; and I had enough of a girl's romantic fancy to fall prostrate before the stern and rugged grandeur of "Mr. Rochester".[15]

Braddon's reading of *Jane Eyre* made such an impression on her that it brought about a new phase of juvenilia:

> the sentimental period, in which my unfinished novels assumed a more ambitious form, and were modelled chiefly upon Jane Eyre, with occasional tentative imitations of Thackeray. Stories of gentle hearts that loved in vain, always ending in renunciation.[16]

This phase took Braddon almost up to the time she went on the stage, but unfortunately she has left no autobiographical record of these years. What is clear, though, is that in no way did Braddon abandon her ambition to be a writer.

When Braddon and her mother went to Southampton, when she was almost eighteen years old and acting with Edwin Holmes's company, her fellow company member Adelaide Biddles (later Mrs. Calvert) testified to her friend's artistic and literary interests:

Miss Seyton played her favourite music for us; she sketched, with her clever pen, our features and our mental peculiarities; she could copy a cartoon of Punch line by line so cleverly that it might almost have been taken for the original drawing. I fancy Mrs. Seyton was a subscriber to Mudie's, for the latest novels were often seen upon their table, whilst many of the standard authors graced their bookcase. Mary and I were omnivorous readers, and in spite of my hard work I managed to rush through a formidable quantity of literature, with which she very kindly supplied me. It embraced everything from Carlyle and Ruskin to Harrison Ainsworth and Fenimore Cooper. I remember, even now, poring over *Sartor Resartus*, with the wretched conviction that I couldn't *quite* understand it.[17]

This at least shows that although far from London, Braddon and her mother were not culturally isolated. The yearly membership for Mudie's at this time was a guinea, and was quite out of reach for the ordinary 'walking lady' who earned less than this in a week, suggesting that Fanny Braddon probably had an income other than what her daughter was earning. Presumably the Cornish Braddons still gave them money, and perhaps they rented out their Camberwell home when away, or still had a lodger using the premises. It also shows that Braddon was interested in many things as a teenager: acting, writing, singing, and drawing and perhaps, like Flora in *A Lost Eden* (1906), she was not quite sure which to pursue. Flora fancies herself, despite her limited talent, an artist and a singer, before deciding to become an actress. Some of Braddon's early sketches still exist, both in the Wolff collection and at Harvard, and they show her interest in theatrical and literary subjects. One fragment of prose from this period has a sketch of Ophelia in a big dress, long black hair and a wreath on her head. A fragment of a play is half filled with sketches, one of which looks like Queen Victoria, and its presence in the middle of a piece of writing perhaps indicates that Braddon was easily distracted from writing to drawing at this time. What remains of a sketchbook in the Wolff collection has twenty nine pages of sketches, mainly in blue ink, which are theatrical rather than naturalistic in look. One is of Edward Bulwer Lytton, a great hero of hers, who she met while she was an actress. The others are of melodramatic subjects, of murders or deathbeds, probably depicting scenes from books or plays, or look as though they could be out of Dumas. Some show beautiful period costumes and several have black people as characters. Flora in *A Lost Eden* is described as showing more enthusiasm than talent:

She brought a collection of pen-and-ink drawings, many of them copies from engravings in books or in the *Illustrated London News*, some of them original, her own ideas of scenes in Scott or Bulwer. Napoleon figured largely, copied from H.K.B.'s illustrations in Lever's novels. There was no more talent in these juvenile efforts than in the average child who loves pictures and tries to imitate the thing it loves. Even the imitative faculty was weak. (p.29)

Even though Braddon did not rate herself as an artist, she remained interested in art, numbering Edwin Landseer and William Frith as friends, and later she hoped that her son William would become a great painter.

Braddon and Adelaide Biddles had much in common, for not only were they both aspiring actresses but both were also aspiring writers. The *Hampshire Advertiser* urged its audience to patronise Adelaide's benefit, for she was no ordinary actress:

Miss Biddles has peculiar claims on the patronage of the play-going public – she is a talented actress in a very wide range of characters, and she adds to her varied accomplishments those of an authoress and a poetess of no mean acquirements, of matured judgement and of refined taste.[18]

Although they were friends it must have been a cause of some annoyance to Braddon that not only was Adelaide Biddles rapidly becoming the most popular young actress in the Southampton company, but she was also, like Braddon, an aspiring playwright and poet, and one whose works were performed by the Southampton company. In October Edwin Holmes put on two of Adelaide's plays, both adapted from serials in the penny part weekly magazine for the lower classes, the *London Journal*. The serials *Minnigrey, The Gypsy Girl; Or, England's Army and Navy* and *Amy Laurence; Or, An Old Man's Love* were by John Frederick Smith who specialised in cheap fiction that would appeal to factory girls, and in Adelaide's adaptation she and her sister Clara took the leads. For her benefit in 1854 Adelaide adapted another serial, *The Wager; or, The Girl, The Wife, and the Heroine*. Surprisingly Mrs. Calvert did not even mention her plays in her autobiography, but as there were comparatively few women playwrights in the nineteenth century it was quite an achievement for her to have had her dramatic pieces staged.[19] Adelaide also beat her friend into print with fiction, for when she went to America after leaving Southampton she found a ready market with the editor of the *American Union* newspaper in Boston, where, for two years, 'I inflicted numbers of short stories upon his readers.'[20] In fact Adelaide said she needed this second income to pay for her stage costumes, and Braddon herself was no doubt disappointed that a career as an actress was not generating the income to support her and her mother as she had hoped.

It certainly seems as if all through Braddon's time on the stage she was very keen to write plays, and to have a play of her own performed. Edwin Holmes, the Southampton manager, wrote the pantomimes for the company, and so her opportunities there were limited. In the Wolff collection there are a number of remnants of plays that Braddon was writing in the 1850s. For example, on the reverse of the Beverley playbill from 1857 in the Wolff collection, incomplete and hard to read, is a play with a French Revolutionary setting, the lead characters being called Florette and Rene. Braddon later told Clive Holland that at this time she attempted, but rarely finished, "nearly every kind of original composition, novels, plays, poems, and history."[21]

At some point in 1854 Braddon had already met Edward Bulwer Lytton and confided in him her literary ambitions.[22] Where this meeting took place is not certain, but it is quite likely that it was through her cousin, *The Times* editor John Delane, who was a friend of Bulwer Lytton's and now lived in the grandeur of Eton Place. From childhood Bulwer Lytton was her literary hero, and she continued to admire him for the rest of her life. She told Joseph Hatton in 1888, "He undertook to correct and criticize my first story (...and) he was the first author of note to give me any real encouragement."[23] At the beginning of 1855, when Mary and her mother were in Scotland, they were clearly trying to cultivate any literary acquaintances they came across, and Braddon was working on poems and plays.[24] In the letter, partly quoted in the previous chapter, to a Mr. Younge, both women addressed him very informally, reflecting the comparatively free and easy world they now moved in. Mrs. Braddon addressed him as 'My "charming brother." ' Younge had obviously been looking over some work of Braddon's, for which both women were very grateful. This Mr. Younge may have been Mr. Anthony Younge, an actor in the provinces specialising in 'old men', who is listed in the *Era* as appearing in Plymouth in 1854 (he became the manager of the Queen's Theatre in Edinburgh in June 1858), and who had had a play published himself in 1850; perhaps he and Braddon acted together towards the end of 1854 and Braddon asked his advice. The play was, as the letter suggests, *The Revenge of the Dead*. Mrs. Braddon concluded her part of the letter, 'I remain (as the old letters say) with sincere wishes for your speedy recovery & success in your literary labour.' Braddon's half of the letter is girlish and teasing, and is worth quoting in full because it surely gives a better

impression of what she was like than most of the surviving letters, of a
far more sober tone, written later in her life:

> I find that Mama has had the supreme impertinence, to tell you in
> her epistle a most horrible claim, about me – in some fine French
> phrase which would have done honour to Sir Charles Grandison or
> Lord Chesterfield – After this with what blushes, must I take up my
> pen – if the nib is not rose coloured pray attribute it to the
> degeneracy of the age in general – not mine in particular. I fancy I
> hear you exclaim poor invalid "Give me Castor oil. Rhubarb
> magnesia – suppose again, cupp me as often as you like, but save
> me from that girl's scrawl." Don't pursue me with her slow-timing
> "Revenges" – I cannot tell you, what pleasure your charming (you
> see that word is tailored for you) letter gave us. Your description of
> the Pacific made me envy your brother, what a refreshing stream of
> Life, his presence will be among the used up nonentities far out at
> sea. The officer will have to exert himself to the extent of a "Haw!
> Haw!" when he hears some of those delightful & most racy
> anecdotes & master Israel the younger will leave off eating to
> listen. It makes one envy the Outward bound, Far Far upon the
> Sea.[25]

The rest of the letter is missing, and the next trace of Braddon's writing
appears two years later, while she was acting in Hull under the
management of Wolfenden and Melbourne at the Queen's Theatre.

One of the most well known residents of Hull was a composer called
Harry Deval, who had trained at the Royal Academy of Music and for
several years in Italy. Made a Chevalier de l'ordre Belge by the King of
Belgium, he had lived in Hull for some years. The composer of a
number of operas, he often wrote his own librettos, but on one occasion
he collaborated with Braddon and she provided the libretto for the
Duchess De La Vallierre.[26] It was also at this time that Braddon's work
began to be published.

Braddon as a Poet in the Provincial Press

On a regular basis for three years Braddon wrote poetry for two
provincial newspapers in towns where she acted. A number of these
were reprinted in *Garibaldi and Other Poems* (1861), but many were
not, and remained unrecorded in any bibliography of Braddon's works.
Mrs. Calvert had testified to Braddon's enjoyment of poetry at
Southampton, adding 'Tennyson, I think, was Mary's chief literary idol;
she could reel off his poetry by the yard.'[27] Whether Braddon was

writing poetry as early as 1853 is not certain, but if she was it was not published. Many provincial newspapers carried a poem in each issue, sometimes by a local poet, but often they were taken from an anthology or more frequently from the most recent issue of a national magazine. Presumably it would not have been easy for Braddon to get her poetry accepted for a provincial newspaper because she was at this time rarely in any town for longer than a few months, so could not be considered local, and in an age when many young ladies wrote poetry as a hobby the local newspapers would probably have had many aspirants. To make any inroad Braddon would have had to display remarkable ability in an unsolicited manuscript, or have someone introduce her to an editor. In the case of her poetry in Yorkshire, and in Brighton, – and later when she first had work accepted by John Maxwell – an introduction of some kind seems to have been pivotal.

The first of the poems appeared in the *Beverley Recorder and General Advertiser* on 9 May 1857.[28] Beverley was a town where Braddon had performed some days earlier in, amongst other plays, Tom Taylor's *Still Waters Run Deep*. The leading actor of the company, Wybert Rousby, was acclaimed in the paper as Beverley's famous son and his two poems 'The Infant' and 'The Man in the Iron Mask' were printed in honour of his return on the second of May.[29] It may well have been through Rousby that initially Braddon's poems were accepted, as unlike many papers of the period the *Beverley Recorder* did not usually carry poetry every week and Braddon had no other connection with the town. These two poems represent Braddon's first appearance in print, the *Beverley Recorder* stated that this was so: 'Her earliest poems were published in the Beverley Recorder under an assumed name,'[30] and Braddon herself also confirmed that the poem 'Rest' was her first publication of any kind:

> To the best of my recollection, the first thing of mine that ever appeared in print was a song in the seventeenth-century style that was published in the *Beverley Recorder*.[31]

Even if it was Rousby who made the initial introduction Braddon soon made friends with the owner of the *Beverley Recorder*, Mr. Ward, writing to his son H.M. Ward almost fifty years later:

> That I, who received such kindness and hospitality from your father and mother, and spent one happy Summer day in the golden time of youth at Beverley, arriving before breakfast with my friend Georgina Ross, Mrs. Kendal's sister, every detail of which day is remembered.[32]

Braddon herself was later the last person to consider herself a great poet, dismissing her poetic output as 'Poet's Corner Verse.'[33] However, in her early twenties she must have been very serious about her poetry, and since she would only have had Sundays off from work she could write a poem for a newspaper more easily than she could make time for a novel. There was probably no financial benefit for her, as Adelaide Calvert only took to writing fiction because there was no payment for newspaper verse.[34]

Straight after leaving the Hull company Braddon joined Henry Nye Chart's company in Brighton. Brighton was probably the most fashionable town she had acted in since Bath four years earlier. It was home to a number of literary figures, including Harrison Ainsworth, the author of such novels as *Jack Sheppard* and *The Tower of London.* Ainsworth would have seen Braddon act many times, as he was often a patron on 'Special' nights. Nor was Brighton cut off from London literary life, as Dickens lectured in Brighton twice during these years. She would have had access to all of the latest books, not only through the local circulating libraries, but also through the good collection at the Royal Literary and Scientific Institution at the Albion Rooms which had been established in 1841, and later became the basis of the Brighton public library. Dr. John Cordy Burrows, knighted in 1873 and responsible for gaining the Royal Pavilion for Brighton, was the treasurer of this institution, and as well as being a respected doctor, he was mayor of Brighton a record three times. He was mayor while Braddon was in Brighton, and unlike some mayors in other towns he fully supported the theatre, becoming a friend of Henry Nye Chart's and of Braddon's. Doubtless Braddon was often a guest at his home, number 62 Old Steine (a statue of him stands nearby to this day). Braddon remained friends with Burrows, dedicating *Dead Men's Shoes* (1876) to him, and he continued to be Braddon's doctor when visiting Brighton, and that of her children, until his death.

When Braddon joined the Brighton company she would have found she was not the only aspiring writer in the company: Walter Baynham adapted a Dickens story for the Brighton company, and later wrote a number of elocution books and *The Glasgow* Stage (1892); Robert Soutar, one of the leading actors, wrote a number of songs and a play while she was in the company, and in the years to come he wrote pantomimes for the Brighton company and published at least one book. From a letter to Braddon from William Sawyer it sounds as though Soutar was not a great favourite of theirs, and certainly he never contributed to any of the journals she was later to influence.[35] Braddon was to remain with Chart's company for three years, three years in which she pursued her long term ambition of becoming a writer; primarily poetry and play-writing, although there is almost certainly some material which remains to be discovered.

A month after her debut in Brighton a third poem appeared by her in the *Beverley Recorder*, the first of six poems she was to write about the Indian Mutiny in the next few months. Of the events which had begun that May in 1857 Braddon later wrote that the Mutiny 'came like a thunderclap upon England at large.'[36] Delhi had been captured by the rebels on the 16 May. 'Delhi' was written just as Delhi was being recaptured by the British columns in mid September, five thousand men in total against fifty thousand within. Braddon chose not to concentrate on the manoeuvres of the assault of Delhi, but on the retribution which followed. The recapture of the king's palace in Delhi had assumed a symbolic importance in the reassertion of Empire, and when the troops entered the city they found it almost entirely abandoned. This happened on the 21 September, and Braddon's poem appeared in Beverley on the 26 September, which means it must have been written before the final fall. Braddon's poem glorifies the destruction of the city in no uncertain terms:

> Down to the ground! Scattered be every stone!
> Annihilation be thy mildest fate;
> And be thine epitaph, these words alone:
> "Here lie the bones of fiends infuriate –
> "Here rot the carcases of a million slaves;
> "And here, *free* Britain's unstained banner waves![37]

The theme of this poem is continued in the next poem she wrote for the *Beverley Recorder*, 'On the Queen's Health Being Drunk Within the Walls of Delhi, After the Battle', in which the soldiers claim they did it for Queen, God and country. Some of it is distinctly gory in its description of the dead enemy:

> Whilest their blood steeps the soil which their deeds have defiled,
> Whilest they lie like slain tigers in ghastly heaps piled,[38]

Braddon continued her Indian Mutiny poems when she found an outlet for publication in Brighton, and more of her newspaper poems were published in the *Brighton Herald* than anywhere else. She gained entry to the *Brighton Herald* through William Sawyer, a young journalist who also had ambitions as a poet and playwright. One of the first plays Braddon appeared in at Brighton was written by Sawyer, *Eight Hours By the Seaside* (the title refers to the number of hours spent in Brighton by day trippers from London who arrived by train), in which Braddon played Aurelia Maggles, and it was probably during rehearsals for this play in September 1857 that she and Sawyer first met. The *Brighton Herald* was a newspaper of liberal persuasion, its offices were in Prince's Place, within easy walking distance of the theatre, and it nearly always carried reviews of the latest plays and magazines. Braddon's work appeared in the weekly poetry section for which Sawyer's wife was also a regular contributor.

William Sawyer (1828-1882) was a young man who had been a local celebrity for some time, having been only eighteen years old when his first work *Stray Leaves* (1846) was published, and this was followed three years later by *Thought and Reverie* (1849). In 1854 while in Oxford he edited *Oxford Wit*, and when he returned to Brighton it was to work for the *Brighton Herald*.[39] Sawyer had known Henry Nye Chart for some years, and at the beginning and end of each season he wrote a poetic address for Chart, or other members of the company, to recite. From those letters that survive from Sawyer to Braddon it is clear that they became great friends in a sort of teasing brother and sister way, and Braddon also became good friends with his wife, mother and sisters. Mary Jane Sawyer was only three years older than Braddon. She had much in common with her husband William, having also published poetry from an early age. She was writing poetry from the age of four, and at the age of fourteen her work was appearing in periodicals. Her only published volume of poetry, *The Quiet Hour*, was published in 1850 under her own name, Mary J. Andrews. However, unlike Braddon, 'M.J.', or 'Bird' as she was known to her friends, was not a prolific writer:

> many of her poems remain unfinished, as she was often – too often – content to set down the initial idea, and leave the working out to that "more convenient season" which never came. (...) During many years it was her custom to contribute a Christmas or New Year poem to the *Brighton Herald*, and it was owing to this custom, which, in time, assumed the form of a duty in her most conscientious nature, that the number of her finished poems is as long as it is. The great charm of her poetry was its singular tenderness and subtle appeal to the heart. Mothers who had lost little ones treasured her lines as expressing the sacredness of their grief, and going to the very depths of their inconsolable agony. All sympathetic natures loved her verses, of which she was herself the humblest critic, rating them far too low in worth, and saying, in her gentle way, when remonstrated with for writing so little, "The world is far too busy to listen to the little notes of a little bird like

me." To speak of her personally, it is enough to say that to know her was to love her.[40]

Soon after her arrival in Brighton, Braddon's uncle, William Braddon was attacked and left for dead after a burglary at his home near Ivybridge.[41] Braddon had only been in Brighton for four months when her first poem was published in the *Brighton Herald* on the twelfth of December. 'Our Heroes', which had also appeared in the *Beverley Recorder* two weeks earlier, was one of Braddon's patriotic verses on the Indian Mutiny, a subject which the newspapers were full of at this time, reflecting the nation's indignation at the uprising. A number of Braddon's poems were carefully attuned to fit current national events, and they were probably her best chance of getting her poems in on a regular basis, as the *Brighton Herald* had several local poets, including William Sawyer's wife. The first of Braddon's poems published while she lived in Brighton celebrated the triumph of General Havelock who had recently liberated Lucknow from the siege. Braddon's poem compares him to the epic leaders of the past, finding their achievements paling in contrast to his:

Go, bid them ransack history, from the first page to the last,
And, if they can, find Havelock eclipsed in all the past![42]

She continued to post poems to Beverley: her next *Brighton Herald* poem, 'Captain Skene', appeared on the 2 January 1858, but had already been printed three months earlier in the *Beverley Recorder*. The demise of Captain Skene must have struck her as a suitably poetic and tragic end, as well as one which extolled death before surrender. Alexander Skene, who had been the Superintendent of the Jhansi District, shot himself and his wife rather than be tortured and killed by the rebels: 'Who shall say from what pollution his fair bride the Saxon saved?' Again she compared modern events to those of the classical age, of 'Roman Glory'.[43] About a month before the poem first appeared, the *Brighton Herald* carried a letter about Captain Skene and the death of his wife entitled 'The Fate of a Heroine'.[44] It is quite likely that Braddon would have seen this letter, and perhaps have got the idea for the poem from it; it was only later that it was accepted that the suicide had not taken place. The Skenes had been murdered with the rest of the British at Jhansi, and the suicide was just one of the myths building up about the Mutiny. Christina Rossetti wrote a similar poem to Braddon's, 'The Death of Captain Skene and His Wife'.[45]

Even Braddon's poem for the new year in the *Beverley Recorder*, 'The Old Year', concentrated on the theme of the Indian Mutiny. News was slow coming to Britain, and so newspapers were full of new information and anecdotes from survivors for months to come. Next came 'Havelock', which the *Brighton Herald* printed within a black border for mourning. Havelock had died of typhoid shortly after the relief of Lucknow, and his death was seen by the country as a disaster, especially as it came so tragically soon after his triumph at Lucknow. Patriotic in the extreme it shows how the mother country sends her men out to protect its satellite:

> When she trusted him firmest, and hoped in him most,
> When she owned him her champion, her saviour, her boast,
> When she watched his career with a fond mother's pride,
> And sent forth her brave children to fight by his side![46]

These poems were by no means unique, other local newspapers carried similar works in their Poet's Corner, and many towns named a road after General Havelock. Braddon herself could not have thought them very good, as she did not reprint them in her book of poems. Braddon's views on the Indian Mutiny seem to have been traditionally hard line. Naturally her poems had to capture the popular mood of retribution, but the same sentiments are echoed in her novel *The Story of Barbara* (1880), which although set in the 1850s was written over twenty years later. It was dedicated to one of the most controversial figures of the Indian Mutiny, the dedication read:

> This book is inscribed to the memory of Major W.S.R. Hodson (a valiant soldier and a skilful commander), who acted with heroic courage and firmness under circumstances of unparalleled difficulty and danger, and who, as the creator of Hodson's Horse, made for himself a reputation that will long survive in India.[47]

This dedication and the opinions expressed in the novel suggest that Braddon shared the popular imperialist sentiment of her poems. *The Story of Barbara*, which in its background detail, is one of Braddon's most autobiographical, shows two teenage sisters, Barbara and Flossie Trevornock, growing up with their mother in a Camberwell villa, just as Braddon had. Like Mrs. Braddon, Mrs. Trevornock advertises for a lodger and in reply comes Captain George Leland of the Honourable East India Company Service. In *The Story of Barbara*, Braddon gives Leland the actions of her dedicatee Hodson. Hodson, who had a reputation for arrogance and a love of looting, had captured three princes who had tortured and killed their British prisoners, and en route, fearing they might be rescued, executed them; even at a time of violent excess on both sides Hodson's actions were widely criticised, and some called it murder. In *The Story of Barbara*, Leland is shown leading 'Leland's Horse', taking part in the siege of Delhi, and capturing three Indian princes, 'human tigers', (p.152) with his hundred men from Humayoon's Tomb, and, fearing their rescue, 'slew them with his own resolute hand'. When a character calls it murder, Barbara defends her lover angrily:

> "It was a sublime act of justice; it was brave, noble, done before the face of the enemy: (...) How dare you call it murder! No more righteous act was ever done." (p.164)

There can be little doubt that these were Braddon's sentiments too and that she felt a need to defend Hodson's actions. She told T.H.S. Escott that she hoped the Hodson family would not object to her use of 'his career for my hero. (...) But as I have praised him up to the skies I hope I shall escape a charge of libel.'[48] From Escott she borrowed Colonel Napier's account, hearing he had 'dealt hardly with Hodson', and after reading it concluded:

> I have been deeply interested in the graphic story of that grand period of British valour – but I am very sorry the Colonel takes such a dark view of Hodson's conduct in making short work of the Princes. I took my view of the action from McDowell's description of the scene – he being at Hodson's side all the time. I see that other contemporary accounts loved Hodson for his pluck & determination & I cannot think that my soldier would have done what he did unless he had seen that a rescue by the mob was imminent[49]

In her novel Leland recalls the classical comparisons Braddon had used in her own poems, saying of the heroes of the Mutiny:

> "Poor Havelock! Ah, Barbara, *that* was a blow! (...) But every soldier in India felt the death of Havelock as a personal loss. Nicolson too, and Peel, and Gerrard, and Adrian Hope. The *Iliad* has not a longer list of heroes." (p.202)

With the regiments that Braddon acted with over the years it is quite probable she knew some of the men involved. Also, her brother Edward was to become a high ranking colonial ruler (who did not have much appreciation of native populations and eventually became the first prime minister of Tasmania[50]) and was in India himself at this time. Braddon and her mother must have been concerned for his safety. During the Mutiny he became involved in the fighting, and served under his superior in the Civil Service, Sir George Yule, in the Bhagulpore region.[51] Two years later he was living in Lucknow itself; and her uncle William had been a judge in India for thirty years. So in many ways Braddon's views were no more advanced than those of her contemporaries, unlike, for example, Wilkie Collins in *The Moonstone*.

In January 1858 Braddon wrote the maudlin 'Lines to the Princess Royal on Her Wedding Day'. As described in the previous chapter Brighton made the day a holiday, and with the special presentation at the theatre Braddon would have been busy herself on the day. No one could regard it as good poetry and it must have seemed twee even at the time:

> Then ring out loud joy-bells, to welcome the dawn:
> Fair sun, shed your light on the glad wedding morn,
> While the first flowers of Spring open their dew-spangled eyes,
> To take a last peep at the Princess we prize.[52]

In February, 'Robespierre at the Guillotine' reflected Braddon's interest in French history, especially at this time that of the French Revolution.[53] One of the plays she was trying to write at this time seems to have had that setting, and one of her notebooks which dates from the 1850s shows that she was reading about French history. Also in February 1858 was 'We May Roam Through This World' and after this no more poems appear for eighteen months.[54] It seems unlikely that the *Brighton Herald* no longer wanted them, but Braddon was later to acquire a patron who was very fussy about what publications her poetry appeared in; perhaps even at this early date he had a say in her work, and declared her work not ready for publication. When her poems started to appear again in September 1859, they were no longer concerned with contemporary events, and included such Tennyson style subjects as 'Queen Guinevere'. Nearly all of these later newspaper poems, ten in fact, were reprinted in Braddon's *Garibaldi* collection.

Braddon certainly wrote some songs for the pantomimes. The pantomime of late 1858 and early 1859, *Red Riding Hood*, was described by the *Brighton Gazette*:

> It was most spiritedly written, and abounded in national and local hits, many of the latter from the pens or tongues of Messrs Soutar and Hall, Misses Thirwall and Seyton.[55]

Out of these names it was probably Braddon and Robert Soutar who did the writing, and they may well have helped to add local touches (as was common in pantomimes) to other productions.

In about 1859 Braddon attempted to write a novel called *Master Antony's Record*, 'begun with resolute purpose'[56] after she had read Thackeray's *Henry Esmond*. It was to be set during the Restoration, 'a brilliantly wicked interval in the social history of England', and for research purposes she:

> made my girlish acquaintance with the Reading-room of the British Museum, where I went in quest of local colour, and where much kindness was shown to my youth and inexperience of the book world.[57]

She had found her inspiration for her novel while staying at the home of her uncle Edward, who was a vicar in Sandwich, in a book of the State Trials, concerning the elopement of Lord Grey with his sister-in-law. The fact that she was able to go and stay with relatives does suggest that the gaps in her theatrical performances probably are periods when she was not acting. It also shows that whatever the opinion of her family over her acting career, she was not excluded from their company. However, 'Master Antony's sentimental autobiography went the way of all my earlier efforts.'[58] The story of Lord Grey still intrigued her four decades later when she used it for her historical novel *London Pride* (1896).

For the 1859 Christmas edition of the *Brighton Guardian* Braddon wrote 'The Peril of Christmas Eve'.[59] It is surprising that for this one poem she switched from the *Herald*, especially as the *Guardian* had been less than complimentary to Braddon's acting and that of the rest of the Chart company. Perhaps it had been considered too long for inclusion in the *Herald*, as at twenty one verses it is the longest by far of her newspaper poems.

Even though Braddon had never managed to complete any of her embryonic novels to date, she now had a commission from a printer in Beverley called Charles Empson to write a lurid novel in penny weekly parts. Until now it has always been believed that Braddon wrote all of *Three Times Dead* (1860) after she left the stage and while she lived in Beverley. Braddon seems to suggest as much in her article 'My First Novel'. But in actual fact at least the first two parts were published while she was still acting in Brighton. This may well have been the novel Mrs. Calvert described her as writing when they acted in *As You Like It* in late 1859. Braddon later said that:

It was but a year or so after the collapse of Master Antony, that a blindly-enterprising printer of Beverley, who had seen my poor little verses in the *Beverley Recorder*, made me the spirited offer of ten pounds for a serial story, to be set up and printed in Beverley, and published on commission by a London firm in Warwick Lane.[60]

The young Braddon was thrilled at the prospect, although she added that with hindsight the idea in business terms of publishing it in such a manner was 'futile':

but to my youthful ambition the actual commission to write a novel, with an advance payment of fifty shillings to show good faith on the part of my Beverley speculator, seemed like the opening of that pen-and-ink paradise which I had sighed for ever since I could hold a pen.[61]

A review of the first two parts was published in the *Brighton Herald* on the 18 February 1860:

This is the commencement of a story, publishing in parts, from the pen of a lady who will be favourably known to our readers from poetic effusions which have from time to time graced these columns. It is not, we believe, Miss Seyton's first essay in the field of prose-fiction; but it is her most ambitious effort, and it affords us much pleasure to be enabled to say that so far as it has gone, her story is of great promise. It exhibits power in the delineation of character and in the conception of striking – not to say startling – incidents, and the interest is strongly sustained. (...) When finished, this will make a capital story for reprint in a Railway book.[62]

The review is intriguing in that it indicates that it was not her first published fiction, and if the review was written by Sawyer or another of her Brighton friends, they would have been in the position to know. In an article written in 1888, Joseph Hatton mentions Braddon wrote short stories and literary sketches while on the stage; possibly there may be stories yet to be found in magazines of the period, and the *Brighton Herald* often carried anonymous book reviews which Braddon may well have contributed to.

Braddon's own feelings on seeing the first part of *Three Times Dead* were of elation, despite the poor production quality of the book. Her copies of the earliest parts must have arrived by post while she was still in Brighton:

> I can recall the thrill of emotion with which I tore open the envelope that contained my complimentary copy of the first number, folded across, and in aspect inferior to a gratis pamphlet about a patent medicine. The miserable little wood block which illustrated that first number would have disgraced a baker's whitey-brown bag, would have been unworthy to illustrate a penny bun.[63]

The look of the illustrations was certainly crude, worse than that for most penny dreadfuls. Empson must have been annoyed by the illustrations too, because a second artist from Hull takes over halfway through, with only marginally better results.

The majority of *Three Times Dead* was written in Beverley after she had left the stage and Brighton and went with her mother to Beverley, where she lived at Beverley Parks:

> Miss Braddon (then better known as Miss Mary Seyton) when she resided in Beverley Parks (...) It was in this house that she wrote her first novel, "Three Times Dead; or, The Secret of the Heath," which was issued by Mr. C.R. Empson, a printer and bookseller in Toll Gavel.[64]

It was not only the writing of her penny part novel that took her to live in Beverley, for Beverley was also the home of her literary patron, whom she later elusively referred to as having been an influence before Empson offered her a deal:

> I had, previously to this date, found a Mæcenas in Beverley, in the person of a learned gentleman who volunteered to foster my love of the Muses by buying the copyright of a volume of poems and publishing the same at his own expense – which he did, poor man, without stint, and by which noble patronage of Poet's Corner verse, he must have lost money. He had, however, the privilege of dictating the subject of the principal poem, which was to sing – however feebly – Garibaldi's Sicilian campaign.[65]

The Actress and Her Patron: Braddon and John Gilby

In Wolff's biography John Gilby remains a shadowy figure, whom we are told was unrequitedly in love with the young Braddon. What is indisputable is that he took a great deal of interest in Braddon and her work; so much so that he invested money in her and became in effect her patron, paying her a wage so that she could leave the stage. By September 1859 she was sending stories she had written to him in Beverley for his approval.[66] He certainly must have spent a good deal of money if he paid her a wage through this time and paid for the publication of her book of poems. It is possible, too, that he used some financial influence to persuade Empson to publish *Three Times Dead*. Finally, almost exactly a year after she had left the stage, there was a terrible breach between Braddon and Gilby, in which Gilby let out a tirade of abuse against Braddon's character and honesty. The crunch appears to have been his hearing of the burgeoning relationship between her and the publisher John Maxwell.

Braddon and Gilby probably became acquainted during her appearance at Beverley, though he could easily have seen her at nearby Hull in 1856. One of the performances in Beverley was for the Masonic lodge, so perhaps Gilby was a member and had been involved with the Masonic amateur dramatics which had been assisted by the managers of the Hull company, Wolfenden and Melbourne (and presumably their actors). Braddon often wrote of the love men in the audience came to feel for actresses they watched, and who then followed them from engagement to engagement. This happens to Eliza in *Aurora Floyd*, which is specifically set in the Yorkshire area, and also in *Lucius Davoren*. Whether these fictional accounts imaginatively represent a fascination Gilby felt for Braddon can never be known for certain; certainly his final letters smack of wounded vanity and jealousy. There is, though, another interpretation which could be put on Gilby's behaviour, an interpretation which Wolff could not have known of. Wolff's source for Gilby having been in love with Braddon comes from one of Charles Reade's many notebooks, in one of which he wrote about Braddon's past. Reade made this entry in 1874, soon after the scandal about the death of Maxwell's first wife:

Her first patron was a simple noble-minded Yorkshire squire, Gilby. He got her "trail of the serpent" published at 2d. a number to assure her wider circulation. Used also to come to London and consult F.G. about the works of a young man, his friend. He was father, lover, and friend. When she fell into the hands of M., he came up dejected, and put questions about M. (F.)G's answers, though guarded, made him sink back into his chair. He then said to tell you the truth, the young man is a young woman I have long loved, and would have asked her to marry me: but I am rich: she was poor. I wished her to have reputation. And everything; that it might be she who did me the favour in marrying me. Ah! I fear I have waited too long. He went away. But presently came limping back. Let me ask you one question. Do you think he is capable – of – seducing her?

"I can't say."

He never came back (...) The excessive delicacy of the Yorkshireman would have cost him almost any woman.[67]

Wolff identifies 'F.G.' as the journalist Frederick Greenwood. This seems likely, as Greenwood carried out a public vendetta against Braddon for years, particularly concerning the publication of *Circe* in 1868. Although he was exposing her plagiarism perhaps it was, in part, an act of vengeance for the sake of his wounded friend. A further motive for Greenwood's attacks in the *Pall Mall Gazette* may be because in the late 1850s he and his brother James worked for Maxwell as contributors to the *Welcome Guest*. It could well be that his grudge was against Maxwell as much as it was against Braddon, and his position on the staff would have made him an ideal informant on the burgeoning relationship between Braddon and Maxwell. If 'F.G.' had been advising Gilby about where to take his protégé, perhaps it was Greenwood who suggested the *Welcome Guest* and John Maxwell as a likely source of employment for a young writer.

John Gilby (1821-1884) lived in Beverley all his life. His father, from whom he had inherited a good income, had been the vicar of the local church, St. Mary's. Gilby used this income to pursue his sporting interests, and he was a well known and successful race horse owner and trainer. Some of his horses, such as Adventurer, Flash in the Pan, Birthright, and Ploughboy, became famous in racing circles. During Braddon's season in Hull he acted as a steward at local races. He clearly discussed racing matters with Braddon, as she herself knew a good deal about horses and the track. In the early 1860s reviewers of her early fiction noted her unusual knowledge about racing, and especially disapproved of Aurora Floyd's unladylike interest in horse racing and gambling. But this knowledge did not come from Gilby, despite the fact that when Gilby died it was suggested that she had learnt all about horse-racing from him.[68] Both of Braddon's parents must have been knowledgeable in order to write their sporting column, and during her years on the stage before she met Gilby she had ample opportunity to go to the races, as evenings at the theatre were frequently held in conjunction with the local race week. The *Beverley Recorder* later denied Gilby taught her about racing, adding darkly and without mentioning she had been an actress, 'even at that early period Miss Braddon knew a great deal of "life" in all its phases.'[69] Gilby was fourteen years older than Braddon and was well educated with a great interest in botany, geology (possessing a fine collection of fossils) and astronomy. He was also disabled. Wolff states that he was paralysed in both legs and had a specially made saddle for when he went hunting. His condition was not quite as bad as Wolff suggests, though, for he was able to walk with the aid of canes:

> He was a terrible cripple, but managed to work his way in and out of the throngs that invariably crowd the stands and enclosures at race meetings with wonderful agility, and for many years went by the cognomen of "the devil on two sticks," through requiring the aid of one in each hand to help him along.[70]

Despite his disability he rode with the local hunt (another thing he and Braddon had in common, as she was devoted to hunting all her life), and he was also keen on shooting and boating. Not long after Braddon's acting appearance in Beverley, the *Beverley Recorder* reported Gilby riding for the Beverley Cup on Fairy;[71] if Braddon now knew him perhaps she went to watch.

Was Braddon in love with Gilby? She must have seen actresses take lovers, but if her novels are anything to go by, it was not something she approved of. Nor did she approve of men who thought actresses, and especially ballet girls, were easy prey because of their low pay and social status. Moreover, unlike most actresses, she always had her mother with her, a mother who was very protective and often suspected the motives of others: 'She was suspicious and was apt to impute motives, and she was generally right.'[72] Any man who wanted to get close to Braddon would have had to make a good impression on Braddon's mother. It seems unlikely that Braddon could have been in love with Gilby: the heroines of a similar age and background in her novels are of a romantic disposition, easily won over by good looks and a Byronic manner (rather like the mysterious men in her newspaper poems). If it is true, as Charles Reade asserted, that Gilby disguised his true feelings, planning to wait until she had achieved literary fame, Braddon may well have been unaware of any feelings he had for her. For a young woman in the 1850s she was in an unusual position: she had male colleagues in the theatre and friends like the journalist William Sawyer, so she would not have considered herself compromised romantically by a friendship with Gilby. These friends called her by her first name, or 'Polly', whereas Gilby called her 'Miss Braddon.' The idea that Braddon should raise herself to his level by making a literary name for herself is an odd one; in Braddon's novels men often want to remove a woman from the stage, but there is not one case of a male character then going on to encourage her to take one of the only other careers that could bring a woman fame or notoriety, that of an author. Also, to believe she was of a lower social position than himself is strange; for even though she had been an actress the social position of her family was a respectable one. But perhaps the idea that she was having to make her own way in the world and had fallen from her level helped Gilby to take an interest in her, and his last letter condescendingly refers to what he had done as a 'gentleman' for 'a woman in your position.'

Wolff marvelled that Braddon did not destroy the letters from Gilby, as she had so many others. He suggests that she may have kept them for the same reasons that Henry Braddon's compromising letters were kept by her mother: as evidence of one who had offended. However, in light of Gilby's later suicide, it seems far more probable she kept them as remembrances of a man who had helped her at the very beginning of her writing career and who came to a tragic end. She certainly must have destroyed a large number of his letters, and perhaps his last vitriolic communication to her was kept by mistake. There can be little doubt that Gilby was a difficult man. His letters at times sound bullying and hectoring. Those that survive are mainly concerned with the publication of *Garibaldi*. Even so, little of the truly personal is in these letters; they do not sound like the letters of a potential lover. The strange passion and later venom of his last letter may have been symptomatic of a disturbed mind, as Gilby was to become more and more prone to mental instability as the years passed. He was later described as having 'a very irritable' and 'uncontrollable temper' and 'All through life he seems to have been subject to fits of almost ungovernable temper'.[73]

At some stage it was decided that with the aid of a wage from Gilby, Braddon would leave the stage to become a full time writer. When she left Brighton she did not stay in Beverley for more than a couple of weeks because her first play, *The Loves of Arcadia*, was about to be performed by Miss Louise Swanborough's company at the Strand Theatre. The Sawyer family remained loyal corespondents. William wrote to her as soon as she had got to Beverley with the encouraging news that he had met John Clarke, a member of Miss Swanborough's company:

Are you in an Asylum. Has the extreme hilarity of your Northern retreat yet affected your mind beyond the limits of reason? I fear that it is so otherwise we should have received a reply to M.J.'s last communication. Came across an apparition. "Here sat the corporeal embodiment of a savage, an actor moreover an actor of "The Strand – the only Temple of the *real* drama in England! In other words it was little Clarke, whom I had met in London, and with whom I now spent a very agreeable evening. We spoke of thee – of the *Loves of a Cadger*, and he was pleased to say Miss Swanborough had faith in it, great faith in it and was disposed to think it will draw for many weeks. So now fortune smiles upon you – go in and win.[74]

He also went on to tell her that he and some of his Brighton friends had started a new comic magazine, and indicated that: 'If you *have* any stray jokes, parodies, com. sketches, or literary fun of any kind on hand, it would be very acceptable.' Unfortunately I have been unable to find out what Sawyer's new comic magazine amounted to. There is no mention of it in the *Brighton Herald*, and as a local production which probably did not last long it is likely that no copies survive. In the Wolff collection there are eight topical comic cartoon sketches by Braddon of swells and the Volunteer Rifles, one with the caption 'If you aspire to glory, join the "Rifles" though presumably they can get on as well without you', which may have been intended for this publication. Sawyer was a now an enthusiastic member and Corporal in the 1st Sussex Rifle Volunteers, writing such pieces as 'How and Why I Joined the Rifles' for the *Brighton Herald*. Mary Jane Sawyer wrote to Braddon on the 2 March, commiserating with what sounds like the latest rejections Braddon had had, but suggesting that there would soon be an introduction to the publisher John Maxwell:

> we received your long epistle last night. (...) but such is life. I will make no further comments but only hope you may wriggle something out of the Maxwell or Wraxwell (sic) – surely perseverance like yours shall somewhere gain its true light. To me you must ever remain a living marvel.[75]

Maxwell was obviously John Maxwell, but the 'Wraxwell' she referred to was Sir Frederick Charles Lascelles Wraxall (1828-1865) who worked for Maxwell for some years, both as a writer and in an editorial capacity on the *Sixpenny Magazine* (where he was deputy editor) and the *Welcome Guest*. The author F.W. Robinson later wrote of him:

> Poor Lascelles Wraxall, clever writer and editor, pressman and literary adviser, real Bohemian and true friend – indeed, everybody's friend but his own.[76]

Wraxall had fought in the Crimea, after which he had returned to London with a hatred of the Government, and became 'sub-editor, and publisher's hack'. When he succeeded to a baronetcy it was worthless because he had already sold his inheritance long before.

At this time Braddon later recalled sending off many manuscripts. One of these was a short story she later reused for *Lady Audley's Secret*:

> at this period of my life, the postman's knock had become associated with the sharp sound of a rejected MS. dropping through the open letter-box on to the floor of the hall, while my heart seemed to drop in sympathy with that book-post packet.[77]

With her mother in London she was obviously having a good time. William Sawyer was coming up to London for a music hall management banquet with his wife, who was complaining that 'for months' she had been promised a visit to London and that her husband's ticket admitted '2 ladies to the Balcony. If we come up together – could you and I go?' Mary Jane, planned to stay with Braddon and her mother, and she was longing to see *Colleen Bawn* amongst other things:

> You see I wish to flutter my gay wings in the sunlight of London – I shall have money in my pocket and William cannot be with me and he would like me to be under protection (...) I promise to be no bother to you - but there is a thirst come over me to do something and be gay – gay.[78]

Although Braddon was doubtless having fun in London, her time was not wholly her own because she had to follow John Gilby's instructions, and of these there were many. The first surviving letter from Gilby was written on 11 March 1860, when Braddon was in London, and where in a few weeks she was to meet John Maxwell. Doubtless she was there to see to some of the arrangements for *The Loves of Arcadia*, although Gilby warned her not to make any financial decisions with Swanborough, as he distrusted her:

> Miss S. dwelt on your being an unknown authoress – she may be very polite, & oily, but I think she is slippery, and I advise you not to go into any business matters with her – Don't be nervous, there is no reason whatever.[79]

He clearly was forever keen for her to improve her education and was also angry that two of his letters had been returned, because, to his dislike, she was still living under the name of Seyton:

> I have just been to church, and I hope I am not angry, but I wish I could show you how you often try to make me so. Here are my 2

letters back by the dead letter office that (I thought) you said you had received – *Business habits these!* (...) Then I rather gather from your letter that you have *not* seen the K. Gardens, or the Nat History at the Museum – Ah! what is the use of writing! What a task shall I have if I try to guide your studies. You know best whether you will be guided or not, but it is the only thing that gives me misgivings and pain.[80]

He seemed to expect her to return to Yorkshire soon, adding: 'I will go and see you as early as possible after yr arrival in Hull. (...) Is your Mama coming to Hull or not?'[81] He was already urging her on to write a new play even before the production of her first: 'I think if you have a proper subject for your own talents you can soon write some more play(s) á la "The Lover", for the country theatres.'[82] It may well have been partly through Gilby's influence, or even financial backing, that Miss Swanborough accepted her play; if Braddon had written a really good play one would have thought Henry Nye Chart would have been interested in producing it. It seems as if Gilby handled all of the arrangements, including the submission of the play to the Strand, and the previous November the *Theatrical Journal* had carried a story about a surprise new play by a mysterious new author which had been accepted by the Strand:

It is stated that at the Strand Theatre the MS. of a new drama has been accepted, sent to the manager, it is said, from a primitive part of Yorkshire, where it had been written by a lady in no way connected with literature.[83]

Gilby objected to Braddon using her stage name when she was in London, angrily remarking that:

you utterly hate & detest yr own name, showing the profound love that you are not even conscious of from its profundity, for your old (name).[84]

He seems to have been anxious that the Strand theatre should promote her play as having been written by a Yorkshire woman with no connections with literature (nor, by inference, with the theatre). It was through Gilby's interference, then, that the separation of M.E. Braddon from her poetic and theatrical predecessor, Mary Seyton, began. It was probably this statement which led many in later newspaper articles to believe Braddon had been brought up in Yorkshire.

Louise Swanborough, the actress manager, certainly seemed to see Gilby as the one with whom to discuss Braddon's financial dealings; if it is true that he was backing the production in some way it certainly shows he was willing to spend a great deal of money to buy her a chance of success, although as the Strand Theatre was quite small by London standards it might not have been as expensive as some. The *Brighton Herald*, no doubt at Sawyer's behest, duly reported the occasion of the first night of her comedietta on the 12 March:

> The comedietta from the pen of Miss Seyton, so long a member of the Brighton company, to which we alluded last week, was produced at the Strand Theatre on Monday night. It is entitled The Loves of Arcadia, and the plot forms an episode in the court-life of Louis XIV. A correspondent, writing from London, says "It was a great success. Everybody was delighted with the charming Dresden china-like character of the piece, which is admirably put on the stage, and was well played. The mounting was superb. There was a crowded house, great applause, and, at the close, loud cries of "Author," when Mr. Parselle came forward and stated that the authoress was not in the house; but he was desired to announce that the piece would be repeated every night during the week.[85]

It was certainly strange that Braddon was not there on the first night, especially as letters from the Sawyers indicate that she had planned to go; one of them wrote:

> (I) hope to have a *full* account of tomorrows trial. You have always shown yourself so free of affection or vanity as to success that I know we shall have from your own hand a fairer report than from any other.[86]

On the reverse of the letter William, regretting he could not come up himself for the first night, said 'I must trust to you for an account of the production of the comedieta.'[87] It is surprising that Gilby did not want to attend with his protégé so they could reap the glory. Perhaps she was there? Although Mr. Parselle, who had played the part of Chevalier de Merrilac, ought to have known whether or not she was there, it is possible she or Gilby had instructed the management that she did not wish to be presented to the audience. On the 18 March 1860, Louise Swanborough wrote to John Gilby soon after the first night, and was still discussing the financial terms. She was not too hopeful as to the possibility of the play having a long run:

I think we may congratulate ourselves upon the success accorded to the "Loves of Arcadia" by the public, the present season (of Lent) is not however too favourable for theatrical matters (...) With regard to the payments weekly or otherwise to be made to Miss Braddon. I regret that my health not permitting me to act more than 4 or 5 times a week will probably make a considerable deduction in the payment to Miss Braddon according to my present arrangement with her, I should therefore propose to purchase the right of acting the piece in London during 3 years for the sum of £20 (instead of the nightly payments as per agreement).[88]

She went on to give Gilby the address of the playwright Stirling Coyne, who was the Secretary of the Dramatic Author's Society, agreeing with Gilby that Braddon ought to join as, 'I fear unless she becomes a member she will have little chance of obtaining any remuneration for her pieces from *country* managers.'[89] Whatever the initial thoughts about *The Loves of Arcadia* were, it only ran for a few days.

Braddon was certainly in London around this time, and about three weeks later she was given an introduction to the owner of the magazine the *Welcome Guest*, the man Mary Jane Sawyer had hoped she would wring some work out of.

'Masterful' John Maxwell[90]

John Maxwell (1824-1895) was an orphan from Limerick. His parents had died while he and his four sisters were still young, and he was forced to make his own way in life when the trust fund which had supported him and his sisters was exhausted. Three of his sisters emigrated to America, where two married and the third became Sister Marie de Chantel, the Mother Superior of a convent in California. His fourth sister, Rosalie, married a Mr. O'Donnell, and moved to England where she often saw her brother and his family. John came to London to open an office in Southampton Street on the Strand when he was only eighteen years old at the request of the family of the Irish poet and novelist Gerald Griffin, to oversee an eight volume edition of his works, edited and with a life written by Griffin's brother, Dr. Daniel Griffin. These appeared under the imprint of Maxwell and Co. and gave Maxwell an occupation for a year, and the edition came out in 1842, after which he worked briefly in journalism and in insurance, probably with an unstable company called the Royal British Bank. At twenty five he was again dabbling in publishing, and the year before, on 7 March 1848, he had married Mary Anne Crowley at St. Aloysius's Chapel, Somers Town, London, the sister of the painter N.J. Crowley. Like

Maxwell, the Crowleys were Irish, and Mary Anne's sister, Eliza Mary, was married to Richard Brinsley Knowles (1820-1882), a barrister and occasional author. Some time after the birth of their seventh and last child Maxwell and his wife separated due, apparently, to the mental instability of his wife. It was the belief of literary London that she spent the rest of her life, insane, in an asylum, but it seems more likely that she returned to Ireland in the care of her family as her brother-in law later stated.[91]

After working as a newspaper agent[92] Maxwell became a contractor for advertisements, principally for the *Illustrated Times*, and he continued to handle the advertising for Ward and Lock's magazines in the 1860s. He had started a short lived newspaper, *Town Talk*, as early as 1858, and William Tinsley states another unsuccessful magazine, the *Cloister*, was aimed at the clergy, by sending the first issue to almost very vicarage in England.[93] At some point he started to work in conjunction with the publishers Ward, Lock & Tyler.[94] For them he brought out magazines, penny part novels such as the works of Dumas, and negotiated with authors and advertisers. W.B. Maxwell described his father when young as 'strikingly handsome',[95] but accounts of his personality and business practice are deeply divided. His skills as a seller of advertising and serial rights for fiction are easy to imagine, as surviving business letters vividly bring to life an adept salesmen, extolling the virtues and commercial value of manuscripts he probably had not read. Robert Buchanan described him as 'a big, burly, florid-faced, loud-spoken Irishman',[96] and one of his other writers, T.H.S. Escott, wrote:

> Hearty of manner, loud of voice, demonstratively Hibernian at times in his accentuation. He proved to me during many years one of the most satisfactory magazine proprietors with whom I have ever done business. I have heard some persons give a less favourable account of him. I do not believe they or anyone had just reason for complaint against John Maxwell. He was not, indeed, a person of superficial polish; nor did he pretend to take other than the commercial view of magazine "copy." But he knew what it would pay him to put before the public. Towards those who could supply this commodity he was fairly liberal and entirely loyal.[97]

Braddon's first meeting with John Maxwell can be precisely dated to early April 1860. She destroyed many of her personal papers after Maxwell died, but she preserved the letter of introduction which first brought her to his office. Louise Swanborough, probably at the behest of John Gilby, clearly arranged an introduction via the writer and playwright Andrew Halliday, who wrote in reply to Miss Swanborough:

> I have much pleasure in forwarding a letter of introduction for Miss Braddon to the proprietor of the "Welcome Guest." She had better call some morning about 11 at the address and take any M.S.S. she may have with her.[98]

The *Welcome Guest* had been founded by Henry Vizetelly in 1858, but, as recorded by Edmund Yates, it soon changed hands:

> In the second year of its existence the *Welcome Guest* was purchased by Mr. Maxwell, and by him issued at an advanced price in a different shape, but without the illustrations; it was under the editorship of Robert Brough, but with much the same staff of authors.[99]

Maxwell had started a number of magazines prior to this date, but without much success, all of them having been short lived. Maxwell was a man with a vision, wanting to bring periodicals within the reach of the lower classes, which he believed to be an as yet untapped part of the market. W.B. Maxwell later wrote that in many ways his father was ahead of his time, and that had he tried this decades later he would have made a great success of the enterprise:

> In some respects he was like a Lord Northcliffe or a Sir Arthur Pearson who had lived thirty years too soon. He had a persistent notion of a periodical very similar to their ones with an irresistibly popular appeal. But he could never quite realise his aim.[100]

At the time Braddon met him, Maxwell had his office at 122 Fleet Street, a few doors from Ward and Lock at 128, and not far from the Shoe Lane office where his business was later based. W.B. Maxwell described it as a 'funny old house' with his 'dingy little office'.[101] Robert Buchanan later recalled that his visits to the *Welcome Guest* office were often tense and unpleasant, not least because he himself was young and poor and desperate to sell his work:

> I was often kept waiting for hours on the premises in Fleet Street, and that I had sometimes to go away angry and disgusted, without an interview at all; now and then, moreover, the great man was crusty, and wouldn't buy what I wanted to sell, so that I had to depart in despair. (...) I had called once or twice to see him, and the

style in which the Publisher's myrmidions received me deepened in me a sultry sense of wrong.[102]

Buchanan went on to relate that his growing anger with Maxwell resulted in a visit to the office with a cudgel, feeling he would be provoked to murder Maxwell, and telling Charles Gibbon 'If he is offensive as usual, I will beat out what brains the ruffian possesses'; the murder was rendered unnecessary when Maxwell was jovial instead of rude, and bought Buchanan's manuscript. Braddon's reception can only be guessed at. Maxwell was not known for his conciliatory nature towards his writers, and seemed to make enemies as often as friends. The novelist 'Rita', who had a bad experience with Maxwell some years later, described her first visit to Shoe Lane:

> I had to wait some time in a dingy little room before I was asked up to the publisher's own office. I stared around with surprise. He sat at a very long table covered with papers. All round the room at various desks were a number of clerks or secretaries to whom he was perpetually addressing remarks, or asking for information during the interview. What an interview it was! Keep to the point he would not. (...) He went on talking grandiloquently about all and everything save the one subject I had come to discuss. Interspersing business details with praises of Miss Braddon (his illustrious wife), foolish compliments as to my youth and looks, and flowery speeches about my sex in general and myself in particular. All this with an audience of sniggering clerks pretending to be busy, but with ears keenly attentive to the matter at issue.[103]

It is likely that things did not go much better for Braddon, and that he was disparaging about her manuscripts – even though she could claim a partly published novel and a forthcoming volume of poetry. In fact he probably did not even read them himself, as his usual practice was to give manuscripts to someone else to judge. But he was also prone to flattery and exaggeration, and Braddon may have found him charming. Presumably he had separated from his wife only two or three years earlier, as his youngest child John, known as Jack, was not quite four years old at this time and was presumably too young to have been sent away to school. Whatever happened at her first interview nothing she wrote appeared in the *Welcome Guest* for some time, which suggests initial rejection. In any case she had to return to Beverley to finish *Three Times Dead* and to complete her book of poems for Gilby, especially the leading verse which Gilby had decided was to be about Garibaldi.

Garibaldi and his cause of Italian independence were astonishingly popular in Britain, and his exploits were related in great detail in newspapers during the period Braddon wrote her epic verse. The poem could not have been more topical: at the moment of Braddon's writing, Garibaldi was intensifying his campaign against the Austrians. In May 1860, with his thousand Redshirts, he began the battle to liberate Sicily and Naples. This enormous poem brought much grief to Braddon, as neither her heart nor her interest was in Garibaldi:

> With the business-like punctuality of a salaried clerk, I went every morning to my file of the *Times*, and pored and puzzled over Neapolitan revolution and Sicilian campaign, (...) How I hated the great Joseph G. and the Spenserian metre, with its exacting demands upon the rhyming faculty. How I hated my own ignorance of modern Italian history, and my own eyes for never having looked upon Italian landscape, whereby historical allusion and local colour were both wanting to that dry-as-dust record of heroic endeavour.[104]

Moreover Gilby sounds like an impossible task master. Because of his financial interest in her work he took every opportunity to assert his views. Whatever his feelings were towards her, he was certainly ambitious for her. Even if Gilby was difficult to please, she obviously enjoyed her six months in Beverley, where she lived first in Beverley and then Black House at Beverley Parks, and Beverley itself remained proud of the link fifty five years later:

> Miss Braddon's association with Beverley was at the very beginning of her literary career. Here she found her first public, and here in the quietness of the old county town her first novel, and her first poems were written and published. She had been writing, it is true, since she was eight, but her readers so far had been the limited public of her friends. Miss Braddon, before taking up literature, had taken to the stage, and acted both in Hull and York. Finding, fortunately, that literature was more her forte, she came, with her mother, to Beverley, and later she moved to the Black House in Long Lane for the sake of seclusion. It was here that she wrote her first novel.[105]

The owner of the Black House was a Mr. Atkinson and Gilby often visited her there while she wrote her novel.[106] One account described Mr. Atkinson as a 'gentleman farmer' who employed her to teach his children, and, if true, this may have been to pay for her and her mother's accommodation.[107] A similar house and location near Beverley, owned by a kindly farmer, was used as a setting in *The Black Band*. Her relations with both newspapers in the town remained good: even though the *Beverley Guardian* had never published any of her work, the binding for *Three Times Dead* was done in their offices. Although no more of her poems were published in the *Beverley Recorder*, she remained friends with the owner of the paper, and socialised with other literary minded men:

> being then a frequent guest with the proprietor's family. The late Dr. Brereton, J.P., and the Rev. Dr. Ryan (minister of Lairgate Chapel) were amongst the friends she was wont to meet at the Recorder office, and with whom she spent each week a few hours in pleasant social intercourse.[108]

Because Braddon used a Beverley Archery Club notebook at this time, with the club entries torn out, Wolff suggested she might have been expelled from the archery club because of her actress past, but there is no evidence to suggest this. On the contrary, it sounds as if she mixed freely in Beverley society (Brereton, for example, had been mayor in 1857 and had encouraged Wolfenden and Melbourne to come to the town; he was also a close friend of Gilby's) and that it was a happy time for her, and she paid tribute to the town's Northern hospitality in *The Black Band* the following year.[109] This happiness was probably in spite of Gilby, whose nagging would have been enough to try anyone.

The novel soon became a release to her, as it meant she could leave the exploits of Garibaldi for the melodramatic excess she so enjoyed:

> I gave loose to all my leanings to the violent in melodrama. Death stalked in ghastliest form across my pages; and villainy reigned triumphant till the Nemesis of the last chapter.[110]

Although Braddon was no longer publishing her poems in Beverley, she was still posting them to Brighton: a further six appeared there between June 1860 and February 1861, four of which also appeared in *Garibaldi*, and the last of which appeared as an advert for the recently published volume. These poems also bear witness to the gradual disappearance of her stage name, Mary Seyton. In September she became Mary Elizabeth Braddon, and in February 1861 M.E. Braddon.

Unfortunately the publication of *Three Times Dead* ended in animosity when first Empson cut his original offer from ten to five pounds, and then he never paid her any more than the fifty shillings she had received for her advance. Braddon remained under the impression that Empson never published it in any complete form, which means Empson never sent her a copy of it bound. In fact he did sell completed copies in red wrappers at two shillings a copy. Not many years afterwards he himself went bankrupt, and the judge observed that it was a pity his now famous first author had not seen fit to bail him out.

Braddon 'left Yorkshire almost broken-heartedly on a dull grey October (sic it was the end of September) morning, to travel Londonwards through a landscape that was mostly under water.'[111] She never returned to the Hull area again, although she continued to use it as a setting for her work for many years to come, including *Dead Mens Shoes* (1876) and 'Prince Ramji Rowdedow' which are both set in Beverley.[112] The next letter which survives from Gilby is from this time, when she and her mother had first moved to Stanhope Street in London. Here she was meant to help Gilby by seeing to some of the instructions to be given to the printers for *Garibaldi*, and Gilby told her he would visit her a week later, but that he himself was 'obliged to attend all the race meetings at this time of year (...) Marshall lost £1110 on the meeting. It was a very bad week for the bookmakers.'[113] On the 9 October he had more instructions for Braddon and her mother:

> Please correct carefully the ms poems & send them to Beverley on Wednesday by book post. If you & yr mama will make the type corrections in the proofs you next receive, I wish you would send me them – you must correct *two* copies, one for me and one for Mr. Strangeways & I will *revise mine after* you have done so (...) I wish you would make me one or two "melodies" from Isiah or elsewhere, but they must be *tip top*, or I shall make spills of them.[114]

Shortly before she moved to London, Braddon's first two stories appeared in the *Welcome Guest*, the second being the ghost story 'The Cold Embrace' which has been anthologised to this day. The *Brighton Herald*, in a piece probably written by Sawyer, noted the *Welcome Guest* in its periodical section once Braddon had become a contributor:

> This magazine, to the development of which poor Robert Brough devoted his latest days, is enlarged and greatly improved. In the current number there is a story, "The Cold Embrace," from the pen of Miss M.E. Braddon, better known to our readers as Mary Seyton, a charming poetess, and formerly Comedienne at the Brighton Theatre. She is, as we are glad to perceive, become one of the staff of the Magazine.[115]

Robert Brough had been a playwright and radical poet (Braddon had acted in several of his burlesques), but his increasing alcoholism had ended in his premature death. His brother Lionel worked for Tinsley and was a friend of Sawyer's, later to become a famous actor and a friend of Braddon. On the 11 October Gilby told her he had lost £130 at Bedford on the races, and two days later he wrote again, complaining about the quality of her proof reading, and urging her to continue working hard. It sounds as though she was writing new poems for the book almost up to the point of it being printed:

> you had missed some important ones – These bad grammas (sic) will be your plague when you have your own ms to correct. (...) It strikes me you must be pretty idle now having no piece of work cut out, & London to amuse you! (...) When will you write a Shakespearian play?[116]

Gilby also displayed a desire for social climbing. He was always urging Braddon to push herself, but clearly not always just for her own benefit; he wanted to get to know influential publishers himself, even badgering Mr. Strangeways, the printer, on the subject:

> Bye the bye do you know of a good author who has employed Murray the publisher, who would introduce me to him? I have written to Mr. Strangeways on the subject.[117]

Gilby continued to demand she write more poetry to fill up space in the volume, obviously deeming some of her newspaper poems not to be of a sufficiently high standard:

> I wish you would write one or two more powerful poems of about 50 to 100 lines, on any thing that will go down, Italy for instance, as I fancy we shall want 100 or 200 lines but I do not know yet.[118]

Braddon decided that her volume needed footnotes, and when Gilby agreed she went to tell the printers, who promptly suspended production while she wrote them. This angered Gilby who had not meant the typesetting to be stopped; and Braddon's claim to be so disabled by an injured foot that she could not go to see the printers to find out what was going on irritated him still further:

> I am so much annoyed that I can hardly write with much patience, but if you have the desire to assist me, I wish you would take a cab (if able) & go down to see them & see it again in progress – I

consider it a most important thing as far as any chance of profit is concerned.[119]

Gilby emphasised that his interest was wholly that of business when he reiterated the importance of profit, and many years later Braddon also claimed that this was his main interest in the volume:

> He looked at the matter from a purely commercial standpoint, and believed that a volume of verse, such as I could produce, would pay.[120]

Although he was angered by the delay, Gilby was also annoyed by the source that had suggested their inclusion to Braddon: 'It is not very flattering to me that you agreed to the notes etc at Mr. Maxwell's suggestion without writing to me by first post.'[121] He was also full of complaints about the printers, 'tell the printers I shall keep them to their agreement, or *find* a *means* of making them respect me a little more', adding he had 'written them a sharp letter.'[122] Mr. Strangeway's letter in reply was polite and cordial, probably in great contrast to the one sent by the impatient Gilby.[123] The following week he wrote to Braddon again, complaining he would never make any money out of the project, and criticising her and her mother's slowness at proof reading, adding sarcastically:

> did you never visit the Strangeways? I do not expect very much in the way of business from ladies, so you may easily please me by a few small "efforts" as C Dickens calls them.[124]

When he wrote to her in early November it sounds as though it was at his request, rather than Maxwell's refusal, that she was turning down any further work with the *Welcome Guest*:

> I need not tell you to make no engagement for some time with the W. Guest people – If your poetry (is) to pay, a few lines of it would be worth all they wd give you in a year.[125]

On the 10 November he wrote again, saying: 'I shd be very happy to re-engage you on as good terms as yr writing warrants, if yr book is well received.'[126] He told her to think of a new important historical subject for her poetry, and sent her a book on astronomy to improve her education. He was a keen and knowledgeable astronomer, having built his own observatory, and possessed all the latest books and instruments. It is quite probable that while Gilby was constantly suggesting worthy and intellectual subjects for her, she was at the same time pursuing work which interested her much more and of which she did not tell him or ask his opinion about.

Her other writing, which she probably found more fun, she discussed instead with William Sawyer. In October Braddon was clearly at work on a pantomime which she hoped that Chart would take at Brighton, and it seems to have been called *Hobgoblobshin*, and which she had sent to Sawyer both for advice and as an intermediary:

> In receipt of Panto. which is clever, "dem'd clever" 'specially for a gal. Yas; and I've got it in copying. It strikes me that the opening drags by reason of a *super* abundance of talkee – talkee among others. There must be songs, I fancy to relieve it at that early stage. The deficiency of incident strikes me throughout: (...) No time must be lost in getting it in as soon as possible. The dialogue is quite brilliant. (...) I don't like the heroine being threatened with corporeal punishment: it's rather in bad taste (...) A copy shall be sent by Monday – or rather the original so that you may finish and send to Creswick – reserving songs. The one you give is very good.[127]

William Creswick was the manager of the Surrey, and had been when Braddon had acted there four years earlier, and she also planned to send it to the theatre in Manchester. However, ten days later Sawyer wrote with disheartening news for its chances in Brighton:

> Have seen Nye C. who from his tone will not accept the Panto. He has handed it over to Sanger. This is a nuisance not his handing it over; but his non-reception but it arises from his *Keating* (may she have ever a cough and never a lozenge) having that one with a Nonsering legend in it. Get the MS as soon as you can and send it to Manchester. I hope you will be more successful with Creswick the creamy.[128]

In the event it was used neither in Manchester nor at the Surrey, but it was surprising Chart did not look more favourably on his former company member's work, especially one who had had a play performed in London. All the same, the conclusion of all future managers who read her work for the theatre, throughout her career over the next fifty years, was that wherever her talents lay it was not as a playwright, and that something was seriously lacking. The Sanger Sawyer was to show it to was Alfred Sanger, the acting manager at Brighton, and whose little daughter Rachel had acted in the last pantomime during Braddon's time with the company. Miss Keating was the doyenne of Brighton pantomimes, having already written three for Chart, and it sounds as though she was disliked by Sawyer and Braddon (Sawyer is referring to a popular brand of cough sweets, Keating's). At this time Braddon was also acting as an intermediary for Sawyer, taking his and Mary Jane Sawyer's poems for consideration at the *Welcome Guest*:

The last letter from Gilby surviving before the publication of *Garibaldi* is from the 20 November, and it sounds as though Braddon was asserting her independence from his patronage. She was acting more on her own initiative, or the advice of someone else, since she was not always sending her work straight to Gilby, and even when she sent revisions to him he inserted his preferred copy:

> It scarcely seems kind of you to have sent the peice (sic) on Isaiah to them without showing it to me. Consider how you increase my letters and trouble. Now I have to send for it from them & return it. (...) Thank you for altering Tired of Life – but I like the old copy the best – so excuse me for sending it. It is more beautiful than the old one. I read it to Mr. B(rereton) & he likes it.[129]

He was still pushing her to try and make influential friends, again comparing her unfavourably to Dr. Brereton's friend Miss Blythe who, he informed her, 'has fairly *wedged* herself into the graces of Mr. Macmillan.' He was cross because she would not be pushy with people in order to advance herself, 'But whether it is your nature or your mama's wish, I don't know (...) It will be curious to see whether Miss Blythe's energy or your talent, carry you on the best. I know which I should bet on.'[130] After this no letters survive until his final break with Braddon three months later. It may well be that it was at this time that she began to fall out with him. She had been sending her poems to Sawyer for his opinion, and he agreed with her that the title poem was very boring. He thought the central poem should have been 'Olivia', describing Gilby's preference as one of the 'greatest blunders of your patron (...) there never was a more lamentable mistake. (...) The subject is one of the most unfortunate'.[131] In another letter, probably referring to Sawyer's opinions on the poems to be selected, Gilby had angrily retorted, 'My dear Miss Braddon, *please* not to be tiresome, but let *me* select the fugitives. (...) I do *not* think Oakey is at all interested in his advice.'[132] Daniel Oakey was a bookseller friend in Westminster who had advised Gilby about possible publishers.

It seems as if later that year Maxwell had promised Braddon promotion, probably as editor of the *Welcome Guest*, although William

Sawyer wrote to her on 3 December 1860, warning her not to take Maxwell's promises too seriously:

> What you tell me of the W.G. is news indeed, only Maxwell is a humbug of the first water – quite a solid gem of "purest ray serene" in the humbug line and therefore all his vows are to be taken *cum grano salis* – rather say a good large lump – a handful at least.
> 'Tis better to have nurtured in your breast
> A vision of the ever Welcome Guest
> Bearing your name and under your control
> Than to have sunk in bitterness of soul
> To the conclusion that your revolutions
> Of pen and brain are doomed (a good rhyme's Proosians)
> Always to be rejected contributions.[133]

Presumably, at this stage, Braddon and Maxwell's relationship was not so close that he had to avoid calling Maxwell a humbug. He was certainly right to remind her that Maxwell's words were not to be trusted, as Braddon did not become editor. He appointed Robert Buchanan, who was six years her junior, and to whom Maxwell sent Braddon to meet at the house he shared with another struggling writer, Charles Gibbon, so that Buchanan could consider her work:

> I remember our first interview on the ground floor of the house where I lived in Stamford Street, Blackfriars. She was a plump, fair-haired unassuming girl, while I was a curly-headed, diffident boy, and she must have been amused, I fancy, by my assumption of editorial airs.[134]

Despite her disappointment she had the short story, 'My First Happy Christmas', in the Christmas issue of the *Welcome Guest*, and which the *Brighton Herald* described as 'a piece of genial writing worthy of Dickens.'[135] William Sawyer had been keen to get a piece in for this edition:

> Could you ask the W.G. people whether they contemplate a Christmas number? I've a long Christmas Card in verse; and something might be done in prose praps.[136]

At about the end of 1860, Braddon and her mother moved to 20 Camden High Street, and she was making friends with George Augustus Sala, who in December became editor of Maxwell's new magazine *Temple Bar*, writing him a girlish, teasing letter. The letter suggests she still spent some of her time in Brighton, assuring Sala she would keep his 'most charming of letters, which I intend to have framed & hung over my mantlepiece in Brighton.'[137] This joking letter to Sala, girlish but calculated to appeal to him, is the sort of letter she had written to Mr. Younge. From the tone of Gilby's letters to her it is hard to imagine her sending such letters to him. Although she had never met Sala, who at this time was very famous, she may have met his mother, Madame Sala, who was a popular singer at the Royal Pavilion during the years Braddon was in Brighton. Maxwell had made Sala editor of his new magazine *Temple Bar*, partly because he was a famous name, and even though Sala was notoriously unreliable with deadlines and was as temperamental as Maxwell.

Garibaldi came out in early February, the British Library copy was deposited on the 8 February 1861. Braddon's preface to *Garibaldi* was surprisingly short and carried no dedication to her demanding patron, reading only:

> In submitting a volume of Poems to the critical Public, the inexperienced author can only appeal to the generous indulgence of that ever-generous tribunal. The wonderful Sicilian campaign, which has made this departing year of 1860 one epic poem, has suggested the brief record here offered to the reader.[138]

It was indeed curious that it carried no words for Gilby, and it was clearly one of the things that rankled when he broke off with Braddon. However, one who was exerting himself on her behalf was John Maxwell who, as Robert Buchanan later recalled, asked Buchanan to write a favourable review for the *Athenaeum* in February 1861, a request his young editor could hardly have refused; although it has to be said that he obviously did not force Buchanan to write a wholly positive review, as it acknowledges the collection had faults. Buchanan also wrote in his review that he deduced from the poems that M.E. Braddon was a young woman, and not a man, even though he knew this before, having met her. The truth was that with her work now appearing in the *Welcome Guest*, Braddon did not need to defer to Gilby's wishes, nor continue to write what were probably very ingratiating letters to her patron. There is a three month gap of letters which no longer survive, but what clearly broke the relationship was her friendship with John Maxwell and her standing up to Gilby's accusations concerning him, while at the same time refusing his corrections of her work. Gilby wrote:

You have so often acknowledged your deficiency in punctuation that I attach not much importance to your opinion of my corrections. (...) My enquiries respecting Mr. Maxwell were conducted in a strictly business manner, and so given to you and it was natural for me to infer, from your having so frequently consulted me on your literary affairs, that you would thank me for making them – I need therefore scarcely notice the sneering language in which you tell me that my information is "vague and undefined, not to say absurd." A contrast no doubt it is to the hundred fulsome and varied expressions of gratitude in the letters which I have in my desk from you (continued as long as you imagined I could be of any service to you) and to your "promise on your honour" to consult me in seeking literary employment, and to take none without my permission!

But my mistake in taking you from your legitimate profession may afford me a not unprofitable lesson – gratitude! why you hardly know the meaning of the word. Honour! Your code of Honour? You have become such an actress that you cannot speak without acting – I have worked as hard and done as much for you as it was possible for a gentleman to do for a woman in your position. (...) I can only feel a pity for you not unmingled with contempt, and wonder if you have one redeeming trait in your character.[139]

He concluded by asking her to return any of his books she still had to Mr. Oakey. Whether Braddon and Gilby ever spoke again is not known. The tone of his final letter and her eventual relationship with Maxwell would suggest not, but the fact that she paid tribute to his generosity as a patron in 'My First Novel' means she bore him no animosity.

Sadly the rest of Gilby's life was neither as happy nor as successful as Braddon's. Gilby committed suicide in 1882 at the age of sixty two. Braddon recalled that when she knew him he was 'at that time' a rich man. But unfortunately by the time of his death this was no longer the case:

On Wednesday morning Mr. John Gilby was found hanging in his residence in Westwood-road. Deceased, who was 62 years of age, had latterly been despondent because of reverses in his position. A few months ago he removed from Newbegin House where he had resided for several years, and this to some extent affected him adversely, while losses in shares had also been a source of anxiety.[140]

He lost most of the money in Kingston Cotton Mills in Hull, and had to move to a smaller house a few months before his death.[141] His housekeeper, Mrs. Saul, who had found the body testified at the inquest that in the early hours of the morning:

> she heard him making a noise and went to quieten him. He said he was wretched and miserable, and she begged him to console himself, as probably before Saturday some arrangement would be made for his comfort. Deceased had been out of spirits for the last seven months, and had spoken about destroying himself. He had also threatened to set the house on fire, and last week he nearly bit her thumb off, but he apologised for this afterwards, and said he was in a temper when he did it.[142]

The *Beverley Guardian* also related his violence against Mrs. Saul: 'A week before his death he seized witness by the wrist, and nearly bit her thumb in two. He had caught hold of her before.'[143] Dr. Stephenson had been about to make arrangements for his entry to the East Riding Asylum or a retreat of some kind because: 'If he was thwarted in the least thing he became violent.'[144] All agreed that he had always had these tendencies.

When Braddon had thought she was going to be made the editor of the *Welcome Guest* she told William Sawyer she would use her new influence to help him bring his own works to a wider public, to which he had said: 'Thanks for your kind promises as to the future. We must live and hope.'[145] Wolff dismissed the assertion in the obituary of Braddon in the *Daily Telegraph* that Sawyer and Braddon left Brighton together to seek literary fortune. But this was not meant literally, and in a way it was true because Braddon did not forget Sawyer's help on the *Herald* and was eager to return the favour by introducing him to her new literary associates on the *Welcome Guest* and *Temple Bar*. When he left Brighton to live in Camberwell it was to work for Maxwell in London and to edit his new venture in cheap periodical literature, *Twice a Week*. According to the *Brighton Herald* he 'quitted Brighton in 1861 to enter upon a literary career in London.'[146] When Maxwell founded *Belgravia* his poetry and essays became a regular feature, and he clearly was a life long and loyal friend. At the end of his life he was editor of the *South London Press* and the comic *Funny Folks*. The author of twenty five novels published in magazines, he was president of the Whitefriars Club at the time of his death. His wife died a year before him, much to his distress, and he himself died suddenly of typhoid at the age of fifty five at his home in Pelham Place West Brompton.

A Trip to Brighton and Three Letters from John Maxwell

Only three letters survive from Maxwell to Braddon, written two months after her disappointment over the editorship of the *Welcome Guest*. Braddon had gone to visit her friends in the Henry Nye Chart company, and was staying at 12 Kensington Gardens in Brighton. Maxwell's letters are already very familiar in tone, addressing her, like Sawyer, and presumably her other Brighton friends, as 'Polly'. They certainly indicate a much closer relationship than the Gilby letters, and would have confirmed Gilby's fears. It was almost a year since she and Maxwell had first met, and Maxwell was in the process of reprinting *Three Times Dead* as *The Trail of the Serpent*. In the first letter, written coincidentally on the 20 February 1861, the same day as Gilby's final letter, Maxwell wrote:

My dear Polly,
Lonely, sad, and very full of thought, I obey your wish that I should write to you this evening. But, oh! how I feel the want of words to express the weariness of soul that arises when, after an arduous day's work – one of unceasing toil – the heart wakes up to find itself *All alone! all Alone!* No kind voice to utter the sweet sounds of sympathy or a soft glance that talks of feelings the lips could only fail in attempting to voice. Well, I am alone! Alone in every sense tonight. And yet no one ever desired loneliness less than I do! but so it is; and to the ordinance of fate I bow with all the resignation I can muster. Most fearfully egotistic and selfish all this sounds. What else could you expect? Asking me to write fresh on the loss of your society, how else can I do but declare the void your absence causes? Of course you will be ready with a toss of the head, curl of the lip, and gentle nervous twitch in an organ that has a natural inclination to turn upwards (horrid impertinence) and with all those graceful accomplishments you will say "It's all very fair Mr. M. but Brighton air is to be preferred to the fetid heated atmosphere of a Turkish bathroom. Moreover, Sir, green-room associations and gossip are somewhat livelier than your dull-pated conversation." Even this can't be helped. Go forth, then, and may every step you take be one of pleasure, every word you hear one of joy, and every acquaintance you meet a friend who can appreciate without loving you, yet love you without offending
Ever faithfully yours, John Maxwell.[147]

The following day he wrote again, in reply to a note from her:

The bright spark of true pleasure derived from your note was allowed but a brief existence this morning. Delivered with it were a host of the most annoying letters I ever got. It would seem as if every wretch who could annoy me got wind of the joy that was sure to arise when I was told by you that an act of mine had afforded "rapture" to your mama, and basely jealous of so innocent a delight, took the opportunity to throw the worst possible annoyance upon me. Thus the joys and griefs of life come so close together we are often barely able to conjure up a smile ere we have to dash away a sorrow.[148]

He went on tell her that he had lined up some work experience at his other magazine, the *St. James's Magazine*, under the editor Mrs. S.C. Hall who, with her husband Samuel, were important literary figures, writing numerous books and editing many annuals:

Today the Agreements between the Halls and the proprietor of the St. James's Magazine were formally executed. Mrs. Hall spoke in the kindliest manner of your gentleness and most unpresuming demeanour. She is well inclined to act matronly towards you and I have encouraged the idea that you are most anxious to profit by her experience and counsel. After no. 1 appears a whole day is expected from you. I was most of all gratified by the candid admission that dear Polly is brimful of unconscious and almost wholly undeveloped power! Think of that coming from such folk.[149]

Maxwell obviously knew the best way to make a good impression on Braddon was to make a good impression on her mother, concluding this letter 'Give my kindest regards to Mama and tell her that her slightest recognition of any act of mine affords the amplest encouragement to do better next time.'[150] Gilby in contrast never sent any greetings to Mrs. Braddon, and the only references to her are when he blames Braddon and her mother for not seeing to the proofs or for not making friends with influential people. The third and last surviving letter from Maxwell was written on the following day, and at the top of the *Welcome Guest* paper he stuck a little clipping from *The Times* advertising that Braddon's story 'The Lawyer's Secret' would be appearing in no. 75 of the magazine. Maxwell had obviously received an angry note from Braddon concerning a letter Maxwell had enclosed with his own:

I sent Russell's letter because it struck me as a curious coincidence that while mama and yourself are criticising him, he should be unconsciously discharging the uninvited duty of critic upon you. It never occurred to me that its coming to you so very abruptly might beget misconception and perhaps create annoyance. I am sure you are incapable of imagining I would send it if I had the slightest idea you could be annoyed thereby. I have never advertised anything written by Mr. Russell; and I have declined the books he has offered to me.

One thousand copies of "The Trail of the Serpent" sold in *seven days*. Pleasant news! I have just sent it out for review.[151]

The identity of Russell was probably the writer William Russell (not to be confused with the later writer of seafaring novels of the same name), whose stories under the pseudonym of Lieut. Warneford were currently appearing in the *Welcome Guest*, and who also wrote under the pseudonym of 'Waters' the sort of low grade detective fiction Maxwell specialised in, books that came straight out as paperbacks or yellowbacks – work he would doubtless have been interested in had Braddon not been cross by Russell's opinion of her own work. In fact Maxwell did not decline Russell's work for long, and his *Experiences of a Real Detective* was serialised in the *Sixpenny Magazine* in 1862 and his Warneford stories appeared in the *Halfpenny Journal*.

When Braddon and her mother returned to London she began to spend one day each week working on the *St. James's Magazine*. The slush pile was dealt with by Mrs. Hall's nephew, Sanford Rochat, and Braddon probably assisted him with this. Mrs. Hall often befriended young writers, and her relations with Maxwell soon became strained. She believed he was exploiting the young poet Robert Buchanan (the editor of the *Welcome Guest*), and after Maxwell dealt with some of his poems submitted to the *St. James's Magazine* 'with an inconsideration amounting to cruelty', Mrs. Hall felt compelled to speak 'very plainly' to Maxwell.[152] Mrs. Hall, who was Irish herself, had known Maxwell's wife, leading to a further awkward exchange, related to another young writer she was helping, Isabella Fyvie Mayo:

He had been married to an Irish lady with whom Mrs. Hall had been acquainted. One day, on going to his office, she inquired after his wife. Maxwell coolly replied: "She is defunct." Mrs. Hall could not believe her ears, and repeated her question, only to receive again the reply: "She is defunct." "Mr. Maxwell," she cried, "surely you do not mean to say that your wife is dead?" "Madam," he returned, with a sardonic smile, "she is *de*-funct!" The poor lady, broken in mind and body, was alive for years afterwards.[153]

Perhaps Mrs. Hall had hoped to remind him of his responsibilities as a husband, and possibly Maxwell had told other people that his wife was dead. Certainly the belief of some of the next generation of Maxwells was that their mother had not at first known of the existence of Maxwell's wife. But, even if this was the case, he could not have hoped to keep the existence of his six surviving children a secret for long. Once the children came to know Braddon they were able to love her as a mother.[154] Only a few months after the letters Maxwell wrote to Braddon when she was in Brighton, she became pregnant with her first child, Gerald. At about this time Maxwell founded two new magazines, in July 1861 the *Halfpenny Journal* which Mrs. Braddon edited and her daughter wrote anonymous fiction for, and the *Sixpenny Magazine* in which was to appear the novel which made her famous, *Lady Audley's Secret*. This novel was to be condemned and praised as one of the leading works of sensation fiction, and it is this development and Braddon's role as a sensation novelist which forms the subject of the next chapter.

Chapter Two Footnotes

1. 'Miss Braddon at Home', *Daily Telegraph*, 4 October 1913, p.9.

2. M.E. Braddon, 'My First Novel', *Idler*, vol. III, 1893, p.20

3. M.E. Braddon, *Before the Knowledge of Evil* (c.1914), unpublished typescript in the Wolff collection, pp.129-130.

4. Clive Holland, 'Fifty Years of Novel Writing. Miss Braddon at Home', *Pall Mall Magazine*, vol. XIV, November 1911, p.702.

5. Braddon, *Before the Knowledge of Evil*, p.169.

6. Ibid. p.170.

7. Ibid. p.171.

8. Mary Angela Dickens, 'Miss Braddon At Home', *Windsor Magazine*, vol. VI, September 1897, p.411.

9. Braddon, 'My First Novel', p.20.

10. Ibid. p.23.

11. Braddon, *Before the Knowledge of Evil*, pp.29-30.

12. Ibid. Clive Holland, 'Miss Braddon: The Writer and Her Work', *Bookman*, vol. XLII, July 1912, p.149, 'Her mother was an unusually cultured woman, possessed of a fine critical taste, and able to express her views in articles, contributed to the magazines and periodicals of the day, and in essays.

13. Holland, Ibid. p.159.

14. Dickens, p.411.

15. M.E. Braddon, 'At the Shrine of Jane Eyre', *Pall Mall Magazine*, vol. XXXVII, 1906, p.174.

16. Braddon, 'My First Novel', p.23.

17. Mrs. Adelaide Calvert, *Sixty-Eight Years on the Stage* (London: Mills and Boon, 1911, p.16.

18. *Hampshire Advertiser*, 4 March 1854, p.5.

19. For details of Mrs. Calvert's plays see: *Hampshire Independent*, 1 October 1853, p.4, 8 October, p.4; *Era*, 26 March 1854, p.11.

20. Calvert, p.36.

21. Holland, 'Miss Braddon: The Writer and Her Work', p.159.

22. Robert Lee Wolff, 'Devoted Disciple: The Letters of Mary Elizabeth Braddon to Sir Edward Bulwer Lytton, 1862-1873', *Harvard Library Bulletin*, vol. 12, 1974, p.149, in a letter dated 13 June (1872) Braddon described herself as first meeting Bulwer Lytton eighteen years earlier, i.e. 1854.

23. Joseph Hatton, 'Miss Braddon at Home', *London Society*, January 1888, p.28.

24. A notebook of the period in the Wolff collection contains a long poem, notes on Napoleon, French practice, and parts of plays including *The Suicide, Or a Tale of the Morgue.*

25. M.E. Braddon to Mr. Younge, 14 January 1855, Wolff collection.

26. James Joseph Sheahan, *General and Concise History and Description of the Town and Port of Kingston-Upon-Hull* (London, Simpkin, Marshall, 1864), p.650. Although Sheahan does not give a date for this opera, it seems unlikely the collaboration and performance took place after Braddon left the Queen's Theatre, as Braddon never returned to the Hull area after the six months in Beverley. Of course it could have occurred during the period of Gilby's patronage, but there is no mention of it in their letters, nor in Braddon's account of the Beverley period. The opera may have been performed at the Theatre Royal in Hull, as Harry Deval had written for that theatre before.

27. Calvert, p.14.

28. Mary Seyton, 'Rest', *Beverley Recorder*, 9 May 1857, p.4.

29. Wybert Rousby, 'The Infant' and 'The Man in the Iron Mask', *Beverley Recorder*, 2 May 1857, p.4.

30. 'The Late Miss Braddon and Beverley', *Beverley Recorder*, 6 February 1915, p.5.

31. M.E. Braddon, 'My First Time in Print', *The Grand Magazine*, vol. I, February 1905, p.33.

32. 'The Late Miss Braddon and Beverley', quotes letter from Braddon to H.M. Ward, 29 December 1914.

33. Braddon, 'My First Novel', p.25.

34. Calvert, p.36.

35. William Sawyer to Braddon, c. March 1860, Wolff collection. I did attempt to find out if Braddon's side of the correspondence could have survived, but Sawyer died childless, his sisters did not marry, and the family of his brother John has also died out.

36. M.E. Braddon, *The Story of Barbara* (London: Maxwell, 1880; repr. London: Maxwell, c.1881), p.151.

37. M.S., 'Delhi', *Beverley Recorder*, 26 September 1857, p.4.

38. Mary Seyton, 'On the Queen's Health Being Drunk Within the Walls of Delhi, After the Battle,' *Beverley Recorder*, 21 November 1857, p.4.

39. 'William Kingston Sawyer', *South London Press*, 4 November 1882, p.1. 'Death of Mr. William Sawyer', *Brighton Herald*, 4 November 1882, p.3.

40. 'Death of Mrs. Sawyer', *Brighton Herald*, 7 May 1881, p.3. From letters it would seem that Mrs. Sawyer lost a baby in 1860. Typical poems by her at this time are 'The Child Asleep' and 'The Dead Baby.'

41. In October 1857 Braddon's uncle William was attacked and left for dead during a burglary at his home, Blacklands at Plympton, near Ivybridge. Braddon, who was a widower of nearly seventy, had been a judge of the Calcutta Sudder Dewanny, the most important of the East

India Company's courts in Bengal. He had dismissed his Swiss valet, James Baudiste, for 'improper conduct towards one of the servant women' and had refused to give him a reference. Baudiste promptly went to the home of another Braddon relative, naval Captain Hewlett, and robbed his servant. He recruited two other men, James Colman and William Browne, and broke into Blacklands in the early hours of Saturday morning. Braddon was found covered with blood, and with serious injuries to his head, in his bedroom. Mary Braddon later stated that her uncle was murdered by his attackers but, although they doubtless left him for dead, he recovered sufficiently (losing the sight of an eye) to testify against the men at their trial the following March. He died later that year. The men were found guilty of the burglary only, and were sentenced to penal servitude for life. 'Burglary and Attempted Murder,' *The Times*, 26 October 1857, p.7; 'The Blackland Outrage', *The Times*, 29 October 1857, p.11; 'The Blacklands Burglary', *The Times*, 11 March 1858, p.12.

42. Mary Seyton, 'Havelock', *Brighton Herald*, 9 January 1858, p.2.

43. Mary Seyton, 'Captain Skene', *Brighton Herald*, 2 January 1858, p.4.

44. 'The Fate of a Heroine', *Brighton Herald*, 5 September 1857, p.4.

45. Michael Edwardes, *Red Year The Indian Rebellion of 1857* (London: Hamish Hamilton, 1973; repr. London: Cardinal, 1975), p.178 reprints this poem and examples of the many others published at the time.

46. Mary Seyton, 'Havelock', *Brighton Herald*, 16 January 1858, p.4.

47. Dedication page of *The Story of Barbara* (London: Maxwell, repr. c.1881), p.2.

48. Braddon to T.H.S. Escott, 16 October 1879, British Library, Escott Papers, Add.Mss.58786.

49. Braddon to T.H.S. Escott, 3 November (1879), Ibid.

50. Edward Braddon was to write that one of the disadvantages of New Zealand for the colonial was, 'it has the Maori, who is a nuisance neither useful nor picturesque', Edward Braddon, *Home in the Colonies*, (Tasmanian Historical Research Association Papers, 1979).

51. 'Death of Sir Edward Braddon', *Tasmanian Mail*, 6 February 1904, p.32. Leaving the East India Railway, Edward Braddon became a Government magistrate in 1857 for the Deoghur district of Santhalia:

He served against the Santhals in their rebellion in 1855, and received the thanks of the Government of Bengal for this, and for raising a Santhal regiment. Sir Edward also served in the Indian Mutiny; under Sir George Yule, in the districts of the Bhagulpore division, and in defending Deoghun against the mutineers, and for his service received the medal and favourable mention in despatches. In 1862 he went to Oudh as Commissioner of Excise and Stamps, which appointment he held until his retirement in 1876, together with additional appointments of Inspector-General of Registration and Superintendent of Trade Statistics. During twenty months of that period he was also Financial Secretary to the Government of Oudh.

Braddon's son, Henry Yule Braddon who was born in Calcutta in 1863, was named after his father and his Indian Mutiny commander. After leaving India, Edward Braddon lived in Tasmania and entered the government in 1879, eventually becoming Prime Minister. He was appointed Agent-General in London 1888-1893, and was fully reconciled with his sister. The author of two books, *Life in India* (1872) and *Thirty Years of Shikar* (1895), he was a contributor to *Blackwood's* and, according to the *Tasmanian Mail*, 'a member of the original staff of the *Pioneer*'.

52. Mary Seyton, 'Lines to the Princess Royal on Her Wedding Day', *Brighton Herald*, 23 January 1858, p.3.

53. Mary Seyton, 'Robespierre at the Guillotine', *Brighton Herald*, 13 February 1858, p.4.

54. Mary Seyton, 'We May Roam Through This World', *Beverley Recorder*, 20 February 1858, p.4.

55. *Brighton Gazette*, 10 March 1859, p.4.

56. M.E. Braddon, 'My First Novel', p.23.

57. Ibid. p.24.

58. Ibid. p.24.

59. Mary Seyton, 'The Peril of Christmas Eve', *Brighton Guardian*, 23 December 1859, p.4.

60. Braddon, 'My First Novel', p.24.

61. Ibid. p.25.

62. *Brighton Herald*, 18 February 1860, p.4.

63. Braddon, 'My First Novel', p.27.

64. *Beverley Recorder*, 24 May 1884, p.4.

65. Braddon, 'My First Novel', p.25.

66. Wolff, *Sensational Victorian*, p.82 records the manuscript of an unfinished short story, 'Kingdom of the Bored', postmarked Brighton, September, and probably correctly assumed the year was 1859.

67. Wolff, *Sensational Victorian*, pp.79-80.

68. *World*, 17 May 1884, p.18.

69. *Beverley Recorder*, 24 May 1884, p.4.

70. *World*, 21 May 1884, p.18.

71. *Beverley Recorder*, 13 June 1857, p.4.

72. Braddon, *Before the Knowledge of Evil*, pp.145-146.

73. 'Suicide of Mr. John Gilby', testimony of Dr. Stephenson, *Beverley Recorder*, 17 May 1884, p.5. and 'Melancholy Death of Mr. Gilby of Beverley', *Beverley Guardian*, 17 May 1884, p.8.

74. William Sawyer to Braddon, c. March 1860, Wolff collection.

75. M.J. Sawyer to Braddon, 2 March 1860, Wolff collection. Wolff misinterprets this letter by believing it was dated 20 November, and thereby attributes Mary Jane's comments to Braddon's disappointment over not being made editor of the *Welcome Guest* – with the correct date this is impossible, as Braddon had not even met Maxwell. Wolff identified M.J. Sawyer as William's sister, but she was in fact his wife. His sisters were called Elizabeth and Fanny and his brother John.

76. F.W. Robinson, 'My First Book', *Idler*, 1893, vol. III, p.210. Wraxall died young, and Folkestone Williams began a subscription for his widow. Braddon told him she was shocked by Wraxall's sudden death, but that her finances were taken up with helping her family and 'it is only right to tell that I only saw the lady once in my life, & that her manner was to me on that occasion by no means conciliatory.' (Braddon to Folkestone Williams, 25 July, Wolff collection.)

77. Braddon, 'My First Novel', p.26.

78. Mary Sawyer to Braddon, 2 March 1860, Wolff collection.

79. John Gilby to Braddon, 11 March 1860, Wolff collection.

80. Ibid.

81. Ibid.

82. Ibid.

83. *Theatrical Journal*, 9 November 1860, p.355.

84. John Gilby to Braddon, 11 March 1860, Wolff collection.

85. *Brighton Herald*, 17 March 1860, p.3.

86. Sawyer to Braddon, c.11 March 1860, Wolff collection. The letter is probably not from Mary Jane as the letter is more formal than hers, but presumably not from Sawyer's mother as Wolff suggests, as the writer had just had a baby. It may have been from his sister-in-law.

87. William Sawyer to Braddon, c.11 March 1860, Wolff collection.

88. Louise Swanborough to John Gilby, 18 March 1860, Wolff collection.

89. Ibid.

90. Braddon uses this term for Maxwell in an unpublished essay, 'A Summer Tour in Belgium Fifty Years Ago' (1914). The essay was intended for the *Strand Magazine*. In her diary, 13 October 1914, Braddon wrote 'Began Belgian article'. The article was to raise £50 for the *Daily Telegraph* war fund for the Belgians. A 2pp. typed extract exists within the Wolff collection, which Braddon had written to the Editor 6 January 1915. As she fell ill, the article was unpublished.

91. Information on Maxwell's first marriage is from Richard Brinsley Knowles's three page privately printed circular, distributed after Mary Anne Maxwell's death, written on 28 September 1874. Doubtless Maxwell's wife was mentally unwell, but evidence is lacking that she was in an asylum. After the separation the circular stated she 'resided thenceforth with her family in the neighbourhood of Dublin.' Nor did she die in an asylum, but at the home of her brother John. This house, 72 Mountain View, Harold's Cross, is listed as belonging to Mrs. Crowley in *Thom's Irish Almanac and Official Directory* for 1859, presumably their mother and where Mary Anne Maxwell most likely lived after the separation. Possibly the asylum was a rumour to make Maxwell's position more sympathetic in London.

92. The Post Office London Directory for 1851, p.876, lists 'Maxwell, John & Co. newspaper agents, 31 Nicholas lane, Lombard Street.'

93. William Tinsley, *Random Recollections of an Old Publisher* 2 vols (London: Simpkin, Marshall & Co. 1900) I, p.62.

94. Ralph Straus, *Sala The Portrait of an Eminent Victorian* (London: Constable, 1942), p.154 mentions the bank, and some other details are from Frederick Boase's *Modern English Biography*, vol. VI (repr. London: Frank Cass, 1965).

95. Maxwell, p.157.

96. Harriet Jay, *Robert Buchanan Some Account of His Life, His Life's Work and His Literary Friendships* (London: T. Fisher Unwin, 1903), p.93. It has to be said that Buchanan was not an easy man to get on with, making more enemies than Maxwell. Later when Tillotson was having trouble with Buchanan and Charles Gibbon, Maxwell said he was not surprised, 'Having been in the past exposed to the predatory practices of both'. (Maxwell to Tillotson, 23 March 1885, *Bolton Evening News* Archive, Bolton Central Library, Greater Manchester.)

97. T.H.S. Escott, *Platform, Press, Politics and Play* (Bristol: Arrowsmith, 1895), p.269.

98. Andrew Halliday to Louise Swanborough, 26 March 1860, Wolff collection. Miss Swanborough forwarded the letter some days later.

99. Edmund Yates, *Edmund Yates: His Recollections and Experiences* 2 vols (London: Richard Bentley, 1884) II, p.41.

100. Maxwell, p.162.

101. Maxwell, pp.162-163.

102. Jay, pp.93-94. On one occasion Maxwell did have to fight a writer. Hain Friswell told Isabella Fyvie Mayo that he had gone to Maxwell's office in anger, only to find him with a woman drinking tea. Undeterred Friswell started his argument:

The altercation between publisher and author grew stormy – violent; I was told that it even went *beyond words*. Presently they arrived at some sort of compromise, and quieted down. Then Mr. Maxwell said, "Mr. Friswell, allow me to introduce you to this lady," naming her. The lady rose, and, curtseying, said: "Have I the honour to meet the author of 'The Gentle Life'?"

103. 'Rita' (Mrs. Desmond Humphries), *Recollections of a Literary Life* (London: Andrew Melrose, 1936), p.43.

104. Braddon, 'My First Novel', p.28.

105. 'Death of Miss Braddon', *Beverley Guardian and East Riding Advertiser*, 6 February 1915, p.2.

106. *Beverley Recorder*, 24 May 1884, p.4.

107. 'Miss Braddon and Hull', *Hull Daily News*, 6 February 1915, p.4.

108. *Beverley Recorder*, 24 May 1884, p.4.

109. Braddon, *The Black Band*, p.210.

110. M.E. Braddon, 'My First Novel', p.25.

111. Ibid. p.30.

112. David Oliver, 'The Late Miss Braddon. An Appreciation', *Hull Times*, 13 February 1915, p.3. Braddon told David Oliver (he who had admired her in the Hull pantomime) that she never returned to Hull again, 'not even on a visit'. In 1908 Oliver sent Braddon an album of photographs of the modern Hull, produced by A. Brown and Sons, so she could see the changes, to which she replied:

> Kingston-upon-Hull is now, indeed, a splendid city, and I greatly admire the wide streets and fine buildings, but it is no longer the old town I knew when there was not a single shop upon the Anlaby-road, only the villas of gentility, and when the streets recalled the Hanoverian Kings.

113. John Gilby to Braddon, 29 September 1860, Wolff collection.

114. John Gilby to Braddon, 9 October 1860, Wolff collection.

115. *Brighton Herald*, 6 October 1860, p.4.

116. John Gilby to Braddon, 13 October 1860, Wolff collection.

117. Ibid.

118. John Gilby to Braddon, 16 October 1860, Wolff collection.

119. John Gilby to Braddon, 21 October 1860, Wolff collection.

120. M.E. Braddon, 'My First Novel', p.29.

121. John Gilby to Braddon, 21 October 1860, Wolff collection.

122. Ibid.

123. Mr. Strangeways to John Gilby, 19 October 1860, Wolff collection.

124. John Gilby to Braddon, 28 October 1860, Wolff collection.
125. John Gilby to Braddon, 5 November 1860, Wolff collection.
126. John Gilby to Braddon, 10 November 1860, Wolff collection.
127. William Sawyer to Braddon, 19 October 1860, Wolff collection.
128. William Sawyer to Braddon, 29 October 1860, Wolff collection.
129. John Gilby to Braddon, 21 October 1860, Wolff collection.
130. John Gilby to Braddon, 20 November 1860, Wolff collection.
131. William Sawyer to Braddon, 29 November 1860, Wolff collection.
132. John Gilby to Braddon, 17 November 1860, Wolff collection.
133. William Sawyer to Braddon, 3 December 1860, Wolff collection.
134. Jay, p.95.
135. *Brighton Herald*, 22 December 1860, p.4.
136. William Sawyer to Braddon, 29 October 1860, Wolff collection.
137. Undated letter from M.E. Braddon to George Augustus Sala. Photocopy of a letter owned by Yale University, in Wolff collection.
138. M.E. Braddon, *Garibaldi and Other Poems* (London: Bosworth and Harrison, 1861).
139. John Gilby to Braddon, 20 February 1861, Wolff Collection.
140. 'Suicide of Mr. John Gilby', *Beverley Recorder*, 17 May 1884, p.5.
141. As creditors the administration of Gilby's estate, amounting to £1302, was granted to Edward Tomlinson of the Borough of Kingston Cotton Mill Company Ltd. Registry of Wills.
142. 'Suicide of Mr. John Gilby', *Beverley Recorder*, 17 May 1884, p.5.
143. 'Melancholy Death of Mr. John Gilby of Beverley', *Beverley Guardian*, 17 May 1884, p.8.
144. Ibid.
145. William Sawyer to Braddon, 3 December 1860, Wolff collection.
146. 'Death of Mr. William Sawyer', *Brighton Herald*, 4 November 1882, p.3.
147. John Maxwell to Braddon, 20 February 1861, Wolff collection.
148. John Maxwell to Braddon, 21 February 1861, Wolff collection.
149. Ibid.
150. Ibid.
151. John Maxwell to Braddon, 22 February 1861, Wolff collection.
152. Isabella Fyvie Mayo, *Recollections of what I saw, what I lived through, and what I learned, During more than fifty years of social and literary experience* (London: John Murray, 1910), p.217.
153. Ibid. p.221.
154. The children of Maxwell and his first wife were Nicholas Joseph, Robert, Elizabeth (known as Bessie), Mary (known as Polly), John (known as Jack) and Katie. Katie was not mentioned in Wolff's account, but a letter from her among Fanny Braddon's papers sounds as if she was the sister of Bessie and Polly. Written on Christmas Day

1866, she says she has had 'a long conversation with Papa, in which he told me what I was only too delighted to hear, your close relationship to us.' It concludes, after effusive messages of love, 'Bessie & Polly both send their most affectionate love to you as well as to dear Papa & Mama.' If the letter, which is addressed to 'Darling Aunty', was to Fanny, it may mean the girls had not been previously told she was Braddon's mother. After the move to Lichfield House, the girls joined the household. As Katie is not mentioned in later letters she was probably the second of the two children to die from Maxwell's first marriage. Polly called one of her three children Katie, presumably in memory of this sister. Robert and John later worked with their father, and ran the publishing business together. All of the children remained close to their step-mother.

Chapter Three
Mary Braddon and the Rise of Sensation Fiction

In the 1860s there was a fascination with sensation in all spheres: art, literature, theatre, actual murders and high profile court trials. The beginning of what soon came to be known as sensation fiction can perhaps be marked with the publication of Wilkie Collins's *The Woman In White* in 1860, but from the late 1850s onwards was a period when many things were being dubbed as 'sensation'. Braddon's former colleagues at the Theatre Royal, Brighton, in 1861, even put on a play with the strange title, *Esmerelda; or, the Sensation Goat.*[1] R.F.Stewart writes in *...And Always a Detective* that the term was applied to anything new or extraordinary, be they circus acts, plays or horrible murders, and that the term probably originated, or was perceived to originate, in America, quoting a poem from *Punch* on this foreign invasion.[2] He also quotes Kathleen Tillotson on the earliest known example of the term 'sensation novel' in the *Sixpenny Magazine* in September 1861; a magazine owned by John Maxwell (although the imprint was that of Ward and Lock) and which serialised *Lady Audley's Secret* between January and December the following year. The *Edinburgh Review* noted:

> Two or three years ago nobody would have known what was meant by a Sensation Novel; yet now the term has already passed through the stage of jocular use (...) adopted as the regular commercial name for a particular product of industry for which there is just now a brisk demand.[3]

It was seen as a distinctly modern phenomenon, a product of the 1860s, with authors eager to jump on the bandwagon to provide and encourage an unhealthy brand of literature. Calling the genre an 'industry', a 'brand', or 'factory-produced', tended to denigrate sensation fiction and set it apart from respectable literature. After her move to London in the autumn of 1860 Braddon was soon to become a part of this new brand of publishing, and along with Wilkie Collins was to become the most important contributor to sensation fiction. This chapter aims to discuss the background of sensation novels and Braddon's leading position within the genre.

1861 and 1862 were busy years for Braddon, and her output was vast. Once free of her patron's influence she was able to concentrate on the sort of writing she really enjoyed, and this sensational fiction – whether for a working class or middle class audience – was marked by exciting plots, colourful characters, and a spontaneity resulting from the speed and ease with which she was to write them. Despite this, at the back of her mind, there was a feeling that she ought to be writing an intellectually worthy novel, but for the moment she had decided this would have to wait, writing to Bulwer Lytton about *John Marchmont's Legacy* and *Eleanor's Victory* in 1863:

> if I live to complete these two I shall have earned enough money to keep me & my mother for the rest of our lives, & I will *then* try & write for Fame, & do something more worthy to be laid upon your altar.[4]

Although one suspects she often told Bulwer Lytton what she thought he would wish to hear, the conflict in her work between popular entertainment and 'Art' remained for decades to come.

John Maxwell may have been useful to Braddon at first as a means of getting her work published in his magazines, but Braddon's writing in the early 1860s was so exactly in tune with the public mood that *Lady Audley's Secret* would have been a 'hit' whoever had serialised it. Maxwell did not have his own publishing house at this time, and most of his ventures were in some way connected with Ward, Lock & Tyler. With her prolific rate of writing Braddon was soon indispensable to Maxwell, and to his newest magazines. She must have saved him money too, as her writing anonymous serials for the very cheapest end of the market, penny and halfpenny weeklies, would hardly have brought her any pecuniary advantage.[5] There can be no doubt she must have been working extremely hard in these early years. At the same time as writing *Lady Audley's Secret*, Braddon also wrote all or part of *The Black Band*, *The Octoroon*, *The Captain of the Vulture*, *The White Phantom* and *The Lady Lisle*.

How *Lady Audley's Secret* came to be written soon became a part of a literary legend which later obituaries liked to suggest had made her famous over night. The publication of her most famous novel was more tortuous than that, and almost did not happen at all. Maxwell had started a new magazine called *Robin Goodfellow*, edited by Dr. Charles Mackay (the father of Marie Corelli) and Lascelles Wraxall, but for some reason, just before the first issue came out, their lead serial had failed to be delivered and Maxwell considered delaying publication. Joseph Hatton later reconstructed what happened next:

> The day before a decision was necessary Miss Braddon heard of the difficulty and offered to write the story.
>
> "But even if you were strong enough to fill the position," was the publisher's reply, "there is no time."

"How long could you give me?" asked the aspiring authoress.

"Until to-morrow morning."

"At what time to-morrow morning?"

"If the first instalment were on my breakfast table tomorrow morning," he replied, indicating by his tone and manner the utter impossibility of the thing, "it would be in time." The next morning the publisher found upon his breakfast table the opening chapters of "Lady Audley's Secret."[6]

Robin Goodfellow folded after only a few issues, and it looked as if the novel would remain unfinished. But some had already read and been so intrigued by the mystery posed that they begged Braddon to finish it. One such reader was the actor J.B. Buckstone, who wrote to Braddon urging her to continue with the story. Buckstone remained such a fan that he and his wife later nicknamed their daughter 'Audley' on account of her round face and blonde hair.[7] The serialisation of the novel started anew, and this time was completed, in another of Maxwell's new magazines, the *Sixpenny Magazine*. In later years Braddon described the hectic writing of *Lady Audley's Secret*:

It was written from hand to mouth, as a serial, wherever I happened to be when the time of publication drew near: in Essex, in Brighton, in Rouen, in Paris, at Windsor, and in London – the closing chapters were finished in the small hours when the first and second volume were in the press, and the publisher was getting clamorous for copy for the third – written anywhere and everywhere, in fact.[8]

It was her visit to Essex which partly inspired the setting for Audley Court and its lime tree walk. People often asked Braddon whether it was based on a real house, many believing it to be Ingatestone Hall in Essex, and she later wrote to the writer Percy Fitzgerald:

Well there never *was*, save in the novelist's imagination. The murderous element in the landscape had to be supplied from the "scene-dock" of fiction. But there was a long, narrow avenue of tall limes, very quiet, very secluded, and aloof from the garden of a dear old oak-panelled grange in Essex, and it seemed to me one summer evening, walking with the master of the house, that this lime-walk suggested something uncanny in the history of domestic crime. So I said to my host, "If I were to take this house of yours as the scene of a novel, would you mind very much if I made the inhabitants a rather bad set of people?" "Mind! People it with fiends if you like, my dear!" said he. Now, that is a verbatim report of a brief question and answer spoken thirty years ago. The story was begun soon afterwards, and I think when it had become widely known as a story, my kind old friend took a fanciful pleasure in identifying his handsome head and patriarchal white beard with the Sir Michael Audley of my first three-volume novel. Many years afterwards, when the house had passed into other hands, my valued friend Mr. Edward Duncan, the well-known water-colour painter sat for some hours on a rainy evening under the arched gate, in order to gratify me with a sketch of Audley Court.[9]

The sketch by Duncan shows Ingatestone by moonlight. A postmark for 14 June 1861 on an unpublished manuscript, 'Tommy and Harry', was sent to George Augustus Sala and puts her at Ingatestone at the right time.[10] The Hall was then divided into homes for several Catholic families, and Braddon's host may have been a friend of Maxwell's.[11] Braddon probably went to Brighton to visit her friends from her years at the Theatre Royal, perhaps this time taking with her John Maxwell, as William Sawyer was about to become Maxwell's employee as editor and chief serial writer of another of Maxwell's ventures into the cheapest of magazines market, *Twice a Week.*[12] Her trips to Paris and Rouen were almost certainly with John Maxwell. At this time George Augustus Sala was panicking over debts and bills at *Temple Bar*, and he wrote to Edmund Yates complaining that he felt left in the lurch by his employer, the now absent Maxwell:

> That duffer M. has been in Paris (...) Maxwell's silence makes me apprehend some sinister designs.[13]

In June 1861, in association with Ward and Lock, Maxwell started a new magazine for the lower classes, the *Halfpenny Journal*, and Braddon became its leading serial writer and her mother became the magazine's editor, writing most of the replies to its readers' problems and queries, and choosing poetry to print from unsolicited manuscripts. She did the same thing for the *Welcome Guest* when it changed its format and price to that of the *Halfpenny Journal*. Fanny Braddon's work for Maxwell, which probably did not include editing the main serials, seems to have remained unknown at the time, but forty five years later the writer George Sims recalled submitting a poem as a boy, and receiving encouraging words from the editor in the 'Answers to Correspondents' section, 'Persevere, and you will probably succeed.' Sims told Braddon of this many years later when they were friends:

And then Miss Braddon gave me a piece of information which, under the circumstances, was quite dramatic. Her mother was editing the halfpenny journal at the time. It was Miss Braddon's mother who generously gave me the first lift on the road to authorship.[14]

Fanny Braddon had proved to be remarkably supportive, and she lived with her daughter and Maxwell at their new home 26 Mecklenburg Square. Presumably her own experience of marriage, and that of her mother, may have made her feel that the legal bond was a bind not necessarily linked with happiness. Their first child, Gerald, was born on 19 March 1862, and within the first couple of months Fanny had to sack the cook for fiddling the grocery expenses and threatening to injure the monthly nurse.[15] Six people lived in the house at this time, Braddon, her mother, Maxwell, and three servants. The children of Maxwell's first family were all at boarding school at this time, presumably even Jack who was only six, the girls at a convent school and the boys at a school at Totteridge.

At this time *Aurora Floyd* was appearing in *Temple Bar*, meaning both of her famous bigamy novels were reaching the public at the same time. Each was independently successful, and the *Court Journal* observed:

The story of "Aurora Floyd" – we do not know who the author is – is carried on with remarkable ability, and is undoubtedly one of the best works of fiction now making their appearance.[16]

With the resurrection of *Lady Audley's Secret* in the *Sixpenny Magazine* it was at last reaching a wide audience, attracting comment for its interesting plot and novelty. The *Court Journal* remarked:

The Sixpenny Magazine contains a very exciting tale, called "Lady Audley's Secret," and we may remark that the attention is concentrated upon the doubt as to whether the heroine has or has not been the perpetrator of a most revolting murder.[17]

William Tinsley later wrote that Maxwell, perhaps not perceiving the enormous potential of the novel, almost published *Lady Audley's Secret* only as a cheap edition, probably in the Ward and Lock shilling library. Tinsley, however, urged his brother to go and buy the book from Maxwell.[18] By the time it appeared in three volumes in September 1862, William and Edward Tinsley had a publishing phenomenon on their hands. The day after publication Tinsley employee Lionel Brough (later a famous actor) called on Braddon to tell her of the incredible sales within twenty four hours. A month later the *Court Journal* observed that Braddon 'seems likely to equal, if not succeed, that of Mr. Wilkie Collins in popular estimation.'[19] Renewing her acquaintance with her literary hero Edward Bulwer Lytton, who would probably have concurred with Robert Audley's decision to commit Lucy Audley to an asylum as he had done the same with his own wife to keep her quiet during his 1858 election campaign, Braddon was granted permission to dedicate the three volume edition to him, 'in grateful acknowledgement of literary advice most generously given to the author'. *Lady Audley's Secret* went through eight editions in three volumes in three months.

John Maxwell and the New Publishers of Sensation Fiction

Braddon's emergence as the 'queen of the circulating libraries' coincided with the success of the new publishers who took the initial risk and published her and other sensation novels.[20] Even Mrs. Henry Wood's *East Lynne* had trouble getting accepted, turned down at first by Chapman and Hall's reader George Meredith. Bentley took it on to spectacular success and their other authors were to include Wilkie Collins, Ouida, Charles Reade and Sheridan Le Fanu's niece Rhoda Broughton. Sensation fiction became associated with a new aggressive style of publishing, which eagerly sought publicity and courted notoriety. Publishers were seen as wilfully catering to public tastes, and ignoring questions of morality in their pursuit of sales. The 'trumpery' of authors of sensation fiction, particularly Braddon, was disliked. The new publishers especially associated with sensation fiction were the Tinsley brothers, whose careers were launched with the success of *Lady Audley's Secret*, which they followed up with a string of sensation novels such as Mrs. Riddell's best seller *George Geith of Fen Court* (1864) (typically containing the heady mix of bigamy and illegitimacy), and eventually *The Moonstone* (1868). The Tinsley brothers (one of whom named his home Audley Lodge when the profits rolled in) and John Maxwell were seen as brash new hustlers, not of the gentlemanly school of publishing; for this new breed, it was perceived, profits and publicity were of prime importance, and to openly seek either was considered somewhat vulgar. The *Athenaeum* berated such a trend in a business which, they claimed, had previously been above this sort of thing:

> This sort of puffery is never used by the great houses (...) we would prefer that the younger members of the publishing trade should

exhibit that perfect decorum before the public which is the habit, as well as the interest, of their more eminent brethren in the craft.[21]

The reviewers for the *Athenaeum* must have been particularly irked when their journal carried an advertisement for Braddon novels which occupied an entire page, and Braddon was the only author to be promoted in this way in 1866.[22] Their criticism was particularly aimed at John Maxwell, who was a master of false reports of sales figures, and who frequently annoyed reviewers when he claimed a third edition on the first day of publication, but without revealing how small the print run of the first had been.[23] Such tactics were to further increase the appearance of success and thus created publishing, as well as fictional, sensation.

Braddon also caused some resentment and hostility because of the vast amounts of money she was making. She accidentally exacerbated matters when the press began to report that like Sir Walter Scott she planned to make £100,000, and she wrote to Sala to ask him to try and counteract the story in one of his columns:

> To speak of myself in the same breath with Walter Scott, the man I worship as second only to Shakespeare! Odious idea! (...) Now one little remark of mine may possibly – owing to the crass stupidity of the people who hear one talk & misunderstand, & don't remember – have been the occasion of this idiotic paragraph. I have often said that I consider one of the most remarkable things in the history of literature the extraordinary spurt of industry by wh Scott – after his financial failure – earned £100,000 for his creditors (...) & my friend has gone away & said Miss Braddon has set her heart upon earning £100,000.[24]

The interest in her comment may have stemmed from Maxwell's own near bankruptcy, and the resulting gossip probably was that she planned to pay his creditors as Walter Scott had, by writing at a prolific rate. It may also explain why reviewers of the 1860s seemed irritated by her vast output. Nor was Maxwell's *Sixpenny Magazine* shy of making the comparison between Braddon and Scott, an anonymous reviewer declaring in a review of *Henry Dunbar*:

> even the popularity of the Author of "Waverley" did not equal that of Miss Braddon, if we measure popularity by numbers.[25]

Braddon's fame soon travelled overseas, most of her 1860s novels were translated into French, and they also appeared in pirated editions in America. Her fame also spread to the colonies, and Braddon's sister-in-law, Georgie, wrote proudly to Fanny Braddon from Lucknow in India in 1863:

> We have been reading "Eleanor's Victory" in "Once a Week" – and thoroughly enjoying it. Mary's style of writing is delightful, and really astonishes one. I feel mightily proud when any one asks if "Miss Braddon the authoress" is any relation to us? – We really do not know which to admire most – her talent or her perseverance.[26]

When Maxwell started his own publishing house in 1864 he usually catered for the lower end of the market, with Braddon his premier author of three deckers. It is quite possible his business could not have survived without Braddon. His main sales were of cheap reprints, in yellowback or paperback form. The books he published were frequently badly reviewed, and included translations of the French novels which were partly blamed for the rise in the craving for immoral literature. Apart from Braddon his writers were almost always poorly paid and considered themselves exploited. Wolff writes that the contributors other than Braddon to *Belgravia* were paid a pittance.[27] The novelist 'Rita' (Mrs. Desmond Humphries), a very popular author, felt deceived as a young woman when Maxwell bought six of her novels (insisting that he must own all future copyright) for just £50. She had been reluctant to agree:

> But he would not allow me to depart. He talked and talked till my brain reeled in confusion. (...) Arguments and persuasions were poured out on me.[28]

It should be remembered that at this time Braddon was paid £1000 by the Tinsley brothers for *Aurora Floyd*, with the copyright reverting back to her after two years. This was a tremendous sum for only her second three decker. In 1864, under the same terms, they paid her £4000 for *Eleanor's Victory* and *John Marchmont's Legacy*. It was only after the brothers balked over an increase in demands that Maxwell started to publish Braddon's three deckers himself, starting with *Henry Dunbar*.[29] It has to be said that Braddon was Maxwell's first, and almost only, writer of distinction. Writing ruefully sixty years later, 'Rita' noted that these very same six books purchased by Maxwell were still in print, and had rapidly been sold on by the publisher without any benefit to herself.[30] Her account of his wheedling and bullying to pressure the young and inexperienced woman to agree to such a contract sounds alarmingly like a villain from a novel by Braddon!

In the early days as owner of the *Welcome Guest*, where Braddon first came into contact with Maxwell, his usual practice was not to read the manuscripts of his writers but to pay for them by the weight, making Buchanan, for one, feel like a 'pauper'. It is unlikely he changed this practice, and nor was this confined to anonymous hacks, as the famous George Augustus Sala complained in a letter to Edmund Yates in 1862 when he was the nominal editor of *Temple Bar*:

> What I wish to tell you about is that hypocritical bandit Maxwell. When he smashed he agreed to pay me a *minimum* of ten pounds a week, cash down, on delivery (...) on my taking him the first chap of Dr. Forster (which I had *scaled*, and which *came* to over the stipulated amount) he began in a most insolent manner to count the number of lines in my M.S. and to express doubts as whether there were ten pounds worth there or not. This of course I could not stand. I flung the cheque in his face, told him he was an impudent fellow, and walked out of the room.[31]

Sala was a great ally of Braddon's in the defence of sensation fiction and a personal friend for thirty five years, but he disliked Maxwell intensely at this time, privately referring to him as 'Don Duffero' and 'flinty Maxwell' and referring to a French liar as a 'Franco-American Maxwell'.[32] It sounds as if the office was often full of tension, especially between Conductor and owner. The situation at *Temple Bar* was obviously bad as Maxwell's financial position worsened, and as the crisis approached Sala was writing a poem to Yates, 'Lines to my publisher', in which he fantasised about Maxwell's death, adding, 'How earnestly I hope that the circulation will go down this month & that Maxwell's creditors won't wait much longer!'[33] In the event Maxwell survived a little longer, but on 15 October 1862 his payments were suspended and he was forced to mortgage all of his magazines to a Mr. Norris.[34] One suspects that the atmosphere in the *Temple Bar* office became even more strained at this time, and Braddon on one occasion took Sala's part, or at least acted as informant against Maxwell to Sala:

> If the scoundrel had not grossly insulted me by giving me the lie when I have Miss Braddon's word that he opened, sequestered & *tore up* a letter addressed to me by a lady, & had done the same thing before, thus laying himself open to a criminal prosecution the shindy would not have assumed such dimensions. As it is it was only by a mercy that Maxwell & self did not finish our little difficulties à la Major Murray.[35]

Many seemed to share Sala's opinion in the publishing world, where Maxwell was renowned for his volatile temper, lack of tact, and dubious business practice. It must have been a difficult time for Braddon, with Maxwell's financial difficulties, her own hard work during this period, and the fact that she was at the time of Maxwell's financial crisis expecting their first child, Gerald, born in March 1862. It was fortunate for their finances that Maxwell and Braddon could not marry, as her earnings would have been sequestered to pay his debts, and when it came to business they did not pretend to be married.[36] With such problems, it may be that some of the hostility directed at Braddon in print partly stemmed from a dislike of Maxwell, against whom many had a grudge, rather than just at Braddon as a purveyor of immoral fiction.

Despite Maxwell's financial problems, he and Braddon must have been heartened by the rapid success of *Lady Audley's Secret* once it was published in volume form. It was followed in quick succession by *Aurora Floyd*, and her use of bigamy in both novels was seized upon as a key part of the formula of the new sensation genre.

What was Sensation Fiction?

Braddon denied that sensation fiction was a new genre when writing a chapter of *The Doctor's Wife* entitled 'A Sensation Author' about a hack author called Sigismund Smith. She argued that the genre had always existed even when the term had not:

> Mr. Sigismund Smith was a sensation author. That bitter term of reproach, "sensation" had not been invented for the terror of romancers in the fifty-second year of this present century; but the thing existed nevertheless in divers forms, and people wrote sensation novels as unconsciously as Monsieur Jourdain talked prose.[37]

This was a subject she was to go back to when the attacks by Mrs. Oliphant in *Blackwood's* began a few years later, when she and George Augustus Sala retaliated with their own essays.

The term 'sensation fiction' came to be applied to many more novels, of a greater variety of styles, than usually accepted by those modern critics who have mostly been interested in the challenging representations of women by Collins and Braddon in their early novels. Consequently there is much generalisation as to what sensation is and the elements it contains. The representation of rebellious women has been hailed especially as a sign of unrest and assertion by women writers and their female readers, and Lyn Pykett has noted Braddon's interest in the secrets of women in her early novels.[38] This may be true, but it would be wrong to suggest that male writers did not also use the vehicle for protest at social strictures, or that many men did not also enjoy reading them, and some of them were just as interested in creating powerful women; Charles Reade, a friend to both Braddon and Collins, is a neglected writer in this area, and Edmund Yates wrote at least one novel close to the sensation pattern.[39] Nor is every Braddon heroine a close sister to Lady Audley or Aurora Floyd. The modern categorisation of sensation fiction as a female phenomenon is not, though, wholly unjustifiable, as this was very much how it was perceived at the time too. Monica Correa Fryckstedt quotes an interesting review of Florence Marryat's *Woman Against Woman* (1866), which indicates a genuine perception that this was a time of increasing change for women:

> It is curious that the most questionable novels of the day should be written by women. To judge from their books, the ideas of women on points of morals and ethics seem in a state of transition, and consequently, in confusion. With the heroes and heroines of women's stories "circumstances alter cases", until it would seem impossible to obtain an absolute rule of life or conduct.[40]

Henry Mansel was the dean of St. Paul's, and in his anonymous article 'Sensation Fiction' in the *Quarterly Review* in 1863 he also includes novels of a much wider range: those based on actual people like Shelley, in *The Last Days of a Bachelor* (1862) by James M'Grigor Allan, fictional accounts of the latest murder cases and those of a more radical nature, 'writing with a purpose' to change laws or social conditions, for the production of which Dickens was a 'grievous offender'.[41] With Shelley's reputation as one who had dared defy society to behave as he pleased, it was not surprising that he should have been attractive as a subject for a sensation novel. Braddon was a great admirer of Shelley, and may have seen some parallels between herself and Mary Shelley. Throughout her fiction, from *Only a Clod* (1865) to *A Lost Eden* (1904), and even her posthumous novel *Mary* (1916), she refers to the Shelleys. Seducers present volumes of poetry to innocent girls, and with the story of Shelley's life attempt to sway their conventional views on sex sanctified only by marriage. The number of novels this occurs in is quite remarkable.

The 'writing with a purpose' style sensation fiction is usually attributed to Wilkie Collins's later fiction, starting with his discussion of the Scottish marriage laws in *Man and Wife* (1870). Braddon used the Scotch marriage laws as late as *The White House* (1906), but unlike

Collins's heroine, Braddon's is no victim, using it to entrap the man she loves. Despite Collins's late conversion to novels with a purpose, it is clear that even in the 1860s it was seen as a characteristic component of sensation fiction. Certainly many of the sensation novelists were interested in using the novel as a vehicle for change. Charles Reade strove to raise public awareness of abuses in regard to private insane asylums in *Hard Cash* (1863), and Wilkie Collins tackled the injustice of inheritance for illegitimate children in *No Name* (1862). Braddon's were less overt in this respect, the plot is never the slave of a cause, but there are patterns of social injustices throughout her novels concerning the interests of illegitimate children, fallen women, the mentally ill, the potential for injustice in criminal cases, and she frequently wrote against the death penalty in her novels. Unlike the others she was probably constricted by her own anomalous social position; to write too overtly with a purpose would make her even more vulnerable to the hints and persecution which were already part of the press coverage of her career. Braddon and Maxwell had all of their six children before they could marry, and she would not have wished to draw further attention to her home life.

The majority of the so-called 'sensation' novels listed by Mansel are from 1862, but *Philip Paternoster* is as early as 1858, and it is surprising that he made no mention of Wilkie Collins's *Basil* (1852); though if he had done so it might have been harder to prove that this growing poison was completely new.

Whatever the social agenda of a sensation novel, its most important role was to thrill, to stimulate the sensations. To be excited, frightened and puzzled was exactly why the reader borrowed the book in three volume form from libraries, and if sufficiently satisfied buy it the following year in a one volume reprint. For those speaking against it, the element of physical and psychological excitement was another example of immoral cravings which were satisfied by sensation authors. In an 1864 sermon against sensation fiction, the Archbishop of York claimed that:

> sensational stories were tales which aimed at this effect simply – of exciting in the mind some deep feeling of overwrought interest by the means of some terrible passion or crime. They want to persuade people that in almost every one of the well-ordered houses of their neighbours there (is) a skeleton shut up in some cupboard.[42]

The belief was that it led people to expect, or more dangerously hope, for the unconventional and to be titillated by unnatural events and irregular behaviour. These were novels that challenged the accepted order and questioned conventional morality, rather than accepting pre-ordained certainties. One of the areas sensation fiction engaged with was the secret desires of characters; one such character, Olivia Marchmont in *John Marchmont's Legacy* (1863), secretly hates the feminine allotted role of charity work and would have excelled in a manly job like a doctor if it was allowed – to the establishment this was rather shocking, and certainly unwomanly.

From the earliest critiques of the 1860s the pioneer sensation novels were held up to be *The Woman in White* and *Lady Audley's Secret*, with Braddon following Collins's example. As a friend and colleague of Dickens, Collins had already attained some level of critical respect, unlike Braddon who had bad reviews for well over a decade from some of the leading journals. Braddon greatly admired Collins and always considered herself indebted in her early works to him, telling fellow novelist Joseph Hatton in the 1887 interview 'Miss Braddon at Home':

> I always say that I owe 'Lady Audley's Secret' to the 'Woman in White'. Wilkie Collins is assuredly my literary father. My admiration for 'The Woman in White' inspired me with the idea of 'Lady Audley's Secret' as a novel of construction and character. Previously my efforts had been in the didactic direction of Bulwer, long conversations, a great deal of sentiment.[43]

Certainly *Lady Audley's Secret* follows Collins in its trick of substituting two similar women and in its use of a young man to unravel the secret, but in many ways it is an inversion, as in Lady Audley Braddon has a wicked heroine who looks like the meek and good Laura Fairlie. Indeed with Lady Audley it almost seemed as if she was taking up Collins's challenge over the characterisation of heroines in 'A Petition to the Novel-Writers' in 1856:

> I know that five feet eight of female flesh and blood, when accompanied by an olive complexion, black eyes, and raven hair, is synonymous with strong passions and an unfortunate destiny. I know that five feet nothing, golden ringlets, soft blue eyes, and a lily brow, cannot possibly be associated by any well-constituted novelist with anything but ringing laughter, arch innocence, and final matrimonial happiness. (...) Although I know it to be against all precedent, I want to revolutionize our favourite two sisters. (...) Would readers be fatally startled out of their sense of propriety if the short charmer with the golden hair appeared before them as a serious, strong-minded, fierce-spoken, miserable, guilty woman? It

might be a dangerous experiment to make this change; but it would be worth trying.[44]

Braddon's other early novel *The Lady Lisle* (1862), and her penny and halfpenny part fiction, were also concerned with the themes of false identity and with the respectable masking the disreputable. In *Birds of Prey* (1867) and *Thou Art the Man* (1894) she used, but only in part, Collins's technique of a character's journal relating part of the narrative. Collins was often taken to task for his complicated structures, but Braddon was never 'complex' to the same degree. Both authors had a keen interest in the theatre, as had Charles Reade, and both revolved plots around secrets. In an uncharacteristically complimentary review of *Eleanor's Victory* (1863) in the *Saturday Review* (quite probably by or arranged by her uncle John's friend Douglas Cook) she and Collins were compared, Braddon winning favour because her emphasis was on entertainment:

> Miss Braddon has peculiarities which make her writing her own, and it would be unfair to say that she imitates anybody. Still, her compositions are so much in that style which Mr. Wilkie Collins has associated with his name that it is impossible not to compare the two writers. Perhaps Mr. Collins still remains the superior in the art of attaching interest to an unimportant secret, but then Miss Braddon eclipses him in the ease with which she works. In her tales there are none of those solemn announcements at each stage by which Mr. Collins compels his readers to understand that the secret which he has invented is unfathomable, and that everything is leading up to it, although no one can see how.[45]

It was seen that the turning point on which a sensation novel always revolves was a secret, but there are usually numerous secrets other than the main plot twist. It is surprising, for example, how often the secret of Lady Audley was misinterpreted; Mansel wrote that the novel was interesting despite the 'transparent nature of the "secret".'[46] Critics usually thought that the secret was the bigamy or the survival of George Talboys. There are in fact various secrets within the text of a Braddon novel, usually unexpressed desires of characters who know they must keep them hidden from respectable society, or a secret in their past which if known would in some way compromise them. The novels were defined as having one secret each, when in fact they are often multiple. The secret revealed which ends a novel, such as the identity of a murderer, is usually relatively easy to guess. If there is one constant factor that does unite the diverse strands of sensation, especially those of Braddon's, it is the concealment of secrets. This is a feature of all her novels, even those which are far less sensational, such as her late historical novels.

Not only were sensational novels perceived to be challenging the position of women, but also the whole order of society. In the early novels the secrets are at the heart of the establishment, in the mansions of the aristocracy or in a normal middle class home. The crimes are within the domestic sphere, and they are firmly set in contemporary times with the railway chase in *Henry Dunbar* (1864), the train crash in *John Marchmont's Legacy* (1863), the use of electric telegrams in *Lady Audley's Secret*, and the ordinary homes of the middle class in the later novels *The Story of Barbara* (1880) and *A Lost Eden* (1904). *Lady Audley's Secret* in particular could not be more up to date, the action is literally set only a couple of months before serialisation. The immediacy is even greater in serialisation as the monthly parts often refer to events of the very month in which they were written. For example, there is a lament on Thackeray's death in the *Temple Bar* instalments of *The Doctor's Wife*, and for the serial reader it reinforced the feeling of the here and now. That 'here and now' is destroyed as a haven of stability; Aurora Floyd, the rich banker's daughter lives in a mansion in rural Kent. That mansion and Audley Court, which had once been a convent, look solidly respectable; the sort of home which should represent the best of society, where nothing evil or mysterious could happen. But the country house and the respectable family behind closed doors are shown to be just the opposite. Things like adultery, secret marriages, or no marriage at all, are all possible, as long as nobody knows. At the beginning of the novel Audley Court is presented as:

> a glorious old place (...) a spot in which Peace seemed to have taken up her abode (...) A noble place; inside as well as out.[47]

However, despite the initial suggestion that this is a secure place, redolent of the past, there is a suggestion that it is too quiet, too perfect and there may be something more:

> It was almost oppressive, this twilight stillness. The very repose of the place grew painful from its intensity, and you felt as if a corpse must be lying somewhere within that grey and ivy-covered pile of building – so deathlike was the tranquillity of all around. (p.24)

That sensation fiction was seen as a symptom of modern times was gloomily accepted by the *Christian Remembrancer* in 1863:

The "sensation novel" of our time, however extravagant and unnatural, yet is a sign of the times – the evidence of a certain turn of thought and action, of an impatience of old restraints, and a craving for some fundamental change in the working of society.[48]

In other words sensation fiction encouraged those who were dissatisfied with the restrictions which society imposed. They particularly disapproved of Olivia in *John Marchmont's Legacy*, a woman trapped in a life of charity work and good deeds, and secretly hating it. A life of charity work and as a support to her vicar father should have been a life of fulfilment in itself. Her father is of an unchristian disposition, emphasising that she is a financial burden and encouraging her into a disastrous, but financially beneficial, marriage.

Sensation fiction was also condemned for its focus on incident rather than character; for hinging upon bigamy or murder. Mansel wrote in 'Sensation Novels' that:

A sensation novel, as a matter of course, abounds in incident. Indeed, as a general rule, it consists of nothing else. Deep knowledge of human nature, graphic delineations of individual character, vivid representations of the aspects of Nature or the workings of the soul – all the higher features of the creative art – would be a hindrance rather than help to a work of this kind (...) "Action, action, action!" though in a different sense from that intended by the great orator, is the first thing needful, and the second, and the third. The human actors in the piece are, for the most part, but so many lay-figures on which to exhibit a drapery of incident (...) Each game is played with the same pieces, differing only in the moves. We watch them advancing through the intricacies of the plot, as we trace the course of an x or y through the combinations of an algebraic equation, with a similar curiosity to know what becomes of them at the end, and with about as much consciousness of individuality in the ciphers.[49]

This idea of characters being part of a puzzle anticipates the detective novels of the 1920s, where on the whole the rule was to neglect character in favour of the all important puzzle. The sensation novelists, despite their interest in puzzles and crime, were not two dimensional in their characterisation in the way that is true of an Agatha Christie novel. The use of crime and murder was none the less disapproved of, and was seen as too influenced by contemporary events described in newspapers.

The 'Newspaper Novel' of 'Real Life' Crime

Newspapers freely related new cases of crime, divorce, infidelity in divorce cases and general scandal. One wonders, when Braddon began *Aurora Floyd*, whether she recalled a newspaper story which occurred in Yorkshire, reported in the *Brighton Guardian* in October of 1858 with the headline, 'Elopement of a Lady of Fortune With a Groom from York'. It detailed the police pursuit of an heiress, the daughter of a magistrate, seen heading for Nottingham with her lover.[50] Although Braddon was not in the habit of writing romans à clef, she knew that a hint of a real life scandal or crime could add a little frisson for catching prospective readers. In her first novel, *Three Times Dead; Or, The Secret of the Heath* (1860), she used a few elements of a recent case, telling George Sims almost forty years later that she wrote it 'very soon after the Sadleir mystery'.[51] John Sadleir had been an M.P. for Sligo who through forgery had swindled a fortune from a Tipperary bank, eventually committing suicide on Hampstead Heath in 1856, and he also provided the inspiration for Dickens's Merdle in *Little Dorrit* (1857) and Charles Lever's *Davenport Dunn* (1859). The suicide Braddon set on the heath was in fact the murder of a long lost twin by the villain who is then free to invent a new identity. Although she may have used a hint of the Sadleir case in the title, and as a detail in the crime, the rest of the book is purely imaginative.

Crime and criminals had always been popular as entertainment; the *Newgate Calendar* from the 1770s onwards had related the lives and trials of celebrated criminals; but there was not much motivation or suspense as the reader knew the sinner would be caught and punished. The murderers and crimes were usually so crass that there was no element of admiration for the intricacy of a crime, nor were the criminals of interest as personalities. By the late 1850s this had changed as there had been a number of high profile trials, and consequently celebrity criminals and murderers. Compared to an earlier period literacy had increased and newspapers were now cheap and available, and crime became a topic of fascination. Penny bloods were also fascinated by real-life criminals and often set them up as heroes, such as Dick Turpin, Charles Pease (a famous burglar), and one who almost seemed real in Sweeney Todd.

Sensation fiction was almost immediately associated with a love of reading about crime, and critics hoped that the public would eventually renounce this craving. The novelist herself, it was suggested, was almost implicit in crime, as it was unnatural to think up such revolting schemes and be sympathetic to a murderer. W. Fraser Rae wrote of Braddon's novel *Henry Dunbar* (1864):

It would hardly have occurred to any other than a "sensation" novelist to make a story like this the subject of a work in three volumes. Few other novelists could have invented anything so diabolical as the murder, or have depicted with seeming complacency the after-life of the criminal. The impression made is, that the murderer was a clever man, and was very hardly used (...) The most astonishing thing about this is, that Miss Braddon should seriously consider a tale of crime as fitted for the "amusement" of anybody. Her notion of what "the general reader" is may be the correct one. We earnestly trust, however, that he does not possess the morbid tastes of Miss Braddon, and is a less contemptible personage than she considers him to be.[52]

Braddon did not glorify criminals, despite the opinion of the critics, but she did attempt to explain them in a way that sometimes made the crime seem justifiable. In *Henry Dunbar*, the man who murders Henry Dunbar and assumes his identity is as much sinned against as sinning. Certainly Braddon's novels contain some crime, but not the excessive amount many suggested. As early as 1866 with *The Lady's Mile* Braddon wrote a novel which contained no crime at all, centred on three women and the marriage market which forces them to marry without love. She worked hard on this novel and, perhaps mindful of the critical reproofs over factual details, she consulted a barrister friend, F.W. James, about legal details and gave a lively portrait of her husband in the character of the Irish barrister Laurence O'Boyneville. Even though there had been criminals in earlier novels of the 1830s, the Newgate fiction of Bulwer Lytton (*Paul Clifford*, 1830) and Dickens's *Oliver Twist* (1838), it was still perceived as a product of the 1860s, primarily created by Collins and Braddon.

What sensation fiction did was bring crime into the heart of the middle and upper class home, which as Henry James noted was more alarming than the earlier thrills provided by the gothic school of Mrs. Radcliffe or Mathew Lewis's *The Monk*:

To Mr. Collins belongs the credit of having introduced into fiction those most mysterious of mysteries, the mysteries that are at our own doors. This innovation gave a new impetus to the literature of horrors. It was fatal to Mrs. Radcliffe and her everlasting castle in the Appenines. What are the Appenines to us or we to the Appenines? Instead of the terrors of Udolpho, we were treated to the terrors of the cheerful country house, or the busy London lodgings. And there is no doubt that these were infinitely the more terrible.[53]

The villains were no longer the residents of a monastery or an Italian prince in his castle, but the meek little governess or paid companion as provided by Lucy Audley and Annie Edwardes's Honoria Forrester in *Miss Forrester* (1865), who in her day was just as shocking as Lady Audley as she plots and schemes and begins the novel by letting her sick employer die. Seeing the beautiful Miss Forrester as part of the trend begun by Lady Audley, the *Athenaeum* critic commented, 'Golden hair is (sic) become as plentiful in the modern female novel, as if some new gold-field had been discovered and thrown open.'[54] Nor were the heroines weakly and passively waiting to be rescued. At the time the genre was defined there were fears of the great unknown: a fear that unsolved murders could happen within the home, that people might be wrongly committed to insane asylums, and that the police could either fail to protect the middle class or would interfere with the middle class, of the working class rising up, or of European secret societies and anarchy. Braddon's penny blood *The Black Band; or, The Mysteries of Midnight* (1861) depicts a dangerous counter-culture in London, a London of plots, robberies, and men and women who will stop at nothing to satisfy their desires. It is significant that a political organisation, the 'Black Band', and their legion of robbers are hidden in catacombs, directly beneath the outward respectability of London.

The Reverend Paget, one of the many who seemed to take sensation fiction far more seriously than readers ever could have done, accused authors (and his anger was reserved for women authors) of supplying would-be murderers with a virtual text book:

> Through their teaching, murder has been made easy to the meanest capacity: the choicest and most scientific modes of destroying life have been revealed to us. (...) For the benefit of students in the science of Toxicology (...) the most approved recipes for poisoning have been set forth with medical and surgical minuteness.[55]

Paget need not have worried. Murders with poisons were frequently fanciful in fiction, with wholly invented and complicated modes of death. In Braddon's *The Black Band*, Colonel Oscar Bertrand is turned from master criminal to jabbering village idiot by a mysterious potion. Would-be poisoners would have done much better to read the newspapers or to read the ingredients on common medicines (opium was a common ingredient even in something as innocuous as cough mixture). To suggest young women would learn to murder from authors such as Braddon was ridiculous: as Richard Altick says, compared to Madeline Smith, Lady Audley 'was a complete bungler.'[56] Nevertheless, the *Saturday Review* glumly observed that 'Mr. Mudie's lending library will soon become a sort of Newgate Calender', and that the modern mix of 'crime and crinoline' in the behaviour of these heroines 'is enough to take away the breath of any quiet middle-aged gentleman.'[57]

It was perceived that the premier crime of the sensation novel was bigamy. Between 1853 and 1863 there were 884 cases of bigamy brought to court in England and 110 in Scotland.[58] There was a great deal of interest in bigamy after the notorious Yelverton trial which ran from the courts to the House of Lords between 1861 and 1864, and transcripts of the trial sold in vast numbers. In reality it was as much a case about the legality of the Scotch and Irish marriages which Yelverton claimed had taken place, but it made bigamy (seemingly a very common crime anyway if one scans papers of the 1850s, one youth according to the *Brighton Herald* acquiring a number of wives before leaving his teens) an extremely fashionable crime, one which everyone knew about from the newspapers. The subject of the Yelverton trial, Theresa Longworth, got in fairly early with the two volume novel *Martyrs to Circumstance* (published in parts by Richard Bentley in 1861), defiantly naming herself on the front cover as the 'Hon. Mrs. Yelverton'. Two novels were closely based on the Yelverton case, J.R. O'Flanagan's *Gentle Blood; or, The Secret Marriage* (1861), the title 'Gentle Blood' refers to Yelverton's comment that because Maria was not of gentle blood she was fair game to make a mistress, and Cyrus Redding's *A Wife and not a Wife* (1867).

But in fiction Braddon became the leading example of an author using bigamy as a leading plot device. In the first year she lived with Maxwell she used bigamy in *The Black Band, Lady Audley's Secret* and *Aurora Floyd*, showing that it was a subject which interested or preoccupied her mind. To do so publicly, in view of her private life, was bold and audacious, but when she started these three novels she had no idea they would make her so famous and that comparisons might be made. There must have been many in literary London who considered Maxwell at least morally a bigamist. When divorce was virtually impossible for most people, and the stigma enormous in any case, there could be vicarious enjoyment reading about those who did dare to misbehave, which as Jeanne Fahnestock comments gave the reader opportunity for fantasy:

Thus in the midst of their devoted family circles, the Victorian husband and wife of the 1860s fantasized on the delights and penalties of having another spouse.[59]

Fahnestock writes that bigamy novels peaked in 1865, and then, because there were so many, began to dwindle.[60] Braddon herself stopped using bigamy in her fiction, and instead she often used the device of a villain luring the heroine into a mock marriage with a friend posing as registrar. This was a device from the days of six volume Minerva Press novels, but in novels like *Dead Sea Fruit* (1868) and *Only a Clod* (1865) Braddon showed how easily an invalid marriage could be procured. A clever villain knew that this was better than genuine bigamy because it did not break the law. Even though Braddon became the most famous writer of bigamy, she wrote more frequently of women duped by a ceremony they thought genuine, or lured away to be mistresses when they expected marriage, as in *To the Bitter End* (1872) and *Mary* (1916), only later to discover their true position and that of any children when the man had tired of them.

There are also examples of details of real life murders being incorporated into sensation fiction. The most famous example is probably that of the Constance Kent case, where a sixteen year old was suspected of murdering her little half brother. Wilkie Collins's readers would have recognised in *The Moonstone* (1868) the details he took from it, especially the crucial evidence of a missing stained night-gown and the conflict between London and local police and that between police and family. Constance Kent revived the spectre of the dangerous female within the home. At first to the public she was the innocent, fragile heroine persecuted by the working class police, but when she rather unconvincingly confessed some years later, she was a creature reviled, and again a warning of the danger of unnatural femininity:

> And yet all the time this miserable girl carried the horrible secret in her possession. Serene, calm, and self-possessed, she stood amid the wreck of the happiness of all belonging to her (...) All this, which one would have thought might have stirred the hearts of the coarsest and vilest profligate, she, the simple maiden of 16 years (...) It is no pleasant reflection that all our maidens, our sisters, and daughters may be Constance Kents, and that a callousness to every moral sense must, in maidenhood, precede the bloom of life and very flower and crowning grace of love and wifedom.[61]

Thus Constance Kent epitomised two sides to femininity, gaining sympathy first as a victim of police machinations, and then revealed as a supposedly homicidal maniac in the guise of a young girl. The changing pattern revolved around a perception of increased instability: working class people were a criminal threat, and women were perceived as being not as controllable, nor as conventionally feminine, as once they had been.

More notorious yet was the Madeline Smith murder trial in Scotland in 1857. Smith was accused of murdering her lover, poisoning him with arsenic, so that he could not tell her parents of their relationship and stop her marriage to a more eligible man. The enormous press coverage and comment which ensued gave rise to the question as to whether *all* daughters were capable of leading such duplicitous lives, and therefore no longer under the absolute control of their families before marriage. Smith may well have inspired Braddon's early villainesses; with her particular brand of manipulation and cool head Smith seemed almost like a character of fiction and had many admirers (including Henry James who jokingly called her 'a rare work of art'[62]). In Braddon's *The White Phantom* (1862-1863), one of the heroines is similarly troubled over the recovery of compromising letters.

How much the cases of Smith and Kent were linked in the public psyche is evidenced by another novel condemned by Mansel, *Such Things Are*, with Madeline Smith and Constance Kent as bosom friends 'vulture-like'.[63] One he does not mention, and probably the most interesting of all, was *Madeline Graham* (1864) by Emma Robinson, a great friend of Braddon's. It was published by Maxwell, being just the type of book that brought the new publishers ill repute, and Robinson (in earlier days a well thought of historical novelist) received savage reviews. It makes no secret of being based on Madeline Smith and has no doubt about her guilt, although her bad ways are shown as having begun by the surreptitious reading of French novels at boarding school and through the influence of a French teacher (whose behaviour doubtless stemmed from a former career as an actress). Unlike the real Smith, Madeline Graham does not have to go to court, not having succeeded in killing her secret fiancé. Knowing all, he and her family force her to marry him, and the book ends with the hint she will be continually punished by him in marriage. Interestingly, most people had wanted Smith to get off, she was big news across the country, and the Beverley local newspaper which printed Braddon's early poems covered all the latest evidence and discussion.[64] Smith was an exact contemporary, both she and Braddon were born in 1835, and both strayed from the expected destiny of upper middle class marriage. That Smith's lover was French must have had something to do with the sympathy for her; many thought she had been taken advantage of by a foreign cad (despite damning letters which showed she was more likely the instigator of sexual relations), just as Aurora Floyd was sympathetic because her lover was working class. The idea that either Smith or Aurora was a willing partner was disturbing, and Smith's defence knew their only chance was to portray her as a victim. Just as women were fascinated by Lady Audley, so they were by Smith, and crowds of women gathered at the courtrooms. The *Daily Express* accused them of having 'dishonoured their sex' by 'eagerly drinking in that filthy correspondence.'[65]

It was not for nothing that Constance Kent and Madeline Smith had such resonance for the Victorian public: they epitomised the fear that outward respectability masked secret desires and crimes. As Mary Hartman points out, referring to Smith and another sexually adventurous young lady, the French Angélina Lemoine:

> In a similar but more immediate way than literature, the trials seem to have supplied a vicarious outlet for frustrations. The accused young women had acted out what the female spectators, in their most secret thoughts, had hardly dared to imagine.[66]

Not surprisingly, some authors cashed in on the notoriety of the new celebrity criminals. Mansel condemned what he termed the 'Newspaper Novel':

> Let him only keep an eye on the criminal reports of the daily newspapers, marking the cases which are honoured with the especial notice of a leading article, and become a nine-days' wonder (...) and he has the outline of his story not only ready-made, but approved beforehand as of the true sensation cast (...) and there emerges the criminal variety of the Newspaper Novel.[67]

He specifically mentions two anonymous novels, *Wait and Hope* based on the discovery of a dismembered body (minus the head) of a man, the identity of which was never discovered by police, the 'carpet-bag mystery of Waterloo Bridge'. This case is referred to by characters in Braddon's later novel *The Story of Barbara* (1880), as one of the most memorable events of 1857, its coverage second only to that of the Indian Mutiny. Flossie goes on about it to take her sister's mind off her former lover in India:

> There had been discovered during the last week the hideous evidence of one of those mysterious crimes which sometimes appall society; and Flossie would talk of no public event save this ghastly discovery of a carpet-bag containing human remains. She

dwelt and enlarged upon this horrible fact with a ghoul-like relish. She brought it forth immediately that public matters were spoken of. Breathe but the name of Sir Colin Campbell, waft but a sigh towards yonder victim at Lucknow, and Flossie flourished her carpet-bag.[68]

Flossie's theory is that he was a spy. A certain piquancy to the case was that the last person seen on the night on the bridge was an old woman carrying a heavy carpet bag.[69] The body was never identified and the case unsolved. It says something about the shared public experience of such cases that Braddon could refer to it twenty three years later and the reader would probably have known which one she meant. Through newspapers famous criminals became familiar and part of shared cultural experience. Braddon wrote of the poisoner William Palmer, recalling in the first person an experience she had in Doncaster, surely from when she was in the town acting with Henry Nye Chart's Brighton company in 1859:

> People are apt to take pride out of strange things. An elderly gentleman at Doncaster, showing me his comfortably furnished apartments, informed me, with evident satisfaction, that Mr. William Palmer had lodged in those very rooms.[70]

Even though newspapers were far more explicit about crime and sexuality than fiction ever was, the reaction to sensation fiction as it began to explore these areas was almost hysterical. George Augustus Sala, making the point that a reader who read newspapers was unlikely to be harmed by the innovations in fiction – importantly he tried to remind people that this was increased realism – wrote in his essay, 'The Cant of Modern Criticism':

> If we read the newspaper; if we read the police reports; if we can laugh at such a case as that of the "Honourable Mrs. Geraldine Meurice," or weep over such a one as that of "Augusta Mitchell;" if we have ever troubled ourself about a Yelverton marriage, a Tichborne baronetcy, a Thellusson will, a Road murder, a Cornhill burglary, a gold-dust robbery, a Roupell forgery, a Simla court-martial, we shall take no great harm by reading realistic novels of human passion, weakness, and error.[71]

Braddon was less directly influenced by actual crime and the newspaper accounts than some of the other sensation novelists. She did not directly turn a real event into fiction as did some of the authors criticised by Mansel. Strangely, one of Braddon's early novels bore a resemblance to a future sensational trial which ran from the 1860s to 1870s. This was the Tichborne case, in which a twenty six stone Australian butcher managed to convince Lady Tichborne that he was the missing, and considerably slighter in figure, heir, her son. Collins may have referred to the case in *Armadale* (1866)[72] but it is eerily similar to the plot of Braddon's early novel *The Lady Lisle* (1862), published several years before the fake heir appeared in 1865. More amazing yet, the false claimant, Arthur Orton, was an admirer of Braddon's novels, having been so struck by one villain's words of wisdom while still in Australia that he copied them out into his pocket book and signed it 'R.C. Tichborne, Bart.' These words were the philosophy of Aurora Floyd's first husband, James Conyers:

> "I should think fellows with plenty of money and no brains must have been created for the good of fellows with plenty of brains and no money." (p.159)

Foolishly Orton left the notebook in Australia, from where it was later posted to the prosecution. When the extract was published, Braddon recognised it and promptly revealed the source when she sent a copy of *Aurora Floyd* to the judge, Lord Chief Justice Sir Alexander Cockburn.[73] It would be fascinating to know if Orton had been further encouraged and inspired in his scheme by reading *Lady Lisle*! Charles Reade went on to dedicate his Claimant inspired novel, *The Wandering Heir* (1875), to Braddon.

Charles Reade was the sensation author most influenced by the newspapers, to the extent of quoting newspaper stories to prove there was nothing unrealistic about his own fiction. He compiled masses of clippings into scrap books, believing the oddest of stories. Reade advised Braddon: 'Never mind the books, read the newspapers.'[74] On one occasion she pasted a newspaper clipping into her notebook, 'The Murderer's Hand', concerning research by a M. Desbarolles on the physiognomy of murderers' hands: his conclusion being that they all had exceptionally broad thumbs![75] However, Braddon does not seem to have often followed Reade's example in her fiction, unlike Wilkie Collins, but she none the less regarded newspapers as an important barometer of modern times:

> I undoubtedly believe that they give the best picture of the events of the day. They really are, as they profess to be, mirrors reflecting the life and views of the period.[76]

The peak of sensation fiction coincided with changes in the divorce laws, which theoretically made divorce accessible to more than just a few aristocrats. A man could easily get a divorce for his wife's adultery, but a woman had to prove an aggravating crime such as incest. There were a number of high profile divorce cases related in newspapers, and because of the increase through the change in the law, divorce provided an opportunity for more exciting plots in fiction. In *The Lady's Mile* Braddon shows a husband trying to frame his wife to prove adultery as grounds for divorce, and in *Dead Sea Fruit* (1868) she shows the plight of a woman separated but legally tied to a husband who is a practised adulterer – divorce and remarriage are impossible for both, and so each awaits the death of the other in order to be free. That women writers were choosing to write about such things, and make the participants the central characters was found by many critics to be shocking.

'It is a shame to women so to write'[77]

Although men were prominent in the sensation genre (Wilkie Collins, James Payn, Sheridan Le Fanu and Charles Reade were the leading male exponents), much of the criticism chose to focus on the fact that women were writing these novels. Braddon and Mrs. Henry Wood were seen as the leaders of the genre, but the most venomous criticism was usually reserved for Braddon. Wood was twenty one years older than Braddon, and although they began to write at exactly the same time, Ellen Wood's sense of morality remained that of the previous generation: underpinning *East Lynne* is the firm conviction that there is no sin without consequence. Strangely, and perhaps as a result of some of the adverse criticism she suffered over immorality, Braddon seemed to rewrite *East Lynne* in her novel *The Lovels of Arden* (1871), but omitting the adultery.

The Reverend Paget wrote a novel which was in part a parody, but also intended as a serious critique of the sensation novel, the women writing them, and those reading them, called *Lucretia; or, The Heroine of the Nineteenth Century* (1868):

No *man* would have dared to write and publish such books as some of these are: no *man could* have written such delineations of female passion (...) No! They are women, who by their writings have been doing the work of the enemy of souls, glossing over vice, making profligacy attractive, dealing with licentious minuteness the workings of unbridled passions, encouraging vanity, extravagance, wilfulness, selfishness in their worst forms (...) Women have done this, – have thus abused their power and prostituted their gifts, - who might have been bright and shining lights in their generation.[78]

Women, if they were writers, ought to be like Charlotte Yonge, encouraging religious feelings and moral improvement. By doing otherwise they were betraying their sex, and their unnatural heroines were setting a bad example to impressionable girls.

One of the most reasoned articles as to why the genre of sensation fiction had come into being appeared in the *World* in 1874, a newspaper which belonged to Braddon's friend Edmund Yates. The author refuted the suggestion that sensation fiction was about crime, and argued that the popular response to sensation fiction was in part a reaction to the moralistic fiction espoused by the likes of Yonge and was:

a protest against and a reaction from the kind of fictions which we may call the novel of the schoolroom. The public had been flooded with milk-and-water romances, "character stories", tranquil tales of home life, the doings and sayings of virtuous, excellent and commonplace people. We are not disparaging the merits of many of these works, which were considerable. But they were absurdly exaggerated by a certain school of critics, who seemed to think that they embraced the sum of those attributes which make up excellence in fiction. It would have been more correct to say that they were pleasantly written, but that they were artistically defective, in as much as they entirely ignored one element in human nature and society. If life were made up of home affections and virtuous emotion, if existence were always fine-weather sailing, if the surface were never ruffled by gusts of passion and by storms of crime, then the novels to which we allude might have been justly extolled as models. But the fact that they are left completely out of sight one side, and that not the least important, of human life and character, soon become recognised. Recognition provoked tedium and ennui, and these culminated in the sensation novel. *Lady Audley's Secret* was the inevitable sequel of the *Heir of Redcliffe*.[79]

In other words it was the end of domestic fiction as epitomised by Charlotte Yonge, who continued to let her father and bishop read and correct her work: feminine docility to please any critic. She disapproved of sensation fiction, and that she believed women writers needed a male to keep them in place is evinced by her dismay on reading an Annie Thomas novel written after Thomas's recent marriage to a vicar. *False Colours* (1865) was about an unmarried mother of an adult son, who passes herself off as a respectable widow. Yonge read Thomas's latest offering in despair, as she had hoped Thomas had 'turned over a new leaf since she was married' and she wondered how her husband could 'have let her write such a book?'[80] Thomas's first works had been published by Maxwell at the same time as Braddon's, publishing her *Lady Lorme* (1862) in the Ward, Lock Shilling Library where it was compared to *Lady Audley's Secret*.

However, these women writers had some editorial freedom as many of them owned and edited their own magazines: Braddon had *Belgravia*, Mrs. Henry Wood the *Argosy*, Mrs. Riddell became part owner and editor of the *St. James's Magazine* in 1867, and Florence Marryat edited *London Society* (1872-1876). Although this allowed them to determine the sort of forum their work appeared in, they still had to consider the sensibilities of those who controlled the lucrative three volume edition market, the owners of the circulating libraries. Charles Reade wrote somewhat resentfully of the circulating libraries: 'They will only take in ladies' novels. Mrs. Henry Wood, 'Ouida', Miss Braddon – these are their gods.'[81] Although this was a distorted view, the women sensation novelists seem to have had an easier time getting beyond Mudie's policy of allowing only fiction suitable for family reading. At no time was Braddon ever banned by Mudie's, and few women writers ever were, although Mudie refused to take Annie Edwardes's *The Morals of Mayfair* (1858) because he thought the title was too salacious.[82] Although Braddon had murderers, thieves and bigamists as central characters, there was still enough morality to make it seem as if Braddon was not necessarily endorsing immorality, and perhaps Mudie did not mind too much what was in the book, as long as the title did not draw obvious attention to it. At the end of the day Mudie's was a business, and as Braddon was one of their most popular authors they purchased over six hundred copies of each of her novels.[83] Even though Mudie's was satisfied, others saw Braddon as a dangerous influence.

Mrs. Oliphant was a trenchant critic of sensation fiction in a series of anonymous articles in *Blackwood's* on modern fiction (interestingly Braddon assumed they were written by a man). She wrote:

> It is a shame to women so to write; and it is a shame to the women who read and accept as a true representation of themselves and their ways the equivocal talk and fleshly inclination herein attributed to them. It may be done in carelessness. It may be done in that mere desire for something startling which the monotony of ordinary life is apt to produce; but it is debasing to everybody concerned.[84]

Braddon herself felt she had received a fairer hearing when some reviewers had at first assumed M.E. Braddon was a man, jokingly telling Edmund Yates:

> It is all Mr. Tinsley's fault for advertising me as 'Mary Elizabeth!' I used to be called *Mr*. Braddon, and provincial critics were wont to regret that my experience of women had been so bitter as to make me an implacable foe to the fair sex. They thought I had been 'cradled into magazines by wrong,' and had learned in the Divorce Court what I taught in three-volume novels.[85]

While Oliphant also criticised other women writers, most of her venom was reserved for Braddon, arguing that the others were her imitators. Oliphant was especially concerned at the sexually outspoken heroines of Braddon, Rhoda Broughton and Annie Thomas, adding insultingly: 'They might not be aware how young women of good blood and good training feel.'[86] With such comments it was not surprising that Braddon felt this reviewer was trying to get at her personally. The expressive natures of sensation heroines were new and alarming, and Braddon was perceived to be the instigator. Yet her heroines were not as sexually expressive as Florence Marryat's or those of Rhoda Broughton. In this respect, Marryat probably went further than any other novelist, male or female, of this period. Monica Correa Fryckstedt credits Marryat with the most sexually pro-active heroine of the period, Henrietta in *For Ever and Ever*.[87] Marryat continued to receive hostile reviews, accusing her of bad taste and immorality, for the rest of her career, long after Braddon was accepted as a gifted novelist. Braddon was more conservative than Marryat and Broughton in depicting sexual attraction, but she probably felt she had to be because of her own socially ambiguous position. In comparison, Broughton, the daughter of a vicar and the grandaughter of a baronet, was a respectable spinster. When Broughton went to live in Oxford she was shunned by many locals who, led by a Miss Smith, mistook her for Braddon.[88] Marryat passed as a widow before her second marriage, although she was in fact a divorcee who had first been pushed into a marriage in India at sixteen years of age. In an interesting reverse of Braddon, Marryat became an actress in her own company after she became a successful novelist.

Braddon was especially vulnerable in the early part of her career to the criticism the difference in her status attracted. Her relationship with Maxwell would have become harder to conceal once she became famous, and the press and public became interested in the private life of the popular young novelist. The critics implicitly suggested that the immorality of her fiction stemmed from deficiencies in her own life: for example, Aurora Floyd's whipping of the Softy caused W. Fraser Rae to comment that Braddon was 'evidently acquainted with a very low type of female character'.[89] An even more barbed insinuation appeared in the following passage in the *Athenaeum* review of *John Marchmont's Legacy*; alleging that the author had a certain ignorance of the words of the marriage ceremony, and which seems too pointed to be coincidental:

> When Miss Braddon knows more about the Marriage Service than she does at present, she will know that these words are uttered by the bridegroom, – not the bride.[90]

Braddon already had two sons by this date, Gerald born in 1862 and Francis born in 1863.[91] A month after the review in the *Athenaeum* Maxwell doubtless made the situation worse when he decided to scotch the rumours, and let it be known that he and Braddon were married. This was duly announced in the society columns of magazines such as the *Court Journal* in January 1864, but was equally quickly denied by Richard Brinsley Knowles, the husband of Mary Anne Maxwell's sister.

Braddon's fellow sensation novelists Wilkie Collins and Charles Reade also had unconventional domestic arrangements, but it seems they never attracted similar public insinuations about their private lives. The other famous female contributor to the genre, Mrs. Henry Wood, was indisputably respectable, extolling conventional morality, and she had first found fame by winning a Scottish temperance fiction competition with *Danesbury House* (1860). However, although it was not uncommon among men to have secret second families, it must have been much more difficult for a woman. Amongst her own circle of friends, the painter William Powell Frith had a second family with his mistress around the corner from his home with his legitimate family, and George Augustus Sala was rumoured never to have been married to his first wife who was of a lower social class.[92] Braddon herself does not seem to have approved of such situations, because they usually meant that a woman was deceived and exploited. In a late playlet, 'A Modern Confessor', she has a wife investigate the background of her future son-in-law, so she can save her daughter the agony she herself experienced as a young bride on discovering her husband already has a mistress and children.[93] In her posthumous novel, *Mary* (1916), there is a real atmosphere of pathos and agony for the unmarried mother heroine, and her horror and humiliation at not having a wedding band. One suspects Braddon would not have approved of Wilkie Collins and his 'morganatic'[94] family because he was single and in the position to marry if he chose. Collins also denied his children his surname, and

Braddon and Maxwell were obviously determined that their children should have the status of legitimate children. They registered their children as a married couple (except for the first, Gerald, who was not registered at all, and possibly Fanny may not have been), for had they not done so the children would have had to have the surname Braddon instead of Maxwell.[95]

It was no wonder that Braddon felt much discomfort about her ambiguous position. If it was not bad enough that the press hinted and criticised her, she had to put up with much from her own family. Braddon and her mother were careful which of their relatives they told about their new family. Their Cornish relatives, like Sarah Cowland and Mary Basden, who were showered with gifts and financial help by Braddon and Maxwell, knew about Maxwell and that Braddon had had a baby; but her brother Edward's wife, Georgie, writing from India asked about the health of 'Margaret & her baby', but seemed to know nothing about Braddon's, or indeed John Maxwell since their love was sent to Fanny and her daughter only. Braddon's older sister Maggie lived in Italy, married to an Italian called Antonio who taught at a college near Naples. From the existing letters from Maggie to her mother it seems as if Maggie was not told of Mary's family for some years, even in 1866 she had not been sent copies of her sister's novels and Maggie was writing as if Mary had only recently married:

> I ought to send her a wedding present tho' I can't do so now I shall hope to one of these days. (...) I have never read "Aurora Floyd", "Eleanor's Victory" and several other works of Mary's, so if ever you have an opportunity you won't forget to send them to me.[96]

Two years later Maggie was dying, and in July of 1868 their brother Edward was with her in Italy, returning from India after many years absence. Maggie wrote to her mother that Edward 'looks young and good looking he has your face precisely every feature shape, and all delight to see him.'[97] She also said Edward would be in England at the end of August, and it must have been then that Edward discovered his sister was not married to John Maxwell and a rift of many years standing took place, with Braddon blaming her brother for the unhappiness he brought to their mother by his anger shortly before her death.

The criticism of women writing immoral and dangerous books came at a time when men believed women could not write great novels because of their lack of life experience and innocence. W.R. Greg wrote in 'The False Morality of Lady Novelists' in 1859:

Many of the saddest and deepest truths in the strange science of sexual affection are to her mysteriously and mercifully veiled and can only be purchased at such a fearful cost that we cannot wish it otherwise. The inevitable consequence however is that in treating of that science she labours under all the disadvantages of partial study and superficial insight. She is describing a country of which she knows only the more frequented and the safer roads, with a few of the sweeter scenes and the prettier by-paths and more picturesque detours which be not far from the broad and beaten thoroughfares; while the rockier and loftier mountains, and more rugged tracks, the more sombre valleys, and the darker and more dangerous chasms, are never trodden by her feet, and scarcely dreamed of by her fancy.[98]

The *Saturday Review*, in its article 'Homicidal Heroines', thought the ignorance of women writers was a particular handicap in novels of crime and sensation because, 'they cannot photograph the wide world; for one hundredth part of its follies or vices or pursuits, unless they are unusually unlucky, they never can have observed.'[99] Braddon was a female writer who did know about the other side of life, the life thought only fathomable to men. As the daughter of separated parents, her career on the stage, and now her relationship with Maxwell, Braddon had been exposed to a life barely glimpsed by most young women of her class, and so she was able to write about some of these unfathomables. Many critics seemed threatened by this aspect in her work. A friend of her uncle's, Douglas Cook, who presumably was well aware of the circumstances in her life which enabled her to write of things not known by other women, wrote favourably of her insight in his review of *Eleanor's Victory* in the normally hostile *Saturday Review*, so it probably counted as something of a defence against the previously raised cudgels:

She alone can write of women's things like a woman, and of men's things like a man. She can talk about gussets, and seams, and dress, and all manner of music; and she can also talk of theatricals, and little Paris dinners, and brandy-and-water, and grisettes, and horses and dogs (...) It is impossible not to be amused with the artless way in which Miss Braddon betrays her intimate knowledge of easy male society (...) It is comical and entertaining to find a lady novelist talking familiarly of the most fatal result of intoxication as "del. trem.", setting down brandy and soda-water as poor stuff (...) It has, we presume, been Miss Braddon's lot to see a phase of life open to few ladies, and she freely draws upon what accident has furnished her with. And it ought to be expressly said that, although she evidently knows how fast young men behave and talk and disport themselves in moments of unrestraint, she never treads even on the borders of indelicacy.[100]

Braddon was able, to some degree, to defend herself once she had her own magazine. Maxwell had been toying with the idea for some time, only too aware that Braddon's name on a magazine ought to ensure the success which thus far had eluded him. *Birds of Prey* had been advertised as early as January 1866 as a forthcoming serial in *Temple Bar*, until Maxwell decided to hold it back as the star vehicle for his new magazine. From 1866 until he sold the magazine to Chatto and Windus in 1876, Braddon 'conducted' Maxwell's magazine *Belgravia*, and as well as being nominal editor she wrote much of the earlier volumes under her own name and that of Babington White. *Belgravia* aimed at a middle class audience, but was more attractive to the eye than *Temple Bar* because it had full page illustrations, and so imitated the already successful format of *Cornhill*. Writing to Bulwer Lytton, asking if he might contribute a poem, 'the merest chip from your quarry of gems', Braddon half apologised for the title, 'Please do not laugh at the snobbery of the title. "Belgravia" is the best bait for the shillings of Brixton & Bow.'[101] Bulwer Lytton did not write anything for the magazine, and, although he must have enjoyed Braddon's flattering letters, he never made much of an effort to meet her. *Belgravia* began in November 1866 and started the serialisation of what was to be a six volume novel, *Birds of Prey* and *Charlotte's Inheritance*. Regular contributors included William Sawyer, Percy Fitzgerald, George Augustus Sala, Maxwell's friend Major Byng Hall (a Queen's Messenger, who wrote articles on antiques and collectables), and young writers like Astley H. Baldwin (a poet and contributor to journals who was born in 1835).

A dinner was held to launch the new magazine at the Langham Hotel, Portland Place, on the night of Tuesday 27 November. Braddon wished Charles Kent could come, but he was prevented by illness, 'There will be many present on that occasion, for whose kindly encouragement I have every reason to be grateful – but there will be no one to whom I owe more gratitude than I do to you after your unfailing & most heartfelt championship.'[102] George Augustus Sala was also unable to attend. Maxwell knew the value of publicity, and everyone in the position to promote the magazine was there. One hundred guests, mainly contributors, other writers, journalists from national and provincial newspapers, and people from the theatre were invited, and although no speeches were given it was described as a lively occasion, the evening rounded off with songs, and one correspondent wrote that 'Another very agreeable feature in the entertainment was the presence of ladies, who mustered in considerable force, and gave a pleasant relief to the broad expanse of black coats and white ties.'[103]

The first issue had already sold well, but Maxwell was irritated by the existence of a rival magazine which had set itself up in direct opposition and chosen an almost identical title, *Belgravia: A Magazine of Fashion and Amusements*. He was soon in dispute with the proprietor, Mr. Hogg, as it had caused confusion with both press and public, and he ensured the interloper discontinued after five issues.

Braddon's role as editor appears to have been a little over emphasised. Although she was editor and shaped much of the look of the magazine, she did not have the time to devote to the day to day running of it, and the contributions were, it seems, usually read and chosen by others. When her friend, the critic Charles Kent, asked her to consider his friend's novel she replied:

> We do not at present contemplate giving more than one long serial in 'Belgravia', as we find that by giving novelettes in three numbers we shall have more field for variety. However I shall have much pleasure in getting Mr. Atherstone's novel carefully read by a much better critic than myself – as I have just at present neither time nor eyesight for the task.[104]

In 1868 the novelist W. Clark Russell, later to become famous as a writer of sea stories, wanted to submit a novelette called 'School for Young Ladies', and he was not sure whether to send it to Braddon:

> I do not know whether I am right in communicating with you or whether I should not address myself to Mr. Cheltenham (sic.) the actual or nominal editor of your magazine.[105]

The letter is marked 'replied' in John Maxwell's writing. The Mr. Cheltnam referred to was Charles Smith Cheltnam. It seems that as when George Augustus Sala was the conductor of *Temple Bar* the celebrity's name took precedence on the title page, but another did much of the editing. In the case of *Temple Bar* it was the less well known Edmund Yates, who later recalled:

> Sala had so much literary and journalistic work that, beyond giving his name to the cover and the supervision to the printed sheets, he left most of the detail to me.[106]

In his memoirs, *Belgravia* contributor Percy Fitzgerald confirmed the role of Maxwell and Cheltnam:

> While Miss Braddon conducted the *Belgravia Magazine*, her busy, untiring husband looked warily after all the business details, finding contributors, etc. He was assisted by Mr. Charles Cheltnam, a dramatist.[107]

Cheltnam, who was married to Leigh Hunt's daughter, also wrote the only play version of *Lady Audley's Secret* to be authorised by its author: the fact that she received no remuneration for the many unauthorised versions always annoyed her. Braddon would not have had time to read all of the manuscripts and see to her own instalments of novels and short stories, and Escott wrote that his work with the magazine was dealt with by Cheltnam. It seems when she did take a stronger editorial line, it was to see to her own interests as a writer, enlisting George Augustus Sala to write defensive articles on her behalf. She also got Sala to write a long and complimentary review of her play *Griselda* (1873), and as the conductor had ordered it he could hardly do otherwise than praise, when in actual fact he had not thought a great deal of it, writing to Edmund Yates on the night he saw it, 'You were at Braddon's first night. Mrs Grizzle is a mull, I fear.'[108]

Although Braddon was too busy with her own writing to read and edit all of the manuscripts submitted by the other contributors, she probably still took a great deal of interest in the look of the magazine and knew the importance of eye catching illustrations and subject matter. Even when she wrote *Eleanor's Victory* in 1863 for a magazine Maxwell did not own, *Once a Week*, she wrote to the artist George du Maurier:

> Launcelot is the young man on the Boulevard. Make him as handsome as the heroine is pretty, if you can please.
>
> I have been delighted with the two pictures I have seen, & I hope the numbers will provide you decent subjects. I will try & make them do so.[109]

As the Conductor of her own magazine, Braddon was also able to fight back against the critics. It is clear from Braddon's letters to Bulwer Lytton that she was greatly wounded by Mrs. Oliphant's accusations. Her friend George Augustus Sala was enlisted to write essays in defence of sensation fiction, arguing against the 'poor canting creature' who had written the *Blackwood's* articles. In 'On the "Sensational" in Literature and Art' Sala pointed out that sensation had always existed in the arts, and some of the greatest writers had been practitioners:

> The only wonder is that the charitable souls have failed to discover that among modern "sensational" writers Mr. Charles Dickens is perhaps the most thoroughly, and has been from the very outset of his career the most persistently, "sensational" writer of the age.[110]

To the name of Dickens he went on to add that of Shakespeare. Sala was an influential defender, and no stranger to literary hackwork himself, and one of the scenes most criticised in *Aurora Floyd*, the whipping of Softy, he defended, adding 'Poor dear Aurora! though she did horsewhip her groom, we all know she was more sinned against than sinning.'[111] This may have been a little unfortunate, for Sala had a lively interest in whipping and masochism; Braddon, though, was probably unaware of this. Sala has been credited with several pornographic novels, and for a hoax correspondence which lasted for a year on the whipping of girls in the *Englishwoman's Domestic Magazine*, and for sharing his interests with Algernon Swinburne.[112] His defence of Aurora's behaviour probably provoked some mirth in Bohemian circles. His second article made the point again that sensation had a long and distinguished lineage. 'The Cant of Modern Criticism' offered a stern rebuttal to Mrs. Oliphant's 'sermon' and called *Blackwood's* a 'decrepit magazine'.[113] He argued that it was nonsense to say English literature was utterly innocent and tame until modern times. To Sala, Braddon's novels were 'indubitably sensational', but he argued that this was a good thing because it made literature more alive and in many ways more, not less, realistic:

> But in all these novels the people walk and talk and act, not like the denizens of some phantom land of anthropophagi, where heads do grow beneath the owner's shoulders, but like dwellers in the actual, breathing world in which we live.[114]

Finally he accused the anonymous author of being driven by one motive only, that of jealousy:

> Hatred and jealousy and spite towards one of the most successful novelists of the age – ill-nature and ill-feeling towards the author of *Aurora Floyd* and a dozen more capital novels shine in every page of the lucubrations of this agreeable soul.[115]

He assumed, as did Braddon, that such narrow minded, and in parts cruel, criticisms could not emanate from a fellow novelist. Braddon clearly remained sensitive about this and other bad reviews for years, parodying them in *Hostages to Fortune* (1875) where Herman Westray gets terrible reviews from the *Censor*:

> in a slashing article three columns long (...) "Extract the acid cynicism and the half-veiled immorality from Mr. Westray's style, and the result is almost as palatable as lemonade without lemon or sugar," says the *Censor*, summing up with the grand air of papal infallibility which distinguishes that journal.[116]

Despite the scandal and the criticism her work had inspired, it must have seemed as if Braddon had at last achieved the financial security she longed for. She was now a major literary figure, and had her portrait painted by William Frith in 1865 which showed her standing by a table, on which were several of her novels and a writing slope. Writing a letter to her at the time he painted her, Frith addressed her as 'My dear Lady Audley' and declared 'we are to go hand in hand to posterity.'[117] That same year Braddon was taking an interest in the work of another artist, Alfred Elmore, who was painting a 'sensation' picture of a young woman outside the gaming rooms at Homburg. Leaning over her shoulder and whispering in her ear was a young man. The painting posed a mystery: the lady could have lost horribly on the gaming tables, been about to commit suicide, or on the verge of losing her virtue to the young man. Braddon must have seen the picture before it was exhibited at the Royal Academy in June 1865, perhaps through Frith who was a friend of Elmore's, for she wrote to him:

> May I venture to submit, in addition to the many titles which will no doubt occur to you for your most interesting picture, the following which may not occur to you.
> "A Perilous Moment." "Trembling in the Balance." "On the Brink" "Lost? or Saved?" "A Dangerous Adonis" "A Woman's Peril."[118]

Elmore selected the suitably ambiguous 'On the Brink' and it became one of the most popular 'sensation' pictures, and it is now in the Fitzwilliam Museum in Cambridge. Coincidentally the picture was selected for the front cover of the Virago edition of *Aurora Floyd*. Braddon herself used the title 'On the Brink' for a chapter in *The Lady's Mile* (1866), when Lady Cecil nearly leaves her barrister husband for another man, and again as the title for a short story which appeared in

Milly Darrell and Other Tales (1873). Elmore was obviously delighted by Braddon and her suggestion, as he gave her a humorous sketch of herself (could it have depicted her as the heroine of the picture?). Braddon wrote to his friend the painter Thomas Creswick:

> It is very cruel of Mr. Elmore to depict me as a Temptress, not withstanding which I shall cherish his cartoon amongst my choicest treasures.[119]

The following year Braddon and Maxwell experienced the sadness of the death of their young son Francis. Some of the time was now spent in Richmond, where they first lived at Dunstable House in Marsh Road (later Sheen Road), and at the end of 1866 Braddon sold government consuls to buy Lichfield House, a magnificent red brick Georgian mansion built for the Earl of Abergavenny, with panelled walls, carved doorways, stables, paddock, kitchen gardens, an orangery and extensive grounds, which had once been the residence of the Bishop of Lichfield. They moved in March 1867 and Braddon wrote to Charles Kent about how busy she was:

> My household is in the business of "moving", and I have no doubt you well know the misery involved in that one word – Every day brings some new trouble. And my literary work scarcely begins till late at night.[120]

Maxwell was an enthusiastic collector of antiques and paintings, as was Fanny, and the house was furnished in a grand manner. The daughters of Maxwell's first marriage returned home from convent school, and Braddon usually rode with her stepchildren in Richmond Park in the morning. The house contained a large library, and Braddon was fond of gardening and made alterations to the grounds. She kept horses and dogs, and in later years was well known for her daring riding during hunts on her horse Vixen.

In late 1868 tragedy struck again when her mother Fanny suddenly died at the age of sixty four, only a short time after they heard that Braddon's sister Maggie had died in Italy. Braddon wrote to Bulwer Lytton in despair at the loss of the mother who had stood by her through so much:

> I cannot tell you how I loved her (...) Thus ends thirty years of the most perfect union, I believe, that ever existed between two human beings of the same sex. I told her every thing, for no act or feeling of mine was complete without her sympathy, & I have rather

endured her reproaches or her anger than lock one secret in my breast.[121]

It was a crushing blow which almost destroyed her health and her work, resulting in a complete nervous breakdown which lasted for the best part of a year. Although Sala was Braddon's friend he still viewed these events with a somewhat cynical eye, gleeful that Maxwell was now getting his come-uppance. Soon after Fanny Braddon's death Sala wrote to Edmund Yates to reveal the latest news after bumping into Maxwell, 'Don Duffero':

Either Don Duffero is the biggest liar out – well he *is* the biggest; but he must be bigger even than himself: which is a paradox, – or the Braddon business has been exaggerated. I think however the first is the case. I met Maxwell today in Fleet Street & asking after Mrs M. he told me that she was "rapidly recovering from a slight attack of nervous prostration into which she had been thrown by the death of her revered parent." He added that "Bound to John Company" was "superb, superb," & then took occasion to ask me when I thought I would turn the "Bargraves" which I did in "Banter" into an entirely new novel altering the names & places. He further took occasion to inform me that he had long been thinking over a variety of schemes by means of which several thousands of pounds might be put into my pocket: remarking parenthetically that he considered me the most brilliant genius of the day, & that my "success" – what success? must be gall & wormwood to *you*, my deadliest enemy. I told him that I had been dining with you on Sunday, whereupon he surveyed me with a wondering eye, and the conversation flagged a little; but happening to notice that I had a new hat he actively observed that I was the best dressed man in London, &, ringing my hand affectionately went over Blackfriars bridge, with a black bag, on his way to the Old Bailey *via* the Waterloo Station. From all which I perpended that Don Duffero is in a tremendous funk. The last run of the ore in the Richmond mine has been worked. It really *does* look like Nemesis. How many more 3 vol novels, each representing a ten-roomed house & an acre of land may he not have calculated upon? When I got to Waterloo 2 hours afterwards I met Clarke a bill discounting friend of Gus Mayhew's and his neighbour at Twickenham. His family doctor is the Maxwell's physician, & according to his showing poor Braddon is altogether off her chump.[122]

Maxwell must have indeed wondered if Braddon would ever recover. It was during this crisis that Braddon gave birth to another child, Rosalie, and her illness must have reminded Maxwell of the illness of his first wife. Feverish, she dreamt she was going to meet her dead uncle William as he emerged from a long passageway out of a ship, and hallucinated about Bulwer Lytton. During her indisposition he was forced to get another writer to complete her current serial in *Belgravia*, *Bound to John Company*. Although Sala chose to concentrate on the distress of Maxwell the slightly shady business man, there seems little doubt that whatever other people thought of Maxwell, Braddon found him a great support. When she had recovered she asked Bulwer Lytton:

> Please do not allude to anything I have said about my long illness in your gracious reply – as that is a point on which my husband is sensitive – and he so good to me that I am bound to consider his feelings on every subject.[123]

For a time after her illness Braddon feared that she would never write again:

> When that unreal world faded the actual world seemed strangely dull & empty and my own brain utterly emptied out – swept clean of every thought. My first efforts to write after that time were beyond measure feeble, and I thought imagination was dead – but, thank Heaven, the knack of copy-spinning, at least, has returned.[124]

When Braddon was fully recovered she was soon able to regain her adeptness at writing, and was as popular and influential as ever.

Despite her success, scandal was once again not far off. Maxwell's wife, Mary Anne, died at the age of forty eight on the 5 September 1874, not at a mental institution, but at Mountain View, Kimmage Road, Harold's Cross. This was the home of her brother John Crowley, formerly the home of their parents, and the village of Harold's Cross was just over two miles from Dublin. Once informed of the death by telegram Maxwell handled the situation badly. He telegraphed John Crowley at ten thirty in the morning on the 7 September, promising money for the funeral, which he planned to attend, adding 'Neither advertise nor telegraph anybody.' At two thirty he telegraphed with an excuse, 'Far from feeling well. Can you arrange without me? Five pounds posted, more shall follow as required. Do things quietly, funeral should be strictly private.' An hour later he send a third telegram, 'If you have written your sister, telegraph requesting her not to advertise death, as I shall do whatever is necessary.'[125] John Crowley, not surprisingly angry, ignored the telegrams and refused Maxwell's request to return what Maxwell now realised would appear insensitive and compromising telegrams. John Crowley informed his sister and Richard Brinsley Knowles, and Knowles published took it upon himself to publish an announcement of death for Mary Anne Maxwell, as the wife of John Maxwell, in several national newspapers. Many of Braddon's friends and acquaintances saw the notice of death and naturally assumed Braddon herself had died, and soon letters of condolence were arriving at Lichfield House. Even more unwisely Maxwell composed a circular on the same day which was distributed around Richmond and to friends in London, reading 'Mr. and Mrs. Maxwell present their Compliments to ------- and beg to disclaim any knowledge of the maliciously-intentioned announcement of a death on the 5th inst.'[126] One of these was shown to Knowles, and with the avowed intent 'due to the name and memory of Mr. Maxwell's deceased Wife, to the feelings of her surviving friends, and to my own character, that some further evidence should be afforded to those whom an attempt has been made to mystify and mislead'[127] wrote a reply in retaliation revealing the full circumstances of the existence of Maxwell's wife. Doubtless the Crowleys had reason to be irritated that their sister's existence had been denied in life and death, and the children of Maxwell's first family, fond of their stepmother as they were, are said to have been pained their father did not attend the funeral, but Braddon was the innocent party in the scandal. She felt the damage to her respectability keenly.

Learning the truth about their employers, all but one of the servants at Lichfield House handed in their notice. When the scandal broke Braddon and Maxwell were fortunate that they numbered so many prominent journalists and newspaper proprietors as personal friends, as this at least prevented too much discussion in British newspapers. Foreign newspapers were not so circumspect, and the *New York Times* carried the front page story from their London correspondent 'Miss Braddon as a Bigamist', in which it stated Mrs. Maxwell had died in an asylum:

> A curious and, I may almost say, characteristic incident has happened to Miss Braddon, the novelist. Having, like so many of her heroines, committed a species of bigamy, she has at last been found out. I say a "species of bigamy", because, far from becoming the wife of two husbands, all Miss Braddon did was to go through some facetious form of marriage with a man who was already married. She thus became, not indeed a bigamist, but, at least, an accomplice in bigamy.[128]

Because of the scandal the family moved to Cheyne Walk in Chelsea for a year, 'for reasons that I never understood' remembered their son William, letting Lichfield House to Lord and Lady Stanley of Alderley.[129] As soon as possible, the marriage took place. Braddon must have confided in her local vicar at Richmond from 1867, Charles Tickell Proctor, for it was he who came to London and married them in St. Brides church off Fleet Street on the second of October 1874. The household was split in its religious affiliations. Braddon and her children attended Protestant churches in Richmond, the Parish Church under Proctor, and later St. John's as she admired the vicar there, Reverend R.B. Harrison. Maxwell and the children of his first marriage attended the Catholic church, where his friend was the priest.[130] Braddon became a prominent friend of the local clergy and the writer Douglas Sladen, who did not attend any church, recalled Braddon inviting him to lunch to meet all of the vicars when he moved to Richmond.[131] Proctor was unpopular with some, described as 'pompous', but Braddon was described as a 'fervent follower and admirer'[132] and had admired his long sermons for some time, described by William as:

> scholarly, eloquent, and cordially sympathetic, (they) pleased her from their very beginning to their almost unreachable end. (...) she listened with a kind of sweet gravity and gentle approval.[133]

Whenever possible William, and Harry Nye Chart, would sit apart from his mother, up in the church gallery, and then sneak out to play on the river bank, returning in time to meet Braddon as she came out.

It would be incorrect to suggest that Braddon's reviews were universally bad; reprints often carry words of praise, especially from the provincial press. There was also a long and complimentary article about her in the influential *Dublin University Magazine* in 1870 which defended her against all charges of immorality.[134] Although the unofficial 'Queen' of sensation fiction, Braddon was also much influenced by, and greatly contributed to, other, related cultural forms of the period. These will be the focus of my next chapter.

Chapter Three Footnotes

1. *Era*, 20 October 1861, p.11.
2. R.F. Stewart, *...And Always a Detective: Chapters on the History of Detective Fiction* (Newton Abbot: David and Charles, 1980), p.41.
3. Stewart, p.44 and p.65. The quotation from 'The Queen's English', *Edinburgh Review*, 1864, is also quoted by Lyn Pykett in her history of the sensation novel, *The Sensation Novel from the Woman in White to the Moonstone* (Plymouth: Northcote House, 1994), p.3.
4. Robert Lee Wolff, 'Devoted Disciple: The Letters of Mary Elizabeth Braddon to Sir Edward Bulwer Lytton 1862-1873', *Harvard Library Bulletin*, vol. 12, 1974, p.13. Letter from Braddon to Bulwer Lytton, 13 April 1863, p.13.
5. P.D. Edwards, *Dickens's 'Young Men': George Augustus Sala, Edmund Yates and the World of Victorian Journalism* (Aldershot: Ashgate, 1997), p.74 notes that Braddon was paid half as much per page than Sala for her *Temple Bar* contributions, even though *Lady Audley's Secret* and *Aurora Floyd* had outsold anything Sala had written.
6. Joseph Hatton, 'Miss Braddon at Home. A Sketch and an Interview', *London Society*, January 1888, p.23.
7. J.B. Buckstone to Braddon, 12 March 1866, Wolff collection.
8. Clive Holland, 'Fifty Years of Novel Writing. Miss Braddon at Home', *Pall Mall Magazine*, November 1911, p.707.
9. Percy Fitzgerald, *Memoirs of An Author* 2 vols (London: Richard Bentley, 1895), I, pp.280-281.
10. Wolff, *Sensational Victorian*, p.437.
11. E.E. Wilde, *Ingatestone and the Essex Great Road* (Oxford: Humphrey Milford, 1913), p.303:

> Miss Braddon laid the scene of her thrilling novel, *Lady Audley's Secret*, at Ingatestone Hall. Her description of Audley Court is, in the main, a correct description of the Hall, though she is in error in stating that the place had at one time been a convent. Miss Braddon stayed in the vicinity whilst writing the book, and reproduces in it a very good picture of the neighbourhood. Perhaps the scene in the lime-walk was suggested to Miss Braddon by the story of William H.F., eleventh Baron Petre, and his wonderful escape from a tragic death under that avenue.

The Post Office Directory listed the residents of Ingatestone, adding the house was 'occupied by several Roman Catholic families; attached is a chapel with a resident priest.' In his introduction to *Aurora Floyd*, P.D. Edwards surmises, from a letter Braddon wrote to Edmund Yates, that she may have considered becoming a Catholic in the early years with Maxwell. Judging by her letter to Bulwer Lytton on the death of her mother she did not consider herself a Catholic by then.

12. Sawyer went to London in 1861 to work for Maxwell. The *Brighton Herald*, 17 May 1862, p.4 revealed that Sawyer was editing *Twice a Week* and contributing the serials *The Flower Girl; A Romance of Real Life* and *Daisy Thorne; or, The Grimwood Mystery*. This magazine, and its successor *Every Week*, where Sawyer contributed *Dead Men Tell No Tales, A Story of London Life*, were run from Maxwell's office at 122 Fleet Street. Unlike the *Halfpenny Journal*, *Every Week* (which cost one penny per issue) refused to take readers' 'matrimonial requests'. Sawyer's anonymous serials were similar in style to those of Braddon's in the *Halfpenny Journal*, and he also contributed serials to the later version of the *Welcome Guest*, including *Jessie Ashton, The Adventures of a Barmaid*. All of Sawyer's serials were published anonymously. That Sawyer left Brighton to work for Maxwell is confirmed in H.C. Porter, *The History of the Theatres of Brighton 1774 to 1886* (Brighton: King & Thorne, 1886), p.132.

13. Judy Mckenzie, ed., *Letters of George Augustus Sala to Edmund Yates* (Queensland: Victorian Fiction Research Guides 19-20, Department of English, University of Southern Queensland, 1993), Sala to Yates, 16 May 1861, p.93.

14. George R. Sims, *Among my Autographs* (London: Chatto & Windus, 1904), pp.113-114. In an earlier article, 'My First Book', George Sims stated he succeeded in having a poem published in the *Halfpenny Journal*, and that the encouraging note from the editor was published in the *Welcome Guest* (in the years when it was published at a halfpenny) - so Braddon's conversation with Sims may have applied to the latter magazine. Almost certainly Fanny Braddon was the editor of both. Readers assumed the editor of the *Halfpenny Journal* was a man, but Fanny Braddon mentioned on at least one occasion in replies to readers that she herself was of Irish birth and another reply described a cook with a tame rat – matching that of her own cook many years earlier, Sarah Hobbs. She also wrote the 'Notices for Correspondents' for the later years of the *Welcome Guest*. Previously it has been believed that Maxwell sold this magazine, and that he and his writers had no more to do with it (he had announced his staff of writers had gone to write for *Robin Goodfellow*). This may have been a ruse to hide assets from his creditors. A further four volumes appeared, 1861-1864, at first seemingly to be under the ownership of George Vickers at Angel Court, the Strand. These four volumes followed the format and style of the *Halfpenny Journal*, and each issue cost a halfpenny (the previous format had cost one penny). The serials were mainly published

anonymously or under pseudonyms. Sawyer wrote for it, as did another Maxwell regular Percy B. St. John, and Sala's *Baddington Peerage* was reprinted as a serial. Possibly Braddon contributed, but if she did she did not use her 'by the author of *The Black Band*' byline. In a letter of December 1862 quoted in this book, Braddon told Bulwer Lytton that she was writing fiction for penny and halfpenny magazines, which would suggest she did write serials for another of Maxwell's cheap publications. A writer to *Notes and Queries* (Mac., 8 May 1915, p.366), writing about *The Black Band*, commented that the 'Bohemian underworld' of the early 1860s thought they detected Braddon's hand in the '*Welcome Guest*, and other periodicals which brilliantly signalized the remission of the Paper Duty.' The most frequent pseudonymous author of serials in the later version of the *Welcome Guest* was Lord Claude Fortescue, author of *Fanny Wyndham; or, Modern Life in London* and *The Black Farm; or, The Idiot Witness*. The first clue of Maxwell's continued involvement in the *Welcome Guest* comes from the fact that readers were asked to write with their problems to the editor at 122 Fleet Street – Maxwell's business address and the same address as the editor of the *Halfpenny Journal*. The *Welcome Guest* continued to promote the *Halfpenny Journal*, and vice versa. By October 1863 the address of the proprietor is 4 Shoe Lane (one of Maxwell's business addresses) and Vickers is described as the printer. More conclusive evidence is provided in the last issue which carried the first part of the serial *The Banker's Secret* by 'the author of "The Black Band" '. In the following issue, 17 December 1864, the *Welcome Guest* was incorporated into the *Halfpenny Journal*.

15. The entry for 26 Mecklenburg Square in *Webster's Royal Red Book* was left blank for some time, although Braddon and Maxwell were living there by the time of Gerald's birth, and Maxwell is not listed until April 1863. *Boyle's Court Guide* begins to list John Maxwell as the resident of 26 Mecklenburg Square in January 1863, and by January 1864 they would have been annoyed to be listed as 'John Maxwell and Mrs. M.E. Braddon.' Braddon mentioned the incident with the cook to Lady Monckton in 1913, letter in the Richmond Local Studies Collections, adding that she had been unable to breast feed and the monthly nurse's 'lapse from strict morality' (about which the cook had taunted her) meant 'she was worth a pound a week as G.M.'s larder'.

16. *Court Journal*, 8 March 1862, p.234.

17. *Court Journal*, 5 July 1862, p.639.

18. William Tinsley, *Random Recollections of an Old Publisher* 2 vols. (London: Simpkin, Marshall & co., 1900) II, p.56.

19. *Court Journal*, 11 October 1862, p.978.

20. The term 'Queen of the circulating libraries' is printed in the adverts of many Braddon yellowbacks, attributing the quote to the *World*.

21. 'Our Weekly Gossip', *Athenaeum*, 28 May 1864, p.743.

22. Monica Correa Fryckstedt, *On the Brink: English Novels of 1866* (Uppsala, Sweden: University of Uppsala, 1989), p.46.

23. This is a frequent complaint in reviews in the *Athenaeum* of early Braddon novels.

24. Braddon to Sala, undated, Wolff collection.

25. 'Henry Dunbar', *Sixpenny Magazine*, vol. VIII, 8 June 1864, p.84.

26. Georgie Braddon to Fanny Braddon, 16 September 1863, Wolff collection.

27. Robert Lee Wolff, *Nineteenth Century Fiction: A Bibliographical Catalogue* 5 vols (New York: Garland, 1981), I, p.152, 'the preposterously low rates paid by Belgravia to contributors other than MEB'.

28. 'Rita' (Mrs. Desmond Humphries), *Recollections of a Literary Life* (London: Andrew Melrose. 1936), p.46.

29. Robert Lee Wolff, *Sensational Victorian: The Life and Fiction of Mary Elizabeth Braddon* (New York and London: Garland, 1979), pp.134-135.

30. Rita, pp.43-44.

31. Mckenzie, Sala to Edmund Yates, c. January 1862, p.99.

32. Mckenzie, letters from Sala to Yates, pp.91-92.

33. Mckenzie, Sala to Yates, September 1861, p.96.

34. For example see the original contract between Braddon and Tinsley for *Aurora Floyd*, dated 20 October 1862, in which 'Mary Elizabeth Braddon of 26 Mecklenburgh Square' is described as 'Spinster and Author.' Maxwell signed the contract as a witness. Wolff, *Nineteenth Century Fiction*, 625f.

35. Frederick Boase, *Modern English Biography* (1921; repr. London: Frank Cass, 1965), vol. VI. Boase states that on the suspension of payments, Maxwell's copyright and stock were valued at the not inconsiderable sum of £23,500. He mortgaged *Temple Bar*, *Welcome Guest* (on which he had lost £2000), *St. James's Magazine* and the *Halfpenny Journal* to Mr. Norris who acted as guarantor to the creditors when he 'surrendered his security' for £6000. According to Boase, Maxwell 'executed a deed of assignment of all his estate and effects' on 1 December 1862.

36. Mckenzie, undated letter from Sala to Yates, p.100. Major Murray was involved in a famous trial in 1861, having killed a rival in self defence. Richard Altick has written a book on the case.

37. M.E. Braddon, *The Doctor's Wife* (London: Maxwell, 1864; repr. London: Ward, Lock & Tyler, c.1867), p.10.

38. For example, Elaine Showalter, 'Family Secrets and Domestic Subversion: Rebellion in the Novels of the 1860s', pp.101-116 in Anthony S. Wohl (ed.), *The Victorian Family* (London: Croom Helm, 1978). Lyn Pykett, *The Improper Feminine: The Women's Sensation Novel and the New Woman Writing* (London: Routledge, 1992), p.84. In later years, although Braddon still had the occasional 'bad' girl, (for example Sylvia in *Taken at the Flood*, 1874) and women with secrets, more often there are men with concealed pasts or crimes.

39. Edmund Yates (1831-1894) wrote a number of interesting novels, including the sensational *A Silent Witness* (1875) which has some similarities to a Braddon novel, with the heroine concealing her father's criminal actions.

40. Fryckstedt, p.57, quotes the *Athenaeum*, 17 February 1866, p.233.

41. Henry Mansel, 'Sensation Novels', *Quarterly Review*, vol. CXIII, April 1863, p.488.

42. W.F. Rae, 'Miss Braddon', *North British Review*, vol. XLIII, p.203. The Archbishop's words were widely quoted, and as late as 1883 John Maxwell thought it was worthwhile printing on business circulars, a sermon given by the Reverend W. Benham on 4 March 1883 at St. Stephen's Church, South Kensington. Praising sensation novels, and condemning those who classed them immoral, Benham concluded, 'I know an aged Prelate, whose praise is widely spread in the Church for his contributions to Sacred Literature, and who is venerated by all who love him for his piety and saintliness, who declares that the writings of the chief of these novelists – I mean MISS BRADDON – are among the best of the works of fiction.'

43. Hatton, p.28.

44. Sue Lonoff, *Wilkie Collins and His Victorian Readers: A Study in the Rhetoric of Authorship* (New York: AMS Press, 1982), pp.27-29 quotes 'A Petition to the Novel-Writers', *Household Words*, 6 December 1856, pp.481-485.

45. Douglas Cook, 'Eleanor's Victory', *Saturday Review*, vol. XVI, 19 September 1863, p.396.

46. Mansel, p.491.

47. M.E. Braddon, *Lady Audley's Secret* (London: Tinsley, 1862; repr. Oxford: Oxford University Press, 1987) p.2.

48. 'Our Female Sensation Novelists', *Christian Remembrancer*, vol. XLVI, 1863, p.210.

49. Mansel, p.486.

50. 'Elopement of a Lady of Fortune', *Brighton Guardian*, 20 October 1858, p.5. 'Miss Braddon and Hull', *Hull Daily News*, 6 February 1915, p.4, stated *Aurora* Floyd 'was founded (it is said) on an incident which occurred at a mansion situated in the western outskirts of Hull.'

51. Braddon to Mr. (George?) Sims, 4 November 1897, Wolff collection.

52. Rae, p.196.

53. Jenny Bourne Taylor, *In the Secret Theatre of Home: Wilkie Collins, sensation narrative, and nineteenth century psychology* (London: Routledge, 1988), p.1 quotes Henry James, 'Miss Braddon', *The Nation*, 9 November 1865, p.594.

54. 'Miss Forrester', *Athenaeum*, 7 October 1865, p.466. *Miss Forrester* was published by Tinsley.

55. F.E. Paget, *Lucretia, or, The Heroine of the Nineteenth Century* (London: Joseph Masters, 1868), pp.297-299.

56. Richard Altick, *Victorian Studies in Scarlet* (New York: Norton, 1970), p.79.

57. 'Homicidal Heroines', *Saturday Review*, vol. XXI, 7 April 1866, pp.403-404.

58. Jeanne Fahnestock, 'Bigamy: The Rise and Fall of a Convention', *Nineteenth Century Fiction*, vol. 136, 1981, p.58.

59. Fahnestock, p.47.

60. Fahnestock, p.55.

61. 'The Road Murder', *Saturday Review*, 29 April 1865, vol. XIX, p.496.

62. Altick, p.189, quotes a letter from James to criminologist William Roughead, 16 June 1914.

63. Mansel, p.501.

64. *Beverley Recorder*, June - July 1857.

65. Mary Hartman, *Victorian Murderesses* (London: Robson Books, 1977; repr. 1985), p.84 quotes *Daily Express*, 11 July 1857.

66. Hartman, p.84.

67. Mansel, p.512.

68. M.E. Braddon, *The Story of Barbara* (London: Maxwell, 1880; repr. London: Maxwell, c.1881), pp.156-157.

69. Altick, p.133.

70. M.E. Braddon, *Aurora Floyd* (London: Tinsley, 1863; repr. London: Virago, 1984), p.244.

71. George Augustus Sala, 'The Cant of Modern Criticism', *Belgravia*, vol. IV, November 1867, p.53.

72. Wilkie Collins, *Armadale* (1866; repr. London: Penguin, 1995), footnote by John Sutherland p.696.

73. Bernard Falk, *The Naughty Seymours* (London: Hutchinson, 1940), p.209.

74. 'Miss Braddon', *Daily Telegraph*, 4 October 1913, p.9.

75. This notebook is in the Wolff collection.

76. 'Miss Braddon', *Daily Telegraph*, 4 October 1913, p.9.

77. Mrs. Oliphant, 'Novels', *Blackwood's Edinburgh Journal*, vol. CII, September 1867, p.264.

78. Paget, p.305

79. 'A Conscientious Authoress', *World*, 16 September 1874, pp.13-14. The essay was probably intended as a critically supportive gesture by Yates after the death notices which had made clear Braddon and Maxwell were not married, and it goes on to emphasise that her novels are suitable reading for anyone: '(the) genuinely healthy tone of Miss Braddon's writing (...) she never writes a line which the most puritanic of parents would wish to keep from the eyes of the most innocent of daughters.'

80. Wolff, *Nineteenth Century Fiction*, vol. I, p.326, quoting Charlotte Yonge, 22 December 1865, quoted from *Notes and Queries*, September 1970, p.341.

81. Alan Walbank, *Queens of the Circulating Library* (London: Evans Brothers, 1950), p. 154.

82. Guinevere L. Griest, *Mudie's Circulating Library and the Victorian Novel* (Newton Abbot: David and Charles, 1970), p. 146.

83. 'Mudie's Library', *Leisure Hour*, 1886, p.188.

84. Mrs. Oliphant, 'Novels', p.264.

85. Edmund Yates, *Edmund Yates: His Recollections and Experiences* 2 vols (London: Richard Bentley, 1884) II, p.172.

86. Mrs. Oliphant, 'Novels', p.264.

87. Fryckstedt, p.110.

88. Michael Sadleir, *Things Past* (London: Constable, 1944), p.93.

89. Rae, p.190.

90. 'John Marchmont's Legacy', *Athenaeum*, 12 December 1863, p.792.

91. The name and year of birth of Braddon's son Francis was unearthed during the research of Norman Donaldson and Garry Hey for Donaldson's introduction to *Lady Audley's Secret* (New York: Dover, 1974). Donaldson, p.xi, states that Francis was born in Chelsea in 1863. Francis Maxwell was christened in January 1863 at St. Anne's, Soho.

92. Straus instituted a search for Sala's marriage certificate for the period Sala claimed he married without success. Mrs. J.E. Panton, the daughter of William Powell Frith, wrote in one of her gossipy volumes of memoirs that a marriage did take place, but not until much later. Panton provides an interesting account of her father's bohemian friends, including Edmund Yates and his wife. Mrs. J.E. Panton, *Leaves From a Life* (London: Eveleigh Nash, 1908), p.170.

93. M.E. Braddon, 'A Modern Confessor', *Pall Mall Magazine*, vol. I, 1893, pp.469-482.

94. Lonoff, p.228, quotes a letter from Collins to Stephen Schlesinger, 26 August 1888, written from Ramsgate where he was living as William Dawson with his 'morganatic family'.

95.. All of Braddon's children were born before her marriage: Gerald Melbourne Maxwell (1862-1933), Francis Ernest Maxwell (1863-1866), Fanny Margaret Maxwell (1863-1955), William Babington Maxwell (1866-1937), Winifred Rosalie Maxwell (1868-1899) and Edward Henry Harrington Maxwell (1870-1933). Both Gerald and William became writers in their own right.

96. Maggie to Fanny Braddon, 3 April 1866, Wolff collection.

97. Maggie to Fanny Braddon, 17 July 1868, Wolff collection.

98. Elaine Showalter, *A Literature of Their Own* (1977; revised London: Virago, 1982), p.26 quotes W.R. Greg, 'The False Morality of Lady Novelists', *National Review*, vol. VII, 1859.

99. 'Homicidal Heroines', *Saturday Review*, vol. XXI, 7 April 1866, p.404.

100. Cook, p.396.

101. Wolff, 'Devoted Disciple', Braddon to Bulwer Lytton, 9 August 1866, p.138.

102. Braddon to Charles Kent, 26 November 1866, Wolff collection.

103. 'From Our London Correspondent', *Western Morning News*, 30 November 1866, p.4.

104. M.E. Braddon to Charles Kent, undated letter, Wolff collection.

105. W. Clark Russell to M.E. Braddon, 13 April 1868, Wolff collection. Maxwell marked the letter 'replied 13'. The novelette was not published in *Belgravia*.

106. Yates, vol. II, p.62.

107. Percy Fitzgerald, *Memoirs of an Author* 2 vols (London: Bentley, 1895), I, p.277.

108. George Augustus Sala to Edmund Yates, 17 November 1873, quoted in McKenzie, p.157.

109. Braddon to George du Maurier, undated letter, author's collection.

110. George Augustus Sala, 'On the Sensational in Literature and Art', *Belgravia*, vol. IV, 1868, p.454.

111. Sala, 'The Cant of Modern Criticism', p.55.

112. Donald Thomas, *Swinburne The Poet in His World* (Oxford: Oxford University Press, 1979), p.46. For more on this aspect of Sala see P.D. Edwards, *Dickens's 'Young Men': George Augustus Sala, Edmund Yates and the World of Victorian Journalism* (Aldershot: Ashgate, 1997).

113. Sala, 'The Cant of Modern Criticism', p.48.

114. Ibid. p.53.

115. Ibid. p.54.

116. M.E. Braddon, *Hostages to Fortune* (London: Maxwell, 1875; repr. London: Ward, Lock & Tyler, c.1876.), p.90.

117. William Frith to Braddon, 25 March 1865, Wolff collection. In his autobiography, *Further Reminiscences* (London: Bentley, 1888) Frith quotes a letter from Braddon at the time when she was sitting. Although she did not appreciate people suggesting plots for her novels, she gave Frith a detailed description for a series of paintings about a wife's adultery in a later letter. (p.402).

118. Braddon to Alfred Elmore, undated c.1865, author's collection.

119. Braddon to Thomas Creswick, envelope dated 17 May 1865, Wolff collection.

120. Braddon to Charles Kent, 19 March 1867, Wolff collection.

121. Wolff, 'Devoted Disciple', Braddon to Bulwer Lytton, 3 November 1868, p.97.

122. Mckenzie, Sala toYates, Tuesday night, c. November 1868, p.118.

123. Wolff, 'Devoted Disciple', Braddon to Bulwer Lytton, 13 June 1872, p.149.

124. Ibid. p.148.

125. Richard Brinsley Knowles, privately printed circular, distributed after Mary Anne Maxwell's death, written on 28 September 1874.

126. Ibid.

127. Ibid.

128. 'Miss Braddon as a Bigamist', *New York Times*, 22 November 1874, p.1.

129. Maxwell, p.13.

130. Interview with the daughter of Braddon's maid Eliza by Rex Sercombe Smith, Sercombe Smith's notebook p.60, Wolff collection. Rex Sercombe Smith began a biography of Braddon in 1936, when he contacted W.B. Maxwell, and may have completed it in the 1950s, as a letter in the Wolff collection from Michael Sadleir in 1957 congratulates him on an essay which was to form the basis of a book. Wolff bought his research papers after he died.

131. Douglas Sladen, *My Long Life* (London: Hutchinson, 1939), p.197.

132. 'Death of Miss Braddon', *Richmond and Twickenham Times*, 6 February 1915, p.6.

133. Maxwell, pp.38-39.

134. C.F. Adams, 'Miss Braddon's Novels', *Dublin University Magazine* vol. LXXV, April 1870, pp.436-445. This essay was printed in its entirety at the back of Braddon reprints in the early 1870s.

Chapter Four
Melodrama, Penny-Part Fiction and French Realism: Mary Braddon's
Negotiation of Other Cultural Forms

Sensation fiction was deemed to be drawn from a disparate group of genres, and in the opinion of critics had been influenced by the worst aspects of French literature, stage melodrama and the working class fiction of the 'penny blood'. This unholy amalgam had created something which was both unhealthy to the development of literature, and also to the moral and intellectual development of the reader. This chapter seeks to explore the influences which helped to shape sensation fiction, and also Braddon's own contribution to melodrama, penny part fiction and French realism. Braddon brought these disparate literary strands together in a way that none of the other sensation novelists did: the links between melodrama were readily perceived by critics, and plays were deemed to be a detrimental influence on literature; she was virtually unique in that she wrote for the penny blood market at the same time as for the middle class subscribers to circulating libraries, the most influential of which was Mudie's;[1] and Braddon had an excellent knowledge of contemporary French literature, which she then tried to rework for a British audience.

The Influence of Melodrama on Sensation Fiction

As a former actress and aspiring playwright Braddon had first hand experience of the theatre, and because of this she understood plays and the effects on an audience of the emotional and moral polarity typical of the drama of the time. She had acted at London's most famous venue for melodrama, the Surrey Theatre, and in the course of her career had acted in some of the most famous melodramas of the period, including two based on novels, *It's Never Too Late to Mend* (after Charles Reade) and *Jack Sheppard* (after Ainsworth).

Sensation fiction has some elements in common with melodrama: it has dramatic incidents intended to thrill, suspense, villainy, virtue and strongly expressed emotion. But sensation fiction and melodrama are far from synonymous. Northrop Frye wrote in his *Anatomy of Criticism* that:

> In melodrama two themes are important: the triumph of moral virtue over villainy, and the consequent idealizing of the moral views assumed to be held by the audience (...) we come as close as it is normally possible for art to come to the pure self-righteousness of the lynching mob.[2]

Watching the stage melodrama the audience might be excited by the exploits of a Jack Sheppard or the wickedness of a villain, but their sympathies would be directed towards the virtuous who were so frequently persecuted. In sensation fiction the moral code is somewhat less clearly defined. The delineation of ethical dilemmas is more complex, in particular when dealing with crime and punishment, and the difference between good and evil characters is less clear; a villain is often as attractive a character as the hero, or their motivation makes them sympathetic as in *Henry Dunbar* (1864). In melodrama, characters are true to their types and are instantly recognisable to the audience, they will not depart from the convention of that character and according to Michael Booth in *English Melodrama*:

> Audiences could enjoy crime and villainy and horror in the full knowledge that the bright sword of justice would always fall in the right place (...) Evil can only destroy itself, no matter how hard it tries.[3]

In melodrama, part of the enjoyment for the audience stemmed from knowing what they would get. In sensation fiction the outcome is less certain. Nothing and nobody is necessarily quite what they seem and appearances should not be trusted. Women can be more assertive than is usual in fiction of the period, because plot devices enable them to take unusually active roles. In Braddon's novels the usual convention of punishing villainy is often transgressed when characters escape legal or moral justice; the form of a melodrama would demand suitable retribution for its climax. For example, when Hazlewood adapted *Lady Audley's Secret* for the stage, Lady Audley is not removed to an offstage asylum but has to die in full view of the audience.

Nonetheless, sensation fiction and its authors had close links to the stage. Charles Reade wrote his fourth play *Masks and Faces* (1852) with Tom Taylor, and adapted this into his first novel, *Peg Woffington* (1853). He often collaborated with Dion Boucicault (Braddon wrote *The Octoroon; or, The Lily of Louisiana* for one of her lower class serials to coincide with the first London production of Boucicault's *The Octoroon; or, Life in Louisiana*) and they also novelised their play *A Terrible Temptation* (1871). Wilkie Collins also adapted his works, such as *The New Magdalene* (1873), and initially planned *Man and Wife* (1870) for the stage before opting to write it as a novel. Collins was also well known for his theatrical collaborations with Dickens.

Even though she was doing nothing that others were not, it was Braddon who was criticised by reviewers for her staginess. Despite her abilities as a playwright she was not responsible for any of the adaptations of her 1860s novels. At the height of her fame as a sensation novelist in the 1860s she wrote a play for the Surrey, *A Model Husband* (1868), which had nothing to do with her sensation novels. As many of the adaptations of her most famous novels were pirated she received no financial benefit from them, which was always a source of annoyance to John Maxwell. Reviewers, however, accused Braddon of always having an eye to adaptation for the stage and of writing her novels accordingly to make them suitable for transfer. The *Athenaeum* reviewer of *Eleanor's Victory* (1863) wrote:

> Truth to nature is sacrificed for the sake of a stage effect, which would *act* well, and produce the startling brilliancy possible only behind the footlights. "Eleanor's Victory" bears indications of great ability turned to vulgar use. Instead of characters, we have stage properties, dresses and decorations which are *not* "altogether new for the occasion", as the playbills have it. Miss Braddon is throughout beset by the consciousness that her story *must* be adapted for theatrical purposes, and to her conviction of this necessity she has sacrificed all the higher qualities of a work of fiction.[4]

The unrealistic was condemned as theatrical, but at the same time sensation fiction was accused of being too realistic and the elements culled from 'real life' were deemed unacceptable in respectable literature. The contradiction therefore existed that sensation fiction concentrated on the sordid elements of real life within the fantasy world of theatre. The *Christian Remembrancer* echoed the dislike of the perceived theatrical elements in Braddon's work, arguing that the characters represented the artificiality of drama:

> the world is essentially a *stage* to Miss Braddon, and all the men and women, the wives, the lovers, the villains, the sea-captains, the victims, the tragically jealous, the haters, the avengers, merely players. We could extract pages, fit, as they stand, for the different actors in a melodrama, vehemently and outrageously unnatural.[5]

Characters in drama were types, not individuals, and the argument was that Braddon chose her types and wrote the plot around them with dialogue to match. Rae said of one of Olivia Marchmont's speeches from *John Marchmont's Legacy*, 'We doubt if, even at the Surrey theatre, anything like it was ever delivered.'[6] As I have already noted, the Surrey theatre was the premier venue in London for melodrama, and whether the critic knew Braddon herself had acted there in 1856 can only be guessed at. A derogatory article in the *Eclectic Review* hinted snidely at her past, in a way which suggested the writer was well aware of Braddon's career as an actress:

> It has more than once occurred to us, as a matter of speculation, whether Miss Braddon has not had a more practical acquaintance with the stage than that which is to be gained by becoming a spectator, however frequently, of theatrical performances.[7]

Admittedly some of the speeches in these novels are melodramatic, whether it is Eleanor in *Eleanor's Victory* (1863), on her knees and swearing vengeance against her father's persecutor, or in her halfpenny part novel *The Black Band* (1861-1852), when the villain Colonel Oscar Bertrand makes his debut in the first chapter as he emerges from behind a pillar to give an aside to the reader. Braddon seems to have been directly influenced by *Jack Sheppard* when she wrote *Three Times Dead* (1860, later retitled *The Trail of the Serpent*). Jack Sheppard's best friend is rescued as a baby thrown into the Thames and is named Thames by his adopted father. Braddon, of course, had played Thames Darrell herself when she was in Brighton, and in *The Trail of the Serpent* baby Slosh is also named after the river his new father rescues him from.

The influence was not all one way though, and the success of the sensation novel was also influencing the popular melodrama. Beth Kalikoff notes the shift towards 'aristocratic' settings in stage melodrama:

> The substitution of an aristocratic setting – the country estate of Sir Michael Audley – for the docks and shops of *Black-Ey'd Susan* (1829) and *The String of Pearls*.[8]

This was probably part of the process which led to the gentrification of the theatres, with high society set dramas and comedies leading to more middle class audiences, with the music halls catering for the working class. Managers could not afford to ignore the massive popularity of sensation fiction, and adjusted melodramas to suit the modern trend. There were three play versions of *Lady Audley's Secret* running in London in 1862 (and doubtless more touring at provincial theatres), and in 1863 there were five versions of *Aurora Floyd*. The most popular version of *Lady Audley's Secret*, and the one Braddon liked, was an unpublished adaptation by George Roberts. It starred Ruth Herbert, an actress manager and famous beauty who had modeled for Rossetti (an interesting irony considering the key Pre-Raphaelite portrait of Lady Audley in the novel, expressing very much Rossetti's images of potentially menacing female sexuality), and who played Eleanor in *Eleanor's Victory* the following year. Although Braddon and Maxwell were later to complain bitterly about all of the adaptations of her novels, at this time she took a great interest in Ruth Herbert's productions, writing to the actress in admiration at her 'grace and self possession. Your charmingly distinct articulation and ever-varying expression of your face', and especially enjoying the 'last shriek of mingled madness and despair at the end.'[9] She urged Edward Bulwer Lytton to go and see it, 'Will you, when you have a spare hour after dinner, drop into the St. James's & see Miss Herbert as Lady Audley. She is very good. Shall I send you a box *undated*? They would all be so honoured by your going.'[10] Braddon further patronised Miss Herbert by taking a box on the first night of *Eleanor's Victory*.

In C. H. Hazlewood's version Lady Audley was given red instead of blonde hair. Beth Kalikoff writes that red hair became a brief fashion for the evil woman in melodrama but:

> later, the female villains of melodrama returned to their traditional raven black tresses (...) Devil figures in medieval dramas and villains like Barabbas in the Jew of Malta always had red hair. Lady Audley's colouring, and that of similar female villains, may stem from this dramatic tradition.[11]

The change of hair colour further demonised Lady Audley, and in a symbolic way which the audience would understand, and this sort of visual symbolism was another area which set the theatre apart from the novel. Interestingly Braddon must have been aware of the symbolism of red hair for villains, because her villain Oscar Bertrand in *The Black Band* wears a red wig. However, in Hazlewood's version of *Lady Audley's Secret* much of the subtlety and suspense of the novel is lost. The melodrama is much cruder. The audience is left in no doubt that Lady Audley pushed her husband down the well, and her madness at the end is fully expressed as a mad soliloquy before dropping dead; not the 'latent' madness described by the doctor in the novel. Just as in one stage version of *East Lynne* when Lady Isabel and William are shown going to heaven on a cloud, the spectacle is all important: Hazlewood's play concludes with a tableau around the body. Villainesses in melodrama were always beautiful, beautifully dressed and bejeweled as part of the spectacle. Heroines of Braddon's fiction like Lady Audley, Aurora Floyd, Eleanor Vane and Olivia Marchmont provided a similar spectacle, with long passages describing their features, clothes, and particularly hair, all such traits suggesting empowerment. In melodrama female villainesses had usually been an appendage of the villain, but after Lady Audley they gained a prominence in their own right.

In contrast Michael Booth writes that the role of the virtuous heroine in melodrama was as:

> an enlargement and identification of that of the hero. Although the weaker vessel in one sense, in another her strength is far greater, and she is more persecuted, far more suffering.[12]

In sensation fiction this is usually quite different, the heroine is not a passive victim but active in her own right. An exception might be Maude in Sheridan Le Fanu's *Uncle Silas* (1864), as she sits and suffers and does not try very hard to escape. If there is a passive heroine in sensation fiction she is juxtaposed with an active one, the passive woman commanding far less of the reader's interest. For example, Laura and Marion in *The Woman in White* or Lucy and Aurora in *Aurora Floyd* and Olivia and Mary in *John Marchmont's Legacy* (1863) are paired in this way. In Braddon's 1860s novels a heroine is often empowered by suffering, she does not remain weak and passive, but can take action, as for example does Margaret in *Henry Dunbar* (1864).

Part of the snobbery of critics over the melodramatic elements in Braddon's novels may have stemmed from the knowledge that Braddon herself had been an actress. In novels like *A Strange World* (1875) and *Hostages to Fortune* (1875) she shows the great disapproval many people felt towards actresses. At the height of the popularity of 1860s sensation fiction Annie Edwardes chose to make a former actress a villainess who rivaled Lady Audley, in *Miss Forrester* (1865). It is perhaps impossible to be sure whether reviewers did know Braddon had acted under the name of Mary Seyton. Her early book of poems, *Garibaldi* (1861), contained poems she had written under the name of Mary Seyton for the *Brighton Herald* between 1859 and 1861; so that when they were republished under her own name it would have been easy for people to work out that Seyton and Braddon were one and the same person. As mentioned in the first chapter, the *Court Journal* had also revealed in a short paragraph Braddon's former identity, and this makes it likely that many critics did know.

Another element sensation fiction has in common with melodrama is the emotional language of some of its characters; words of love or hatred are released, not stifled. Michael Booth writes that:

> The lack of emotional and physical restraint in melodrama must have offered a satisfying release for all kinds of feeling, and the

removal of controls operating oppressively in real life may have been another cause of popularity.[13]

Restraint in the sensation novel is often the cause of the secret on which the plot turns or the cause of much misery, but the reason for the restraint has been the strictures of society. Those who do speak are punished for it; for example in *John Marchmont's Legacy*, Olivia Marchmont's life is ruined because she cannot declare her love for a man. But when she does declare herself she is then reviled by him, because to do so is a masculine prerogative. The only time she can express herself forcibly over her ambitions and frustrations is within the private sphere of her mind, or at times of near madness. It was this emotional release and freedom of expression that some critics found objectionable about the sensation novel, as well as the introduction of the improbable.

Braddon herself seems to have been irresistibly drawn to melodramatic situations even when she when she was writing her 'serious' fiction. Just as melodrama was a term of abuse when applied to a novel, even now when a novel is described as having melodramatic situations or dialogue, it is not quite thought equal to the realistic and that one has to apologise for it in some way. Even Braddon's biographer Robert Lee Wolff preferred to extol the merits of *Ishmael* (1884), *Joshua Haggard's Daughter* (1876) and *The Cloven Foot* (1879) to those novels which are more obviously sensational. I would argue that it is Braddon's use of popular culture and her fondness for melodrama that partly makes her such an enjoyable writer to read.

Michael Booth, in *English Melodrama*, gives a list of typical melodrama titles, titles which often promise a mystery:

Coelina, or The Child of Mystery, The Woman With Two Husbands, The Man With Three Faces, Thérese, or the Orphan of Geneva, The Madwoman of Wolfenstein.[14]

These are very similar to the sort of titles used for working class fiction sold in weekly penny parts, and *Lady Audley's Secret* would not seem out of place amongst them. Many of Braddon's novels were rushed on to the stage in the 1860s, including some of her lower class anonymous fiction. *The Black Band* was swiftly adapted in London at the Pavilion theatre, Whitechapel, and in Liverpool, and it was recommended to the readers of the *Halfpenny Journal* while the serial was still appearing. The editor replied to one correspondent:

Dicky Sam of Liverpool. – Thanks for your information. We were not aware that the dramatic version of "The Black Band" had been produced at Liverpool with so much success. It has been played at the London theatres with equal popularity.[15]

This shows that rather than one sphere especially affecting another there was a great deal of cross fertilisation. In London *The Black Band* was staged at the Pavilion Theatre, Whitechapel, and the theatre must have had some kind of arrangement with the *Halfpenny Journal* as their play *Cora; or, The Octoroon Slave of Louisiana* (an original work, but intended as a 'spoiler' before Boucicault's *The Octoroon* opened in London) provided the inspiration for Braddon's *The Octoroon; or, The Lily of Louisiana*.[16] As was mentioned in the first chapter, one melodrama Braddon appeared in at Brighton in February 1860 was called *Quicksands and Whirlpools* which was based on a serial by Percy B. St. John in the lower class magazine the *London Journal*, and Adelaide Calvert also adapted several such serials for the stage. Braddon used melodrama plots and titles for her working class fiction, and when she wrote *Oscar Bertrand; or, The Idiot of the Mountain* (1863-1864), she took the title *The Idiot of the Mountain* from a melodrama by W.E. Suter performed at the Surrey Theatre in 1861.

The Influence of Working Class Fiction and Braddon's Own Contribution to the 'Literature of the Kitchen'

In December 1862 Braddon wrote confidentially to her literary mentor Edward Bulwer Lytton:

> P.S. I do an immense deal of work which nobody ever hears of, for Half penny & penny journals. This work is most piratical stuff, & would make your hair stand on end, if you were to see it. The amount of crime, treachery, murder, slow poisoning, & general infamy required by the Half penny reader is something terrible. I am just going to do a little paracide (sic) for this week's supply.[17]

In that month the now famous and successful author of *Lady Audley's Secret* would have been completing the final monthly instalment of *Aurora Floyd* for *Temple Bar*, and the week's supply of 'paracide' must have been *The White Phantom*, a novel which also contained a character called Aurora, which was appearing anonymously in the *Halfpenny Journal; A Magazine For All Who Can Read*. At this time it was not widely known that Braddon was moonlighting amidst the mysterious world of lower class magazines and penny part novels; but the connection between sensation fiction and its humbler relations had already been made.

Early sensation fiction was seen to be influenced by working class fiction, and penny part fiction, known as penny bloods, were thought to be infiltrating respectable serials and three volume novels.[18] The *Westminster Review*, in its review of Collins's *Armadale* in 1866, declared:

> now we have a Sensational Mania (...) its virus is spreading in all directions, from the penny journal to the shilling magazine to the thirty shillings volume.[19]

This image of a virus with a contaminating influence was common. The noble art of literature, which was meant to illuminate, was being cheapened and was becoming a form driven only by an urge to entertain. Worse still, the influence was from working class entertainment. Working class readers were seen as mysterious and incomprehensible by the middle class journals, and were dubbed 'The Unknown Public' by Wilkie Collins.[20] The cheap penny bloods, especially those from the 1840s and 1850s, seethed with crime and shocking incident. One example is G.W.M. Reynolds's *Mysteries of the Court of London* (sold in weekly parts from 1849 until 1856) which, with its high life intrigues and murderous women, may have paved the way for Collins, Braddon and Ouida. This massive work by Reynolds was inspired by the works of Eugene Sue, particularly *The Mysteries of Paris*. The influence of French authors such as Sue, Dumas and Scribe, then, appeared in penny fiction almost twenty years before the French influence of authors like Zola in the middle class fiction of George Moore. According to Louis James, 'from about 1844 the main outside influence on English lower-class fiction was from France.' James also notes that Paul de Kock, for example, was mostly read by the lower classes because he was considered too coarse and indecent for loftier taste.[21] The advantage of French fiction from a publisher's point of view was that it was cheaper to pay for a translation than for an original work. The numerous translations of works like Sue's *The Wandering Jew* suggests that these French novels were very popular with the unknown public.

By the 1860s the home grown penny part novel had taken over more or less, with many British authors, such as James Rymer, working on as many as ten novels at a time. These works were characterised by numerous incident, and sensation fiction was accused of doing the same thing; but the penny dreadfuls were much cruder and genuinely do have an almost complete reliance on action over characterisation. They consisted of about five pages per week, with the text set in double or triple columns, and a crude woodcut appeared at the top of each issue. There are numerous short paragraphs, little in the way of description or characterisation, and dialogue takes up most of the page (as authors were paid by the line, dialogue was the easiest way to fill a page). When penny part fiction was not published in a journal, but on its own, an instalment would end in the middle of a sentence to make sure it was purchased the following week.

As a child Braddon had enjoyed reading such penny part fiction, as her mother's cook, Sarah Hobbs, supplied her with copies of Reynolds's magazine. This must have stood her in good stead for her first works of fiction. Braddon's first novel *Three Times Dead; or the Secret of the Heath* (1860, soon re-titled and reissued as *The Trail of the Serpent*) appeared in penny parts in Beverley. Her instructions had been to create a heady mix of popular authors, including the pioneer of English penny fiction, Reynolds:

> The Beverley printer suggested that my Warwick Lane serial should combine, as far as my powers allowed, the human interest and genial humour of Dickens with the plot-weaving of G.W.M. Reynolds.[22]

The style was influenced by Dumas in its high society Parisian episodes and by Dickens with the town being called Slopperton-on-the-Sloshy and its attempt at comic characters. The setting is partly working class, and it is these characters who are most sympathetic, in part catering for its audience. It is crammed full with impossible incident. None of the characters are terribly well developed, and coincidences abound: twins separated at birth, assumed identities, poisonings, characters thought dead not dead. The villain Jabez North shares the characteristic of later Braddon characters in that he seems to be a pillar of the community, but he is a wicked man who has been able to pass as the epitome of respectability. That staple of sensation fiction, the lunatic asylum, also appears, and if one wishes to trace Braddon's progression as a novelist increasingly interested in naturalism one could compare the stereotyped depiction of the lunatic asylum and its inmates (who all fancy themselves to be famous people) to that in *Strangers and Pilgrims* (1873); in the later novel the heroine has two mental breakdowns, one after the death of her baby and the second after meeting her old lover, and the novel impresses with its detailed and realistic asylum scenes and portrayal of mental illness. By 1873 Braddon had undergone the trauma of losing a child and a nervous breakdown after the death of her mother, and the serious note and greater insight in her fiction probably derives from some of the changes in her own life. When *Three Times Dead* was renamed *The Trail of the Serpent* and reissued for the second time in book form in London in 1866, the *Spectator*, recognising its origins, and admitting Braddon's subsequent improvement as a novelist, pointed out the similarity of such fiction to stage melodrama, adding neither genre was equal to real literature:

> We dare say they would dramatise well for a suburban theatre, under the title of *The Bloodstained Usher; or, The Mysterious Murder of Marwood*, but they bear no relation whatever to literary art.[23]

John Maxwell saw the 'unknown public' as a new and ready market for magazines, and the first volume of the *Sixpenny Magazine*, which serialised *Lady Audley's Secret*, was dedicated to Gladstone for repealing paper taxes and so allowing such cheap magazines. Maxwell also founded several ephemeral magazines which serialised lower class fiction in the early 1860s: the *Halfpenny Journal* (1861-1864), *Twice a Week* (1862) and *Every Week* (1862-1863). The first was edited by Fanny Braddon, doubtless with assistance from her daughter who was the chief serial writer, and the last two were edited by William Sawyer, Braddon's friend from her days in Brighton, and he wrote most of the serials for them.

Braddon and her mother used the 'Answers to Correspondents' section of the *Halfpenny Journal* to publicise the work of friends Braddon had made while on the stage; for example they did this in the second issue with William Sawyer, about whom the Editor replied to an alleged letter from a 'Brightonian':

> The sketches of Parisian life, now appearing in the *Brighton Herald*, are from the versatile pen of Mr. William Sawyer, who is not only a very charming poet and witty prose writer, but who is also a distinguished member of the Rifle Brigade.[24]

In other weeks Braddon plugged the appearance of a former Brighton company member, Margaret Eburne, now acting in Hull, and also the work of Wybert Rousby. Her serial *The Black Band* also contained a character called George Melville, presumably named after the popular handsome leading actor she had worked with at Brighton. Magazines like the *Halfpenny Journal* sought not just to entertain, but also to improve the education of its readers with advice on etiquette, education and handwriting. With this emphasis on self-improvement the penny bloods in journals tended to avoid the more salacious aspects of more notorious titles, such as James Rymer's *Varney the Vampire* (1847) and Thomas Prest's *The String of Pearls* (1846) which introduced the legend of Sweeney Todd. Because of the emphasis on 'self-improvement', more traditional morality prevails, with no lurid sex scenes or titillating woodcuts. This was certainly the case with the *Halfpenny Journal; A Magazine For All Who Can Read*, which was a co-production of Maxwell and Ward and Lock. It was set up to compete against the brand leader and pioneer in this area, the *London Journal*, and *Reynolds's Miscellany*. It closely copied the format of these magazines, but at half the price (and half the number of pages). Reynolds had been especially keen on the self-improvement aspect, but his journal also had a political edge with his strong Chartist sympathies. The *Halfpenny Journal's* advice page included a matrimonial section in which readers sent in details and asked the editor to find them a spouse. This was clearly extremely popular and today gives a wonderful insight into the aspirations and working habits of the 'unknown public'. The *Halfpenny Journal* also followed Reynolds's paternalistic attitude towards its readers, and morality is extolled in the fiction and non fiction. Hard work, honesty, and good behaviour is rewarded. Despite this, in many ways the plots would not have been considered moral enough by the standards of middle class fiction. In *The Black Band*, one of the heroines, Clara, escapes rape twice (once by her uncle), her friend Lolota becomes the mistress of a Marquis and, far from being punished, eventually marries him. Another heroine has an illegitimate child, and prostitution is mentioned rather than hinted at. These characters alone, along with a villainess called Lady Edith Vandeleur who makes Lady Audley look like a candidate for canonisation, would have sent a reviewer apoplectic if he had come across it in a three decker. Nearly all of the serials in the first two years of the *Halfpenny Journal* were written by Braddon anonymously, which must have saved Maxwell money as one assumes Braddon would not have needed payment once her career had taken off. Further savings were made by encouraging contributions from poetically inclined readers.

The longest of these lower class serials by Braddon was *The Black Band; Or, The Mysteries of Midnight* (1861-1862), written under the pseudonym Lady Caroline Lascelles and running for fifty two weeks at two chapters an instalment. This pseudonym was suggested, perhaps with mischievous intent, by Maxwell's editor Frederick Wraxall, but the name was dropped without explanation after eleven instalments, perhaps when Braddon and Maxwell realised that a real Lady Caroline Lascelles was very much alive, and 'a respectable Victorian grandmother.'[25] However, the intriguing pseudonym had already attracted the curiosity of readers, and the editor replied to a reader calling themselves Esholt: 'We are not permitted to enter into any details of the family of Lady Caroline Lascelles.'[26] The brief use of this pseudonym was to continue to haunt Braddon and Maxwell, although Maxwell himself claimed that the aristocratic nom de plume 'was discarded, as it was found that "fine words butter no parsnips".'[27] In common with other penny bloods there is an astonishing rapidity of incident, with numerous robberies, seductions, murders and plots. In her later novel *The Doctor's Wife* (1864) Braddon created Sigismund Smith, whose career echoes her own as he progresses from penny bloods to sensational three deckers. Smith describes his own novel in penny numbers, *The Smuggler's Bride*, proudly stating it 'teems with suicides':

> There's the Duke of Port St. Martin's, who walls himself up in his own cellar; and there's Leonie de Pasdebasque. the ballet-dancer, who throws herself out of Count Caesar Maraschetti's private balloon; and there's Lilia, the dumb girl, – the penny public like dumb girls, – who sets fire to himself from the – in fact, there's lots of them.[28]

The weekly format must have dictated much of the content, with the need to make sure the reader continued to buy succeeding issues.

At the centre of *The Black Band* is the Austrian Colonel Oscar Bertrand, the leader of the Black Band, a political organisation dedicated to robbery around the world. Membership is signified by a band of black on the member's left wrist. It is an early example of the sort of anarchy plots which became popular as a response to national paranoia towards the end of the century, most famously in Joseph Conrad's *The Secret Agent*. To leave or to betray the organisation is death, and the tentacles of the Band extend everywhere as Bertrand explains to Lord Lionel:

> "I am the centre of a system so vast in its operations, that it extends over the greatest part of civilized Europe. I am the captain of a company so large that there are men in it upon whose faces I have never looked, and never expect to look. It is a company which, though continually at war with society, can yet – secure in its internal strength and the unfailing prudence of its operations – afford to defy society year after year. Recall to your recollection some of those gigantic robberies which have startled the wealthiest cities of Europe – robberies in which a skill has been displayed partaking almost of the supernatural – robberies which have defied the determination and the perseverance of the cleverest police in

Europe, and which have remained undiscovered until this hour. Remember these, and you may form some idea of the resources of the mysterious company of which I speak."[29]

During Braddon's six month stay in Beverley, where she wrote *Garibaldi and Other Poems* (1860) at the behest of her patron, she had spent weeks poring, without enthusiasm, over books and papers about the struggle for Italian independence from the Austrians. Nevertheless, Braddon decided to use some of this material in *The Black Band*, and with her Garibaldian sympathies she naturally chose to make her villain an Austrian. At the time these secret societies were common, and had been from the beginning of the nineteenth century in Italy. The Black Band and the political society they work against in Italy, the Mountaineers who are fighting for Italian independence from the Austrians, were probably inspired by the Camorra in Naples which made money from extortion and robbery and thus financed its campaign of murder. Wilkie Collins had used a vengeful Italian secret society in *The Woman in White*; Count Fosco is assassinated by one, but the Black Band is portrayed as a threat to all of Europe. This theme of European insecurity was exploited sixteen years later when Vickers reissued the novel as an abridged yellowback, with an advertising blurb quoting a speech by Disraeli on the renewed danger of secret societies and their terrorist activities.[30]

The Black Band gives the reader a voyeuristic portrayal of decadent upper class life, intertwining the plot with the worthy working class. One of Braddon's sympathetic put-upon heroines is Clara Melville, a working class ballet girl who is the prey of a dissipated lisping aristocrat, Sir Frederick Beaumorris. Clara and Bertrand's long-suffering wife, Ellen Clavering, act as a contrast to the wicked Lady Edith Vandeleur who is locked up by her husband as a mad woman after she tries to poison him so she can marry Lord Lionel Willoughby. Lady Edith is a sister of Lady Audley, with her ambitions over-ruling morality, as well as one of her own crimes being bigamy. Lady Audley was of more humble origins, but Lady Edith is the daughter of an Earl. Both women present a beautiful exterior to the world (though Edith's is dark and dramatic, not insipid and babyish), which conceals inner evil. The reader is assured that any working class girl would be superior to Lady Edith in morality:

> "Goodness, virtue, truth!" she cried, with a sneer; "will those win me admiration or respect? No! I must be able to outdo them all in pomp and splendour, and then, though they may hate me, they will bow to me, and lick the dust under my feet."

If anybody who beheld this lovely creature (crowned with snow-white flowers, emblems of the purity which was a stranger to her guilty soul), could have known the secrets of her wicked heart, how loathsome would her grandeur and beauty have appeared!

How far before her the poorest cottage girl, walking barefoot over her native heath, whose heart could glow with a sincere affection, and whose soul could scorn a falsehood! (pp.21-22)

There are other similarities to *Lady Audley's Secret* with the confining of Lady Edith to Robert Merton's castle to save public face, and also because he assumes a wife trying to kill a husband must be mad, just as Lady Audley's assertiveness and self-motivation are attributable only to a mad woman. Lady Audley is confined to an asylum, 'Buried Alive' as the chapter is entitled, and Lady Edith is literally buried alive in the chapter 'The Burial of the Living'.

The worthy working class prevail and are leading characters in this and other Braddon bloods, such as *The Factory Girl* (1863). A fairy tale element tends to take over when they often turn out to be deposed aristocracy. However, just as would be the case with Lady Audley, it was the wicked characters who attracted the interest and admiration of the readers: the advice columns of the *Halfpenny Journal* are littered with corespondents using the nom de plumes of 'Lady Edith' and 'Oscar Bertrand'.

In the middle class three volume sensation novel, sympathies shift to suit the audience, the upper classes are infiltrated by the wicked governess Lady Audley and it is Aurora Floyd who is taken advantage of by the groom. Both spheres, however, are interested in what happens when the two worlds meet. In middle class fiction ordinary working class characters are of less importance as individuals, only in so far as they affect their social betters. At the height of 1860s sensation fiction the working class, usually in the guise of servant or police, signifies danger and lack of security in the middle class or aristocratic home.

Even when Braddon achieved success she still secretly contributed to the lower class market. The *Halfpenny Journal* was not ultimately successful as a publishing venture, folding after four years. Sigismund Smith, fictional author of such works as *The Smuggler's Bride* in *The Doctor's Wife* knew, just as his creator did, exactly what the penny dreadful reader demanded:

Sigismund Smith was the author of about half a dozen highly-spiced fictions, which enjoyed an immense popularity amongst the classes who like their literature as they like their tobacco – very strong. Sigismund had never in his life presented

> himself before the public in a complete form; he appeared in weekly numbers at a penny (...he) perhaps produced more sheets of that mysterious stuff which literary people called "copy" than any other author of his age. (pp.10-12)

He is paid one pound per page and, like Braddon, dreams of writing a great novel. Despite the sensational character of his fiction, his admirers are disappointed at how ordinary he is as a person. He writes for the publisher 'Bickers', which was clearly meant to be George Vickers, who later reissued *The Black Band* in 1877. When journals such as the *Athenaeum* discovered Braddon wrote for both, she received a great deal of criticism, not helped by Maxwell's attempts to deny that Braddon was the author of these or of those she wrote under the name of Babington White.[31] The *Athenaeum* chose to misread Braddon's humorous portrait of Sigismund Smith, accusing her of hypocrisy in condemning Sigismund for supplying to 'the lust of his ignoble readers', arguing his trade was the same as Braddon's.[32] Critics might like to think that such fiction was only enjoyed by the working class, but the appearance of similar features in middle class fiction proved otherwise. W. Fraser Rae in his 1865 article 'Sensation Novelists – Miss Braddon' in the *North British Review* commented that:

> Others before her have written stories of blood and lust, of atrocious crimes and hardened criminals, and these have excited the interest of a very wide circle of readers. But the class that welcomed them was the lowest in the social scale, as well as in mental capacity. To Miss Braddon belongs the credit of having penned similar stories in easy and correct English, and published them in three volumes in place of issuing them in penny numbers. She may boast, without fear of contradiction, of having temporarily succeeded in making the literature of the Kitchen the favourite reading of the Drawing Room.[33]

Many critics differed from Rae over the easy simplistic language, and thought she was a talented writer wasting her time on rubbish. Others delighted in spending half of their review berating her spelling and grammar, or finding obscure factual errors. Braddon had Sigismund Smith say "What the penny public want, is plot, and plenty of it; surprises, and plenty of 'em; mystery, as thick as a November fog." (p.40). The irony, as Braddon must have known, was that this had also proved to be the case at the middle class circulating libraries. Bored with novels which acted almost as conduct books for young ladies, they now enjoyed a plot with mystery and strong passions. That the middle class shared this delight was a constant source of annoyance to critics, and the author was blamed for supplying to such cravings. Braddon again made the point that there were similarities between the two markets when Smith reappears in *The Lady's Mile* (1866) as Sigismund Smythe, and like Braddon he is now a writer of three volume novels.

Penny bloods were prouder of their dependence on actualities than middle class fiction was. In penny parts if the fiction was based on real life this was something of a selling point. In the *Halfpenny Journal*, at the start of Braddon's *The Octoroon; or the Lily of Louisiana, A Story of the Present Day* (1861), the editor praised its authenticity and compared it to *Uncle Tom's Cabin*, knowing its working class readers would sympathise with slaves, especially now the Civil War had started:

> The Octoroon appeals straight to the heart and sympathies of every reader, however circumstanced, or wherever placed in our social system. Therefore, let all our Subscribers unite in helping us to make this Tale known: for, upon their co-operation may turn the mitigation of slavery, if not the total abolition of the hideous traffic in Human Beings that the exigencies of Slavery both foster and sustain.[34]

There was some two way traffic, from respectable literature to penny parts. James Payn and Collins were puzzled as to who the 'unknown public' actually were. Collins believed they were the newly literate classes, who needed to be educated into reading good books. In 1883 Thomas Wright tried to reclassify these readers, pointing out they were not wholly working class: many were schoolboys looking for exciting plots as he had done, others were the genteel poor who could not afford better, and some were young ladies whose family had just enough money for them not to have to go to work. Wright's findings are confirmed by the replies to readers in the *Halfpenny Journal*: the readers included schoolboys, clerks, reasonably well educated young women of the lower middle class, as well as those claiming an income of one hundred pounds per year. When they could afford to they would read middle class fiction, most having read Dickens and Bulwer Lytton. Sensation novelists were also great favourites when reprinted as yellowbacks:

> With the leading living novelists whose works run into fancy boards editions they are well acquainted, familiar as household words among them are *It is Never Too Late to Mend*, *Hard Cash*, *The Woman in White*, *No Name*, and the earlier works in the

Braddon series. Of recognised novelists, Miss Braddon was until within the last few years first favourite with the unknown public.[35]

Wright also comments on the love for Ouida and her overblown aristocrats amongst this audience, suggesting bloods were now imitating her;[36] however, this style had always existed in penny bloods and Ouida, who was notorious for her inaccuracies, probably is another example of penny part fiction brought to the middle classes.

A year after publication as a three decker, *Lady Audley's Secret* was serialised in the *London Journal*.[37] This was the longest running magazine (1845-1912) carrying fiction for the lower classes. In 1866 it reprinted *Aurora Floyd*, three years after its appearance as a three decker. This proves sensation fiction, even the same books, were being read by all strata of society. In 1849 J.F. Smith had been the star contributor of the *London Journal*, and it was he who brought the circulation to one hundred thousand per week. He aimed the magazine particularly at work-girls in the North.[38] The only obstacle for the lower classes was cost, they could not afford to subscribe to Mudie's, and so would have to wait until cheap reprints appeared.

In the British Library some of the original covers of the *Halfpenny Journal* are bound in with the issues of that magazine, and on these there are adverts for cheap paperbacks ('French style') of *The Lady Lisle* and *The Captain of the Vulture* by M.E. Braddon. As these adverts do not reveal that M.E. Braddon was the main contributor to the magazine, it shows that even at this early stage she was keeping her Braddon work separate from the hack work.

Sensation fiction, especially Braddon's, was condemned for encouraging immoral and even criminal behaviour in young women. The *Medical Critic and Psychological Journal* examined this issue in an article of 1863, and came to the conclusion that young ladies would not be harmed by their reading.[39] The fact that a medical journal was even discussing the issue at all shows how seriously the possibility was taken. The fear that women might become uncontrollable was soon joined by the argument that working class boys were becoming corrupted by penny part fiction. Much as modern films are blamed for the behaviour of the young, so penny bloods and dreadfuls were blamed for encouraging criminality in boys. In 1869 the journalist James Greenwood wrote of a prison governor who was so convinced of this that:

This is a fact generally known among the juvenile criminal population, and they never fail to make the most of it when the time comes. I went the rounds of his jail with this governor on one occasion when the 'boy wing' was occupied by about forty tenants, and in each case was the important question put, and in the majority of cases it was answered, 'It was them there penny numbers what I used to take in, sir,' or words to that effect; and the little humbug was rewarded with a pat on the head, and an admonition 'always to speak the truth.'[40]

In 1866 *The Wild Boys of London; or The Children of the Night* was published, a gripping story concerning boy criminals living in the sewers and their regular fights with the police.[41] When reissued some years later it was suppressed by the police halfway through its run because of fears that their behaviour was being emulated. Religious groups, such as the Religious Tract Society, soon joined the campaign and published rival cheap papers of stories to win readers away from sin. However, it is interesting that sensation fiction and penny fiction was seen as inflammatory to the behaviour and morals of two sections of society who were seen, in varying ways and degrees, to be about to rebel from their allotted spheres: women and the working class.

Braddon's Interest in and Use of French Fiction

Sensation fiction was also deemed to incorporate some of the worst vices of French literature, with a 'foreign' sensuality. Unlike the earlier gothic novel the action was not set in the faraway Italian castles of Mrs. Radcliffe. but in the heart of England. This in itself was contradictory to the accusation of foreignness levelled at sensation fiction. Wilkie Collins may have had a foreign villain, Count Fosco in *The Woman in White*, and so did Braddon with the Austrian Colonel Oscar Bertrand in *The Black Band*, but on the whole the settings of sensation novels could not be more English. There was, however, a definite influence from France; Wilkie Collins got his idea for *The Woman in White* from a French book of trials, and Braddon was probably the first British author to try to bring the influence of Flaubert to the reading public with *The Doctor's Wife* (1864), her adaptation of *Madame Bovary*. She was also interested in other French authors, like Balzac and Zola, but her admiration was also mixed with some ambivalence. Wilkie Collins was also an admirer of Balzac, writing an article on him for *Household Words* in 1859. Balzac was morally ambiguous and generally not thought to be in good taste. Even if French literature was admissible as art, it was essentially so foreign that its influence not only should not be seen in English literature, but could not because of the difference in national psyche. A review of Collins's *No Name* in 1863 confirmed the view that sensation fiction was influenced by French fiction, but could never be so wholly, because English fiction would have to leave so much out, especially in regard to sex:

> It is a plant of foreign growth. It comes to us from France, and it can only be imported in mutilated condition. Without entering on the relative morality or immorality of French and English novelists, one may say generally that, with us, vicissitudes of legitimate love and decorous affection; while in France they are based upon the working of those loves and passions which are not in accordance with our rules of respectability.[42]

Braddon had been encouraged to read Balzac by George Augustus Sala in the early 1860s, and they planned to collaborate on a novel which would use French and German sources for its inspiration, Hugo's *Les Miserables* and Goethe's *Faust* (the type of plagiarism Sigismund Smith calls a 'combination novel'). It would have been called *Dr. Forster*. Sala wrote to Maxwell:

> But if you want to resuscitate *Temple Bar* and make a tremendous hit, let Miss Aurora buckle to, and do with me my long contemplated and gigantic *duel* (sic) romance of Dr. Forster. It is the legend of Faust and Mephistopheles adapted to modern life, but with a concurrent legendary setting in Germany. (...) the *Misérables* would be the model and Goethe's *Faust* the plot, Aurora would be tremendous at dialogue and love-making, and the painting and decorations would belong to me. Done together in Fleet Street, the copy would never be late, we ought to give a lot every month.[43]

This project never came to fruition, perhaps because Sala's main interest in the collaboration was that Maxwell should let him off completing the serial *Captain Dangerous*. It was not until 1891 that Braddon wrote *Gerard or The World, The Flesh and the Devil*, based on *Faust* and Balzac's *La Peau de Chagrin*, although Sala wrote his version, *The Seven Sons of Mammon*, in 1862. Braddon's attempt was somewhat unsuccessful, although she was probably able to be more open about areas such as illegitimacy than she would have been if she had written it thirty years earlier. *Gerard* was set during the decadent 1890s of London. Unlike her earlier French inspired works, such as *Circe* (1867) which she had controversially plagiarised from Octave Feuillet's *Dahlia*, the adaptation is fully acknowledged within the text as Gerard constantly compares his experiences with the heroes of the two source works.

Braddon's interest in Balzac in the 1860s was reflected in a number of her early novels. *Birds of Prey* (1867) and *Charlotte's Inheritance* (1868) contain the same characters over six volumes, and Braddon may have had in mind Balzac's sequence novels. The villainous dentist, Philip Sheldon, rejects English novels because:

> the heroes of them were impracticable beings, who were always talking of honour and chivalry.[44]

Sheldon regains an interest in fiction when he takes up French novels, and he is impressed when he came across Balzac:

> He had been riveted by the hideous cynicism, the supreme power of penetration into the vilest corners of wicked hearts (...) "That man knows his fellows," he cried, "and is not hypocrite enough to conceal his knowledge or to trick out his puppets in the tinsel and rags of false sentiment in order that critics and public may cry, 'See, what noble instincts, what generous impulses, what unbounded sympathy for his fellow-creatures this man has!' " (vol. I, p.239)

Braddon greatly admired Balzac, and like the fictional Sheldon was bored with the domestic and honourably motivated characters of English fiction. Braddon, like others, initially saw Balzac as the 'high priest of the naturalistic school'[45] before the emergence of Flaubert and later still, Zola. In the sensation fiction of the 1860s, reading French novels usually indicates a moral failing, rather than just an adventurous taste in books. Robert Audley lays them aside when he becomes a citizen upholding law and the family. In *Birds of Prey* the chief villain reads them, as does the con-man Valentine Hawkhurst. But when Valentine renounces his wicked ways and falls in love with a pure and innocent girl, he finds Balzac no longer to his liking:

> "I'm sick of them all," he thought; "the De Beauseants, and Rastignacs, the German Jews, and the patrician beauties, and the Israelitish Circes of the Rue Taitbout, and the sickly self-sacrificing provincial angels, and the ghastly *vieilles filles*. Had that man ever seen such a woman as Charlotte, I wonder – a bright creature, all smiles and sunshine, and sweet impulsive tenderness; an angel who can be angelic without being *poitrinaire*, and whose amiability never degenerates into debility? There is an odour of the dissecting-room pervading all my friend Balzac's novels, and I

don't think he was capable of painting a fresh, healthy nature. (vol. II, p.49)

Like Robert Audley, Valentine becomes an accepted member of society and his French novels are laid aside. Braddon, while admiring Balzac personally, could not bring herself to go as far as to recommend him to her readers at this time. Later Braddon realised Balzac was not as revolutionary as she had originally thought, and that, unlike Zola, something of fantasy, the ideal and beauty, was retained:

> Balzac was not a realist in the modern sense of the word. He was an analyst but not a naturalist. The atmosphere of romance pervades all his books; (...) Let him descend ever so deeply into the gloomy basement of the social fabric there is always the counterbalance of beauty, luxury, refinement somewhere in the picture. There is always something to gladden the eye and soothe the senses.[46]

However, in the 1860s, Mrs. Oliphant felt that the French influence had been kept at bay until now. Writers were no longer practicing self-restraint:

> That corruption which has so fatally injured the French school of fiction has, it has been our boast, scrupulously kept away from ours. It was something to boast of. We might not produce the same startling effects; we might not reach the same perfection in art, which a draftsman utterly free of all constraints, and treating vice and virtue with equal impartiality, may aspire to; but we had this supreme advantage, that we were free to all classes and feared by none. Men did not snatch the guilty volume out of sight when any innocent creature drew nigh, or mature women lock up the book with which they condescended to amuse themselves, as they do in France.[47]

Even though she admitted it often meant sacrificing art, purity was more important. Paradoxically Oliphant suggested this restraint made the British freer because people had been used to discussing what they read in front of their family. She pointed to *Jane Eyre* as the beginning of all that was wrong now, with 'what advanced critics call her "protest" against the conventionalities in which the world clothes itself.'[48]

Braddon attempted to incorporate some of what she admired in French literature when she adapted Flaubert's *Madame Bovary* (1857) for a British audience in 1864. This was daring when one considers that even in France Flaubert's novel had been taken to court for immorality.

Braddon marked the publication of Flaubert's novel as a further step in the progression of French realism:

> The appearance of *Madame Bovary* opened new vistas and revealed wider horizons. The novelist of the old school was left a long way behind by the physiologist, the analytical student, the vivisectionist of the present. In cold blood and with a passionless pen Gustave Flaubert traces the degradation of a selfish and vain young woman.[49]

Set in the early 1850s, Braddon had to tone down the sensuous elements in *The Doctor's Wife*, her Madame Bovary, Isabel Sleaford, can no longer be a woman driven by her search for sexual passion, but a complete innocent whose naiveté allows her almost to become a man's mistress. She is in love with romance, but excludes sex as she thinks her worldly admirer only wants a romantic friendship in which literary appreciation will form a large part. Like Madame Bovary, Isabel has wasted many hours in the dangerous female pastime of reading, although these writers are no more dangerous than Bulwer Lytton, Thackeray and Dickens, and her dream is to be rescued from Camberwell by a duke. By making these respectable writers inflammatory to Isabel's imagination, Braddon was probably making a point: attributing such damaging influence on a young girl to the triumvirate rulers of nineteenth century fiction showed how ridiculous such claims were when they were made about her own work. If Braddon had been serious she would have had Isabel reading penny dreadfuls and French fiction (as Braddon's great friend Emma Robinson did in her novel *Madeline Graham*). Isabel's innocence is unconvincing, as the reader is asked to believe that a married woman who reads about and admires Steerforth (not David Copperfield) does not imagine that her lover will make any demands on her and will be content to swap books. Braddon insists that Isabel is too innocent to understand he wants her to run away with him and become his mistress:

> the possibility of deliberately leaving her husband to follow the footsteps of this other man, was as far beyond her power of comprehension as the possibility that she might steal a handful of arsenic out of one of the earthenware jars in the surgery, and mix it with the sugar that sweetened George Gilbert's matutinal coffee. (p.239)

Unlike Madame Bovary's lovers, Roland Landsell, an aristocratic poet, is sincerely in love with Isabel and would have married her had she been free. She certainly could not have taken a second lover like Madame Bovary did, of which, because it was devoid of love, Braddon wrote, 'The second liaison is gross and shameless.'[50] Because Braddon had to make Isabel an innocent if she was to remain acceptable as a heroine, she has to make the lover in love with her childishness. Isabel worships Roland as she would a hero in a novel, any passion on her part would have been inadmissible, unless at the end she became disfigured and died in a particularly grisly fashion. Moreover, in a further attempt to bring in a moral element, Roland has a penitent deathbed scene, when he retracts his atheism and takes all of the blame for his romance with Isabel, "She was a child, and I mistook her for a woman" (p.331). Braddon was well aware that she could not give her lovers a happy ending because of the disapproval of the critics, but this did not stop the readers of the serialisation in *Temple Bar* from hoping that they would. One admirer wrote from Ireland in reply to a letter from Braddon:

> (I) am counting the days till the September no. reaches our remote regions. I am *so* sorry for Roland & Isabel but I am sure you are right – & it would never do to sacrifice Public Opinion for the sake of ideal characters, tho' you make them so *real*, one feels sure they are living, & loving & suffering somewhere. If they may not be happy *together* I trust Roland doesn't marry Lady Gwendoline, that would be *too* much.[51]

Despite the difficulties of adapting the novel, Braddon worked harder on this than with any of her previous books, though as usual with serialisation at this time she was unsure how it would end until the last instalment. Braddon wrote to Bulwer Lytton after he had read the first instalment and guessed its origin:

> The idea of the Doctor's Wife *is* founded on "Madame Bovary" the style of which book struck me immensely in spite of it's (sic) *hideous* immorality. There seems an extraordinary Pre-Raphaelite power of description – a power to make manifest a scene in an atmosphere in a few lines – almost a few words – that very few writers possess – and a grim kind of humour equal to Balzac in its way.[52]

Naturally Braddon was protecting herself by adding that it was not unqualified approval she felt for Flaubert, but without the 'hideous immorality' it was no longer *Madame Bovary*, and the reader is asked to believe that the widowed Isabel spends the rest of her life spending the fortune she inherits from her lover on good works and becomes a sensible woman:

> useful, serene, almost happy (...) she is altogether different from the foolish wife who neglected all a wife's duties (...) the chastening influence of sorrow has transformed a sentimental girl into a good and noble woman – a woman in whom sentiment takes the higher form of universal sympathy and tenderness (p.348)

Wolff reads this as being her punishment, that she is still trapped in a dull life, although contemporary critics with their usual perversity insisted Braddon was rewarding the wicked woman. Doubtless the young and impoverished Isabel would have not been displeased at the idea of being a rich widow, but Braddon was hardly at liberty to condone this.

Where Braddon is most successful is depicting the empty and useless life of a girl who has not been educated, and Isabel's unhappiness manifests itself in depression or in fantasies of a better life. However, undeniably, the novel contains some of Braddon's finest writing to date, especially in her descriptions of everyday life in the early 1850s and in terms of characterisation. Apart from her early hack work it is her first attempt to describe lower middle class life, and scenes such as Isabel and her husband on honeymoon with nothing to say to each other and nothing in common are poignant. There is little of Flaubert's attention to country life and the doctor, George Gilbert, did not interest her deeply. He is good but dull: there are no descriptions of gory operations, and he could just as easily be a clerk or lawyer. Yet, it was this very aspect of Flaubert which so greatly appealed to Braddon:

> To such a story as this Gustave Flaubert lent the grace of his admirable style, a style in which every sentence was the result of intense thought and study, an almost religious devotion to art for arts sake. Every line is true and clear as the lines of a marble figure. (...) The story passes before the reader in a series of word pictures.[53]

In the end it was the situation of Madame Bovary which interested her most. Still Braddon was unable to leave out sensation: Isabel's father is the leader of a gang of forgers and, by one of the coincidences beloved of sensation fiction, Isabel's admirer Roland had testified against him in court years earlier, resulting in a fatal attack by her father. Sexual immorality was not permissible, but crime to spice up a novel was. The changes to suit English morality were not enough, and *The Doctor's Wife* and its heroine were still considered immoral, because even if she did not commit adultery and remained pure, the thought of the sin was enough and the heroine was not punished for that sin. The *Athenaeum* reviewer, calling it 'immoral and foolish', wrote:

> By disappointing her heartless seducer, and making her false wife stop short of adulterous intercourse with the man she prefers to her generous and devoted husband, Miss Braddon lays claim to rank amongst writers of morality (...) Miss Braddon is under the impression that her heroine is guiltless of conjugal infidelity, because she confines herself to sinning in thought, and to certain acts which dishonour the husband without entitling him to the relief of the Divorce Court.[54]

It was telling that their greatest sympathy rested with her husband, who is not the brightest or most interesting of husbands, and is of less importance than the husband of Emma Bovary. It is hard to imagine what critics would have made of a more faithful version of *Madame Bovary*, if Braddon and any publisher had dared to bring it to them. Even as late as 1905, the novelist Mrs. Cashel Hoey commended Braddon for the metamorphosis:

> To the sickening commonness and boredom which developed the vileness of *Madame Bovary* we owe Miss Braddon's charming story *The Doctor's Wife*.[55]

Interestingly when Braddon came to write her essay 'Emile Zola and the Naturalistic School', in her discussion of *Madame Bovary* she did not mention her own use of the novel, but instead suggested George Eliot had made use of the novel in *Adam Bede* (1859), both in style and morality, her words, in part, could have applied to her own novel:

> There is a curious resemblance too in the characters of Emma Bovary and Hetty Sorel, (...) but in the English writer there is at least some touch of tenderness, and there is also the reticence which marks the wide gulf between French and English fiction.[56]

French fiction was, by the time of sensation fiction, increasingly available in cheap translations. There was much discussion about this freedom of availability; discussion circled round whether they could be procured by schoolgirls, and whether adulterous women and murderesses had been influenced by reading them. Mansel too resented the French novel, especially the freedom of availability at railway bookstalls where they could be procured by innocents:

> We have ourselves seen an English translation of one of the worst of those French novels devoted to the worship of Baal-Peor and the recommendation of adultery, lying for sale at a London railway-stall, and offered as a respectable book to unsuspecting ladies; and the list now before us furnishes sufficient proof that poison of the same kind is sometimes concealed under the taking title of the circulating library.[57]

To be freely available and on public display was bad enough, but Mansel presents women as victims by suggesting they are 'unsuspecting', rather than just buying what they would like to read. With his list of sensation novels, with *Lady Audley's Secret* and *Aurora Floyd* prominent, he was implying that this was the new French fiction, and that the circulating library which was meant to protect its readers was letting it in. Thus three deckers were extolling French themes of immorality, and he cites as an example the anonymous *Recommended to Mercy* (1862), which had a mistress as the heroine: 'This is a favourite theme with French novelists of a certain class.'[58] Sinners were now being made more attractive than the conventional heroine of the past.

In *Hostages to Fortune* (1875) Braddon examines the phenomena of French drama being rewritten, or rather censored, for a London audience. The actress manager Myra Brandreth wants strong drama and decides on a French play, 'L'Ange Déchu'. She refuses the urging of her translator to 'whitewash' it, persuading him they will somehow smuggle it through the Lord Chamberlain's office. Myra argues that it is the usual changes which make English drama unrealistic through ridiculous incidents. Braddon would doubtless have said this also applied to sensation fiction, where love affairs could be permissible by accidental bigamy. Myra says to change the status of characters would render the play into:

> A purely English style of construction, in which probability is sacrificed to propriety. In order to escape the charge of immorality, we make our plots more improbable than the wildest fairy tale. Now your French dramatist starts with a motive strong enough to overturn a family or an empire, and builds his dramatic edifice upon a substantial foundation.[59]

The play is denounced by the press who advise audiences to avoid the Frivolity theatre 'as a pest-house infected with French poison' (p.350). Society, 'always ready for a sensation', flocks to see the play.

Braddon knew only too well about the common practice of borrowing French plays for the London stage. The early effect of this practice was that Braddon too was tempted to plagiarise for her novels. French plots were clearly of great interest to her, but with her own seemingly fathomless imagination, it seems at first odd that she should have done it. *Dead Sea Fruit* (1868) was another 1860s novel she took from a French source. Mrs. Cashel Hoey pointed out that a novel as late as *Mount Royal* (1882) was in part an adaptation of a novel called *Le Baron Trèpassé*.[60] In *Hostages to Fortune* Braddon gave a clue as to why she might have resorted to this. A playwright finds himself desperate for money, bereft of ideas, and so resorts to using a French play:

> The crowd of images, the wealth of incident, the variety of subject, which used to throng the chambers of his mind, inhabit there no longer. He is obliged to resort to other men's invention for suggestions that may assist his wearied fancy, and with this view reads innumerable French and German novels, (...) groping for some available notion in the kennels of continental fiction – a novel which he can condense and crystallise into a drama, or a drama which he can develop and widen into a novel. (p.211)

Writing so much at once in the 1860s – numerous three deckers, penny bloods, revising other people's books for Maxwell and her own illness – she may have had trouble keeping up with the frenetic pace. Braddon overstepped the line with *Circe* (1867), a novel which she wrote as Babington White, and which was so directly plagiarised from Octave Feuillet's *Dahlia* (1857) that it was considered to be dangerously close to a translation. This was immediately spotted and used by high class journals to expose her as Babington White and as a literary thief. She also used Frederic Soulié's fiction for her penny blood work, writing in December 1864 to Bulwer Lytton:

> I have read Soulié, at least many of his stories, and have helped myself very freely to some of them for my Anonymous work. He is certainly magnificent for continuous flow for invention – incident arising out of incident.[61]

What Braddon had at first failed to realise was that what was acceptable in the free and easy world of the theatre was altogether a different matter to literary critics.

The later French influence on Braddon was very different, and was that of Zola. In a 1911 interview she said:

"I have read most of Zola's books at one time or another, and although, of course, I admit that they have many faults of taste from an English point of view, I have found them intensely interesting, and have always recognised the power behind his pen. I began to read Zola while I was writing my story 'Ishmael'."[62]

With Zola came an increased interest in realism, but Zola was still a controversial figure in unexpurgated form, and the publisher Vizetelly was sent to prison as late as 1889 for publishing him. Braddon admired him greatly, but in interviews always added that she had some reservations about the morality of some of his work. In 1885 her knowledge of French literature was so highly regarded that T.H.S. Escott asked her to write an article for the *Fortnightly Review*. Although surprised by his 'flattering' suggestion, and admitted she had thought about writing about Zola and Daudet for some time, she felt she could not write from the condemnatory viewpoint he initially required:

But, alas, I could not write such a paper as you suggest – for I owe so much to French literature and I am such an ardent admirer of the great French novelists that to depreciate their work would be to turn upon my chief benefactors.[63]

Although she had reservations as to whether she possessed the 'critical faculty' to write literary criticism, she was keen to write the proposed article on Zola and Daudet:

taking them as the only great novelists who have arisen in Europe since the death of Dickens & Thackeray – & as far & away over the heads of our English fiction-mongers – writing of course with due reprobation of Zola's hideous & needless coarseness & taking him at his best in "Le Bonheur des Dames" – where to my mind he most nearly touches Balzac – & where he shows perhaps for the first time that he can describe a passionate, yet not impure, love.[64]

Escott obviously was either reassured by this approach, or perhaps had assumed when he first approached her that she would wish to concentrate on the immorality of French literature, and she began to work on 'Emile Zola and the Naturalistic School.' Braddon was enthusiastic, but she was also apprehensive about the subject matter, still scarred by the accusations of immorality which had dogged her over twenty years earlier and the gossip over her belated marriage ten years previously, and she asked Escott, 'Must the article be signed?

That is a serious question for me in writing of Zola. A woman cd only approach with lightest touch some of those questions wh he handles so boldly.'[65] She researched her essay carefully, reading everything she could by Zola, admitting to Escott she had found it harder to write than fiction, and adding 'the whole leaves an envious impression of perverted genius.'[66] She told him that while she had intended to examine in depth the work of several authors, in the end the piece was dominated by Zola and because this had 'obliged' her to 'write boldly' she had decided 'I *cannot* possibly put my name to the paper' and asked him to publish it anonymously.[67] Clearly anxious, she then decided she would use:

> an old *nom de plume* which I have always repudiated when brought home to M.E.B. but which seems to me better than using a new one. Should you like to use the paper please kindly let the authorship remain a secret between you & me. I have written from an entirely masculine standpoint, & quite oblivious of Podsnappery.[68]

The surviving manuscript reveals that this pseudonym, heavily scored out in ink, was to be that of Babington White. It seems surprising that Braddon was prepared to use this name, after the furore twenty years earlier over the publication of *Circe*, but she changed her mind yet again when John Maxwell decided to write to Escott and told him he thought the article ought to be published under her own name. A few days later Braddon wrote to Escott, 'Since my husband wrote to you I have reflected upon his wish to have the article published with my name, & that reflection has induced me to desire to withdraw the article altogether.'[69] Although Maxwell handled the negotiations for book and short story sales, Braddon had often published essays anonymously or under her initials in the *World* without his assistance. Perhaps he thought the essay was too long, and that Braddon would not receive sufficient remuneration unless her name was on it. Whatever his reason, and he clearly did not understand her reservations, his interference meant she preferred not to publish the article at all. She told Escott, apologetically, that had she kept to her original intention, and concentrated on Daudet and the Goncourts, she could have allowed the essay to appear under her name, but her fascination for Zola had 'impelled' her to concentrate on him. She admitted her fear over what people might say was her principle reason for the withdrawl:

> Now I know this little world of ours so well that, altho' I quite agree with you that a woman of my age who has practiced the

profession of literature for nearly a quarter of a century has earned the right to read every thing, I am sure there wd be all kinds of illnatured remarks made upon the conjunction of my name & Zola's – to say nothing of those respectable personal friends who wd be shocked at my familiarity with certainly the coarsest writer of *any* epoch.[70]

The manuscript of a draft version of 'Emile Zola and the Naturalistic School' exists, and in this she expressed her reservations that Zola's realism had gone too far. She thought that in *Le Fortune des Rougon* he could not depict a pure love without 'sounding the depths of sensuality and reducing womanhood to the level of brute beasts.'[71] Some of his imagery she found 'distinctly immoral'[72] and in *La Curée*:

It is all morbid anatomy: as one reads, one imagines M. Zola, cool as a cucumber, revelling in his demonstrations of humanity's vileness. (...) He delights in descriptions of diseases.[73]

English literature had to wait for George Moore and *The Mummer's Wife* (1885) for similarly realistic details of illness and the like. In Braddon's work the horrible is touched upon, but not to the excess she deplored. With regards to female sexuality, despite what the critics said, she did not depict morally vacuous, sexually active women. A woman becomes a mistress because she is in love, because she has been duped by a 'profligate', and there are always consequences. They are not women who took a lover for adventure, money, or caprice, and they expect marriage to be the natural result. The nearest she ever came to a Nana was in the character of Kate, the street urchin turned actress, in the late novel *Our Adversary* (1909). Here Braddon showed an avaricious woman, but unlike Nana whom she described as 'not a creature with a heart and a conscience (...) She is vice incarnate',[74] Kate has more redeeming qualities and goes back to her first lover, the father of her child at the end of the novel. Braddon deplored Zola's lack of restraint, and she found much of his writing too explicit. But still she read and admired him.

She also borrowed Zola's interest in theories of heredity. For example in *The Golden Calf* (1883), one of her finest novels in terms of characterisation, Braddon gives a detailed examination of a failed marriage and the effect an alcoholic husband has on himself and his wife. Towards the end Braddon has the alcoholic husband (who is possibly mentally ill as well) burn down the house, and his wife is rescued from the flames by an admirer who had disguised himself as a hermit to be near her. It makes for a disappointing ending in a novel which is characterised by its realism to suddenly subside into coincidence and melodrama. It is a rare case in a Braddon novel that melodrama should seem out of place, but the mix of the realistic with the sensational jars where mystery has previously been almost excluded. Probably her most successful Zola-inspired novel was *Ishmael* (1884), set during the unrest before and after the rise of Louis Napoleon. Robert Lee Wolff, who seems to have felt that the non-sensational novels must be worthier than those that are, counts this as one of her best novels. It is an interesting novel, but it is toned down Zola, and has the slightly studied air of one who has read much about the period and setting. Although poverty and degradation are shown amongst the poor, Braddon counterbalances this with clean living, hard working poor people. The hero, Ishmael, goes to Paris and becomes an ardent republican and finds his friends among left wing workmen. In middle age Ishmael speaks publicly and ardently against Marxism, and here Braddon's own belief in paternalistic Toryism seems to be intruding.

Braddon's study of French literature was assiduous, and she was still having lessons to improve her accent in her seventies. She spoke excellent French and frequently visited France. When the playwright Tom Taylor died she purchased his entire collection of French literature. Braddon's novels were also popular in France in translation – even *Madame Bovary* in the form of *The Doctor's Wife* returned to France as the two volume *Le Femme du Docteur* translated by Charles Bernard Derosne in 1867 – and a short novel was serialised in *Figaro*. Braddon was able to write in several styles and her use of Zola during the 1880s seems to have been another attempt to write 'serious' fiction, just as *The Doctor's Wife* had been during the 1860s and the historical novels were to be in the 1890s. In between she continued to write novels of mystery and secret relationships: it was these that made her popular then and which make her readable now.

Braddon's increased realism was also an acknowledgement that sensation fiction was no longer such a novelty, and that characterisation was as important as incident. In an interview of 1913, Braddon reflected on the shift in her literary technique:

> "No, no golden-haired heroines now," was the reply to a natural question. "The days for golden hair have passed away. Less detail of heroines is wanted now and more character study. Readers are not satisfied with incidents alone; they like to see character evolve as events move."[75]

Braddon's sensation fiction succeeded in combining influences from several existing cultural forms, but in doing so she also contributed to each of them. In the early 1860s she helped to found the new sensation genre, but this too never went away and eventually developed into the detective fiction which is still with us, and to the history of which Braddon is also an important contributor.

Chapter Four Footnotes

1. The only other writer to do this was Elizabeth Grey (1798-1869), who wrote penny bloods, gothic novels, and society novels.

2. Northrop Frye, *Anatomy of Criticism* (Princeton, New Jersey: Princeton University Press, 1957), p.47.

3. Michael Booth, *English Melodrama* (London: Herbert Jenkins, 1965), p.14.

4. 'Eleanor's Victory', *Athenaeum*, 19 September 1863, p.361.

5. 'Our Female Sensation Novelists', *Christian Remembrancer*, vol. XLVI, 1863, p.210.

6. W.F. Rae, 'Miss Braddon', *North British Review*, vol. XLIII, 1865, p.195.

7. 'Miss Braddon: The Illuminated Newgate Calendar', *Eclectic Review*, vol. XIX, January 1868, p.31.

8. Beth Kalikoff, *Murder and Moral Decay in Victorian Popular Literature* (Michigan: UMI Research Press, 1986), p.82.

9. Virginia Surtees, *The Actress and the Brewer's Wife* (Wilby, Norwich: Michael Russell, 1997), p.61.

10. Robert Lee Wolff, 'Devoted Disciple: The Letters of Mary Elizabeth Braddon to Sir Edward Bulwer Lytton 1862-1873', *Harvard Library Bulletin*, vol. 12, 1974, p.15. Letter from Braddon to Bulwer Lytton, May 1863.

11. Kalikoff, p.82.

12. Booth, p.30.

13. Booth, p.30.

14. Booth, p.30.

15. 'To Correspondents', *Halfpenny Journal*, vol. I, 17 February 1862, p.272.

16. For more on this see the introduction by Jennifer Carnell for Mary Elizabeth Braddon, *The Octoroon; or, The Lily of Louisiana* (Hastings: The Sensation Press, 1999).

17. Robert Lee Wolff, 'Devoted Disciple', p.11, Braddon to Bulwer Lytton, December 1862, p.11.

18. 'Penny bloods' are for adults, the term 'penny dreadful' should be applied to those serials particularly directed at a predominately boy readership. For this definition see John Springhall. ' "A Life Story for the People" Edwin J. Brett and the "Low-Life" Penny Dreadfuls of the 1860s', *Victorian Studies*, vol. 33, Winter 1990, p.277.

19. R.F. Stewart, *...And Always a Detective: Chapters on the History Of Detective Fiction* (Newton Abbot: David & Charles, 1980), p.46 quotes from 'Armadale', *Westminster Review*, October 1866.

20. Wilkie Collins, 'The Unknown Public', *Household Words*, 21 August 1858, pp.217-222.

21. Louis James, *Fiction for the Working Man 1830-1850* (Oxford: Oxford University Press, 1963), pp.136-137.

22. M.E. Braddon, 'My First Novel', *Idler*, vol. III, 1893, p.25.

23. 'The Trail of the Serpent', *Spectator*, vol. XLX, 11 August 1866, p.891.

24. 'Notices to Correspondents', *Halfpenny Journal*, vol. I, 8 July 1861, p.16.

25. A letter from Mrs. Wyndham, a great grand-daughter of Lady Caroline, *Times Literary Supplement*, 15 May 1944, p.235.

26. 'To Correspondents', *Halfpenny Journal*, vol. I, 25 November 1861, p.176.

27. Letter from John Maxwell, *Athenaeum*, 23 March 1867, p.387.

28. M.E. Braddon, *The Doctor's Wife* (London: Maxwell, 1864; repr. London: Ward Lock & Tyler, c.1867), p.11.

29. M.E. Braddon, *The Black Band; or, The Mysteries of Midnight* (Halfpenny Journal, vol. I, 1861-1862, p.2; repr. Hastings: The Sensation Press, 1998), p.6.

30. M.E. Braddon, *The Black Band; or, The Mysteries of Midnight* (London: George Vickers, 1877), the title page read:

> There are Secret Societies, an element which we must take into account, and which at the last moment may baffle all our arrangements; Societies which have regular agents everywhere, which countenance assassination, and which, if necessary, could produce a massacre.

> Lord Beaconsfield, speaking as Prime Minister of England at Aylesbury, September 20 1876.

31. See, for example, 'The Manufacture of Novels', *Athenaeum*, 16 February 1867, 26 February p.290, 9 March p.323, 16 March p.354, 23 March p.387. In 'English Authors in America', *Athenaeum*, 11 May 1867, pp.623-624, the American publishers Hulton & Co. drew attention to Maxwell's dealings in the States, pointedly referring to Braddon and 'her friend'.

32. 'The Doctor's Wife', *Athenaeum*, 15 October 1864, p.495.

33. Rae, p.204.

34. *Halfpenny Journal*, vol. I, 11 November 1861, p.160.

35. Thomas Wright, 'Concerning the Unknown Public', *Nineteenth Century*, vol. XIII, February 1883, p.288.

36. Wright, p.290.

37. Robert Lee Wolff, *Nineteenth Century Fiction: A Bibliographical Collection* 5 vols. (New York: Garland, 1981), I, p.131.

38. James, p.42.

39. 'Sensation Novels', *Medical Critic and Psychological Journal*, vol. III, 1863, pp.513-519.

40. Richard D. Altick, *Victorian Studies in Scarlet* (New York: W.W. Norton, 1970), pp.73-74 quotes James Greenwood, *The Seven Curses of London* (1869).

41. For a brief account of *The Wild Boys of London* see W.O.G. Lofts and D. Adley, 'A History of "Penny Bloods" ', *Book and Magazine Collector*, no. 32, November 1986, pp.48-55.

42. Nicholas Rance, *Wilkie Collins and Other Sensation Novelists* (London: Macmillan, 1991), p.31 quotes a review of *No Name*, Reader, 3 January 1863.

43. Letter from George Augustus Sala to John Maxwell, c. October 1862, Wolff collection.

44. M.E. Braddon, *Birds of Prey* 3 vols. (London: Ward, Lock & Tyler: 1867), I, p.238.

45. M.E. Braddon, 'Emile Zola and the Naturalistic School', unpublished manuscript, 1885, Wolff Collection. It is difficult to give page numbers for these quotations, because the manuscript is made up of two unmatched drafts which do not run on consecutively.

46. Ibid.

47. Mrs. Oliphant, 'Novels', *Blackwood's Edinburgh Journal*, vol. CII, September 1867, p.257.

48. Ibid.

49. Braddon, 'Emile Zola and the Naturalistic School'.

50. Ibid.

51. C.J. Devon to Braddon, 22 August 1864, Wolff collection.

52. Wolff, 'Devoted Disciple', letter from Braddon to Bulwer Lytton, Summer 1864, p.22.

53. Braddon, 'Emile Zola and the Naturalistic School'.

54. 'The Doctor's Wife', *Athenaeum*, 15 October 1864, p.495.

55. Mrs. Cashel Hoey, 'A Glance at Miss Braddon's Work', *World*, 25 April 1905, p.713.

56. Braddon, 'Emile Zola and the Naturalistic School'.

57. Mansel, p.493.

58. Mansel, p.493.

59. M.E. Braddon, *Hostages to Fortune* (London: Maxwell, 1875; repr. London: Ward, Lock & Tyler, c. 1876), p.349.

60. Hoey, p.713.

61. Wolff, 'Devoted Disciple', Braddon to Bulwer Lytton, December 1864, p.28.

62. Clive Holland, 'Fifty Years of Novel Writing. Miss Braddon at Home', *Pall Mall Magazine*, November 1911, p.703.

63. Braddon to T.H.S. Escott, 6 December (1884), British Library, Escott Papers, Add.Mss.58786.

64. Ibid.

65. Braddon to Escott, 22 December (1884), British Library.

66. Braddon to Escott, no date, British Library.

67. Braddon to Escott, no date, British Library.

68. Braddon to Escott, no date, British Library.

69. Braddon to Escott, 12 May (18850, British Library.

70. Braddon to Escott, no date, British Library.

71. Braddon, 'Emile Zola and the Naturalistic School'.

72. Ibid.

73. Ibid.

74. Ibid.

75. 'Miss Braddon', *Daily Telegraph*, 4 October 1913, p.9.

Theatre Royal,
WINCHESTER.

Open every Evening for a Short Season only.—Lessee and Manager, Mr. EDWIN HOLMES, No. 4, Monument Terrace.

PERFORMANCES FOR WEDNESDAY AND THURSDAY, SEPTEMBER 14th and 15th.

On WEDNESDAY EVENING, Sept. 14,

Will be performed SHAKSPEARE'S Historical Play of

RICHARD III.

Or, THE BATTLE OF BOSWORTH FIELD.

King Henry the Sixth, - - - Mr. RAINFORD
Edward, Prince of Wales, Miss C. BIDDLES | Richard, Duke of York. Miss ADELAIDE HOLMES (her first appearance)
Richard, Duke of Gloucester, afterwards King Richard III. **Mr. HOLMES** | Duke of Buckingham, - Mr. GREATREX
Henry, Earl of Richmond, Mr. C. A. CALVERT | Lord Stanley, Mr. BISSON | Duke of Norfolk, Mr. J. G. MONTAGUE
Sir Richard Radcliffe, Mr. BRANDON | Sir William Catesby, Mr. POWELL | Tyrrell, Mr. H. SIMPSON | Tressel, Mr. LAVINE
Lord Mayor of London, Mr. C. YOUNG

Elizabeth, Queen of Edward IV. - Mrs. RAINFORD | Lady Anne, Miss ADELAIDE BIDDLES | Duchess of York. - Miss SIDNEY

A PAS DE DEUX, MISS LOUISA SIDNEY AND MR. LAVINE.

To conclude with the laughable new Farce of

POP GOES THE WEASEL.

Mr. Josiah Scraggs, Mr. RAINFORD | Augustus Smuggins, Esq. Mr. C. A. CALVERT | Mr. Wolfenden Shark, Mr. BRANDON
Mr. Verdant Fig, Mr. POWELL | A Mysterious Stranger, Mr. GREATREX | Jacob Timid (servant to Scraggs), Mr. J. G. MONTAGUE
Louisa Scraggs (a romantic young lady), Miss ADELAIDE BIDDLES

To conclude with the popular Dance of "Pop goes the Weasel."

On THURSDAY EVENING, Sept. 15th,

Will be repeated the popular new Drama, by Miss ADELAIDE BIDDLES, entitled

MINNIGREY

THE GIPSY GIRL;
Or, ENGLAND'S ARMY and NAVY.

Geoffrey Howard, under the assumed name of Hanway, - Mr. RAINFORD | Edward Howard, his grandson, - Mr. POWELL
Gus, formerly a gipsey boy, Mr. CALVERT | Blue Peter, a young sailor, Mr. BRANDON | Frederick Hill, an officer, Mr. GREATREX
Paul Kemp, Lieutenant of the Press Gang. - Mr. H. SIMPSON | Jack Williams, a Private Soldier - Mr. LAVINE
Bill Blowhard, a Trumpeter, Mr. J. G. MONTAGUE | Bing, a Surgeon, Mr. YOUNG | Soldiers, Sailors, Peasants, &c. &c,
Minnigrey, formerly a Gipsy Miss CLARA BIDDLES | Agnes, a Portuguese Peasant Girl - Miss ADELAIDE BIDDLES
Molly Turpin, a Sutler, great, great, great grand-daughter of famed Dick Turpin - Miss MARY SEYTON
Alice, the Nurse of Minnigrey Mrs. RAINFORD | Peasant Girls - Misses LOUISA SIDNEY, SEYTON, &c.

In Act 2 a Double Military Hornpipe by Miss L. Sidney & Mr. Lavine.

A CHARACTERISTIC PAS DE DEUX, by Miss Louisa Sidney and Mr. Lavine.

To conclude with the very laughable Farce of THE

WANDERING MINSTREL.

Mr. Crincum, Mr. BISSON | Tweedle, Mr. POWELL | Herbert Carrol (with a song), Mr. GREATREX
Jem Baggs (the Wandering Minstrel), Mr. J. G. MONTAGUE.
Mrs. Crincum, Miss RAINFORD | Julia, Miss M. SEYTON | Peggy, Miss C. BIDDLES

MISS BRADDON IN HER DARING FLIGHT
1868

1874

ANNESLEY BANK

1892

'MISS BRADDON' BY YOSHIO MARKINO, c.1914

Chapter Five
Detectives and the Detection of Secrets and Crime: Braddon's Contribution to the Detective Genre

In previous chapters I have discussed Braddon's use of popular culture in her work, but she is also an important contributor to the history of a genre which remains to this day one of the most popular of all, that of detective fiction. Nearly all of Braddon's novels contain an element of crime and detection, if only because there is always at least one character with something to hide and in fear of exposure. This chapter seeks to trace the beginnings of detective fiction within sensation fiction, and Braddon's own innovative work. Braddon also provides a number of early detectives, both in her working class and her middle class fiction. I shall discuss in turn her use of the professional detective, the amateur male detective and the amateur female detective, each section examining the progression of each type of detective chronologically.

Sensation Fiction to Detective Fiction

It is to sensation fiction that one should look for the origins of the detective novel. Almost always these novels never quite reach the stage of becoming a full detective novel, in which the whole point should be to set up a puzzle for either an amateur detective or a professional detective to solve. Nevertheless, sensation fiction frequently presents the reader with a puzzle, a detective figure and a solution, even if this was not the primary aim of the author. Sensation fiction's preoccupation with secrets, and the revelation of those secrets and of crime, are often so intrinsic to the plot that they must be considered as the antecedents of the emergent detective novel. Sensation novels by Braddon and others are often close to the formula of detective fiction. Ultimately, though, they will disappoint the reader who desires to be baffled by a seemingly unfathomable mystery and then to follow the detective as he deciphers clues and brings the culprit to justice. Even if Braddon and other sensation novelists had desired to take the novels along this logical path, they might have been deterred by critics who believed that the process of introducing crime and detectives into mainstream fiction had already gone too far. To many contemporary critics sensation fiction was feeding a dangerous and unhealthy craving for violent crime and the depiction of immoral and unwholesome characters. They believed this to be a grossly inaccurate picture of the true English home. The *Westminster Review* wrote that:

> It would be absurd to conclude that every English family circle must include at least one murderer or murderess, and one maniac, because Wilkie Collins and Miss Braddon have found it convenient thus to represent the social existence of English people.[1]

However, at the time of the emergence of sensation fiction the press reflected society's fears that there were murders occurring which the police seemed to have no ability to solve. Cases such as that of Constance Kent and the dismembered body of the Waterloo Bridge murder, which were considered police failures, and later their inability to find Jack the Ripper, all gave rise to a fear that the order of society was being undermined by a counter-world of danger and criminality. The unsolved crimes also gave the public ample opportunity to play detective and discuss their theories, as Braddon observed in *Beyond These Voices* (1910):

> There is nothing that English men and women enjoy more than the crime which they call "a really good murder." (...) Every man is at heart a Sherlock Holmes, while every woman thinks herself a criminal investigator by instinct.[2]

Newspapers not only gave increasing coverage to cases of murder, and trials, but also the first celebrity members of the police emerged; inevitably police began to appear in fiction to a greater degree than they had previously. The *Eclectic Review* observed that Braddon's novels were 'Works answering all the purposes of lengthened Police reports.'[3] This was nothing but hyperbole, as Braddon's novels were far from being a catalogue of crime. Fiction was now reflecting the interest which newspapers had already exploited when, encouraged by the greater levels of literacy, they soon discovered that crime sold copies. The nineteenth century also saw a growing interest in urban crime, and books written about criminal physiognomy assured readers that criminals could be identified by physical and cranial characteristics. Poorer members of society and the areas where they lived in London were mapped out in sociological investigations by Mayhew, Rowntree and Booth.[4] Life-styles which were previously undocumented and a mystery were now revealed. Crime and disease were perceived to emanate from the poor, just as the sensation novel was perceived to have brought crime into the parlour from the working class fiction of its servants.

If bigamy was the first crime exploited by sensation fiction, it was not long before authors used a whole range. Braddon's characters commit forgery, murder, impersonation and theft, but she usually deals with these crimes in conjunction with the detection of secrets emanating from broken moral laws. Her main concern is how crime affects the family, and how the family must contain the secret within itself to prevent public exposure. In many ways it was hardly surprising that Braddon should have been so preoccupied with family secrets and concealed relationships, when throughout the 1860s, and right up until her marriage in 1874, she must have been in dread of gossip about her own family life.

Of all of the sensation novelists Braddon was the one most associated with crime and criminal life. When Wilkie Collins wrote *Armadale* (1866) he was seen to be following Braddon's lead, rather than the other way around as was usually thought.[5] Florence Marryat, Annie Thomas and Rhoda Broughton managed without using any crime at all; their fiction was more concerned with the emotions of romantic sensation. Probably Braddon's only rival to claim the title as the first woman to write detective fiction is the American author Anna Katharine Green (1846-1935) who wrote *The Leavenworth Case* (1878), and many others which were popular on both sides of the Atlantic. Following in Braddon's footsteps, Green chose a lawyer to be the detective in her first successful novel. Braddon's first novel of crime and detection, *Three Times Dead* (1860), preceded Green's by eighteen years.

Sensation fiction revolved on secrets and their exposure, and it was thought by some critics that the number of secrets in each novel was increasing to a ridiculous degree. The *North British Review* wrote of *Eleanor's Victory* that 'Lady Audley contains one secret only: this one contains three.'[6] The natural progression of revealed secrets and revealed murderers evolved into whodunits or whydunits, and the solution to a mystery was to become the whole raison d'être of most of the detective novels of the future. As sensation novels were perceived to be evolving into detective fiction, critics were increasingly hostile towards the formulaic mechanics of the novels. They argued that sensation novels of crime worked as formulaic genre, with puzzles and mystery more important than characterisation, and this development was to be resisted. Genre was seen to be at odds with literature. The idea that authors were beginning to extol and define the new genre was to be deplored:

> One eminent member of the craft goes so far as to talk of the science – perhaps the word used was the philosophy – of detection, as if it were a subject on which public lectures were read at Scotland Yard by a well-paid professor.[7]

Braddon herself referred to the science of detection by the police in *The Black Band; or, The Mysteries of Midnight* (1861-1862), describing the work of the police as:

> that wonderful science which tracks the dark pathway of crime with such marvellous success, that we come at last to look upon the detective officer as the magician of modern life.[8]

Today *The Notting Hill Mystery* (1862-1863) by Charles Felix is generally regarded as the first detective novel proper, thus preceding *The Moonstone* (1868).[9] *The Notting Hill Mystery*, which was serialised in *Once a Week* shortly before *Eleanor's Victory*, is written as a series of letters from an insurance company agent to his employer, as he sets about proving the guilt of the mysterious mesmerist Baron R. who poisoned his wife by administering the poison to her long lost twin. It precedes methods of 1920s detective fiction by providing within the text a marriage certificate, and a plan of a house. While a strong case has been made for *The Notting Hill Mystery* as the first detective novel, it does have faults which perhaps preclude it, and so leave *Lady Audley's Secret* in a strong position to claim that laurel. There is no characterisation in *The Notting Hill Mystery*, and more importantly there is no arrest or moral acknowledgement of justice, as not surprisingly murder through mesmerism could never be proved. The detective is a shadowy figure, his reports are business-like, revealing no part of his personality.

There were also other early works which sounded as though they ought to be detective fiction, such as *Recollections of a Detective Police-Officer* (1856) by 'Waters' (the pseudonym of William Russell), which purported to depict real cases. In more mainstream fiction Inspector Bucket in *Bleak House* (1853) was probably the most notable example, and he at least gets to arrest the murderer of Tulkinghorn, the French maid Hortense, which is more than Braddon allows most of her policemen to do. The gradual appearance of policemen in fiction was a response to real-life events, as in 1844 the Home Secretary, Sir James Graham, organised a few policemen to solve crimes, 'The Detective Police' (later the Criminal Investigation Department of Scotland Yard). The fictional representation frequently reflected the uncertainty and hostility the public felt about the social status and competence of the police. The 1860s was a time before professional detectives could be seen either as hero or as the leading character in a novel. This conflict is further represented by the preference of Braddon, and most succeeding crime writers, to use an amateur detective to investigate mysteries within and affecting the family.

Braddon was a significant contributor to the emergent detective fiction, even if she did not at first see it as a separate and distinctive genre. Amateur and professional detectives frequently appear in her work, and are often as much in opposition to each other as they are to the criminal. Usually she used a male amateur detective, but there are also a number of women. In her later newspaper fiction Braddon continued the progression from sensation fiction to detective fiction: *Wyllard's Weird* (1885), *Cut By the County* (1886), and *The Day Will Come* (1889) all have a strong detective element. Detective fiction by this date was the most popular type of light reading, and was especially suited to newspaper fiction with its weekly instalments (the instalments were monthly in her magazine *Belgravia*), leaving the reader to wonder what would happen next. In this Braddon was succeeding in keeping up to date, as in the 1890s detective fiction became even more popular. The *Strand* magazine, which started in January 1891, contained detective stories by Arthur Conan Doyle, Grant Allen, Arthur Morrison, and L.T. Meade, to name but four. They were both popular and respected, and unlike their predecessors were not criticised for providing puzzles, mystery, exciting events, and pure entertainment.

Class and the Professional Detective

As long as there has been detective fiction an author has had to decide whether to use an amateur detective or a professional detective. In the nineteenth century a professional detective in fiction, and this especially applies to Braddon's works, fell into three categories: the police, a retired policeman hired in a private capacity, and lastly the agent of a private enquiry office.[10] The most famous policeman of 1860s fiction is Wilkie Collins's Cuff in *The Moonstone*, but he is not the all knowing detective who would become pre-eminent by the end of the century as exemplified by Sherlock Holmes.

It has to be stated that Braddon's treatment of the professional detective differs wildly as to what audience she was writing for in the 1860s. The difference is quite remarkable, showing as it does the relationship between class and popular literature and the snobbery which almost had to permeate the middle class form. What it meant, however, was a delay to the development of detective fiction because authors such as Braddon became reluctant to introduce policemen as central characters in middle class fiction. Braddon's first novel created an interesting detective, Joe Peters, in *Three Times Dead* (1860), later retitled as *The Trail of the Serpent* (1861). As mentioned in the previous chapter, this novel was published in Yorkshire in penny parts and aimed at a lower class audience. Here Braddon was able to present a policeman who was definitely working class. The working-class policeman was problematic to Braddon and to other writers, who were unsure of their place in the middle-class novel. In this early novel Braddon is less inhibited and more sympathetic in her treatment of the professional detective. Of course there was also working class hostility towards the police as persecutors and enforcers of unpopular laws, as James Walvin writes in *Victorian Values*:

> But in the early years of their establishment in a number of towns the police incurred a marked degree of plebeian hostility. (...) Working-class communities felt themselves to be the permanent object of suspicious scrutiny by a vigilant and unsympathetic police force.[11]

As Beverley was a small town this hostility was perhaps less likely to be present, but Braddon gets round this problem by making her policeman an underdog within the force, the rescuer and adopter of an illegitimate child, and on the side of justice rather than just victimising the first suspect. He is also dumb, making him the ultimate in the silent watcher of society, hearing and seeing what no one else does, partly because people assume he is deaf as well as dumb. The dumb witness had been used as a device in Gothic melodrama, but a dumb detective is distinctly unusual and Braddon handles the character of Peters with aplomb. He has all the advantages of an amateur detective as people do not suspect him of being a policeman. His anonymity is a key asset. Peters first appears with the arrest of Richard by Jinks:

> Mr. Jinks's quiet friend was exactly one of those people adapted to pass in a crowd. He might have passed in a hundred crowds, and not one of the hundreds of people in any of those hundred crowds would have glanced aside to look at him. [12]

Peters communicates in sign language and is a very low underling in the police force. Official justice is shown to be frequently wrong, and Peters (even though he is the representative of the law) knows that the wrong man is being tried for the murder. Through his help the young man is committed to an insane asylum while Peters searches for the real murderer. As an early work some of the plotting is extremely crude; for example, Richard destroys the letter from his uncle which would prove his innocence by accidentally setting it alight while using it as a taper for his cigar just *after* he is arrested by the detective Mr. Jinks! A baby, Slosh, is rescued from the river and brought up by Peters to be a detective, and aged ten he helps his adopted father catch the murderer.

The murderer turns out to be his real father, but the enthusiastic Slosh has no sentimental misgivings: "I'd hang my grandmother for a sovering, and the pride of catching her, if she was a downy one." (p.211) With Slosh, Braddon shows the son of a hardened murderer becoming a detective, and so debunking the theories of inevitable heredity which were current at the time. Slosh also represents the key difference between a Braddon professional and amateur detective: the professional will not allow personal considerations stand in the way of public retribution. Braddon's amateur detectives always put the personal and family interests first. Peters is the last policeman Braddon gives such a prominent role for almost forty years, and the later Faunce is not given such a detailed or intriguing home life.

What is even more noticeable is the different treatment of the police in Braddon's lower class serial work, which appeared anonymously in the lower class magazine the *Halfpenny Journal*. The journal had a paternalistic self-improvement approach, and doubtless this may be partly why Braddon presents the police in such a good light. In *The Black Band; or, The Mysteries of Midnight* (1861-1862) the police are shown as the only form of protection against the machinations of the criminal political organisation the Black Band:

> The detectives were soon at work: that wonderful police, without which there would be safety neither for life nor property in the streets of civilised London, was put in motion, and every step was taken likely to lend to the clearing-up of the mystery.
>
> Gambling houses were broken into by the fearless members of that band, who are always ready to encounter danger, and who are unrewarded by glory or honours.
>
> There are medals for the man who cuts down his enemy upon the battle field; but there is no medal for the policeman who, alone, and in the dead of night, enters some den of infamy, and struggles, single handed, with a gang of desperate thieves. (p.46)

The police are commended as the brave upholders of civilised life, whereas in her middle class novels they come under suspicion from those they are supposed to be helping, as they are seen as being primarily motivated by the prospect of financial reward. In *The Black Band*, however, Inspector Martin and Sergeant Boulder drift in and out of the complex and multi-charactered story. They are first employed by the Italian consul who believes:

> "Nothing is hopeless to the detective police of London, (...) I know these men to be two of the cleverest detectives in London. They

scent a crime as the thorough-bred hound scents a fox. What is as dark as midnight to us may be as clear as dawn to them. Without them we cannot stir a step; with them we may do anything." (p.197)

It is hard to imagine Sir Michael and Robert Audley making such a statement of confidence, nor the many other middle and upper class families in Braddon novels who will do almost anything rather than allow the police to enter the home. Boulder and Martin are not the central characters, but they are indisputably on the side of right. There is none of the ambiguity over class and suspicion of their motives that permeates the three decker novel. In *The Black Band* they have the attribute of mystery, they are unlike other men on account of their detective abilities:

> They were unalike in every particular, except in the one respect of a certain grave and reflective look in the face of each, utterly different to any expression ever seen in the countenances of other men.
>
> To the eye of the initiated, "Detective" was written in unmistakable characters in the thoughtful lines about their mouths, and in the wrinkles clustered round their eyes.
>
> Inspector Martin was a short wizen little man, whose insignificant appearance was of the greatest use to him in his professional capacity. He was a man who might have passed anywhere, by reason of that very insignificance of appearance.
>
> Sergeant Boulder, on the contrary, was tall and stalwart, broad-shouldered and strong-limbed. He had come off victorious in many a personal encounter with some of the most powerful ruffians that had ever picked oakum in Cold Bath Fields, or ornamented the Hulks by their presence. Heaven help the delinquent who fell into the grasp of Joseph Boulder. He was known to his colleagues as the Lion of the Detective Force. (p.198)

At first the Prince who has been robbed can hardly believe that the quiet Martin and burly Boulder can be the famed police. They admit that the robberies of the well organised band are as competent as themselves, and may 'defy detection'. Characters such as Ellen Clavering, whose baby has been kidnapped, have implicit confidence in them, unlike in the three volume novel where it is assumed they will fail. Contrary to the situation in the middle class sensation fiction where a policeman has little opportunity to speak, these two policemen speak naturally as working men of their class, and they feel no embarrassment at their profession. Indeed, it is they who are at times mysterious and superior, because they are all knowing and they present 'rather a patronizing air' towards the Prince and the Consul (p.201). Boulder says to his colleague:

> "if they succeed in throwing dust in our eyes we ought to be ashamed of ourselves. I feel that my honour as a detective officer is concerned in unearthing them, and by the Heaven above me I'll do it!" (p.200)

The police are significantly absent from *Lady Audley's Secret* where there was ample opportunity to introduce them (the missing George, Lady Audley's arson, her attempted murder of her blackmailer, to name but three instances), and they are virtually excluded from *Aurora Floyd* too. Joseph Grimstone of Scotland Yard appears late in the novel to investigate the murder of the first husband of Aurora, but he is also in the pay of Aurora's husband, John Mellish. This is a reminder of the difficult position of a detective employed by the authorities who then hired him out to a private patron, as is the case with Dickens's Mr. Bucket who works for the villain Tulkinghorn. The power of the wealthy individual was demonstrated in *The Moonstone* with the hindrances Cuff encounters before being sacked. Although Aurora is the prime suspect in the murder, and in theory ought to be arrested for questioning, she is not even interviewed by Grimstone, and so the mistress of the house is safe from the authority of the police. Grimstone's role is relegated to some minor detecting concerning some buttons which will implicate the Softy. The introduction of Grimstone does not really add anything, except as a realistic plot requirement that an official investigator would have to become involved at some point. Grimstone suffers as Cuff suffers, the family have a greater power within the home than the police. He receives none of the admiration received by Joe Peters in *The Trail of the Serpent* or Boulder and Martin in *The Black Band*. In *Aurora Floyd* and most succeeding novels of the 1860s, such as in *The Lady's Mile* (1866), where a private detective disguises himself as a butler to get evidence against the lady of the house so her husband can divorce her, the presence of the professional detective is peripheral. One of the disadvantages of a policeman like Cuff was that he could be hired or sacked at will. He was not allowed to be a genius who will enter a family and restore the order of society. If he had done so in the 1860s it would not have seemed credible to the reader.

The involving of the police or a private detective is an infringement of the home. Just as a companion or governess is an intruder not quite of the class of the family, so does the policeman or detective suffer discrimination and resentment from the wealthy who will close together to keep them out and to keep secrets within the home and within the family. Anthea Trodd writes that while the policeman might be looked down upon, he was also an object of fear:

> When the policeman's enquiries took him to the door of the middle-class home, however, he became a different figure. The fiction and journalism of this period yield ample proof of widespread middle-class fears of police intrusion and surveillance.[13]

Just as the middle and upper class family resent the police as a lower class intruder, so critics treated the fictional policeman as a lower class intruder into respectable literature. Braddon's reluctance to give a high profile to any detective in her middle class fiction was perhaps due to the snobbery of critics, with the perception that to introduce them lowered quality fiction. Mrs. Oliphant wrote:

> We have already had specimens, as many as are desirable, of what the detective policemen can do for the enlivenment of literature: and it is into the hands of the literary detective that this school of story-telling must inevitably fall at last. He is not a collaborator whom we welcome with any pleasure into the republic of letters. His appearance is neither favourable to taste nor morals.[14]

The 'school' was the sensation genre, and although Oliphant used the appearance of the detective as another contributing factor in the disintegration of morality in literature, she was right to see a future trend that sensation fiction would eventually be replaced by detective fiction. To have a policeman in a novel was in itself fairly new, although the role allocated to them was nearly always much slighter than the critics perceived. In the 1860s the genre of 'detective fiction' did not yet exist; R. F. Stewart finds the earliest use of the phrase, defining it as a separate genre, in a review in the *Morning Post* in 1888 of H. F. Wood's *The Passenger from Scotland Yard* which stated: 'It would seem as if on this side of the Channel we are destined to have a school of "detective fiction".'[15] The reference to France was important because both sensation fiction and the detective fiction of the 1880s were perceived to have been inspired by French literature. The interest in the police had begun much earlier with extensive newspaper accounts of their investigations, and in 1850 Dickens published ' "Detective" Anecdotes' in *Household Words* about Inspector Charles Field. In *Bleak*

House four years later he presented one of the first fictional incarnations with Bucket.

At times Braddon seemed unsure how to introduce viable detectives into the middle class novel, and when she does she seems too influenced by Collins's Cuff. She also continues to echo fears of whether detection is a respectable profession. Unlike Boulder and Martin in *The Black Band*, Mr. Carter in *Henry Dunbar* (1864) conceals his work from his wife:

> "To this day she don't know what my business really is – she thinks I'm *something* in the City, bless her dear little heart!"[16]

This is reminiscent of a later Sherlock Holmes story, 'The Man With the Twisted Lip', where a man tells his wife he is working in the city, when he is in fact leading a double life as a beggar. Part of the revulsion of feeling the middle class novel expressed was due to the fear that a detective was uncomfortably close to a criminal. In early French true-life fiction the criminal and the policeman are vitually interchangeable, as in the ghosted autobiography of Eugène François Vidocq. Vidocq was a criminal who in 1811 became the first chief of the Sûreté and whose men were also former criminals. The tales of Vidocq were just as popular in Britain, appearing in numerous editions and made into a successful melodrama by Douglas Jerrold. Vidocq's behaviour and status as a former criminal informed much of the prejudice against the police. However, the idea of setting a thief to catch a thief remained so pervasive that this prejudice remained for a long time. The quandary of whether a detective should be likeable, or just tolerated as a necessary evil, is expressed by Clement Austin in *Henry Dunbar* (1864). Austin thinks about the falseness and degradation it requires, while at the same time he is aware that the police are needed for the protection of society:

> The man had an enthusiastic love of his profession; and if there was anything degrading in the office, that degradation had in no way affected him (...) if he had to affect friendly acquaintanceship with the man he was hunting to the gallows (...) if at times he had to stoop to acts which, in other men, would be branded as shameful and treacherous, – he knew that he had done his duty, and that society could not hold together unless such men as himself (...) were willing to act as watchdogs. (vol.II, p.149)

Just as in *Bleak House* and *The Moonstone*, Bucket and Cuff, while important, are not the heroes, neither are Braddon's professional detectives such as Carter in *Henry Dunbar*. R.F.Stewart writes:

> it may be asked (...) why no novelists cleared the stage by making the police detective the hero, who can then capture, providentially or otherwise, both criminal and heroine. The answer is best given by asking another equally naive question: can you imagine a Bucket or a Cuff wooing, let alone winning, an Esther Summerson or a Rachel Verrinder?[17]

Rachel Verrinder has to marry the hero, and that is Franklin who is a gentleman. The marriage plot is often at the heart of a sensation novel, a rite of passage which is a reward for the male amateur detective or a consolation to the female detective. As Stewart says, it would have been impossible for a romance between the daughter of the house and the hired policeman. Of course Aurora Floyd married her groom, but that led to disaster.

There was also the suspicion, both in real life and in fiction, that a working class detective was not intelligent enough to solve crimes, and much attention was paid to their failures. Wilkie Collins based Cuff on Sergeant Whicher who, like Cuff, was dismissed upon accusing the daughter of the house. Cuff is not an all-knowing detective, in fact much of what he deduces is wrong. It seemed, to the press in real life, that case after case remained unsolved. In *Henry Dunbar* Braddon depicts this sense of hopelessness when the police provide no suspect for the murder:

> By slow degrees the gossips resigned themselves to the idea that the secret of Joseph Wilmot's death was to remain a secret for ever. Two or three "sensation" leaders appeared in some of the morning papers, urging the bloodhounds of the law to do their work, and taunting the members of the detective force with supineness and stupidity. (vol. I, p.205)

In real life criticism of the low intelligence of the police was widespread. They were seen as little better than manual labour and not capable of solving the more unusual sort of crime. An article in the *Saturday Review* called 'Detectives in Fiction and in Real Life' was dismissive of any resemblance between real life policemen and their fictional counterpart policemen in terms of ability:

to any one who has any practical acquaintance with the proceedings of detectives and with the transactions which they try to detect, this detective-worship appears one of the silliest superstitions that ever were concocted by ingenious writers (...) hardly anything that can be fairly described as remarkable or even peculiar ability is ever shown by the police in finding out a crime.[18]

The writer went on to point out that in real life criminals are usually caught by following 'mechanical precautions', through their links in the underworld or tracing bank notes, and as long as the perpetrator is only the most obvious suspect they will get him:

but when a crime is committed out of the common routine, and by a person who does not belong to the class of criminals; it is wonderful how helpless they are.[19]

What the writer really meant was that they would be unable to solve any case which was alien from their own class. The simple and sordid crimes amongst the working class were their natural level, for it was from this class they originated. As a character type they were deemed to lack sufficient imagination to put themselves in the place of the person they are investigating.

The distaste for the professional detective is clearly reflected in one of the few changes Braddon made from newspaper serialisation to book form. In *A Strange World* (1875) a policeman called Paufoot is renamed Smelt. The investigating amateur is called Humphrey Clissold in the serial, but becomes the perhaps more heroic sounding Maurice Clissold in the book.[20] Braddon rarely revised her later work to any great degree, so it is surprising she inserted this snippet of prejudice. What her own views were is difficult to gauge, as Braddon changed her views to suit her readership.

As detective fiction became popular as a genre in its own right, Braddon soon changed direction again, with a novel which contains more detection than any of her previous works. The status of the professional detective also improves, he is not the incompetent interloper he once was. The Paris detective Félix Drubarde in *Wyllard's Weird* (1885) is described by the lawyer Distin as:

"one of the cleverest police-officers in Paris. (...) he hears of events so quickly that it might be supposed he had a network of speaking-tubes all over the city."[21]

Distin assures the amateur detective Heathcote that Drubarde will not swindle him financially, "In fact the man is a gentleman, in his own particular line. He has made an independence, and he only works as an amateur." (p.83) He is trying to convince Heathcote that the professional is an honorary amateur, thus eliminating the mercenary element, with the advantage that Drubarde has those links with the working class which often preclude the amateur. However, despite Drubarde's independent income, he remains proud of his policeman past, even his apartment is decorated with newspaper engravings of past triumphs:

> all representing notorious crimes. "The Murder in the Rue de la Paix," "Germainne La Touche stabbed in the kitchen of the Red Cross restaurant by her lover, Gilles Perdie," (...) They were hardly pleasing subjects in abstract; but to Félix Drubarde they were all delightful; for they recalled some of the most profitable hours of his life. (pp.111-112)

Like the later Faunce, he has volumes of crime reports in beautiful bindings, a contrast to Braddon middle class characters who bind Shelley and Byron in elaborate bindings. Drubarde defines imagination (p.126) as the most important quality for a detective, but in the end he refuses to see a link between the two murders. At this point Heathcote dismisses him as an old worn out 'sleuthhound' (p.142).

In *The Day Will Come* (1889), the police once more get nowhere with the case. Again they are the intruders in an aristocratic home after a murder. They are disliked because it is a paid job and they see it as a sport. Mathew Dalbrook thinks of a local policeman with feelings of resentment at his intrusion, even though a murder has just been committed in the house:

> It was of the reward the man was thinking, no doubt – congratulating himself perhaps upon the good luck which had thrown such a murder in his way. And presently the man from Scotland Yard would be on the scene, keen and business-like, yet full of a sportsman's ardour, intent on discovery, as on a game in which the stakes were worth winning. Little cared either of these for the one fair life cut short, for the other young life blighted.[22]

Luke Churton, the London detective, fails, although his instinct is right that the solution is to be found within secrets of the family, observing, "There is something in the lives of most of us that we would rather keep dark" (p.105). Partly his failure is because he misreads the family situation: blinded by admiration for class, he befriends the murderer because she is 'a lady born and bred' (p.106). Even at this late date Braddon shows a policeman who is unable to operate within the sphere of his social betters. However, the reason for this is that she used an amateur detective as her hero in this novel, and therefore Churton has to be inept.

John Faunce in *Rough Justice* (1898) was Braddon's last professional detective of any importance. His prominence is Braddon's acknowledgement of what was by now the most popular genre with the public, detective fiction in a one volume novel or short story. Faunce is also fascinated by crime in fiction and fictional detectives:

> "Balzac was a born detective (...) It is only natural, perhaps, that a man of my calling should take a keen interest in stories of crime than in any other form of fiction; and I am not ashamed to confess a liking for those novels in which some mystery of guilt is woven and unravelled by the romancer (...) I have hung spellbound over Bulwer's "Lucretia", over "Armadale", and "The Woman in White", over "Martin Chuzzlewit", "Bleak House", and the unsolved problem of "Edwin Drood"; and inspired by this recreational reading, I have been beguiled into writing a detailed account of all those cases in which I have been engaged that have offered any kind of interest to the novel-reader."[23]

However, Faunce's tastes are essentially old fashioned, since all of the books he loves are thirty or forty years old. Just as Braddon was having trouble in keeping up to date with modern detective fiction, so does Faunce's reading reflect this. Where was Faunce's collection of Dick Donovan novels, or Grant Allen's, or Conan Doyle's Sherlock Holmes, a character who now dominated the genre and had firmly established the detective as hero? Faunce keeps scrapbooks, compiled by his wife, of all the latest crimes, just as Charles Reade did and advised Braddon to do. Faunce is shown to be tactful and humanitarian in his questioning, but in *Rough Justice* he is not infallible in his deductions. When retired he tends his roses in Putney, but unlike Collins's Cuff, he is not content to remain at home tending them but agrees to work privately to help Arnold prove his innocence. Towards the end he is relegated from the plot and it is Arnold who confronts the murderer, Greswold. It is not until he reappears in *His Darling Sin* (1899) that Faunce fully solves the case, rather than an amateur hero or heroine. When a policeman took centre stage in *His Darling Sin* Braddon was responding to public taste as much as anything else, as by that date there was a plethora of professional detectives created by other writers. The

Spectator referred to Faunce as 'the inevitable detective'.[24] Unlike Carter of *Henry Dunbar* of thirty years earlier Faunce does not feel he has to be ashamed of his career:

> Although a man of respectable parentage, good parts and education, he was not in the least ashamed of having been for many years a respected member of the Police.[25]

Even so, Braddon still feels the need to emphasise the fact that Faunce does have the instincts of a gentleman, and he does come from a respectable family. This makes it possible for him to work among the upper classes. There is no possibility of Faunce entering one of these homes as an ambiguous mix of policeman and potential criminal. One of the people he encounters sees him as a living incarnation of Bucket and Cuff and observes "There is no question of class distinction with a clever man like that." (p.120) As an indication of how times had changed, the novelist Haldene also tries to solve the mystery entrusted to Faunce, but fails. In an earlier novel he would have displaced Faunce and succeeded.

Faunce is very much a professional detective of the 1890s, as adept at unearthing clues in Algiers as in a theatre or the poorest areas of London. He is also well-read and intelligent. At first Haldene is affronted that the policeman is as clever as himself (p.180). Faunce is a good man, going far beyond duty to help some of the impoverished people he encounters. In *Rough Justice*, Braddon uses Faunce to show the desperate lives of many of the poor, to whom drug abuse is the only relief. However, Faunce continues to show up the limitations of the professional detective of sensation fiction. He is not a sufficiently interesting character to carry the plot, having none of the eccentricities of the great detectives. Faunce was in part an example of changing attitudes towards the police, as they came to be seen as an upholder and protector of law and personal property. But like many of her contemporaries Braddon was unsure how a man who was not a gentleman could deal with the guilty secrets of those who were his social betters.

Despite the growing acceptance of the police, in fiction the amateur reigned for decades, his position consolidated above all by Sherlock Holmes. Even in the 1930s an amateur had to prove stupid police wrong by aristocratic genius, as in the case of Dorothy L. Sayers's Lord Peter Wimsey helping out Chief Inspector Parker, or Agatha Christie's Poirot and Inspector Japp. Even when an author of the 'Golden Age' of detective fiction did use a professional detective they preferred to use upper class men, such as Ngaio Marsh's Inspector Alleyn who is the son of Lady Alleyn and has a Russian butler. When judged alongside these later writers Braddon created policemen such as Peters, Boulder and Martin, and Faunce with less snobbery than they ever did.[26]

The Gentleman Amateur Detective and Joshua Slythe

In the 1860s the belief of readers, writers and critics was that a policeman could not possibly make the leap from solving humdrum everyday crime to that of more unusual crimes. Among the upper classes in sensation fiction, secrecy and discretion was paramount. No doubt a reader might have been bored with the hum drum proceedings of a realistic police investigation, without the leeway for breaking rules that an amateur has. The law has limitations, as Walter Hartright observes in *The Woman in White* (1860):

> The law would never have obtained me my interview with Mrs. Catherick. The law would never have made Pesca the means of forcing a confession from the Count.[27]

More importantly the amateur detective, knowing the prejudice he and others feel against the professional detective, is reluctant to cast himself in that role. Walter Hartright knows that he is being followed by Sir Percival's men and that he and Laura are in danger. Despite this he will not degrade himself by wearing a disguise, as this would make him deceitful and false to himself and too close to the behaviour of a detective or spy:

> But there was something so repellent to me in the idea – something so meanly like the common herd of spies and informers in the mere act of adopting a disguise – that I dismissed the question almost as soon as it had risen in my mind. (p.502)

In his book ...*And Always a Detective*, R.F. Stewart describes *Lady Audley's Secret* as 'the sensation novel to begin all detective novels.'[28] He justifies this on the grounds of Robert Audley's methods of detection, but it should also be stated that Robert Audley sets the pattern for many later gentleman amateur detectives since he is a barrister with a small private income:

> But he had never had a brief, or tried to get a brief, or even wished to have a brief in all those five years.[29]

He has, therefore, no need to investigate for sordid financial reasons. Sherlock Holmes was the premier genius amateur detective, and because he has a private income he can choose cases out of interest, not out of the sordid motive of a fee.

Braddon, the daughter of a solicitor herself, frequently chose a legal career for an amateur detective; Heathcote in *Wyllard's Weird* (1888), like Robert, finds himself peculiarly suited to detection:

> The detective instinct, which is a characteristic of every well-trained lawyer's mind, had been suddenly developed into almost a passion. (p.125)

The law was a profession of gentlemen, but still allowed an enquiring mind which was one of the key attributes of a detective. Robert Audley, despite his previous indolence, sees his interviewing in the terms of a lawyer. When he questions Lady Audley's maid Phoebe he finds her as impenetrable as her mistress:

> "No," he murmured again; "that is a woman who can keep a secret. A counsel for the prosecution would get very little out of her." (p.133)

Robert Audley also feels well prepared by some of his light reading, "I haven't read Alexandre Dumas and Wilkie Collins for nothing". (p.402)

Robert Audley's natural aptitude for detection is shown before he has any need to use these abilities when he and George first visit Helen Talboys's old father:

> "I've a strong notion that that old man didn't treat his daughter too well," thought Robert, as he watched the half-pay lieutenant. "He seems, for some reason or other, to be half afraid of George." (p.44)

Because Robert is going to be the detective figure he has powers of observation not open to his friend. His first feeling towards Lady Audley is one of attraction, saying to George: "I feel like the hero of a French novel; I am falling in love with my aunt." (p.56) The portrait of Lady Audley shows him the other side of her nature, a powerful sexualised one, and from then on he is threatened by her. It is important that the detective and the criminal should be pitted against one another, and Lady Audley and Robert recognise each other as adversaries. The adversarial nature of their relationship is delineated early on when Robert presents her with "circumstantial evidence" which she pretends, as "a poor little woman" (p.119), she cannot understand. Both take refuge in traditional sex roles, Robert as masculine and assertive, Lady Audley feigns weakness and ultra femininity. One of his first deductions (and Robert himself *does* call them deductions) is after George goes missing. When admiring Lady Audley's wrists, he notices recent bruising, bruising she claims is several days old:

> It was not one bruise, but four slender, purple marks, such as might have been made by the four fingers of a powerful hand that had grasped the delicate wrist a shade too roughly (...) "I am sure my lady must tell white lies," thought Robert, "for I can't believe the story of the ribbon." (p.88)

The reader and Robert Audley think she has George's blood on those hands. Robert shows detective abilities, as he notices clues that no one else does, and Braddon succeeds especially in details like this because the reader follows his thoughts, sharing his investigation, and is taken in by the same red herring. He begins to keep a list of clues and deductions, a 'Journal of facts connected with the disappearance of George Talboys, inclusive of facts which have no apparent relation to that circumstance.' (p.100) This list of clues would give credit to any future amateur detective. He gathers and interprets evidence, as when he finds a half burnt telegram in the hearth of Lucy's father, 'He carefully folded the scrap of paper, and placed it between the leaves of his pocket-book.' (p.94). Robert is not an all knowing detective, he knows no more than the reader. The reader sometimes knows more, but never all, and Robert is sometimes wrong in his deductions. However, he is so impressed with himself that ' "Upon my word," he said, "I begin to think that I ought to have pursued my profession, instead of dawdling my life away as I have done." ' (p.100)

Robert is further spurred on when he meets Clara, George's sister, and finds her attractively like George; even her handwriting is a feminine version of his (p.209). The fact that Clara lives with a dictatorial father lends a quest element to his investigation, where at the end his reward will be to rescue and marry Clara. In almost all cases a Braddon male amateur detective sees his task as a quest which will win him a wife; a woman detective's aims are quite different.

Robert is different to other Braddon male amateur detectives since he is avenging another male. Most of the others are specifically aiming to win a wife, to prove a woman's innocence in some way, or to avenge the wrong done to a woman. For example, in *A Strange World* (1875), it initially looks as though Maurice Clissold will be another Robert Audley when his best friend is murdered, and at first he himself is the prime suspect. However, instead of continuing to investigate the murder he soon becomes more concerned with investigating the origins of the actress he wishes to marry, so that he can prove her legitimacy and good birth.

One of the few early occasions when the reader briefly enters Lady Audley's thoughts is when Robert is watching her:

> Robert turned away from the lovely face, and shaded his eyes with his hand, putting a barrier between my lady and himself; a screen which baffled her penetration and provoked her curiosity. Was he still watching her, or was he thinking? and of what was he thinking? (p.217)

He puts a barrier between them, just as Lady Audley has created one so no one knows her true self. Again this demonstrates Robert's abilities as a detective, but Lady Audley's thoughts have to be hidden from the reader or there would be no secrets to reveal. Unlike Sir Michael, Robert penetrates beyond the mask, and has become her pursuer determined for vengeance on behalf of his friend George Talboys, even though this goes against the grain of his character to date:

> With Mr. Robert Audley's lymphatic nature, determination was so much the exception, rather than the rule, that when he did for once in his life resolve upon any course of action, he had a certain dogged, iron-like obstinacy that pushed him on to the fulfilment of his purpose. (p.89)

Lyn Pykett sees Robert Audley as feminised, but gaining a masculine identity through his struggle with Lady Audley and his eventual entrapment of her.[30] This is reasonable enough, but at the same time, his inactivity as a barrister and his general laziness enable him to take on the role of gentleman detective. In the nineteenth century, an alternative to a working class professional was the gentleman with private means, and Robert Audley investigates one of the earliest country house murder mysteries.

A reluctance to allow the police and courts to deal with criminals is a recurrent feature in Braddon's novels. Lady Audley is found not to have succeeded in her attempted murder; this means she can be dealt with within the family, and the scandal concealed. Robert Audley arranges for her to be removed to an asylum abroad. Lady Audley had earlier threatened Robert:

"I would warn you that such fancies have sometimes conducted people, as apparently sane as yourself, to the life-long imprisonment of a private lunatic asylum." (p.273)

Eventually, it is Robert who does exactly what she had threatened him with, arranging for Lady Audley, who may be as sane as himself, to be committed to an asylum. The novel also provides the classic denouement to a detective novel, as Robert brings Sir Michael into the library to hear Lady Audley's "confession" (p.346). Sir Michael orders Robert to deal with the problem, to him she no longer exists. Most importantly Robert restores order, and the criminal intruder is removed from the aristocratic home. The last two chapters are entitled 'Restored' and 'At Peace'. In traditional detective fiction the role of the detective is to restore order. The displacement caused by the crime, or Lady Audley herself in this case, is removed and society returns to its earlier state. Despite Robert's position of power through his knowledge of guilt, Lady Audley realises his powers are limited, because she knows his desire to protect the privacy of the family is greater than the desire for officially meted out justice: 'she knew that he could do no more without bringing everlasting disgrace upon the name he venerated.' (p.372). It is because the disappearance of George Talboys was investigated by a family member, and not an outside investigator, that the scandal can remain enclosed within the family. Robert is still able to remove her from society anyway and, as Dr. Mosgrave says, "Whatever secrets she may have will be secrets for ever!" (p.381)

Lady Audley's Secret was first serialised in Maxwell's magazine *Robin Goodfellow*, but as the magazine folded after thirteen parts it re-ran and was completed in the *Sixpenny Magazine*. However, Braddon must have been writing *Lady Audley's Secret* concurrently with *The Black Band; or, The Mysteries of Midnight* in the *Halfpenny Journal*, as both novels started appearing in instalments in July 1861.

As remarked in the first section there are great differences between Braddon's treatment of the professional detective in her lower class fiction. In *The Black Band* Braddon has a very different kind of amateur detective, who makes a marked contrast to Robert Audley. This is all the more interesting when it is considered they were written at exactly the same time. 'The Lawyer's Hack' is Joshua Slythe, a clerk who makes a tatty contrast to his aristocratic employer Weldon Hawdley. He is used on the 'dark cases' which need detective work. 'The junior clerks whispered among themselves that Joshua Slythe was a spy – an amateur police-officer.' (p.278) Unlike Robert, Slythe has clearly been involved in many cases and rescues Sir Arthur Beaumorris by infiltrating an insane asylum in disguise. Such subterfuge is part and parcel of being a detective, but amateur gentleman detectives are reluctant to tell lies or adopt other identities. Although in his official capacity, as a lawyer's clerk, Slythe does some detective work on behalf of his employer, he also gets involved with inter-linking cases out of interest and a wish to help. Once Robert Audley solves his case he is no longer a detective. Decades later, when amateur detectives reappeared in subsequent novels, a different author might have chosen to resurrect a character like Audley for succeeding mysteries. When Slythe foils a plot to poison the ballet girl, Clara, actor Antony Verner is suitably amazed at his detective abilities:

> "Merciful powers!" exclaimed Antony Verner; "what an extraordinary being you are. Piece by piece you unroll an intricate scheme of villainy, which I could never have unravelled." (p.396)

Slythe infiltrates the Black Band itself when he is mistaken as a robber, and gathers information for the police to enable Inspector Martin to catch them:

> The best years of his life had been devoted to the unravelling of mysteries and the discovery of secrets, and he felt that he was now on the high-road to the disentanglement of a web of dark and unknown crimes. (p.505)

At the end of the novel a grateful Sir Arthur Beaumorris says to the 'ferret-eyed, shabbily dressed' Slythe that there must be no class distinction between them, and that Slythe must come to live with him at the castle. This would never have happened in a three volume novel, and forms, in part, the fantasy world of penny part fiction where fortune was just around the corner, and even the poorest might turn out to be the lost heir to an Earldom.

The reintegration into society of the aimless hero through detection occurs again to a lesser extent in *Birds of Prey* (1867) when Valentine Hawkhurst, who has been a lazy conman, redeems himself by tracing a family line to find a missing heir, all to marry the girl he loves. Although lethargic like Robert Audley, his detective process is more about his redemption, since his own behaviour has been more criminal than heroic. In doing so he exposes Philip Sheldon, a murdering society dentist. That Sheldon is the epitome of respectability is a pattern for murderers in Braddon's novels. Valentine, the detective figure in *Birds of Prey*, is an outsider, really a criminal, who becomes respectable. Robert Audley, by contrast, is part of an important family. Because of Valentine's criminal past he is less scrupulous about how he obtains his information than the gentleman amateur detective would be, and so exemplifies the theory about Vidocq, that a detective needs some thing of the criminal about him. Valentine moves into detection by starting genealogical research for three thousand pounds to find the Haygarth heir. He sees himself as on a quest, as a prince in a fairy tale sent on a journey full of danger:

> Valentine fancied himself in the position of this favourite young prince. The trackless forest was the genealogy of the Haygarths; and in the enchanted castle he was to find the crown of success in the shape of three thousand pounds, if he were so fortunate as to unravel the tangled skein of the Haygarth history.[31]

His investigation is written as a journal, tracing the events of decades earlier, trying to find letters before a rival con man gets to them: an authenticating device is added by Braddon, the letters are in an antiquated eighteenth century style. Valentine's success at unravelling forgotten family secrets reforms him as a character:

> "I do not think I can ever be a thorough Bohemian again. These lonely wanderings have led me to discover a vein of seriousness in my nature which I was ignorant of until now." (vol. III, p.56)

In the sequel, *Charlotte's Inheritance* (1868), Valentine rescues Charlotte before Philip Sheldon, her stepfather, can finish poisoning her. Valentine maintains secrecy to the extent of deciding never to tell his innocent wife of Sheldon's designs on her life. Once Valentine has married into the family he has joined the closed circle of secrecy, the family he had once investigated is now his own family and their interests are his interests.

Succeeding novels involve a process of detection, but it is usually for the hero's personal gain, not to protect society. For example, one of the heroes in *Lucius Davoren* (1873) seeks to prove the death of the missing husband of the woman he wants to marry. *A Strange World* (1875) starts out as a detective novel, but Braddon does not succeed because of the lack of red herrings, and the identity of the murderer is transparent. In *Cut By the County* (1886) there is some interesting detective work by a former army officer (how to tell if footprints are made by a gentleman's boot, for example), but his motive, again, is to protect a respectable family from scandal without involving the police.

A prominent male amateur detective is lacking until *Wyllard's Weird* (1885) which has Heathcote, a former solicitor, as the amateur. This novel was Braddon's response to the popularity of the detective story, but many saw it as a revival of sensation fiction. The *Athenaeum* wrote in its review of *Wyllard's Weird*:

> It is obvious that current fiction is suffering from a revival. The tales of mystery and murder which went out of fashion as art came in are beginning to captivate once more (...) It was not to be expected that the author of 'Lady Audley's Secret' should look on while others won success in the field where she had triumphed twenty years ago.[32]

In *Wyllard's Weird* there are four detective figures. As well as the amateur there is a criminal lawyer, an English policeman and a famous French policeman. Heathcote, the amateur, is the one to succeed, partly because of the trust people felt for him when he was a solicitor:

> the fact of his good birth and ample means, had made him a chosen repository of many a family secret which would have been trusted to very few solicitors (...) and his advice, shrewd lawyer though he was, always leaned to the side of chivalrous feeling rather than to stern justice. (p.24)

It is the disregard for strict justice which makes Heathcote suitable as an amateur detective in a Braddon novel, since his priority will be to protect a good family name and not necessarily turn the murderer over to the police and vulgarity of the press. He takes on the task because he is asked to by his former fiancée Dora, a married woman, whom he still loves. Although he thinks as an amateur detective he cannot succeed where the police have failed (p.74), Heathcote, in common with other male amateur detectives, sees himself as a knight on a quest:

> In the good old days of chivalry her knight would have deemed it an honour to bleed and perish for her sake far away in Palestine (...) I have put on my lady's colours, and I will work for her as faithfully as if my love were not hopeless. (p.93)

The idea of the detective seeing himself as a knight has some similarities with Raymond Chandler's Philip Marlowe. Heathcote comes to have a flair for detection and is spurred on by the failure of the British police to solve one murder, and takes on a second which the French had failed to solve years earlier. It is his taking on the second case, which has seemingly no link to the first, which marks Heathcote as a member of the new type of detective emerging in the mid 1880s. Heathcote precedes the first appearance of Sherlock Holmes in *A Study in Scarlet* in *Beeton's Christmas Annual* for 1887 by two years. He has taken on a case that has no personal interest for him, and for the pleasure of beating the police:

> He no longer limited his desire to the unravelling of the web of Léonie Lemarque's fate; he ardently longed to discover the mystery of Marie Prévol's murder – to succeed where one of the most accomplished Parisian detectives had failed. (p.125)

Although it seems unlikely Heathcote could succeed where the famed French police have failed, there is no stopping an English solicitor in love. He succeeds because people will talk and confide in him rather than the socially ambiguous police. He is able to get information from the poor by being kind and financially generous, and the Bohemian artists who would provide no statements to the police on principle also talk to him, thinking he might become a patron. No sphere is closed to him. Unlike the professional detective he gains interviews with the nobility, writing to the aristocratic mother of one victim:

> "I am an Englishman of good birth and education, and I shall know how to respect any confidence with which you honour me." (p.297)

Yet Heathcote brings no murderer to justice. He feels like a judge, and lets a triple murderer evade justice because the man is terminally ill, to protect his good name, and because he loves the wife, Dora. In Braddon's novels the detective usually is the judge, and his knowledge and decision is more important than that of society. Wyllard committed the first two murders out of sexual jealousy, but the third is to protect his secret double life and to maintain the respectable facade. Despite his crimes his wife is able to forgive him, and it is for her sake that Heathcote maintains the secret that the financier was not the man everyone believed. This happens again in *Rough Justice* (1898) when Arnold is content to obtain a signed confession from the murderer Oliver Greswold, so that he can prove his own innocence to the woman he loves; but he takes it no further than that, saying:

> "You have got off very cheap, Mr. Greswold, for your wife's sake. I leave you to your conscience and your God." (p.385)

Like Wyllard, Greswold's good name is left intact. If the amateur detective is a gentleman and the criminal is a gentleman, the tacit agreement seems to be that these two forces will combine and maintain secrecy.

The Female Detective as Avenging Angel

The appearance and development of the female detective in Victorian fiction was slower in happening than that of the male, which was not surprising when it is considered that opportunities for them were more limited. Detective work, by its very nature, needed more freedom of movement than was usually possible for women. Despite this, several detectives put in an appearance during the early 1860s. A forty year old widow and former actress called Mrs. Porchal appeared in *Revelations of a Lady Detective* (1861) by W. S. Hayward who, according to A. E. Murch:

> solve(d) various fairly simple problems, and was distinguished by her regard for 'lady-like conduct' and her personal appearance, rather than by any detective skills.[33]

Three years later a nameless female detective was created by Andrew Forrester Junior in *The Female Detective* (1864). Like all detectives, Forrester's heroine is aware of the social ambiguities of her profession, but although 'her trade is a despised one (she is) not ashamed of it.'[34] Both of these characters are connected to the police force, even though there were no women in the police at this date. Because of this official connection they ought to be considered as early professional detectives. Braddon never created a professional woman detective, but in her work she has a number of women characters who, when circumstances require it, chose to do some amateur investigating. Not all of them call it that, but they do become preoccupied with investigating the past secrets of their family, secrets which they themselves have been excluded from. Braddon was a significant contributor to the development of the genre, with her depiction of more than one female amateur detective who eschews domesticity for action. Usually the first female amateur detective in a novel is attributed to Wilkie Collins with Valeria Woodville in *The Law and the Lady* (1875).[35] Valeria sets about proving the innocence of her husband who was tried in Scotland for poisoning his first wife and is stigmatised by the Scottish verdict of not-proven. Her husband leaves her when she discovers this, and so she also has to win him back by proving his innocence. Eustace is a very weak figure, feminine compared to Valeria's assertion. In Collins's earlier novel *The Woman in White*, Marion almost becomes a detective, when she climbs out of her bedroom window to listen to Fosco and Sir Percival plotting, but as a result of getting wet she becomes ill and her narrative ends – as does her role as detective.

Braddon created two women in the early 1860s who, like Valeria, are drawn out of the traditional feminine role in order to help a loved one. This allowed them to become active as an amateur detective, through morally justifiable motives, such as loyalty to a parent. In *Eleanor's Victory* (1863) Braddon created her first, and most successful, female amateur detective. Eleanor is certainly as much of a detective figure as Valeria Woodville. Eleanor Vane becomes an amateur detective when she is urged in her elderly father's suicide note to take revenge against the man who cheated him at cards. She is only fifteen years old at this point, and has been provided with a cause:

> "I don't know who he is, or where he comes from; but sooner or later I swear to be revenged upon him for my father's cruel death."[36]

That Eleanor becomes an amateur detective is seen by her friend Dick, a theatrical scene-painter, as incredibly shocking and unnatural:

> "by such an investigation as will waste your life, blight your girlhood, warp your nature, unsex your mind, and transform you from a candid and confiding woman into an amateur detective. Suppose you do all this, and you little guess, my dear, the humiliating falsehoods, the pitiful deception, the studied baseness, you must practice if you are to tread that sinuous pathway, – what then?" (p.173)

This dislike is intrinsically linked with ideas of femininity: Dick's fear is that by becoming false in some way while gaining information she will become desexed. It was exactly such action which helped Robert Audley assert his masculinity; but the same assertion in a woman is undesirable. Activity and knowledge are detrimental to femininity. This argument against activity in literature is expressed by E. S. Dallas in *The Gay science* in 1866:

> When women are thus put forward to lead the action of a plot, they must be urged into a false position. To get vigorous action they are described as rushing into crime, and doing masculine deeds. Thus they come forward in the worst light, and the novelist finds that to make an effort he has to give up his heroine to bigamy, to murder, to child-bearing by stealth in the Tyrol, and to all sorts of adventures which can only signify her fall (...) It is not wrong to make a sensation; but if the novelist depends upon the action of a

woman, the chances are that he will attain his end by unnatural means.[37]

Still, as Lyn Pykett writes: 'However, as in other women's sensation novels, without the heroine's "unwomanly purpose" there would have been no story.'[38] Eleanor is undeniably active, but she is taking that action because she was urged to by her father. As Dick had feared, her role now is to deceive, but she is also able to use the advantages of her sex to find out information that Dick, as a man, has been unable to. She learns to use her good looks to advantage at a shipping office, where Dick was rebuffed when he tried to obtain information from staff:

> Perhaps for the first time in her young life the young lady was guilty of a spice of that feminine sin called coquetry. She was armed, therefore, with all the munitions of war without which a woman can scarcely commence a siege upon the fortress of man's indifference. (p.170)

Here Braddon suggests that the delightful weakness and allure of femininity is in itself duplicitous. Women are shown to be stronger and more resilient than men believe. In using her personal charms to obtain information Eleanor precedes Valeria, who also uses her good looks in exchange for information. An amateur detective such as Robert Audley has the authority of his sex and position to gain information, the female amateur detective has to rely more on subterfuge and her physical presence. Dick, who knows the theatre, had thought Eleanor would make a good actress, a skill and former profession that George Sims was later to make use of for his female amateur detective.[39] Eleanor has already created a false identity for herself when she becomes a companion, and so keeps her true self and feelings a mystery. She also considers pretending to love her suspect, Launcelot Darrell:

> No! not for the wide world – not even to be true to her dead father – could she be so false to every sentiment of womanly honour! (p.177)

Unlike Wilkie Collins's Magdalene Vanstone, she holds back from actually marrying her enemy to achieve these aims. Braddon assures her readers that Eleanor is not unfeminine enough for that. To have allowed her heroine to marry her suspect would probably have alienated critics and some readers. It would have been seen as the act of a villainess, not a heroine. Eleanor marries another man she does not love in order to stay near her suspect, but she thinks she can make him a good wife later; Braddon shows Eleanor's behaviour to be thoughtless rather than calculated as Magdalene's had been. Magdalane's behaviour was criticised by reviewers, and in view of her own personal situation at this time Braddon was probably reluctant to incur similar wrath.[41] Eleanor's detective work is more emotional, and partly based on fate and intuition. For example, Eleanor, presumably led by feminine intuition, is convinced her enemy will cross her path and that she will physically detect his presence. She is proved wrong and allows the man to propose to her, 'No instinct in her own breast had revealed to her the presence of her father's murderer.' (p.151) Rather than having to locate a missing witness, Eleanor herself is that witness, she has to uncover her own unconscious and recover the lost memory of the man she saw with her father.

> "It can only be from discoveries I make in the present that I shall be able to trace my way back to the history of the past." (p.166)

However, Eleanor is not the confident, logical detective that Robert Audley was. Despite having already taken a false identity, married a much older man purely to stay near her suspect, Braddon states Eleanor is incapable of the necessary spying:

> Miss Vane was not a good schemer (...) she did not possess one of the attributes which are necessary for the watcher who hopes to trace a shameful secret through all the dark intricacies of the hidden pathway which leads to it. (p.168)

Despite Dick's fears, her femininity has not been compromised, but she is constantly struggling with her conscience over her deceit:

> She hated herself for her hypocrisy. Every generous impulse of her soul revolted against her falsehood. But these things were only a natural part of the unnatural task which she had set herself to perform, (p.212)

At this stage she feels she is not up to the job, feeling she is too emotional and too impulsive, and by implication needs a masculine mind to help. She writes to Dick:

> "Your brain is clearer, your perception is quicker than mine. I am carried away by my own passion – blinded by my indignation. You were right when you said I should never succeed in this work." (p.211)

Dick gathers much of the evidence and is critical of her ineffective methods of watching her suspect because it lacks methodology: "You go cleverly to work, Mrs. Monckton, for an amateur detective!" (p.215). It is on Dick's initiative that they search through the suspect's sketchbooks, finding a sketch of Paris with her father in it on the very day he died with the false name (p.222), providing almost an early photo-fit! This, and the spying that Dick carries out, is exactly the sort of behaviour he had warned Eleanor about at the beginning, but Eleanor has been unable to do it alone. Although Dick is necessary for practical assistance, Eleanor has the problem of how to punish a man whose crime is moral and beyond the reach of the law. She has to wait for a further crime, and when it comes Eleanor, not Dick, is the one to spy and steal the genuine will. That Eleanor is the one to have a personal interest in the case, takes the important action, gathers evidence, and finally proves her enemy's guilt, marks out Eleanor as the detective figure in the novel.

When the man she suspects was the cause of her father's death, Launcelot Darrell, feels Eleanor, as the representative of justice, finally has the evidence to denounce him, he feels, 'IT had come: detection, disgrace, humiliation, despair'. (p.376) At first it seems the exultant Eleanor will exact her long awaited revenge, "Now, the proof of your crime is in my hands (...) Cheat, trickster, and forger; there is no escape for you now." (p.377) But it is not to be. By the end of the novel she has come to accept her responsibilities as a wife, and her duty as a woman. The 'victory' of the title is a moral victory over her own worst nature. She forgives the man she has devoted her energies to entrapping. She chooses not to expose the secrets of his past, and can forgive without demanding retribution. She does not demand his exclusion from society, as Robert had with Lady Audley or Valentine had with Philip Sheldon. In doing so Eleanor gains the feminine qualities she had previously lacked. Robert asserts his masculinity by his actions against Lady Audley, but Eleanor has to learn to forgive, a feminine quality. In the end Eleanor Vane does not commit any crime, and realises retribution against Darrell can only be 'left to the only Judge whose judgements are always righteous.' (p.400). Dick says:

> "This is your victory, my dear. This is the only revenge Providence ever intended for beautiful young women with hazel-brown hair." (p.397)

The forgiven Laurence Darrell marries her husband's ward and becomes a successful painter of 'sensation' pictures. By this intermarriage Launcelot, like Valentine in *Birds of Prey*, is rehabilitated within the family. The *North British Review* was unimpressed by such leniency:

> The moral of the story seems to be, that to cheat an old man at cards and to forge a will are no impediments to attaining distinction in the world, and, indeed, are rather venial offences.[41]

But such an ending does fit the pattern for detective fiction in so far that order has been restored. In the end, as Launcelot committed a further crime, he could have been dealt with by the police, or he could have killed himself or become suddenly seriously ill. Despite the fact none of these happens, the order of society is still restored because Launcelot is integrated, as is Eleanor. The review by or arranged by Cook was probably nearer the mark when he wrote that Braddon had ended her novel:

> In order not to offend the moral sense of a Christian public, Eleanor has to forego her vengeance in the moment of her triumph.[42]

The avenging angel becomes the angel of the house. Doubtless Braddon may have become reluctant to foist another 'beautiful fiend' on the reading public after the criticism of Lady Audley and Aurora Floyd.

It must be significant that in the next few books after *Lady Audley's Secret* and *Aurora Floyd* she veered away from bigamy heroines, and the type of heroines which had been criticised, and tried to make them more acceptable. Despite her actions Braddon is constantly stressing Eleanor's goodness, and there is never really any expectation of her murdering Launcelot. If she is unusually active she cannot help it, as she has never had anyone to guide her: her mother is dead, her half sister will not receive her, and her father is an irresponsible dreamer in his seventies. The relationship between Eleanor and her father is not unlike Little Nell and her grandfather in *The Old Curiosity Shop* with his uncontrollable gambling, fantasies of wealth and plans for Eleanor to be an heiress: he even calls her Nell. He is also one of the first of the unreliable father figures in Braddon's novels. Unlike Lady Audley, Eleanor is not governed by self interest, her ambitions are wholly centred around what she can do for her father. Therefore, it is only as an extension of being a good daughter that Eleanor carries out his wishes beyond the grave.

Because it is for the sake of a relative, for the sake of female justice, activity is more acceptable than in the case of a heroine of self interest like Lady Audley, or one of sensuality like Aurora Floyd. The reckless side of Eleanor's nature she has inherited from her unsuitable father:

> (Richard) recognized the taint of her father's influence in this vision of vengeance and destruction (...) Eleanor's teacher during her most impressionable years. It was scarcely to be wondered at, then, that there was some character flaws in the character of this motherless girl, and that she was ready to mistake a pagan scheme of retribution for the Christian duty of filial love. (p.123)

Therefore, once the task is achieved she has to learn to become what society expects of a woman. Her youth has been spent among Bohemians, gamblers, poor lodgings, and people of the theatre. She has not had anyone to tutor her in the rules of society (p.91). At the end of the novel she becomes a good and loyal wife to a rather unsympathetic character, and comes to respect his judgement more than her own, even when he is patently wrong. He is her education:

> Eleanor's intellect expanded under the influence of this superior masculine intelligence. Her plastic mind, so ready to take any impression, was newly moulded by its contact with this stronger brain, (p.120)

He can make her into what a proper father should have done. Eleanor (and the detective) is domesticated. If Eleanor is to be viewed as an early female detective it could also be said that her renouncing of vengeance makes her conform not just to the good angel, but also to the later rule that a good detective must uphold law and rules of society, not break them.

In *Henry Dunbar* (1864) Braddon again shows a loyal daughter, urged into action by filial loyalty. Joseph Wilmot has told his daughter "the secret of my life" (vol. I, p.27) and she too has learnt to hate the name of the man who has wronged him, "Henry Dunbar. I will not forget that name." (vol. I, p.30) They live under the assumed name of Wentworth and she works as a piano teacher. She believes her missing father has been murdered by his former employer Henry Dunbar, who let Wilmot go to prison for a forgery he had done for Dunbar. When Margaret starts investigating she associates herself with her father's criminal life by signing her deposition for the magistrate as Wilmot, 'she signed it with her father's real name, the name that she had never written before that day.' (vol. I, p.171). By doing so she associates herself with her father's criminality, and it also signifies her own transformation from ordinary girl to active detective. To do so she has to become resilient, surprising her fiancé when he hears she has a 'strong will':

> "Margaret has a strong will!" exclaimed Clement with a look of surprise; "why she is gentleness itself." (vol. II, p.102).

She pursues Henry Dunbar to an inn and to his ancestral home, and refuses with disgust his messages offering money:

> "All the wealth of this world cannot buy peace for Henry Dunbar, or forgetfulness. So long as I live, he shall be made to remember. If his guilty conscience can suffer him to forget, it shall be my task to recall the past. I promised my dead father that I would remember the name of Henry Dunbar: I have had good reason to remember it." (vol. I, p.207)

Dunbar is trapped in the house, knowing Margaret, his pursuer, is waiting at the gates. In the course of her investigation she discovers that the aristocracy have the power to evade justice. The courts care nothing for the murder of a poor man, and have no wish to inconvenience a millionaire. Margaret rapidly changes her mind when she discovers it is Henry Dunbar who is dead; her father had killed him and taken his place. She no longer believes he should face official justice. She helps him to escape and they disappear. Margaret is transformed from the amateur detective, a representative of the moral justice and authority the police will not use, to assisting a murderer and becoming herself a fugitive from justice. She helps her father to salvation when they start a new life, where he goes to church twice a day, and his gravestone reads, 'Lord have mercy upon me, a sinner!' (vol. II, p.307) His penitence is emphasised by Margaret:

> "If my father had failed to escape, and had been hung, he would have died hardened and unpenitent. God had compassion on him, and gave him time to repent." (vol. II, p.311)

Margaret has been more than a match for the police. Mr. Carter of Scotland Yard feels especially humiliated at being outwitted by a young girl:

> To have been hoodwinked by a girl, whose devotion to the unhappy wretch she called her father had transformed her into a heroine – to have fallen so easily into the trap that had been set for

him, being all the while profoundly impressed with the sense of his own cleverness. (vol. II, p.278)

Mr. Carter is right to note that it was devotion to her father that made her a heroine. Margaret is one of a long line of daughters of disreputable fathers. It was a subject Braddon returned to over and over again, and must represent the conflict she felt for her own father, the man who had failed to provide for his family and had been disreputable in his business dealings. Like Eleanor, once it is over, Margaret returns to the expected convention of home and marriage. The *Saturday Review* disliked the book and found the end immoral, as did the *Athenaeum*: 'He was sorry for what he had done! There's a moral for you!'[43]

By not demanding retribution for a criminal Braddon again incurred the wrath of critics. In *To the Bitter End* (1872), Braddon shows the consequence of an amateur detective demanding vengeance, when a father searches for his dead daughter's seducer. Tragedy ensues, because he identifies and murders the wrong man. The figure of justice has committed a worse crime than the man he was seeking.

In allowing many of her criminals to escape official justice Braddon breaks the rules of later detective fiction, where the punishment of the criminal and the restoration of the order of society is the climax of the novel. Because of Braddon's reluctance to have a criminal executed, there is often repentance or suicide. Although the refusal to punish the villain, or the tendency of the detective to keep the identity of the culprit secret, is contrary to the rules of the 'Golden Age' of detective fiction of the nineteen twenties and thirties, not all late nineteenth century detective stories follow these rules either; just as Braddon's detectives act as judge, so does Sherlock Holmes dispense justice in 'The Blue Carbuncle', and in 'A Case of Identity' he lets the culprit go.

Both Eleanor, Margaret and other amateur detectives created by Braddon, both male and female, are in the position to decide whether the perpetrators of crime should be revealed or kept secret, and usually the secrecy is maintained. In both of these cases families could be tainted by association, and so the family is protected by dealing with the secret or crime within that confine. The protection of the status of the bourgeois family is paramount, even if it involves the whole family concealing further secrets or even breaking the law. The preservation of secrets unifies a family in secrecy. There is a strong feeling that despite crime the rest of the family should not be stigmatised. If the crime were revealed, such stigmatisation would be inevitable; society's judgement would be harsh, and so the secret is kept. In *Henry Dunbar*, Margaret has committed a felony by helping a murderer to escape, but it is this action which allows her to maintain respectability herself. She is able to stay at the mansion her father had taken as an impostor, and her children mingle with those of the daughter of the man her father murdered. No one knows of her previous identity, because she has been able to suppress the crime:

> and none of the Maudesley servants who wait on the beautiful young matron have the faintest suspicion that they are serving the daughter of Henry Dunbar's murderer, the false master of the Abbey, (vol. II, p.313)

As a good middle class daughter she could never have turned her father in as "a downy one" as young Slosh does in *The Trail of the Serpent* (p.211). However, there is no doubt that Braddon's own humanitarian views also contributed to her reluctance to hang villains. Eleanor and Margaret, like Robert Audley, become detectives not by inclination, but as a duty to someone they love. Whereas, he stays active after it is over and begins his career proper, Eleanor and Margaret, who have both had unconventional backgrounds, retreat into the happy ending of the domestic life which would have been their lot had they had an ordinary upbringing.

Eleanor and Margaret are Braddon's main contributions to creating a woman detective. Some later characters do an element of detecting; in *Just As I Am* (1880) a working class woman tries to prove her father was innocent of murder, and conducts interviews with witnesses and takes a job as a servant to obtain information. She does not succeed in discovering the murderer's identity, and again the upper class murderer and his good reputation are preserved by one of his own class who allows him to repent at leisure (this time in a monastery). In *One Life, One Love* (1890) Daisy turns detective to discover the secrets of her family which have been kept from her. She discovers, by looking through twenty year old newspapers that her father was murdered. Gradually she learns her beloved step-father had committed the crime, to gain her mother. Through Daisy, Braddon shows the limitations of the female detective; to garner information Daisy has to break from her middle class life and brave the worst streets of London, where she finds, to her horror, men think she is sexually available. Although it sounds as if Daisy is an important female detective, her investigation in fact takes up only a small part of the novel, and more time is spent on her love life.

Braddon's Contribution to the Development of Detective Fiction

After *His Darling Sin* (1899), Braddon gave up her experiment of trying to write an up-to-date detective novel, and her later works are concerned with secrets within Edwardian society. For example, in *Beyond These Voices* (1910) the murder of a banker is never officially solved, although a James Japp of the C.I.D. (the same name Agatha Christie chose for her inspector in the Poirot novels) puts in a brief appearance. Braddon prefers to make it a novel of character rather than a detective novel, concentrating on the feelings of guilt and conversion to Catholicism of the banker's wife, whose lover had shot him.

Braddon never created a detective akin to Dupin or Holmes, and her detectives continue to fall into two types: the amateur who is personally affected by the case in some way, and the decent policeman with a resemblance to Wilkie Collin's Cuff. Braddon's preference for the amateur detective was nothing unusual, and even when detective fiction was a popular genre in its own right the amateur detective remained pre-eminent. The belief of the public and the creator of fiction was that a policeman could not possibly make the leap from solving humdrum crime to the more unusual crimes of the higher classes in sensation fiction. As a character type they were deemed to lack sufficient imagination to put themselves in the place of the person they were investigating, and were not going to possess the interesting and eccentric personalities of their amateur counterparts. The Victorian fictional solution to creating a viable detective was to have one of unusual brilliance; a man who accepted a professional fee, but was not doing it for the sake of financial reward, and more importantly yet, a gentleman. Holmes and Edgar Allan Poe's Dupin are apart from people, and unlike Braddon's amateur detectives do not get emotionally involved. Julian Symons in *Bloody Murder* writes that:

> Part of Holmes's attraction was that, far more than any of his later rivals, he was so evidently a Nietzschean superior man. It was comforting to have such a man on one's side.[44]

The amateur detective of sensation fiction was also comforting because there was no sordid exchange of money, and a gentleman would not expose a family's secrets to public gaze.

In *Wyllard's Weird* Braddon creates a situation, which was to become classic in detective fiction: a number of people in a confined space, one of whom must be the murderer. Braddon has twelve passengers on a train to Cornwall, one of whom must have thrown a girl out to her death. But unlike a later novelist – Agatha Christie for example in

Murder on the Orient Express – Braddon does not centre her novel on these twelve people. She only identifies and follows three, one of these becomes the amateur detective, so leaving only two possible suspects. She further gives it away with the very title, alerting the reader that there is something strange about the seemingly respectable landowner and financier Julian Wyllard. Braddon's working title had been *A Double Life* which would have been much more suitable, applying to either suspect. It is hard to believe Robert Lytton's (Bulwer's son who wrote poetry under the pseudonym Owen Meredith) assertion that he had not guessed the solution until the end.[45] A.E. Murch suggests that Braddon was influenced in this novel by French detective fiction, especially the sections where Heathcote investigates in Paris:

> Miss Braddon unravels the sensational clues in a manner very reminiscent of Gaboriau or Fortuné du Boisgobey. In so doing, she may have had in mind a wish to please her wide circle of French readers, for she was proud of the success of French translations other novels, and was in close touch with literary circles in Paris.[46]

Braddon would certainly have been familiar with these authors, but the French authors relied less on the amateur detective. The murders in her later novels such as *Like and Unlike* (1887) and the bodies are described more graphically, and it may be this facet was derived from French novels. Yet Braddon never has a professional or an amateur detective who is adept at disguises, unlike French detectives who excelled at it or Tom Taylor's Hawkshaw in the play *Ticket of Leave Man* – as does the later Sherlock Holmes. With Braddon's theatrical skills it is a pity she never created an actress amateur detective, who could use her skills to investigate. The nearest she comes to it is when Margaret in *Henry Dunbar* disguises herself as a maid to throw the police off her father's track. Justina, an actress, in *A Strange World* would have made an ideal one, as she guesses from the beginning of the novel who the murderer is, but her future husband Maurice Clissold does not take her theory seriously. Braddon may have created a detective who had these abilities in an anonymous short story in Braddon's Christmas annual *Mistletoe Bough* called 'A Terrible Experience', which, if it is by Braddon, is Braddon's best contribution to the type of detective fiction which had become popular in the late 1880s, providing as it does a French policeman who is a master of disguise, and a woman thief who is also adept at disguises.[47]

Sensation fiction of the 1860s was already criticised for promoting puzzle over character, so at this stage a novelist was unlikely to push it any further by making a novel where the whole point was the puzzle. A three decker novel could never have been purely puzzle, because as it was so long it had to be full of character and love plots to fill up the space. If detective fiction is the exposé of the solution of a puzzle, the whodunit in a crime or murder, sensation fiction is instead the revelation of secrets, and how the suppression of secrets affects the security of the family. A reader looking for puzzle solving is likely to be disappointed, because there is no challenge and will find the detective – professional or amateur – rather slow. Braddon was not very adept at keeping the murderer a secret from the reader. She does drop red herrings, the wrong person is often accused, but the reader never senses any danger. As puzzles they rarely work on the level of the classic detective novel, but are saved by interesting characters. It could be said that this would not have been the case for contemporary readers who would not have been so used to predicting the patterns of authorial deception, but reviewers of the time commented that the veil was too transparent.[48] One fan felt so cheated by *Sons of Fire* that he wrote to complain to Braddon that the mystery was obvious after only the tenth chapter, and her reply suggests that she had no great interest in baffling her readers:

> as the dram. pers. are then all on the scene of action, and the experienced novel reader ought to be able to foresee the drift and end of the story. I am sorry – for your purpose – the story is rather a psychological romance – than a complicated mystery: but still there is the grand question for your readers to solve – Which man will the heroine marry in the last chapter?[49]

Braddon probably never surpassed the mystery of what was Lady Audley's secret, the reader thinks they know it when in reality they do not. In this novel Braddon showed that the streets of London were not the only places to hold dark secrets and danger. She observed:

> No crime has ever been committed in the worst rookeries about Seven Dials that has not been also done in the face of that sweet rustic calm which still, in spite of all, we look on with a tender, half-mournful yearning, and associate – with peace. (p.54)

This was over thirty years before Conan Doyle had Sherlock Holmes similarly remark that the countryside also contained the potential for evil:

"It is my belief. Watson, founded upon my experience, that the lowest and vilest alleys of London do not present a more dreadful record of sin than does the smiling and beautiful countryside."[50]

The other situation she may well have created, as well as the amateur detective in a country house mystery, is the classic denouement used to end so much later detective fiction, when Robert Audley announces his findings and exposes Lady Audley to the upholder of society, Sir Michael Audley.

Chapter Five Footnotes

1. R..F. Stewart, *...And Always a Detective: Chapters on the History of Detective Fiction* (Newton Abbot: David and Charles, 1980), p.41 quotes 'Novels With a Purpose', *Westminster Review*, July 1864.

2. M.E. Braddon, *Beyond These Voices* (London: Hutchinson, 1910), p.185.

3. Stewart, p.67 quotes 'Miss Braddon', *Eclectic Review*, 1868.

4. Henry Mayhew, *London Labour and the London Poor* (1861-1862); B.S. Rowntree, *Poverty: A Study of Town Life* (1901); Charles Booth, *Labour and Life of People, London* (1891).

5. Monica Correa Fryckstedt, *On the Brink: English Novels of 1866* (Uppsala, Sweden: University of Uppsala, 1989), p.64 quotes 'Armadale', *Westminster Review*, vol. 86, July 1866, p.270.

6. W. Fraser Rae, 'Sensation Novelists: Miss Braddon', September 1865, *North British Review*, vol. XLIII, p.190.

7. 'Detectives in Fiction and in Real Life', *Saturday Review*, vol. XVII, 11 June 1864, p.712.

8. M.E. Braddon, *The Black Band; or, The Mysteries of Midnight* (*Halfpenny Journal*, vol. I, 1861-1862, p.115; rcpr. Hastings: The Sensation Press, 1998), p.219.

9. Julian Symons, *Bloody Murder* (1972; revised, London: Penguin, 1985), p.52. *The Notting Hill Mystery* was serialised in *Once a Week* in 1862-63. It was published in book form in 1865.

10. The private enquiry agent of novels such as *To the Bitter End* (1872) gets even less of a chance to do his work. In general such agents do so little that this one case will suffice. Mr. Kendal is occupying a fallen place in society as he is a former solicitor who 'took to drinking, and went altogether to the bad; then came up to London, and set up as a private enquirer.' (repr. London: Ward, Lock & Tyler, c.1874, p.159) Despite these failings Kendal does his work competently, before being sacked by his client, who has too personal an interest in the case and cannot leave it to a hired hand.

11. James Walvin, *Victorian Values* (London: Sphere, 1987), p.72.

12. M.E. Braddon, *The Trail of the Serpent* (London: Ward, Lock & Tyler, 1861; repr. London: Simpkin, Marshall, c.1905), p.25.

13. Anthea Trodd, *Domestic Crime in the Victorian Novel* (London: Macmillan, 1989), p.7.

14. Mrs. Oliphant, 'Sensation Novels', *Blackwood's Edinburgh Magazine*, vol. XCI, May 1862, p.568.

15. Stewart, p.27.

16. M.E. Braddon, *Henry Dunbar*, 2 vols. (Leipzig: Tauchnitz, 1864), II, p.160.

17. Stewart, p.187.

18. 'Detectives in Fiction and in Real Life', *Saturday Review*, vol. XVII, 11 June 1864, p.713.

19. Ibid.

20. The novel was serialised in thirty three parts between 18 April and 5 December 1874 in the *Bolton Weekly Journal*.

21. M.E. Braddon, *Wyllard's Weird* (London: Maxwell, 1885; repr. London: Simpkin, Marshall, c.1905), p.82.

22. M.E. Braddon, *The Day Will Come* (London: Simpkin, Marshall, 1889; repr. London: Simpkin, Marshall, c.1890), p.56.

23. M.E. Braddon, *Rough Justice* (London: Simpkin, Marshall, 1898), p.106.

24. 'His Darling Sin', *Spectator*, vol. LXXXXIII, 4 November 1899, p.662.

25. M.E. Braddon, *His Darling Sin* (London: Simpkin, Marshall, 1899), p.178.

26. For details on the snobbery in the detective fiction of the 1920s and 1930s see Colin Watson, *Snobbery With Violence* (London: Methuen, 1971; repr. 1987).

27. Wilkie Collins, *The Woman in White* (1860; repr. London: Penguin, 1982), p.640.

28. Stewart, p.202.

29. M.E. Braddon, *Lady Audley's Secret* (Oxford: Oxford University Press, 1987), p.33.

30. Lyn Pykett, *The Women's Sensation Novel and the New Woman Writing* (London: Routledge, 1992), p.103.

31. M.E. Braddon, *Birds of Prey* 3 vols. (London: Ward, Lock & Tyler, 1867) II, p.37.

32. 'Wyllard's Weird', *Athenaeum*, 21 March 1885, p.371.

33. A.E. Murch, *Development of the Detective Novel* (London: Peter Owen, 1958), p. 163.

34. Michele Slung, ed., *Crime on Her Mind: Fifteen Stories of Female Sleuths from the Victorian Era to the Forties* (London: Penguin, 1977), p.15.

35. Patricia Craig, and Mary Cadogen, *The Lady Investigates: Women Detectives and Spies in Fiction* (Oxford: Oxford University Press, 1996), p.21. Jenny Bourne Taylor, ed., Wilkie Collins, *The Law and the Lady* (Oxford: Oxford University Press, 1992), p.xv.

36. M.E. Braddon, *Eleanor's Victory* (London: Tinsley, 1863: repr. Ward, Lock & Tyler, c.1867), p.77.

37. Quoted in Winifred Hughs, *The Maniac in the Cellar: Sensation Novels of the 1860s* (Princeton: Princeton University Press, 1980), p.42.

38. Pykett, p.86.

39. George R. Sims, *Dorcas Dene Detective* (1897) is mentioned by Craig and Cadogen, p.23.

40. For the criticism of Magdalene see Audrey Peterson, *Victorian Masters of Mystery* (Frederick Ungar: New York, 1984), p.53.

41. W. Fraser Rae, p.191.

42. 'Eleanor's Victory', *Saturday Review*, 19 September 1863, p.397.

43. 'Henry Dunbar', *Saturday Review*, vol. XVIII, 9 July 1864, p.64. 'Henry Dunbar', *Athenaeum*, 21 May 1864, p.703.

44. Symons, p.65.

45. Letter from Robert Lytton to Braddon, 28 August 1885, Wolff collection.

46. Murch, p.156.

47. 'A Terrible Experience', *Mistletoe Bough*, 1889, pp.33-54. Wolff attributes this anonymous story to Braddon in his catalogue.

48. 'A Strange World', *Athenaeum*, 16 February 1875, pp.225-226.

49. Letter from Braddon to an unknown correspondent, 13 December 1894, Wolff collection.

50. Richard Altick, *Victorian Studies in Scarlet* (Norton: New York, 1970), p.275, *Strand Magazine*, June 1892. Altick does not give the title of the story.

Chapter Six
The Years of Success and Security:
The Later Years of Braddon's Life and Career

By the 1880s Braddon was a respected literary figure. She mixed in high society, and she and John Maxwell were prominent and respected figures in Richmond. Maxwell became involved in local government for the Conservatives, and was an active member of the Richmond Vestry which oversaw local interests and founded various institutions; in 1878 he campaigned to extend the opening hours of Kew Gardens.[1] He also urged that measures be taken for the purification of the Thames, writing to *The Times* about the matter. He developed several plots of land in the Richmond area with houses,[2] including most of the area round King's Road and many of the roads between Queen's Road and the town in the 1870s, naming roads after his wife's novels, including Audley Road and Marchmont Road. He bought property in Earls Court as late as 1890, and in 1892 Braddon noted in her diary 'Max bought two small lots land behind Bolton House £120.'[3]

Braddon and Maxwell also socialised with their aristocratic and titled neighbours at their second home near Lyndhurst in the New Forest. Maxwell built many of the houses at Bank, their own was named Annesley Bank and was enlarged from a cottage into a large and substantial property. Making changes to many of the cottages in Bank, Braddon wrote to Bram Stoker that the rural residents 'do not altogether appreciate improvements wh involve cleanliness & order on their parts.'[4] Since the inhabitants had their homes bought for building land, and were moved to another hamlet Maxwell had bought, Gritnam, perhaps their lack of appreciation is not to be wondered at. Many of their literary friends visited them there, and Joseph Hatton remembered Henry Labouchere writing an entire issue of *Truth* one evening. The area gave Braddon ample opportunity to indulge her passion for fox and deer hunting, on her horses Peggy and Vixen, and she did this as often as three times a week.

If anyone remembered the scandals of the past, it did not seem to matter. In 1883 a painting was exhibited to admiring crowds at the Royal Academy, when William Powell Frith painted Braddon for a second time, as one of a select group of notables in 'A Private View at the Royal Academy in 1881'. Braddon was depicted with many of the most famous personages of the day, including Gladstone, Browning, George Augustus Sala, Anthony Trollope, Oscar Wilde and Angela Burdett-Coutts.

However, as a writer she had not lost the ability to shock and offend reviewers. *Like and Unlike* (1887) was found to be too unpleasant by the *Athenaeum* reviewer who wrote:

> The murder this time is a trifle too shocking, and the concealment too ghastly.[5]

The murder which was 'too shocking' was the bludgeoning to death of an unfaithful wife by her upper class thug of a husband, who then wrapped her body in a blood soaked carpet before dumping her in a river. It is months before the decomposing body is discovered, identifiable only by her beautiful hair. The description is far more graphic than it would have been in the 1860s. On the whole, however, reviews were friendly by this date, as were articles about her; this was due partly to the fact that many of the journals were now being edited by her 1860s friends. There were other authors now considered controversial, and Braddon was older and some of her books display more conservative attitudes (especially concerning class) than she is often given credit for.

After *Belgravia* was sold to Chatto & Windus in 1876, Braddon no longer had an editorial staff, and she seems to have read and chosen most of the work for her annual *Mistletoe Bough*. She was very much aware that commercial interests had to prevail in her selection of manuscripts, telling Charles Kent that she feared his wife's story was not 'strong enough for an Annual wh has to Fight so many "blood & thunder" rivals.'[6] As with the early volumes of *Belgravia*, it is difficult to ascertain how much she was writing of her Christmas annual, since nearly all of the stories were anonymous, and hardly any of them could be identified if she had not collected some of them into volume form. *Mistletoe Bough* remained very much a family affair, with her daughter Fanny writing some of the stories, and, through an astonishingly generous gift from his father, her son, W.B. Maxwell, became the proprietor of the annual on his twenty first birthday. William thought the magazine old fashioned, and disliked taking on his father's role of calling on businesses to canvas for advertising. Sales fell and, preferring hunting to publishing, the annual came to an end.

Spencer Blackett took over the publishing business of John and Robert Maxwell in 1887, and in 1889 Jack Maxwell died at the age of thirty three, leaving his widow Alice and two young children. William said his brother had 'literally worked himself to death.'[7] John Maxwell continued to bullishly negotiate his wife's contracts with newspaper proprietors, but although Braddon always spoke fondly of her husband, none of John Maxwell's children were close to their father.

Interviewing their daughter Fanny Selous, then in her nineties, in 1958, Rex Sercombe Smith observed, 'Mrs Selous was lively & interesting & didn't like her father whom she distinctly referred to as Mr. Maxwell.'[8] Maxwell was financially generous to his children, and William later admitted they took advantage of this. At the same time they were embarrassed by him, made fun of his shop talk, and often tried to avoid him when he wanted to spend time with them.[9] Their relationship with their mother was close, and William recalled that when they were children:

> Hers was naturally a happy disposition. She rejoiced in laughter, and taught us children to love innocent mirth. She used to read to us; she walked with us, played with us, took us out for drives, but a good while elapsed before we knew that she had other more important tasks and that she belonged to the public as well as us. (...) One of the amazing things about her was that she got through her immense amount of work as if by magic. She never seemed to be given any time in which to do it. She had no stated hours, no part of the day to be held secure from disturbance and intrusions. She was never inaccessible. Everybody went uninvited to her library, we children, the servants, importunate visitors. I don't remember that she ever refused to come away from the quiet dignified room if we asked her. And she never failed to be available as a companion to my father when he wanted her, and no matter for how long.[10]

Despite his ill health in the 1890s, John Maxwell found retirement difficult, and insisted on keeping himself busy. He became easily anxious, pacing the house as he looked for things to do, while Braddon pleaded 'Dear Max, you have *nothing* to think about – only to rest and to take things easily.'[11] Later his behaviour became more irrational, Braddon described him as highly *emotional*', and it has been suggested that he was suffering with Alzheimer's. William said:

> When illness tightened its hold on him all the old good-humour vanished and his temper became very bad. Life under the same roof with him was often difficult. Trifles irritated him; grievances that were not very substantial made him beside himself. He had brief storms of unreasonable anger. He rated the servants for imagined faults. Sometimes all through a meal he made people uncomfortable – and most of all my mother, who was very unhappy in seeing the unmistakable evidence of the deterioration of mind

that such excesses afforded. She used to implore me never to forget that he was not always like this.[12]

Towards the end, his temper changed, he became quiet and gentle, only brightening in his wife's presence. Eventually he succumbed to influenza on 3 March 1895 while they were staying at Annesley Bank. Gerald, who was in New York acting in Augustin Daly's production of *The Gentleman of Verona,* was unable to attend his father's funeral, which was conducted by Maxwell's friend and local Catholic priest Father O'Connell.

After John Maxwell's death, Braddon's writing commitments seem to have lessened, and her diaries indicate that she enjoyed an active social life. In 1887 she had told Joseph Hatton she devoted most of the hours from ten till seven to literary work for four days a week, spending two days a week riding and hunting.[13] In 1897 Mary Angela Dickens wrote that she now worked from eleven until one.[14] Braddon also showed she was quite capable of overseeing her business affairs, as she took over the management of some of her first editions and all of the one volume reprints of her novels. Her son, W.B. Maxwell, wrote:

> Her position in this respect was I think unique. For in fact she was her own publisher. She bought the paper, gave orders to printers and binders, and finally sent the bound and wrappered books to Simpkin, Marshall, and Company for distribution.[15]

In the 1860s Braddon had expressed her desire to Bulwer Lytton that she intended to write a novel for the sake of 'fame', rather than popularity. Then she had begun *The Doctor's Wife* with that intention, and later came *Ishmael* (1884). Her final attempt to write what she considered to be her serious fiction were a number of historical novels: *Mohawks* (1886), *London Pride* (1896), *In High Places* (1898) and *The Infidel* (1900). She considered these to be her best works, and she certainly worked harder on them than any of her other novels. But to readers at the time, as well as to the modern reader, they seem dry, humourless and lacking in pace and excitement.[16]

In her last years she continued to write novels, although they were not best sellers. They were well received, but reviews of them were brief, and these late novels were not given the great prominence of the first two or three decades. One was *The Rose of Life* (1906), the central character of which was based on Oscar Wilde. Wilde's mother had been a friend of Braddon's, and Wilde became a regular visitor to Lichfield House in the 1880s, reading the Maxwell family 'Lord Arthur Saville's Crime' and 'The Canterville Ghost' before publication. One of

Braddon's notebooks lists characteristics and witty epigrams for Daniel Lester to say, and this reveals that her original intention had been to make him 'gallant to his wife – yet leaving her for the night club – the company of profligate women.'[17] The final novel has no profligate women (or men); Lester's fall is through theft.

However, Braddon was praised for the consistently high standard she had sustained over so many years. By now the reviewers were the people who had enjoyed reading her when young. As a reviewer of *The White House* (1906) wrote with a tinge of regret:

> she seems to have abandoned those frankly sensational methods which, as some of us can testify, imparted a 'fearful joy' to the childhood of a generation now matured.[18]

These later novels do not show any falling off in terms of ability, which is remarkable when one considers she continued writing after a stroke. In November 1908 she was confined to bed and was given morphine injections every night. Although respected she was perceived as being a writer of a previous generation, as were some of her views. Some of her criticisms of the modern novel are reminiscent of the criticisms she herself received as a young woman:

> "That many of the books of which I hear – I seldom read any of them myself," she said in parenthesis – "should be published at all is a scandal; that they should be written by women is even worse – it is a disgrace."[19]

In old age she was praised for traditional domestic values, Mary Angela Dickens writing:

> Miss Braddon has never allowed her special work as a novelist to crowd out of her life her everyday work as a woman. She has responded, as the simplest matter of course, to all the demands made upon a wife and mother.[20]

She told Alice Hastings (the daughter of William Frith), a little patronisingly, she admired her for being such a 'clever housekeeper', adding 'I only wish I had more time for housekeepng, wh I am very fond of – especially dusting & furniture polishing.'[21] She was indeed beginning to sound a little old fashioned in her views, and the novelist and suffragette Beatrice Harraden worried she might cause offence when she asked Braddon for a signed novel for the Women's Social and Political Union fair.[22] Although Braddon expressed her belief in 1913 that women should have the vote, she disagreed with the militant wing of the suffrage movement:

> Certainly, I think women ought to have a vote when every half-educated man, every clodhopper may have his say in the government of his country. Suffragists, I think, are both self-sacrificing and daring. Militants, however, have gone the wrong way about asserting their rights. Nothing is to be gained by the destruction of private property, and those actions have done nothing more than alienate even those who are in sympathy with the movement.[23]

The woman who had become a teenage actress and then travelled to London to write for magazines said in old age:

> Modern tendencies may be a little too much towards the liberty of the individual. Bachelor girls, perhaps, are just a trifle too appreciative of their freedom. I think, however, that they will eventually learn that home and home ties are best for them.[24]

Despite this, she wrote interesting novels even in her seventies; particularly outstanding are *A Lost Eden* (1904), *Dead Love Has Chains* (1907) and *The Green Curtain* (1911). She lived to see a film version, a 'picture play', of *Aurora Floyd* in 1913. When the First World War broke out Braddon was on holiday in Bexhill-On-Sea with William and Sydney, and their children Barbara and Henry. Although he was in his forties William was determined to join up and Braddon interested herself in the plight of Belgian refugees, having a family come to live with her at Lichfield house. In December 1914 she was still fit and active and her agent, A.P. Watt, was pleased when she told him she had just finished *Mary*, and he was keen to find a newspaper in which to serialise it.[25]

A fortnight before her death she became weaker, and remained at home, but still busied herself gathering things to send to her grandson, Austin Lachlan, who was at the front with the Gloucestershire Regiment, and who was injured a few days before her death. A week later she had a stroke and was confined to bed. Douglas Sladen visited her, and he noted her depression over William being away with the army, to the extent of wishing it was one of her other sons.[26] Her family were with her when she died shortly before eight in the morning on the 4 February 1915, including William who was now a lieutenant in the Royal Fusiliers, and had been stationed in Colchester, Fanny, Edward (a barrister) and Gerald, who was now the theatre critic for the *Daily Mail*.

The *Daily Mail* commented that although the height of her fame had been forty years earlier, and despite the war, most of the evening papers carried the news of her death as the headline on the evening news-bills.[27] The obituaries commemorated Braddon affectionately as one of the last great Victorian novelists.

A few days later the *Thames Valley Times* commented that the funeral on the 8 February reflected Braddon's love of music and flowers. The coffin was of panelled English oak with brass fittings and the plate bore the inscription, 'Mary Elizabeth Braddon, Died February 4th 1915, Aged 77 years.' The long cortege left Lichfield House shortly before two o'clock in the afternoon, two of the carriages were filled with flowers, and the hearse contained yet more wreaths. Shops were closed, their windows covered by black shutters, and houses drew their blinds as people lined the streets. Before the service Ambrose Porter played Beethoven's Funeral march, Chopin's Prelude in C Minor, and Mendelsohn's Funeral March. The coffin was carried up the aisle while 'Blest are the Departed' was played and the service was conducted by Max Binney, the vicar of Richmond, assisted by Braddon's friend Reverend J.H. Champion McGill, the vicar of Isleworth, and Reverend Beckwith. Three hymns were sung, 'The Saints of God', 'Now the Labourers Task is O'er', and 'Peace, Perfect Peace.' The coffin was carried from the church to the accompaniment of Chopin's March Funebre, and many people were waiting outside the church to watch and gather at the cemetery. Her funeral was attended, and flowers sent, by her many friends and relations, including Florence Haydon who had acted with her in Brighton, and Madge Kendal, whose sister had acted in Hull with Braddon so many years earlier. Kendal's wreath read:

Oh, tell me not that years will give
Oblivion as they fly
The hope whereby alone I live
Is one with memory.[28]

In October of that year a portrait in bronze by John E. Hyett was unveiled at the Parish Church in Richmond by two of her grandchildren, and Braddon's last novel, the melancholy *Mary*, was published posthumously in 1916.

One of Braddon's greatest strengths was as a brilliant plotter, and naturally the sensation novel provided ample opportunities for elaborate plots. Although it has been claimed that Braddon moved away from sensation, this really is not the case. However, her writing style, particularly her dialogue, became less melodramatic and her characters written with a greater psychological perspective. Her descriptive powers certainly improved as she matured, but the novels of the 1860s which made her name still remain exciting and readable. Nor is it true that she abandoned sensation and melodrama; readers loved it and Braddon was clearly at home writing it.

Her achievements were numerous. Although Braddon did not become a famous and acclaimed actress in the 1850s, she was obviously good enough to remain in almost constant employment, despite initial disadvantages. There can be no doubt that her career on the stage helped to shape her as a writer, not only in terms of plots and settings, but it also gave her an insight into what the reading public would most enjoy.

Braddon had enough judgement to realise that her talents did not lie as a poet, and so she made a seemingly effortless move to writing cheap penny and half penny part fiction. Braddon was always adept at adapting her writing to whatever audience she was writing for, and she proved that every strata of society enjoyed stories of a dramatic and mysterious nature. In the early 1860s there was a dividing line between inexpensive lower class fiction and the middle class novel of the circulating library; Braddon made this transition, and in doing so she wrote some of the most successful and well known novels of her generation. Despite hostility from some critics over the sensational aspects in her life and work, Braddon insisted on defending her fiction in *Belgravia* and her readers did not abandon her. She managed to maintain this popularity for decades, and always attempted to remain up to date with plots of modern life. Braddon also provides an interesting example of the literary market place, with the weekly and monthly serialisation of her work, and her own later management of reprints.

She achieved great popularity as a novelist, but she had such ability that she remains of importance and interest today. Even though a number of her novels have been reprinted in recent years, there are many others of such an exceptionally high quality that they do not deserve to be neglected. The relationship of her novels to popular culture makes her especially interesting; she was writing books for the people rather than the elitist few. It is also partly her early life, her courage to become an actress when few women took such a step, her determination to become a writer, and her brave relationship with John Maxwell, which commands our respect and admiration today.

Chapter Six Footnotes

1. Somers T. Gascoyne, *Recollections of Richmond It's Institutions and Their Development* (Richmond: Frederick W. Dimbleby, 1898), p.43.
'Death of John Maxwell', *Richmond and Twickenham Times*, 9 March 1895, p.6:

> Until seven or eight years ago Mr. John Maxwell was amongst the foremost of our public men in Richmond. The mental and physical vigour which raised him to high position in the publishing world were amply exercised as a member of the Richmond Vestry, at that time the chief local authority in the district. His bold and vigorous speeches will long be remembered by those who heard them. At public meetings respecting local matters his voice was generally heard, and he frequently took part, as a Conservative, in political gatherings, where his incisive and sometimes vehement speeches were always effective.

2. 'Death of John Maxwell', *Richmond and Twickenham Times*, 9 March 1895, p.6.
3. Diary, 7 October 1892, Wolff collection.
4. Braddon to Bram Stoker, 6 April ny, Bram Stoker Correspondence, Brotherton Library, University of Leeds.
5. 'Like and Unlike', *Athenaeum*, 1 October 1887, p.435.
6. M.E. Braddon to Charles Kent, 13 July 1881, Wolff collection.
7. W.B. Maxwell, *Time Gathered* (London: Hutchinson, 1937), p.159.
8. Notebook of Rex Sercombe Smith, 1 July 1958, p.110, Wolff collection. The children believed that Maxwell had not told Braddon he was already married.
9. Maxwell, pp.279-281.
10. Maxwell, p.163.
11. Ibid.
12. Ibid.
13. Joseph Hatton, 'Miss Braddon at Home', *London Society*, January 1888, p.28.
14. Mary Angela Dickens, 'Miss Braddon At Home', *Windsor Magazine*, vol. VI, September 1897, p.418.
15. Maxwell, p.144.
16. The writer of 'Miss Braddon, An Enquiry', *Academy: A Weekly Review of Literature and Life*, vol. LVII, 14 October 1899, p.432, observed of *Ishmael* and *London Pride*, 'They are good novels, and more than a proof of versatility, but they are scarcely "Braddon." '

17. Notebook in Wolff collection covering the Edwardian period, including notes for 'Naomi', a late play version of *Henry Dunbar*, and songs for a new adaptation of the *Loves of Arcadia*.

18. 'The White House', *Athenaeum*, 8 December 1906, p.730.

19. Clive Holland, 'Fifty Years of Novel Writing, Miss Braddon at Home', *Pall Mall Magazine*, November 1911, p.707.

20. Dickens, p.416.

21. Braddon to Alice Hastings, 10 November ny, Wolff collection.

22. Beatrice Harraden to Braddon, 28 November ny, Wolff collection.

23. 'Miss Braddon at Home', *Daily Telegraph*, 4 October 1913, p.9.

24. Ibid.

25. A.P. Watt to Braddon, 18 December 1914, Wolff collection.

26. Douglas Sladen, *My Long Life* (London: Hutchinson, 1939), p.198.

27. 'Death of Miss Braddon', *Daily Mail*, 5 February 1915, p.3.

28. *Era*, 10 February 1915, p.8.

Appendix One
Calendar of Mary Braddon's Theatrical Career

This calendar is intended to be as comprehensive as possible, giving details of the towns where Braddon acted, the plays put on by the various companies and, where known, the parts she played as Mary Seyton. This gives an indication of the large number of plays which formed the repertoire of provincial theatre companies in the 1850s. Information on what roles Braddon played has mainly come from newspapers and collections of playbills. When Braddon played a particular role, she usually played that same role for succeeding performances that season. The author of the play, where known, is given on the first occasion the title is mentioned, as well as the number of acts and whether it was a comedy, farce, drama or tragedy etc. As well as those roles listed she probably played Constance in *The Love Chase*, as a notebook of the period has the first act copied out with the part of Constance underlined.

1852

THEATRE ROYAL, BATH
LESSEE AND MANAGER, MRS. MACREADY
Braddon probably acted in Bath for the season beginning in the autumn of 1852. She may not have played large enough roles to be reviewed or mentioned on playbills, and so I have not given full details of the productions at Bath in 1852.

1853

I have given some details of the productions in Bath for the second half of the season. It is by no means complete, but gives some indication of what was performed.

THEATRE ROYAL, BATH
LESSEE AND MANAGER, MRS. MACREADY
Saturday 8 January
> Grand Juvenile night
> *Children in the Wood* (D)
> *The Miller's Daughter* ('grotesque ballet')
> *A Day After the Fair* (F 2a C.A. Somerset)

Saturday 15 January
> *Uncle Tom's Cabin* (D 2a Edward Fitzball)

Jamie of Aberdeen (ballet)

Saturday 22 January
    Uncle Tom's Cabin
    The Corsican Brothers (D 3a Dion Boucicault)

Thursday 27 January
    Queen Mab and Harlequin and the Golden Pippin; or, The Fairy
    of the Enchanted Beehive
    Barber Bravo
Friday 28 January
    As Thursday
Saturday 29 January
    The Bride of Lammermoor (D 3a)
    Queen Mab
Thursday 3 February
    Queen Mab
Friday 4 February
    Queen Mab
Saturday 5 February
    Queen Mab
Monday 7 February
    Daytime juvenile performance
    Queen Mab
Saturday 12 February
    Time Tries All (C 2a John Courtney)
    Uncle Tom's Cabin

Saturday 26 February
    Hamlet
    Your Life's in Danger (F 1a Maddison Morton)

Saturday 19 March
    Time Tries All
    Uncle Tom's Cabin

Saturday 2 April
    The Second Part of Uncle Tom's Cabin

Saturday 9 April
    The Second Part of Uncle Tom's Cabin

Thursday 14 April

The Second Part of Uncle Tom's Cabin

Friday 29 April
Gentleman amateurs of Bath
    The Rivals (Sheridan)
    The Rough Diamond (C 1a J.B. Buckstone)
Saturday 30 April
    Benefit of Miss Clara St. Casse
    Uncle Tom's Cabin
    Buffo Scena
    Milliner's Holiday (F 1a J. Maddison Morton)
    Swiss Cottage (C 1a T.H. Bayly)

Wednesday 4 May
    Benefit for Mr. Melville
    Richlieu (D 5a Bulwer Lytton)
    The Full-Dress Rehearsal

Saturday 7 May
    Money (C 5a Bulwer Lytton)

Wednesday 11 May
    Benefit of Mr. Salmon, leader of the band
    Trevanian (D)
    Rural Felicity (C J.B. Buckstone)

Friday 13 May
    The Flowers of the Forest (D 3a Buckstone)
    The Little Devil; or, My Share (D Benjamin Webster)

Saturday 21 May
    Patrons Col. Pinney M.P. and Officers of the 2nd Royal Somerset
    Militia
    London Assurance (C 5a Dion Boucicault)
    band
    Corsican Brothers

Tuesday 24 May
    Benefit of Mr. Chute
    St. Cupid; or, Dorothy's Fortune (C 3a D. Jerrold)
    Don Caesar de Bazan (D 3a G. Beckett and Mark Lemon)
End of season.

THEATRE ROYAL, SOUTHAMPTON
LESSEE AND MANAGER, EDWIN HOLMES

Saturday 13 August

My Wife's Mother (C C.J. Mathews)

Raymond and Agnes; or, The Bleeding Nun of Lindenburg (D 2a Edward Fitzball)

Dancing by Miss Louisa Sidney and Mr. Lavine

Sparks in the Dark

Monday 15 August

Patrons Commodores and members of the Royal Southern Yacht Club

John Bull; or, The Englishman's Friend (C 5a Colman)

comic singing by Mr. J.G. Montague,

dancing by Sidney and Lavine

The Haunted Inn (F 1a R.B. Peake)

Thursday 18 August

The Momentous Question (D 3a Edward Fitzball)

Box and Cox (F 1a J. Maddison Morton)

Boots at the Crown (F 1a Charles Selby)

Saturday 20 August

Minnigrey, The Gypsy Girl; or, England's Army and Navy (Adelaide Biddles)

The Sleeping Draught (F 2a Samson Penley)

Also this week: *The Farmer's Story* (D 3a W. Bayle Bernard)

Monday 22 August

Benefit of Mr. Holmes (last night before season)

The Lady of Lyons (D 5a Bulwer Lytton)

Love, War, and Physic (F 1a R. Jephson)

dancing

White Lies; or, Sudden Thoughts

THEATRE ROYAL, WINCHESTER
LESSEE AND MANAGER EDWIN HOLMES

Tuesday 23 August

The Lady of Lyons

Dance by Sidney and Lavine

The Sleeping Draught

Wednesday 24 August

The Stranger (D 5a August von Kotzebue)

Thursday 25 August

Patron the Mayor

The Honeymoon (C 5a John Tobin)

Monday 29 August
   The Lady of Lyons
   Dance. Comic song by Mr. Brandon
   The Momentous Question (D 2a Edward Fitzball)
Tuesday 30 August
   Patrons Mayor Crofton and Officers of the 20th Regiment
   Band music
   John Bull
   Dance by Miss Sidney
   Katherine and Petruchio (C 3a David Garrick adap.)
Wednesday 31 August
   The Honeymoon
   White Lies
Thursday 1 September
   The Stranger
   Dance
   Boots at the Swan

Monday 5 September
   Minnigrey
   pas de deux
   Pop Goes the Weasel
Tuesday 6 September
   Minnigrey
   dance
   Rappings and Table Movings (F 1a Howard Paul)

Monday 12 September
   The Rajah's Daughter
   singing and dancing
   Uncle Tom's Cabin
Tuesday 13 September
   Therese
   singing and dancing
   Uncle Tom's Cabin
Wednesday 14 September
   Richard III
   Pop Goes the Weasel
Thursday 15 September
   Minnigrey **(SEYTON PLAYED MOLLY TURPIN AND A
   PEASANT GIRL)**

dance

The Wandering Minstrel (F 1a Henry Mayhew) **(SEYTON PLAYED JULIA)**

Friday 16 September

Funds for the Jewry St. Improvement Committee

The Poor Gentleman (C George Colman) **(SEYTON PLAYED DAME HARROWBY)**

An epilogue, a song, brass band

Raising the Wind (F 1a James Kenney) **(SEYTON PLAYED MISS PEGGY PLAINWAY)**

Saturday 17 September

Uncle Tom's Cabin

Monday 19 September

Lover's Vows (Mrs. Inchbald) **(SEYTON PLAYED MADAME KARL)**

Harlequin Open Sesame and the Forty Thieves, or the Fairy of the Lake **(SEYTON PLAYED FAIRY PEASEBLOSSOM)**

Tuesday 20 September

George Barnwell (T 5a George Lillo) **(SEYTON PLAYED LUCY)**

Saturday 24 September

Harlequin Open Sesame

panorama of the funeral of the Duke of Wellington

Friday 30 September

Benefit of Mr. Holmes

Heir at Law (C 5a George Colman) **(SEYTON PLAYED CAROLINE DORMER)**

dance

No! No! No! (F) **(SEYTON PLAYED DOLLY)**

comic song, poetic address, Winchester amateur band

Young England (F Maddison Morton) **(SEYTON PLAYED MRS. DASHALONG)**

THEATRE ROYAL, SOUTHAMPTON

Start of winter season

Monday 3 October

Minnigrey

A comic song by Mr. Brandon, dance by Sidney and Lavine

Pop Goes the Weasel

Meet Me By Moonlight (F Thomas Parry)

Tuesday 4 October

As Monday, except last
The Wandering Minstrel

Saturday 8 October
Last 2 nights of panorama of Wellington's funeral
Harlequin Open Sesame
Monday 10 October
Amy Laurence; or, An Old Man's Love (Adelaide Biddles)
Damon and Pythias (T 5a)
panorama and address by Miss Biddles
Harlequin House

Saturday 15 October
The Blind Boy (D 2a J. Kenney)
Amy Laurence
The Wandering Minstrel
Also this week: *The Innkeeper of Abbeville* (D 2a George Soane), *Ambrose Gwinett* (D 3a Douglas Jerrold)
Monday 17 October
Clari, the Maid of Milan (operatic play, Howard Payne and J.R. Planché)
The Little Jockey; or, Youth, Love, and Folly (F 1a William Dimond)
Ben the Boatswain; or, Ashore and Afloat (D 3a T.E. Wilks)

Wednesday 19 October
The Green Bushes (D 3a Buckstone) **(SEYTON APPEARED)**
His First Champagne (F 2a W.L. Rede)
Thursday 20 October
As Wednesday

Saturday 22 October
The Farmer's Story
Ben Bowling
Monday 24 October
The Maid of Honour; or Love, Fidelity, and Revenge (D)
The Maid With the Milking Pail (C Buckstone)
My Poll and My Partner Joe (D 3a J.T. Haines)
Tuesday 25 October
(as Monday)
Wednesday 26 October
The False Friend; or, The Peasant Boy **(SEYTON PLAYED OLYMPIA)**

Thursday 27 October
  The False Friend
also this week: *Robert Macaire* (D 2a), *Green Bushes*
Saturday 29 October
  The False Friend
  The Maid of Honour
Monday 31 October
  A Maiden's Flame
  A Legend of Lisbon
  The Female Duellist
  The Queen's Page
Tuesday 1 November
As Monday but ending with:
  High Life Below Stairs (F 2a James Townley)
Wednesday 2 November
  Faith and Falsehood
  The Dream at Sea (D 3a Buckstone)

Saturday 5 November
  The Village Phantom; or, Ernestine the Somnambulist
  Guy Faux; or, Gunpowder Treason (D)
Also this week: *The Fate of a Bushranger*
Monday 7 November
  Crazy Ruth; or, The Prophet of the Moor
  Ladies at Home; or, Gentleman We Can't Do Without You
  Mr. and Mrs. White; or, on a Trip to Richmond
Tuesday 8 November
  Crazy Ruth
  Ladies at Home
  The Queen's Page
Wednesday 9 November
  Linda, The Pearl of Savoy

Saturday 12 November
  The Broken Hearted; or, The Gypsy Queen
  The Middy Ashore (F 1a W. Bayle Bernard)
  The Rajah's Daughter
Also this week: *The Minute Gun at Sea*

Monday 14 November
  Victorine (D Buckstone)
  The Poor Soldier (operetta)
  Wilful Murder (F 1a Thomas Higgie)

Tuesday 15 November
First two as Monday and
Fortune's Frolic (F 1a)
Wednesday 16 November
The Last Link of Love
The Lonely Man of the Ocean (D 3a Thomas Blake)
Thursday 17 November
William Tell (D 4a Sheridan Knowles)
Green Bushes
Friday 18 November
The Castle of Andalusia (O'Keefe)
The Last Link of Love
Saturday 19 November
Linda, the Peal of Savoy
All in the Wrong; or, The Mistakes of a Night (C 5a A. Murphy)
Monday 21 November
Hamlet
The £100 Note; Or, Boots and Conundrums (F R.B. Peake)
Tuesday 22 November
Romeo and Juliet
The Hypocrite (5a Isaac Bickerstaff)
Wednesday 23 November
Jacob Faithful; Or, The Life of a Thames Waterman (after Marryat)
The Female Duellist
Fortune's Frolic
Thursday 24 November
Jacob Faithful
Love and Charity (D 1a Mark Lemon)
The Lottery Ticket (C 1a Samuel Beazley)

Saturday 26 November
Romeo and Juliet
The Poor Soldier
Monday 28 November
Macbeth
Blanche Heriot; or, The Churtsey Curfew
The Curfew Bell
Tuesday 29 November
Macbeth
The Village Phantom
Wednesday 30 November
Martin Chuzzlewit
The £100 Note

Saturday 3 December
    Nicholas Nickleby (D 3a Andrew Halliday)
    Exchange no Robbery (C 3a Theodore Hook)
    The Queen's Page
Monday 5 December
Patron: US consul J.R. Croskey
    King John
    The Soldier's Progress
Tuesday 6 December
As Monday
Wednesday 7 December
    Benefit for Widows and Orphans Fund of the Ancient Order of
    Foresters
    The Jew of York! Or, The Days of Robin Hood
    dance by Miss Sidney
    Dominique the Deserter (C 1a W.H. Murray)
    The Little Jockey (F 1a William Dimond)
    The Maid of Judah

Saturday 10 December
    Martin Chuzlewit
    The Soldier's Progress
Monday 12 December
    Richard III
    The Mistress of the Mill (C 1a M.T. Moncrieff)
    The Irish Tutor (C 1a Richard Butler)
Tuesday 13 December
    Othello
    The Irish Tutor
    The Captain is Not a Miss (F 1a T.E. Wilks)

Thursday 15 December
    Hamlet
Friday 16 December
    Macbeth
Monday 19 December
    Benefit of Mr. Holmes
    Rob Roy; Or, Auld Lang Syne (D 3a)
    Love and Charity
    singing and dancing
    The Wizard's Stone; Or, The Banks of the Itchen 1000 Years Ago
    (local author)

Monday 26 December
>reopens
>*Speed the Plough* (C 5a Thomas Morton)
>*Harlequin Blue Beard and the Magic Key; Or, The Genius of Improvement*

Saturday 31 December
>*Guy Mannering*
>*Harlequin Blue Beard*

1854

Monday 2 January
>*The Cedar Chest; or, The Lord Mayor's Daughter*
>*Plot and Counterplot*
>*Harlequin Blue Beard*
Tuesday 3 January
>As Monday
Wednesday 4 January
>Juvenile night
>*Harlequin Blue Beard*
>*The Wizard's Stone*
Thursday 5 January
>As Wednesday
Friday 6 January
>*The King's Wager* (D 3a T.E. Wilks)
>*Harlequin Blue Beard*
Saturday 7 January
>*Richard III*
>*Harlequin Blue Beard*
Monday 9 January
>*The Flying Dutchman; or, Phantom Ship* (C 3a Fitzball)
>*Kate Kearney Married; or, The Pride of Killarney*
Tuesday 10 January
>(As Monday)
Wednesday 11 January
>Juvenile Night
>*Harlequin Blue Beard*
>*Bombaster Furioso; or, The Doleful Lover* (F 1a W.B. Rhodes)
>*The Doleful Lover*
Thursday 12 January
>(Juvenile night as Wednesday)

Saturday 14 January
The Flying Dutchman

Monday 16 January
The Mountaineers; or, Love and Madness (D 3a Colman)
Where Shall I Dine (F. G.H. Rodwell)
All in the Wrong
Tuesday 17 January
Grand Amateur Performance led by Capt. Disney, with ladies of the company.
The Wreck Ashore (D 2a Buckstone)
Don Caesar de Bazan
Wednesday 18 January
Juvenile night
Harlequin Blue Beard
Thursday 19 January
(As Wednesday)

Saturday 21 January
Harlequin Blue Beard (matinee only)
Monday 23 January
Benefit for Mrs. Holmes
Henri Quatre; or, Paris in the Olden Time (Morton)
Aladdin; or, The Wonderful Lamp
Wednesday 25 January
The Diamond Ring; or, He Would be a Sailor
The Flying Dutchman

Friday 27 January
Patron B.M. Willcox M.P.

Monday 30 January
Guest Star Charles Pitt
King Lear
High Life Below Stairs (F 2a James Townley)
Tuesday 31 January
Richard III
Past Ten o'clock (F T.J. Dibdin)
Wednesday 1 February
The Egyptian (5a J.H. Wilkins)
The Cedar Chest
Thursday 2 February
Richelieu; or, The Conspiracy (D 5a Bulwer Lytton)

Raising the Wind
Friday 3 February
    Benefit for Charles Pitt
    The Wonder (C 3a Susannah Centlivre)
    The Brigand (D 2a J.R. Planché)
Saturday 4 February
    King Lear
    Sharp and Flat
Monday 6 February
    Patrons Sir Edward and Lady Butler
    The Honeymoon
    Betsy Baker (F 1a J. Maddison Morton)
    The Wandering Minstrel
Tuesday 7 February
    The Diamond Ring
    The Mountaineers
Wednesday 8 February
    Benefit for Oddfellows Widows and Orphans Fund. Patron Sir
    A.J.E. Cockburn M. P. Attorney General
    The Wreck Ashore; or, A Bridegroom from the Sea
    The Rival Pages
    Dance by Montague and Sidney, song by Mr. Brandon
    Exchange No Robbery; or, Village Bathing
Thursday 9 February
    Harlequin Blue Beard
Friday 10 February
    Harlequin Blue Beard

Monday 13 February
    Life in Russia; or, The Serfs of Muscovy
    Whitebait at Greenwich (F 1a J. Maddison Morton)

Wednesday 15 February
    Benefit for Mr. Montague (stage manager)
    Man and Wife; or, More Secrets Than One (C S.J. Arnold)
    Singing and dancing
    Black Eyed Susan (D 2a Jerrold, sexes reversed)

Saturday 18 February
    (matinee only)
    Harlequin Blue Beard
    Jealous Man! (C 5a George Colman)
Monday 20 February

Elizabeth; or, The Exiles of Siberia
Rory O'More (D 3a Samuel Lover)
Tuesday 21 February
    Elizabeth; or, The Exiles of Siberia
    Crazy Ruth
Wednesday 22 February
    Patrons Robert and Mrs. Wright
    Married Life (C 3a Buckstone)
    Four Sisters; or, Woman's Worth, and Woman's Ways (F 1a W.
    Bayle Bernard)
    His First Champagne
Thursday 23 February
    Harlequin Blue Beard (25th and last time)
Friday 24 February
    Fashionable Amateur Gentlemen
    You Can't Marry Your Grandmother (C 2a T.H. Bayly)
    Raising the Wind
    The Rendezvous (F 1a R. Ayton)
Saturday 25 February
    Othello
    Kate Kearney Married

Monday 27 February
    Benefit for Mr. Collings (box book keeper)
    She Stoops to Conquer (Goldsmith)
    Othello Travestie
Tuesday 28 February
    Man and Wife
    Black Eyed Susan (sexes reversed)

Thursday 2 March
    Benefit for Charles Calvert
Friday 3 March
    The Duel; or, My Two Nephews (C R.B. Peake)
    Electricity; or, The Doctor Dosed (comic ballet)
    The Brigand
Saturday 4 March
    The Duel
    Electricity
    Crazy Ruth
Monday 6 March
    The Lady of Lyons
    The Brigand

Tuesday 7 March
   The Corsican Brothers
   The Hypocrite
Wednesday 8 March
   Benefit for Mr. Skinner
   Who Wants a Guinea (C 5a Colman)
Thursday 9 March
   Benefit for Adelaide Biddles
   The Wager

Saturday 11 March
   Speed the Plough!
   The Cedar Chest
Monday 13 March
   The Battle of Austerlitz; or, The Soldier's Bride (D 3a J.T. Haines)
   The Green Hills of the Far West
Tuesday 14 March
   (As Monday)
Wednesday 15 March
   Benefit for Mrs. J.W. Simpson
   The School for Scandal

Friday 17 March
   Benefit for Mr. and Mrs. Rainford
   Woman and Her Master, or, The Miser's Progress (by Mr.
   Rainford, adapted from the *London Journal*)
   Raby Rattler; or, Life in England, Ireland and Australia
Saturday 18 March
   Man and Wife
   Raymond and Agnes
Monday 20 March
   *Woman and Her Master; or, The Peer, The Poisoner and the
   Maniac* (D 3a H. Young)
   The Outlaw Chief
Tuesday 21 March
   Jane Shore (T 5a Nicholas Rowe)
   Woman and Her Master
Wednesday 22 March
   The Black Doctor (D)
   The King's Gardener (C 1a Charles Selby)
   Don Juan
Thursday 23 March
   The Poor Gentleman

One O'clock; or, The Knight and the Wood Demon (D 3a)
Friday 24 March
    Benefit for Mr. E.V. Gregory
    The Will and the Way (Mrs. Gregory)
Saturday 25 March
    The Foundling of the Forest (D William Dimond)
    The Girl, the Wife, and the Heroine (Biddles)
Monday 27 March
    Gil Blas (D 3a)
    The Sea (D 2a C.A. Somerset)
Tuesday 28 March
    The Will and the Way
    The Wandering Minstrel
Wednesday 29 March
    Benefit for Mr. G.J. Hall (leader of orchestra)
    Esmerelda, or the Hunchback of Notre Dame (D 3a)
    Shylock
Thursday 30 March
    The Battle of Austerlitz
    The Outlaw Chief
Friday 31 March
    Benefit for Mr. Everill
    The Struggle for Gold! or, The Sea of Ice (D 5a Edward Stirling)

Monday 3 April
    Benefit for Mr. Holmes
    The Czar and the Sledge Driver
    Willikin and His Diana (T 3a J. Stirling Coyne)
    Lucille, or the Story of a Heart (D 3a Bayle Bernard)
Tuesday 4 April
    Hamlet
Wednesday 5 April
    Minnigrey

Friday 7 April
    Secrets Worth Knowing (C Thomas Morton)
    The Waterman
    Farewell address.

THEATRE ROYAL, READING
Season: Monday 15 May to c. 23 June

THEATRE ROYAL, ABERDEEN The season began in Aberdeen on Tuesday 17 October. Local newspapers carry virtually no information on the theatre.

1855

THEATRE ROYAL, ABERDEEN
Braddon was still in Aberdeen on 14 January, the day she and her mother wrote to Mr. Younge.

THEATRE ROYAL, STAMFORD
LESSEE AND MANAGER, HENRY JOHNSON
Monday 19 March
    Start of season.
    Rob Roy
    Dancing Mad (ballet)
    The Lottery Ticket
Tuesday 20 March
    The Merchant of Venice
    Mr. and Mrs. White

Friday 23 March
    The Sea of Ice

Monday 26 March
    The Hunchback of Notre Dame
Tuesday 27 March
    Richard III
    Mischief Making (F 1a Buckstone)
Wednesday 28 March
    The Sea of Ice
    The Windmill (F 1a Edward Morton)

Friday 30 March
    John Bull
    A ghost story performed by Mr. Selwyn
    The Widow's Victim (F Charles Selby)
Also this week: *'Twas I*

Monday 9 April
    Therese or the Orphan of Genoa (D 3a J.P. Payne)
    The Vale of Gems, or Harlequin Sinbad the Sailor
Tuesday 10 April

The Hunchback of Notre Dame

Friday 13 April
    Patron Mayor William Smith
    Faint Heart Never Won Fair Lady (C 1a J.R. Planché)
    The Vale of Gems, or Harlequin Sinbad the Sailor
also this week: *The Miser Murderer*

Monday 16 April
    The Dumb Girl of Genoa (D 2a John Farrell)
    Illustrious Stranger (F 1a J. Kenney and J. Millingen)

Wednesday 18 April
    Benefit of Mr. Selwyn
    The Soldier's Daughter
    Ben Bolt

Monday 23 April
    Benefit of Mr. and Mrs. C. Stanton
    Don Caesar De Bazan
    Robert Macaire (D 2a)

Wednesday 25 April
    Benefit of Mr. Warlow
    The King's Wager
    Brother Bob and Sister Fan
    The Day After the Fair (F 2a C.A. Somerset)

Friday 27 April
    Benefit of Mr. Johnson, Manager
    The Rake's Progress (D 3a W.L. Rede)
    The Manager in Distress (F 1a Colman)
End of Season.

THEATRE ROYAL, GLASGOW
LESSEE AND MANAGER, MR. GLOVER

THEATRE ROYAL, SOUTHAMPTON
LESSEE AND MANAGER, EDWIN HOLMES
Monday 3 September
    The Lady of Lyons
    The £100 Note
    Loan of a Lover (F 1a Planché)

Tuesday 4 September
The Rivals
Wednesday 5 September
His First Champagne
Thursday 6 September
Sweethearts and Wives (C 2a James Kenney)
Plot and Counterplot (C Charles Kemble)

Monday 10 September
Kenilworth (D)
Monsieur Desarais and his performing dogs.
The Anchor of Hope (D 2a Edward Stirling)
The £100 Note
Tuesday 11 September
The Anchor of Hope
M. Desarais
A Roland for an Oliver (F 2a J. Maddison Morton)
Singing and dancing each night.

Saturday 15 September
The Corsican Brothers
Plot and Counterplot
Monday 17 September
Richlieu
Honest Thieves (F 1a T. Knight)
Tuesday 18 September
Hamlet
Return from Russia
Wednesday 19 September
Louis XI (D 5a W.R. Markwell)
Thursday 20 September
Romeo and Juliet
Friday 21 September
Love (5a Knowles)
Louis XI
Saturday 22 September
Douglas (T 5a John Home)
Charles II
Mr. and Mrs. White
Also this week: *The Iron Chest* (D 4a Colman)
Monday 24 September
Guests for week Mr. and Mrs. Charles Pitt
Macbeth

Black Eyed Susan
Tuesday 25 September
  Civilisation (D 5a J.A. Wilkens)
  An Object of Interest (F 1a J.H. Stocquler)
Wednesday 26 September
  Ingomar the Barbarian (D 5a Maria Lovell)
  Hunting a Turtle (F 1a Charles Selby)
Thursday 27 September
  Civilisation
  The Widow's Victim
Saturday 29 September
  Macbeth
  The Rough Diamond
Monday 1 October
  The Carpenter of Rouen (D 4a J.S. Jones)
  The Irish Tutor (C 1a Richard Butler)
  Robert Macaire
Tuesday 2 October
  The Carpenter of Rouen
  Your Life's in Danger
Wednesday 3 October
  Southampton Amateurs with company ladies
  Richlieu
  The Wandering Minstrel
  (SEYTON APPEARED IN THESE)
Thursday 4 October
  The King's Wager

Saturday 6 October
  Carpenter of Rouen
  The Anchor of Hope
Monday 8 October
  Faustus and Mephistophiles; or, The Sorcerer and His Victim
  ballet
  All in the Wrong
Tuesday 9 October
  Faustus
  A Roland for an Oliver
Wednesday 10 October
  Clari; or, the Maid of Milan
Thursday 11 October
  As Wednesday
Saturday 13 October

Faustus
Your Life's in Danger
Monday 15 October
   Pizarro (T 5a Sheridan)
   Sailor of France (D 2a J.B. Johnstone)
Tuesday 16 October
   Faustus
   Black Eyed Susan
Wednesday 17 October
   The Daughter of the Regiment (D 2a Fitzball)
   The Charcoal Burner (D 2a George Almar)
Thursday 18 October
   Ben Bolt

Saturday 20 October
   Clari; The Maid of Milan
   The Irish Tutor
   All in the Wrong
Monday 22 October
   The Battle of Austerlitz; or, A Soldier's Pride
   The Minute Gun at Sea
Tuesday 23 October
   The Battle of Austerlitz
   The White Slave (D 2a Edward Stirling)
   The Hunchback of Notre Dame
Wednesday 24 October
   The Irish Lion (F 1a Buckstone)
   How to Beat the Russians
   (SEYTON APPEARED IN THESE)
Thursday 25 October
   The Carpenter of Rouen
   Faustus

Monday 30 October
   Joan of Arc (D 3a Fitzball)
   Cinderella; or, The Little Glass Slipper (Holmes)
   Blue Jackets (F 1a Stirling)
Tuesday 31 October
   Joan of Arc
   Cinderella
   Ben Bolt
   Le Barbiere di Cadis

Friday 3 November
    Southampton Amateurs and company ladies
    Married Life
    The Spitalfields Weaver (C 1a T.H. Bayley)
    My Fellow Clerk (F 1a John Oxenford)
Also this week: *Young Husbands and Married Daughters* (C 2a J. Daly)
Monday 5 November
    Guy Faux
Saturday 10 November
    Cinderella
Monday 12 November
    The Orphan of Geneva
    The Field of Forty Footsteps (D 3a William Farren)
    Will Watch
Tuesday 13 November
    as Monday

Also this week: *The Happiest Day of My Life* (F 2a Buckstone), *The Lonely Man of the Ocean* (D 3a Thomas Blake)
Monday 17 November
    The Black Doctor
    Hush Money (F 2a Charles Dance)
    Only a Halfpenny (F 1a Oxenford)
Tuesday 18 November
    Only a Halfpenny

Monday 26 November
    Richard III
    The Eton Boy (F 1a Edward Morton)
    How to Settle Accounts with your Laundress (F 1a Stirling Coyne)
Tuesday 27 November
    Isabelle (D 3a Buckstone)
Wednesday 28 November
    Romeo and Juliet
Thursday 29 November
    Faustus
    The Black Doctor
Friday 30 November
    Southampton Amateurs with ladies of company
    The Black Domino (D 3a T.E. Wilks)
    Monsieur Jacques (D 1a Morris Barnet)
    My Wife's Second Floor (F 1a J. Maddison Morton)

Monday 3 December
Alice Gray; or, The Suspected One (D 3a J.T. Haines)
The Soldier's Progress
Tuesday 4 December
Alice Gray
George Barnwell
Wednesday 5 December
The Flowers of the Forest
Mistletoe Bough
Thursday 6 December
Isabelle
Love's Dream; or, The Sleep-Walker

Monday 10 December
Mr. Holmes's Benefit
Still Waters Run Deep (C 3a Tom Taylor)
The Muleteer of Toledo (C 2a J. Maddison Morton)
Catching a Captain
Tuesday 11 December
Young Husbands and Married Daughters
The Flowers of the Forest
Wednesday 12 December
The Odd Fellow's Benefit for Widows and Orphans Fund
The Prisoner of War (C 2a Jerrold)
Perfections
Amateurs and Actors (F 1a R.B. Peake)

Monday 17 December
Rory O'More
The White Slave
Tuesday 18 December
The Midnight Hour (F Mrs. Inchbold)
The Lonely Man of the Ocean
closed until panto.

Wednesday 26 December
The Englishman in India (D Dimond)
Harlequin and the Sleeping Beauty in the Woods; or, The Rival Fairies (Holmes)

Monday 31 December
Patrons Hon. Sir Edward and Lady Butler
The Governor's Wife (C. 2a T. Mildenhall)

Harlequin and the Sleeping Beauty

1856

Monday 7 January
  Trafalgar Medal (D 2a Buckstone)
  Harlequin and the Sleeping Beauty
Tuesday 8 January
  The Governor's Wife
  Harlequin and the Sleeping Beauty
Wednesday 9 January
  Juvenile night
  The Gypsy Queen
  Harlequin and the Sleeping Beauty
Thursday 10 January
  as Wednesday
Thursday 11 January
  The Wandering Minstrel

Monday 14 January
  bespeak of R. Wright
  A Husband at Sight (F 2a Buckstone)
  His First Champagne
  Dominique the Deserter

Wednesday 16 January
  Ancient Order of Foresters and Orphans Fund
  The Vampire
  Lover's Quarrels (F)
  The Devil to Pay

Monday 21 January
  Mr. Collings's benefit (box book keeper)
  The Rivals
  Gwynneth Vaughan (D 2a Lemon)

Thursday 24 January
  Southampton Amateurs
  Love and Marriage; or, Southampton in the Days of Good Queen Bess (Dr. C. Oswin)
  Bamboozling (F 1a Wilks)
  The Spectre Bridegroom (F 2a W.T. Moncreiff)

Monday 28 January
  Gentleman amateurs
  Still Waters Run Deep
  The Brigand
Thursday 31 January
  Southampton amateurs
  Othello
  Love and Marriage

also this week: *The Jewess, The Bride of the Isles*
Monday 4 February
  Benefit of Mrs. Holmes
  The Old English Gentleman
  Giraldo (C 3a Hy Welstead)
  Nice Young Ladies

Thursday 7 February
  The Old English Gentlemen
  Gwynneth Vaughan

Monday 11 February
  Benefit of Mr. Skinner (box check taker)
  Belphegor (D 3a Webster)
  The Rival Pages
  The Crown Prince (D 2a T.E. Wilks)
Tuesday 12 February
  The Rivals
  Luke the Labourer (D 2a Buckstone)

Thursday 14 February
  Benefit of Mr. G. Teague (Harlequin and ballet master)
  The Green Hills of the Far West
  Harlequin and the Three Wishes

ROYAL SURREY THEATRE, LONDON
LESSEES MESSRS. SHEPHERD AND CRESWICK
Monday 3 March
  Jasper Langton; or, a Duel to the Death (F J.S. Coyne)
  The Sailor of France **(SEYTON PLAYED MADELINE)**
  The Waiter at Cremorne (D William Suter)
Tuesday 4 March
  As Monday
  (SEYTON PLAYED MADELINE)

Wednesday 5 March
>Benefit of Mr. Widdicombe
>*Town and Country* (C Thomas Morton)
>*A Concert*
>*Richard Ye Thirde* (burlesque)

Thursday 6 March
>*Jasper Langton*
>*The Sailor of France* (**SEYTON PLAYED MADELINE**)
>*The Irish Tutor*

Friday 7 March
>Benefit of Mr. J. Neville
>*Black Eyed Susan*
>*La Somnambula*
>*The Scapegoat of Paris*

Saturday 8 March
>*Town and Country*
>*The Sailor of France* (**SEYTON PLAYED MADELINE**)
>*The Waiter at Cremorne*

Monday 10 March
>*Jasper Langton*
>*Brother Bob*
>*Paris in 1792*

Tuesday 11 March
>As Monday

Wednesday 12 March
>*The Beggar's Petition*
>*Precious Betsy*
>*Maid of Genoa*

Thursday 13 March
>As Monday

Friday 14 March
>As Monday

Saturday 15 March
>*Othello*
>*The Waiter at Cremorne*
>*Brother Bob*

Monday 17 March
>(Easter Monday and through the week)
>*How We Live in the World of London* (Johnstone) (**SEYTON PLAYED CLARA**)
>*Tufflehausen; or, The Lawyer's Secret*

Monday 23 March (and through the week)
>*How We Live in the World of London*

Steelhard
Tufflehausen
The Tailor and the Cobbler
Monday 31 March (and through the week)
How We Live in the World of London
Tufflehausen
The Tailor and the Cobbler
Monday 7 April
How We Live in the World of London
Tufflehausen
The Postman's Knock **(SEYTON APPEARED)**
Monday 14 April
As 7 April
Monday 21 April
How We Live in the World of London
Sarah's Young Man (F 1a Suter) **(SEYTON PLAYED
ARAMINTA)**
Postman's Knock
Monday 28 April
How We Live
Sarah's Young Man
Two Polts (F 1a John Courtney) **(SEYTON APPEARED)**
Wednesday 30 April
As Monday.
Monday 5 May
Benefit for Mr. Creswick
Richlieu
Black Eyed Susan
Tuesday 6 May
How We Live in the World of London
Wednesday 7 May
Virginius; or, The Roman Father (T Knowles)
last two as Tuesday
Thursday 8 May
Benefit for Sarah Thorne
The Lady of Lyons
The First Fratricide; or, The Death of Abel
The Waterman
Friday 10 May
As Tuesday
Monday 12 May - 17 May
Jack Sheppard **(SEYTON PLAYED WINIFRED)**
Your Life's in Danger **(SEYTON PLAYED THE COUNTESS)**

May 18 - 25 May
As previous week
Monday 26 May - 31 May
Martin Chuzzlewit **(SEYTON PLAYED CHARITY)**
The Thumping Legacy (F 1a J. Maddison Morton)
Twice Killed (F 1a Oxenford)

Monday 2 June
Guest stars James Anderson and Miss Elsworthy
Othello
The Floating Beacon (D 2a Fitzball)
Tuesday 3 June
Ingomar
Black Eyed Susan
Wednesday 4 June
Julius Caesar
The Floating Beacon
Thursday 5 June
Ingomar
Black Eyed Susan
Friday 6 June
Julius Caesar
The Floating Beacon
Saturday 7 June
Othello
The Floating Beacon
End of Season.

QUEEN'S THEATRE, HULL
LESSEES, MESSRS. WOLFENDEN AND MELBOURNE
Monday 28 July
Beginning of season,

Friday 1 August
The Flowers of the Forest

Friday 8 August
Grand Fashionable Night
Charles XII
Speed the Plough

Tuesday 12 August
Esmerelda

Friday 15 August
   Grand Fashionable Night
   The Corsican Brothers
   Wandering Minstrel

Monday 25 August
   Guest star for six nights Mr. Addison
   The County Squire (C 2a Dance)
   The Courier of Lyons (D 4a Charles Reade)

Friday 29 August
   Patrons Hull Cricketers
   Guy Mannering
   A Roland for an Oliver

Friday 5 September
   Benefit for Mr. Addison
   School for Scandal
   Gwynneth Vaughan; or, The Tar of Many Weathers
(in preparation *Blythe Hall* from the *London Journal*)

Friday 12 September
   Seven Poor Travellers (2a C. Duval after Dickens)

Monday 15 September
   How We Live; or, A Peep into the Great World of London
Friday 19 September
   How We Live
   The Seven Poor Travellers

Monday 22 September
   The Jewess

Friday 26 September
   The Jewess

Friday 3 October
   Benefit of Mr. T. Lyon
   Cahill Ckvye Darvey; Or, He of the Red Hand

Friday 17 October
   The Fall of Sebastopol; or, The Return of our Heroes (last night)

Aladdin

Wednesday 22 October
  Guy Mannering
Friday 24 October
  Aladdin
Monday 27 October
  Guest stars Brothers Hutchinson and Delevanti family

Friday 31 October
  Benefit of Hutchinson brothers

Monday 3 November
  Red, White and Blue (ballet)

Friday 7 November
  Benefit of M. Allano

Friday 14 November
  Benefit of John Holmes (treasurer)
  Dred
  Jack Long of Texas (D. n.a.)

Wednesday 19 November
  Patron Mayor W.H. Moss and Sheriff
  Benefit for Widows and Orphans Fund of the Kingston Unity

Friday 21 November
  Benefit of Mr. A. Wood
  Dick Tarleton (from *Cassell's Family Paper*)
  Mary Price; or, The Memoirs of a Servant Girl

Friday 28 November
  Benefit of Mr. Claire, Hutchinson, Delevantis and Mat Graves

Monday 1 December
  Guest star, Ira Aldridge for five nights

Friday 5 December
  Benefit of Ira Aldridge
  The Mummy (F 1a W. Bayle Bernard)

Monday 15 December

Patrons: Officers and Members of the Independent Order of Odd
Fellows
The Druids Brass Band
Doom of Barostein
Loan of a Lover
Luke the Labourer
(closed for pantomime machinery)

1857

THE QUEEN'S THEATRE, HULL
Friday 2 January
> *Humpty Dumpty! Crook'd Back Dick and Jane Shore; or,*
> *Harlequin Pearl Prince and Grape* **(SEYTON APPEARED)**

Wednesday 7 January
> Patron Mayor M. Ross
> *Humpty Dumpty*
Friday 9 January
> Patron: Lieut. Mordock of Royal Artillery, Commander of the Hull
> Garrison
> *Humpty Dumpty*
Friday 16 January
> *Humpty Dumpty*
Friday 23 January
> *Humpty Dumpty* (last juvenile night)
Friday 30 January
> Benefit of M., Mdme. and Tom Thumb Delevanti
> *Raphael's Dream* (with jester W.F. Wallett)
Friday 13 February
> Jubilee Gala and Presentation
> *Humpty Dumpty* (47th night)
> fourth night of guest star W.F. Wallett
> *The Man With a General Face*
Friday 20 February
> Patrons: Shipwright's Benevolent Association
> *Sixteen-String Jack*
Friday 27 February
> Farewell Benefit of Mr. Harwood
> *The Merchant's Stead*
Friday 6 March
> Grand Fashionable Night
> *Surgeon of Paris* (D Jacob Jones)

Wednesday 18 March
    Benefit of the Widows' and Orphans Juvenile Fund
    William Tell (D 5a Knowles)
    Lady of the Lake (D T.J. Dibdin)
    Crinoline (F 1a Robert Brough)
Friday 27 March
    Benefit of Mr. N.T. Hicks
Wednesday 1 April
    Richelieu
Friday 3 April
    Grand Fashionable Masonic Night, Minerva Lodge
    Ingomar
    A Wonderful Woman (C 2a Dance)
    Did You Ever Send Your Wife to Cottingham (F 1a Stirling Coyne)
Monday 6 April
    Guest star, the comedian Mr. Addison

Friday 10 April
    Mr. Addison's Benefit
    Old Parr and the Cabin Boy (D 2a Lemon)
    Tax Oblige Benson
Monday 13 April (Easter Monday)
    Son of the Night
Friday 17 April
    Mons. Jullien and His Monster Band and Mdm. Gassier
Monday 20 April
    London Grand Opera Company
Friday 24 April
    London Grand Opera Company with Rebecca Issacs

ASSEMBLY ROOMS, BEVERLEY

Monday 27 April
    Ingomar
    A comic song by Mr. Rorke.
    Pas Seul (Miss Macready)
    Away With Melancholy (F 1a J. Maddison Morton)
Tuesday 28 April
Wednesday 29 April
    Evening by desire and under patronage of the mayor.
Thursday 30 April
    Benefit for Mr. Rousby
Friday 1 May
    Under the Patronage of the Worshipful Master Officers and

Masonic Brethren of Constitutional Lodge no. 371
Still Waters Run Deep **(SEYTON PLAYED MRS. STERNHOLD)**
The Wonderful Woman **(SEYTON PLAYED HORTENSE)**
Saturday 2 May
Richard III
singing and dancing
Ben Bolt

QUEEN'S THEATRE, HULL
Monday 4 May
Guest Star Wybert Rousby
Friday 8 May
The Outcast
Still Waters Run Deep
The Love Knot; or, Marguerite's Colours **(SEYTON PLAYED HELEN DE MONTBRUN)**
Monday 11 May
Evadne; or the Hall of Statues (R.L. Sheil T 3a) **(SEYTON PLAYED OLIVIA)**
Lady of Lyons
Friday 15 May
Benefit for Miss Marriott
Friday 22 May
Guest stars for 2 nights: Mr. & Mrs. Charles Dillon, & Mr. Barret
Othello
Also this week *Macbeth*
Saturday 23 May
Belphegor (Charles Webb)
Three Musketeers
Friday 29 May
Benefit for Mr. Clifton and Mr. Rosier
Monday 1 June
Guest stars for 6 nights, Miss and Mr. Alfred Raynor
Friday 5 June
Ingomar
The Holly Tree Inn
Saturday 6 June
Last Night of Season (but days 'after-season')
Monday 8 June
Allied Metropolitan Dramatic Company engaged for 2 weeks.
Friday 12 June
Grand Fashionable Night

The School for Scandal
The Corsican Brothers (Nye Chart playing all parts)
Young England (F Maddison Morton)
This week company also performed: *Richelieu, Secret Services* (D 2a
J.R. Planché), *Forty and Fifty* (F 1a T.H. Bayly), *That Rascal Jack* (F 1a
Thomas Greenwood)
Friday 19 June
Speed the Plough
Saturday 20 June
Therese; or, The Orphan of Genoa (D 3a John Payne)
That Rascal Jack
The Broken Sword (D Dimond)
Monday 22 June
Guest stars for 12 nights, Mr. and Mrs. Leigh Murray and the
London Dramatic Company.
The Marble Heart (D 5a Selby)
His First Champagne
Wednesday 24 June
The Discarded Son (D 3a Webster)
Belphegor
Friday 26 June
Grand Fashionable Night
To Parents and Guardians (C 1a Taylor)
2 songs
A Novel Expedient (C 1a Webster)
Katharine and Petruchio
Saturday 27 June
The Lady of Lyons
Belphagor
Friday 3 July
Patron Lady Clifford Constable
Benefit for Leigh Murray
Still Waters Run Deep
His First Champagne
Saturday 4 July
Victorine (D Buckstone)
William Tell
Monday 6 July
Benefit in memory of treasurer, John Holmes
Peter Bell the Wagoner (D 3a Buckstone)
a musical melange
Rent Day (C 3a Jerrold)

THEATRE ROYAL, BRIGHTON
LESSEE AND MANAGER, HENRY NYE CHART
Saturday 1 August
New Season
> *The Wife; A Tale of Mantua*
> *The Prince of Happy Land* (Planché) **(SEYTON PLAYED**
> **FAIRY PINEAPPLE)**
Monday 3 August
> *The Love Chase* (C 5a Knowles)
> *Cure for the Heartache* (C Thomas Morton)
Tuesday 4 August
> *Cure for the Heartache* **(SEYTON PLAYED ELLEN)**
Wednesday 5 August
> *Cross of Gold; or, A Woman's Love and a Soldier's Honour*
> *Spoiled Child* (F 1a Bickerstaff)
Thursday 6 August
> *Married Life* **(SEYTON PLAYED MRS. DOVE)**
> *The Prince of Happy Land*
> *Sudden Thoughts* (F 1a T.E. Wilks) **(SEYTON PLAYED**
> **CLARISSA)**
> *Grandfather Whitehead* (Lemon) **(SEYTON PLAYED LOUISA**
> **DRAYTON)**
Friday 7 August
> *The Lady of Lyons*
> *The Prince of Happy Land*
Saturday 8 August
> *The Lady of Lyons*
> *The Prince of Happy Land*
Also this week: *Katherine and Petruchio* **(SEYTON PLAYED**
BIANCA)
Monday 10 August
> *Ingomar*
> *The Prince of Happy Land*
Tuesday 11 August
> *The Lady of Lyons* **(SEYTON PLAYED WIDOW MELNOTTE)**
> *The Prince of Happy Land* **(SEYTON PLAYED PINEAPPLE)**
Wednesday 12 August
> *Ingomar*
> *The Prince of Happy Land*
Thursday 13 August
> *A Life's Trial* (D 3a W. Bayle Bernard)
> *The Prince of Happy Land*
Friday 14 August

As Thursday

Monday 17 August
Love's Sacrifice (D 5a G.W. Lovell)
A Life's Trial
Tuesday 18 August
Fortunio and his Seven Gifted Servants (Planché)
Wednesday 19 August
Crinoline **(SEYTON APPEARED)**
Thursday 20 August
Married Life
Crinoline
Fortunio
Friday 21 August
The Wife
Fortunio **(SEYTON PLAYED PERTINA)**
Saturday 22 August
Crinoline
Also in the week: *The Midnight Watch, Spoiled Child, Don Caesar de Bazan.*
Monday 24 August
Sea and Land (D 3a Lemon)
Crinoline

Thursday 27 August
Sea and Land
Crinoline
Married Life
Friday 28 August
The Child of the Regiment
Crinoline
Fortunio and His Seven Gifted Servants
Saturday 29 August
Sea and Land
Crinoline
During the week: *Love's Sacrifice, Midnight Watch* (D 1a Maddison Morton), *Life's Trials, Married Life. Crinoline* was performed every evening.
Monday 31 August
Victims (C 3a Taylor) **(SEYTON PLAYED MRS. SHARP)**

Thursday 3 September
Victims

ballet
The Child of the Regiment
Friday 4 September
The Child of the Regiment; or, The Daughter of a Thousand Fathers **(SEYTON PLAYED THE DUCHESS)**
Victims **(SEYTON PLAYED MRS. SHARP)**
Saturday 5 September
Black-Eyed Susan
Monday 7 September
Romeo and Juliet **(SEYTON PLAYED LADY CAPULET)**

Wednesday 9 September
Much Ado About Nothing
Eight Hours at the Seaside (William Sawyer) **(SEYTON PLAYED AURELIA MAGGLES)**
Thursday 10 September
Victims
ballet
Conrad and Medora **(SEYTON PLAYED GULNARE)**
Friday 11 September
Victims
Conrad and Medora
Saturday 12 September
The Cross of Gold
Conrad and Medora
The Pilot
Also this week: *Victims, Child of the Regiment, Sea and Land*

Thursday 17 September
Romeo and Juliet
Herr Kratky Maschick playing his cor-melodian
Conrad and Medora
Friday 18 September
Herr Kratky Maschick
Also this week *Pizarro, The Spaniard in Peru* (T 5a), *Much Ado About Nothing, Romeo and Juliet, Victims.*
Monday 21 September
Ocean Life (D 3a Haines)
Conrad and Medora
Tuesday 22 September
Merry Wives of Windsor
Conrad and Medora

Wednesday 23 September
  Pizzaro
  Conrad and Medora
Thursday 24 September
  Merry Wives of Windsor
  Herr Kratky Maschick
  Conrad and Medora
Friday 25 September
  School for Scandal
  Herr Kratky Maschick
  Conrad and Medora
Saturday 26 September
  Victims
  Ocean of Life
Monday 28 September
  Richelieu
  Herr Kratky Maschick
  Susan Hopley; or, The Vicissitudes of a Servant Girl (D 3a G.D.
  Pitt)
Tuesday 29 September
  Merry Wives of Windsor
Wednesday 30 September
  School for Scandal **(SEYTON PLAYED LADY SNEERWELL)**
Thursday 1 October
  Merry Wives of Windsor
  Victims
Friday 2 October
  Richelieu
  Conrad and Medora
Saturday 3 October
  Merchant of Venice
  Susan Hopley
Also this week: *Child of the Regiment*
Monday 5 October
  The Gamester (T 5a Edward Moore)
Tuesday 6 October
  Merchant of Venice

Thursday 8 October
  Grand Fashionable Night
  Merchant of Venice
  The Volunteer Waltzes
  Distinguished Connexions (Captain Murray) **(SEYTON PLAYED**

MISS JANE BEAUFORT)
Roland for an Oliver
Friday 9 October
  The Gamester
  Victims
Saturday 10 October
  All in the Wrong
  The Corsican Brothers
Monday 12 October
  Jessy Vere; or, The Return of the Wanderer (D 2a C.H.
  Hazlewood)
Tuesday 13 October
  All in the Wrong (C 5a A. Murphy)
  Distinguished Connexions
Thursday 15 October
  Patrons Royal York Lodge
  All in the Wrong **(SEYTON PLAYED CLARISSA)**
  The Volunteer Waltzes
  Band of 6th Inniskilling Dragoons
  Fortunio
Friday 16 October
  A Cure for the Heartache
  Distinguished Connexions
  The Invisible Prince (Planché)
Saturday 17 October
  Pizarro
  Laid Up in Port; or, Sharks Along Shore (D 3a T.H. Higgie)
Monday 19 October
  Othello
Tuesday 20 October
  All in the Wrong

Thursday 22 October
  She Stoops to Conquer
  Make Your Wills (F 1a E. Mayhew and G. Smith)
  The Invisible Prince
Friday 23 October
  The Invisible Prince **(SEYTON PLAYED FAIRY GENTILLA)**
  Othello
Saturday 24 October
  The Invisible Prince
  Jack Sheppard

Also this week: *Hamlet, Distinguished Connexions, Laid up in Port; Or, Sharks Along Shore, Mary the Maid of the Inn*
Monday 26 October
    Richard III
    My Poll and My Partner Tom
Tuesday 27 October
    She Stoops to Conquer **(SEYTON PLAYED MISS NEVILLE)**

Thursday 29 October
    Benefit for Cicely Nott
    The Serious Family (C 3a)
    Loan of a Lover
    Child of the Regiment
Friday 30 October
    Othello
    Married Life
Saturday 31 October
    Richard III
    Jessy Vere
Also this week: *All in the Wrong, Conrad and Medora, The Invisible Prince*, after-pieces were *Jack Sheppard, My Poll and my Partner Tom* (D 3a J. T. Haines), *Make Your Wills!, Distinguished Connexions*
Monday 2 November
    Henry IV part I
    Richard III
Tuesday 3 November
    Henry IV
    Richard III
Wednesday 4 November
    The Serious Family
Thursday 5 November
    Masks and Faces (C Charles Reade and Tom Taylor)
    Wilful Murder (F 1a Higgie)
    Make Your Wills
Friday 6 November
    Masks and Faces **(SEYTON PLAYED KITTY CLIVE)**
    Victims **(SEYTON PLAYED MRS. SHARP)**
Saturday 7 November
    The Stranger (D 5a Kotzebue)
    The Dream at Sea
Monday 9 November
    The Hunchback (D 5a Knowles)
    Martha Willis (Jerrold)

Tuesday 10 November
  All in the Wrong
  Masks and Faces **(SEYTON PLAYED KITTY CLIVE)**
Wednesday 11 November
  Richelieu
  The Serious Family
Thursday 12 November
  A Pretty Piece of Business (C 1a Morton)
  A Wonderful Woman
  Done on Both Sides (F 1a Maddison Morton)
Friday 13 November
  Henry IV part 1
  Martha Willis
Saturday 14 November
  The Honeymoon; Or, How to Rule a Wife **(SEYTON PLAYED
  ZAMORA)**
  The Mutiny at the Nore (D Jerrold)
Monday 16 November
  Macbeth
Tuesday 17 November
  The Honeymoon
  Henry IV
Wednesday 18 November
  Macbeth
Thursday 19 November
  Grand Special Night Benefit for Mr. Wheeler
  Our Wife; Or, The Rose of Amiens (C 2a Maddison Morton)
  Lend Me Five Shillings
  The Green Bushes
Friday 20 November
  The Hunchback
  The Brigand
Saturday 21 November
  The Iron Chest (D 4a Coleman)
  The Green Bushes
Monday 23 November
  Venice Preserved; Or, A Plot Discovered (T 5a Thomas Otway)
  The Hut of the Red Mountain; Or, Thirty Years of a Gambler's Life
  (D 3a H.M. Milner)
Tuesday 24 November
  Macbeth
  Done on Both Sides
Wednesday 25 November

Masks and Faces
The Lady of Lyons
Thursday 26 November
   A Pretty Piece of Business **(SEYTON PLAYED CHARLOTTE SHEE)**
   Our Wife
   The Mutiny at the Nore
Friday 27 November
   gentlemen amateurs of the Inniskilling Dragoons and ladies of company
   Still Waters Run Deep
   Little Toddlekins (C 1a Charles Mathews) **(SEYTON PLAYED ANNIE BABBICOMBE)**
   Band
Saturday 28 November
   The Hypocrite
   Macbeth

Tuesday 1 December
   Eight Hours at the Seaside **(SEYTON PLAYED AURELIA)**

Friday 4 December
   The Rivals
   Eight Hours at the Seaside
   The Spoiled Child
Saturday 5 December
   Eight Hours at the Seaside
   Jack and Jack's Brother; or, The Gipsy and the Orphan
Also this week: *King Lear, Don Caesar de Bazan, The Wandering Boys; or, The Castle of Olival* (D 3a John Kerr)
Monday 7 December
   Birds of Prey (Charles Wray)
Tuesday 8 December
   Birds of Prey
Wednesday 9 December
   Benefit for Mr. G.K. Maskell
   The Country Squire
   Poor Pillicoddy (F 1a Maddison Morton)
   The Lonely Man of the Ocean
Thursday 10 December
   Poor Pillicoddy
   Birds of Prey
   Eight Hours at the Seaside

Friday 11 December
Patron, the Mayor
Double Faced People (C 3a John Courtney)
Eight Hours at the Seaside
Done on Both Sides
Every night but one had *Eight Hours at the Seaside*
Saturday 12 December
Hamlet
Wednesday 16 December
benefit of Henry Nye Chart
Love's Telegraph
That Rascal Jack
St. Mary's Eve; A Story of the Solway (D 2a W. Bayle Bernard)
Thursday 17 December
As Wednesday
(closed until boxing night)
Tuesday 22 December
amateur gentlemen performing
Delicate Ground; or, Paris in 1793 (C Dance)
The Hunchback
Saturday 26 December
Birds of Prey **(SEYTON PLAYED HELENNE DE GUERANDE)**
King Blusterbubble and Grummo the Giant; or, Harlequin Prince Honorbright and the Dwarf Monarch of the Ruby Mines (C.A. Somerset) **(SEYTON PLAYED FAIRY QUEEN PHANORA)**
Also at this time: *The Country Squire, Poor Pillicoddy*

Thursday 31 December
Serious Family
King Blusterbubble

1858

THEATRE ROYAL, BRIGHTON
Friday 1 January
Done on Both Sides
King Blusterbubble
Saturday 2 January
Married Life
King Blusterbubble
Monday 4 January
Lord Darnley; or, The Keeper of Castle Hill (D 2a Wilks)

(SEYTON PLAYED LADY MARGARET)

Tuesday 5 January
    King Blusterbubble
    Lord Darnley

Wednesday 6 January
    King Blusterbubble **(SEYTON PLAYED PHANORA)**
    Love's Telegraph
    Masks and Faces

Thursday 7 January
    Love's Telegraph
    Masks and Faces

Friday 8 January
    Where There's a Will There's a Way (C 1a Maddison Morton)
    A Day Well Spent (F 1a Oxenford)

Saturday 9 January
    The Dream at Sea
    King Blusterbubble

Monday 11 January
    Clara, The Maid of the Inn

Tuesday 12 January
    King Blusterbubble
    The Lady of Lyons **(SEYTON PLAYED WIDOW MELNOTTE)**
    Poor Pillicoddy

Wednesday 13 January
    Poor Pillicoddy **(SEYTON PLAYED MRS. O'SCUTTLE)**

Thursday 14 January
    Love's Telegraph

Friday 15 January
    first juvenile night
    King Blusterbubble
    The Hunter of the Alps (D 2a Dimond)

Saturday 16 January
    The Crown Prince
    King Blusterbubble
    Ingomar

This week's shows concluded with: *Slasher and Crasher* (F 1a Maddison Morton), *Eight Hours by the Seaside*

Monday 18 January
    Ingomar

Tuesday 19 January
    Ingomar
    King Blusterbubble

Wednesday 20 January

King Blusterbubble
Crown Prince
Thursday 21 January
    The Lady of Lyons
Friday 22 January
    Love's Telegraph
    King Blusterbubble
Saturday 23 January
    Third grand juvenile night
    King Blusterbubble
    Carpenter of Rouen
Monday 25 January
    Wedding day of Princess Royal, theatre free.
    Bridal Morn; or, The Happiest Day of My Life (Buckstone)
    (SEYTON PLAYED MRS GRIMSLEY)
    Our Wife
    Eight Hours By the Seaside (with new song by Sawyer)
    Slasher and Crasher **(SEYTON PLAYED DINAH BLOWHARD)**
Tuesday 26 January
    Afternoon performance of King Blusterbubble
    Double Faced People
    King Blusterbubble
Wednesday 27 January
    Benefit of M. Allano
Friday 29 January
    Hearts are Trumps (D 3a Lemon)
    King Blusterbubble
Saturday 30 January
    St. Mary's Eve
    King Blusterbubble
Monday 1 February
    The Island of Silver Store; or, The Prisoner's Perils (new play
    Walter Baynham after Dickens)
Tuesday 2 February
    Benefit for Brothers Ozmond
    King Blusterbubble
    Ozmond's Roman Brothers and Mdm. Ozmond on tightrope.
Wednesday 3 February
    Miss Sanger's benefit
    King Blusterbubble
    St. Mary's Eve
Thursday 4 February

Mr. Cooper's Benefit
Nicholas Nickleby (D 3a Halliday)
Bengal Tiger (F 1a Dance)
The Soldier's Progress; or, The Horrors of War (D 4a Courtney)
Friday 5 February
    The Island of Silver Store
    Brothers Ozmond
    Slasher and Crasher
    Hunter of the Alps
Saturday 6 February
    Nicholas Nickleby
    The Island of Silver Store
Monday 8 February
    Gentlemen amateurs from London with company ladies
    Benefit of treasurer, John Chart **(SEYTON APPEARED)**
    The Wonderful Woman
    To Paris and Back again for five pounds, and founded on Fact
Tuesday 9 February
    Miss Adelaide Bowering's Benefit
    The Provoked Husband; or, A Journey to London (C 5a Vanbrugh)
    The Spitalfield's Weaver
    The Sea! The Sea!
    The Spectre Bridegroom **(SEYTON PLAYED GEORGIANA)**
Wednesday 10 February
    Benefit of Roberts Tindell and Mrs. Woollidge
Thursday 11 February
    Benefit of George Melville
    Still Waters Run Deep
    Belphegor The Mountebank
    The Dress Rehearsal (after Sheridan's *Critic*)
    Interludes by Robin Steer
Friday 12 February
    Benefit of Mr. T. Phillips
    The Lost Ship; or, The Man O' War's Man and the Privateer (D 3a
    W.T. Townsend)
Saturday 13 February
    Hearts are Trumps
    Slasher and Crasher
    George Barnwell
    The Provoked Husband
Also this week were: *Hearts are Trumps, The Island of Silver Store*
Monday 15 February
    Benefit of Henry Nye Chart

London Assurance (C 5a Boucicault)
Boots at the Swan
Tom Cringle's Log

THEATRE ROYAL, COVENTRY
Tuesday 16 February
Beginning of season.

Friday 19 February
 The School for Scandal
 Our Wife
Saturday 20 February
 The Provoked Husband
 The Carpenter of Rouen
Monday 22 February
 The Lady of Lyons

Friday 26 February
 The Rivals
 A Pretty Piece of Business
 The Crown Prince
Saturday 27 February
 Tom Cringle's Log
Monday 1 March
 Hamlet
 Black-Eyed Susan
Tuesday 2 March
 The School for Scandal
 Slasher and Crasher
Wednesday 3 March
 Birds of Prey
 That Rascal Jack
 All in the Wrong
Thursday 4 March
 Grand Special Night for Charles Dresser, Mayor
 Money
 Boots at the Swan

Saturday 6 March
 Miseraldi; or, The Dying Gift (**SEYTON PLAYED RICARDO**)
 My Wife's Dentist (F 1a T.E. Wilks)
 Lord Darnley
Monday 8 March

Flowers of the Forest

Robert Macaire

Tuesday 9 March

Romeo and Juliet **(SEYTON PLAYED PARIS)**

A Pretty Piece of Business

Wednesday 10 March

Grand night for the Company of Proprietors

Love Chase

Young England **(SEYTON PLAYED MRS. DASHALONG)**

Thursday 11 March

No performance.

Friday 12 March

Victims **(SEYTON PLAYED MRS. SHARP)**

Lend Me Five Shillings

Young England

Saturday 13 March

Othello

Dominique the Deserter

Monday 15 March

Love's Sacrifice **(SEYTON PLAYED HERMINIE)**

The Dumb Girl of Genoa

Tuesday 16 March

Bespeak of the officers of the 15th Hussars

Victims

Rural Felicity (C Buckstone)

Wednesday 17 March

Money **(SEYTON A PRINCIPAL)**

My Wife's Second Floor

Thursday 18 March

No performance.

Friday 19 March

Benefit for Mr. John Robinson, bill deliverer.

The Wife or a Tale of Mantua (D 5a Knowles)

Victorine

Saturday 20 March

The Corsican Brothers

The Momentous Question (D 2a Fitzball)

Monday 22 March

a celebrated Adelphi drama

Tuesday 23 March

Fashionable night for Lord Leigh and Trinity Lodge

The Hunchback

Done on Both Sides

Wednesday 24 March
>*The Serious Family*
>*The Corsican Brothers*

Thursday 25 March
>Race night, patrons the race stewards
>*The Hunter of the Alps*
>*Rural Felicity*
>*Wilful Murder*

Friday 26 March
>*My Wife's Dentist* (F 1a Wilks) **(SEYTON APPEARED)**
>*The Victims*
>*My Sister Kate and My Man Tom* (C 1a Lemon)

Saturday 27 March
>*Jane Shore* (Nicholas Rowe)
>*Laid Up In Port; or Sharks Along Shore*

Also at this time: *Green Bushes, The Lonely Man of the Ocean*
Closed for Passion week.

Monday 5 April
>*Conrad and Medora; Or, the Cruel Corsair and the Little Fairy at the Bottom of the Sea* (William Brough)

Wednesday 7 April
>*Lady of Lyons*
>*Conrad and Medora*

Thursday 8 April
>No performance.

Friday 9 April
>*Child of the Regiment*
>*My Sister Kate*
>*Conrad and Medora*

Saturday 10 April
>*The Stranger*
>*Conrad and Medora*
>*Medea* (Robert Brough)

Tuesday 13 April
>George Melville's Benefit
>*Ingomar*
>*The Daughter of the Regiment* (1 act only)
>*The Critic* (Sheridan)

Wednesday 14 April
>*All That Glitters Is Not Gold* (C 2a Thomas and John Madison Morton)
>*The White Horse of the Peppers* (D 2a Lover)

THEATRE ROYAL, LEAMINGTON SPA
Thursday 15 April
> *The Rivals*
> a farce

THEATRE ROYAL, COVENTRY
Friday 16 April
> *The Victims*
> *The Happiest Day of My Life* (F 2a Buckstone)
Saturday 17 April
> *The Factory Girl; or, All That Glitters Is Not Gold* (Jerrold)
> *The Happy Man* (F 1a Lover)
> *The Wandering Boys*
Also in past two weeks: *Richard III, Romeo and Juliet, Macbeth.*
Monday 19 April
> *Pizzaro* **(SEYTON APPEARED)**
> *Pauline, or The Lone Chateaux* (D 3a Oxenford) **(SEYTON APPEARED)**
Tuesday 20 April
> Benefit of Adelaide Bowering
> *Masks and Faces*
> *A Rough Diamond* (C 1a Buckstone)
> *Sea and Land*
Wednesday 21 April
> *The Rivals* **(SEYTON APPEARED)**
> *The Happy Man*
Thursday 22 April
> No performance.
Friday 23 April
> Benefit for Coventry Philanthropic Institute
> *Henry IV* **(SEYTON PLAYED EARL OF WESTMORELAND)**
> *Slasher and Crasher* **(SEYTON PLAYED DINAH BLOWHARD)**
Saturday 24 April
> *Merchant of Venice*
Also this week: *Victims, The Happiest Days of Our Life, All that Glitters is Not Gold* **(SEYTON WAS A PRINCIPAL IN THESE)**.
Monday 26 April
> Mr. Dewar's benefit
> *Still Waters Run Deep*
> *Crinoline*
> *The Thirteenth Chime; or, the Monk the Mask and the Murderer*

Tuesday 27 April
    Benefit of Mr. Steele
Wednesday 28 April
    The Provoked Husband
    Rent Day

THEATRE ROYAL, LEAMINGTON SPA
Thursday 29 April
    The School for Scandal
    Hunter of the Alps

THEATRE ROYAL, COVENTRY
Friday 30 April
    Benefit of Miss Weston and Robert Tindall
    Nicholas Nickleby
    Crinoline
    Belphegor
Saturday 1 May
    Venice Preserved
    Black-Eyed Susan
Also this week: *Richlieu* **(SEYTON PLAYED FRANCOIS)**, *Honesty the Best Policy.*
Monday 3 May
    The Courier of Lyons
    Susan Hopley

Wednesday 5 May
    A Cure For the Heartache
    Deaf as a Post (F 1a John Poole)
    The Rake's Progress (D 3a W.L. Rede)

THEATRE ROYAL, LEAMINGTON SPA
Thursday 6 May
    All in the Wrong
    a laughable interlude, and a comic drama

THEATRE ROYAL, COVENTRY
Friday 7 May
    She Stoops to Conquer
    Weak Points (F 2a Buckstone)
Saturday 8 May
    The Courier of Lyons

338

Also this week: *Spoiled Child, The Robber's Wife* (D 2a Isaac Pocock)
Monday 10 May
   Benefit for Henry Nye Chart
   London Assurance **(SEYTON PLAYED PERT)**
   A Gentleman in Difficulties (C 1a Bayly)
   Blanche Heriot; or the Chertsey Curfew
Wednesday 12 May
   The Hypocrite

THEATRE ROYAL, ROYAL LEAMINGTON SPA
Monday 17 May
   Still Waters Run Deep
   The Wandering Boys
Tuesday 18 May
   Masks and Faces
   Young England
Wednesday 19 May
   No performance

Monday 24 May
   Where There's a Will There's a Way
   Crinoline
   St. Mary's Eve
Tuesday 25 May
   Love's Telegraph
   The Bengal Tiger
   Just Arrived From India
   My Sister Kate

Tuesday 8 June
   guests: Mr. and Mrs. Barney Williams, supported by the Brighton
   company
Wednesday 9 June
   The Irish Tutor
   An Hour in Seville
   The Latest from New York

THEATRE ROYAL, COVENTRY
Monday 14 June
   The Queen's Visit, Or the Peasant's Journey from Village to Court
   (John Morton)
   wandering minstrels

Friday 18 June
>*The Man of Many Feelings* (C 3a Stirling Coyne)
>*Adventures of His Grandfather*
>*The Unfinished Gentleman* (F Selby)

THEATRE ROYAL, BRIGHTON
Saturday 31 July
Opening night of season.
>*The Lady of Lyons* **(SEYTON PLAYED WIDOW MELNOTTE)**
>*The King's Gardener* **(SEYTON PLAYED LOUISE DE LA VALLIERE)**
>*Child of the Regiment* (an act) **(SEYTON PLAYED DUCHESS DE GRANDLETE)**
>Speech given by Harry Nye Chart, written by Sawyer

Monday 2 August
>*Fraud and its Victims* (D 4a J. Stirling Coyne) **(SEYTON PLAYED ISABELLE)**
>*The Hunter of the Alps*

Tuesday 3 August
>*Fraud and its Victims*
>*My Sister Kate* **(SEYTON PLAYED MISS PEMBERTON)**

Wednesday 4 August
>*Plot and Passion* (D 3a Taylor)

Thursday 5 August
>*The Queensbury Fete*

Friday 6 August
>*The Man of Many Friends*
>ballet
>*Nothing Venture Nothing* Win (C 2a Stirling Coyne)
>*Eight Hours at the Seaside*

Saturday 7 August
>*Nothing Venture Nothing Win*
>*Fraud and its Victims*

Also this week: *Slasher and Crasher*, *The Swiss Cottage* (C 1a T.H. Bayly)

Monday 9 August
>*Lalla Rookh* (Robert Brough)
>*Richlieu* **(SEYTON PLAYED FRANCOIS)**

Tuesday 10 August
>*Nothing Venture Nothing Win*
>*The Queensbury Fete*
>*Lalla Rookh* **(SEYTON PLAYED LALLA ROOKH)**

Wednesday 11 August

340

The School for Scandal
Lalla Rookh
Thursday 12 August
Richlieu
Friday 13 August
Lady of Lyons **(SEYTON PLAYED WIDOW MELNOTTE)**
Lalla Rookh
Monday 16 August
A New Way to Pay to Old Debts (C 5a Massinger)
Lalla Rookh **(SEYTON PLAYED LALLA ROOKH)**
Tuesday 17 August
Plot and Passion
Lalla Rookh
Wednesday 18 August
The Queensbury Fete
Lalla Rookh
My Friend the Major (F 1a Selby)
Thursday 19 August
Nothing Venture Nothing Win
Lalla Rookh
A Hard Struggle (D 1a Westland Marston)
Friday 20 August
Fraud and its Victims **(SEYTON PLAYED ISABELLE)**
Lalla Rookh
Ruth Oakley (D 3a Thomas Williams and Augustus Harris)
Saturday 21 August
Ruth Oakley
Lalla Rookh
Also this week: *Nothing Venture Nothing Win*
Monday 23 August
Lalla Rookh
Tuesday 24 August
Lalla Rookh
Wednesday 25 August
Guest star for 3 nights Ira Aldridge
Othello
Lalla Rookh
Thursday 26 August
The Slave; or, The Mother and Her Child (D Thomas Morton)
The Padlock
Lalla Rookh
Friday 27 August
The Merchant of Venice

Othello
The Mummy **(SEYTON PLAYED LUCY)**
Lalla Rookh
Saturday 28 August
    Our Wife
    Lalla Rookh
    Black Eyed Susan
Special guest this week was the Ira Aldridge who played Othello, Gambia in *The Slave*, Mungo in *The Padlock*. He left on Friday. Also this week: *Ruth Oakley, Fraud and its Victims, Armand; or, The Peer and the Peasant* (D 5a Anna Cora Mowatt).
Monday 30 August
    Guest star for 6 nights Sir William Don
    Used Up (C.J. Mathews)
    Rough Diamond
Tuesday 31 August
    The Evil Genius (C 3a W. Bayle Bernard)
    Whitebait at Greenwich **(SEYTON PLAYED LUCRETIA SMALL)**
    My Friend the Major **(SEYTON PLAYED TODHUNTER)**
Wednesday 1 September
    Married Life **(SEYTON APPEARED)**
    An Alarming Sacrifice (F Buckstone)
    A Hard Struggle
Thursday 2 September
    Love and War
    Serious Family **(SEYTON PLAYED MRS. CHARLES TORRENS)**
    Box and Cox
Friday 3 September
    Single Life (C 3a Buckstone)
    ballet
    Done on Both Sides
    Whitebait at Greenwich
Saturday 4 September
    Guy Mannering
Monday 6 September
    Guest stars George Vining and Miss Castleton of Royal Olympic Theatre
    Retribution (D 4a Taylor)
Tuesday 7 September
    Still Waters Run Deep
    ballet

The Young Widow (F 1a J.T. Rodwell)
Boots at the Swan
Wednesday 8 September
Still Waters Run Deep
Subterfuge (C 1a)
Boots at the Swan
Thursday 9 September
Going to the Bad (C 2a Taylor)
Friday 10 September
Going to the Bad
Retribution
Saturday 11 September
The Serious Family
The Corsican Brothers
Guest stars for this and following week, George Vining, Miss Castleton.
Afterpieces were: *The Married Rake, Susan Hopley, Subterfuge, The Young Widow, Boots at the Swan* (three times).
Monday 13 September
The Hunchback
Courier of Lyons **(SEYTON PLAYED JANETTE)**
Tuesday 14 September
Going to the Bad (Tom Taylor)
ballet
Still Waters Run Deep
Wednesday 15 September
Going to the Bad **(SEYTON PLAYED MISS DASHWOOD)**
The Corsican Brothers **(SEYTON PLAYED ESTELLE)**
Thursday 16 September
Benefit of George Vining and Miss Castleton
Patrons: officers of the 11th Hussars
The Jealous Wife **(SEYTON PLAYED LADY FREELOVE)**
A Double Victory (C Oxenford)
London Assurance
Friday 17 September
The Lady of Lyons
The Queensbury Fete
Saturday 18 September
Armand (D)
The Slave
Also this week: *Retribution, The Hunchback*
Monday 20 September
Macbeth

Perdita
Tuesday 21 September
Macbeth
Perdita **(SEYTON PLAYED HERMIONE)**
Wednesday 22 September
Richlieu **(SEYTON PLAYED FRANCOIS)**
Perdita
Thursday 23 September
Patrons: Gentlemen Amateur Cricketers of Brighton
Plot and Passion
Perdita
Friday 24 September
Miss Hunt's Benefit
From Village to Court **(SEYTON PLAYED BERTHA, COUNTESS OF LINDENBURG)**
Box and Cox
Perdita **(SEYTON PLAYED HERMIONE)**
Saturday 25 September
Perdita
Merchant of Venice
Monday 27 September
Rob Roy
Perdita
Tuesday 28 September
Armand **(SEYTON PLAYED JAQUELINE)**
Perdita
Wednesday 29 September
Rob Roy
Perdita
Thursday 30 September
The Man of Many Friends
Perdita
Friday 1 October
Romeo and Juliet
Perdita
Saturday 2 October
A Hard Struggle
The Sea; or, The Ocean Child
Monday 4 October
The Fire Raisers (F 1a Selby)
The Flying Dutchman
Tuesday 5 October
Romeo and Juliet

Perdita
Wednesday 6 October
　The Rivals
　The Flying Dutchman
　Tom Noddy's Secret (F 1a Bayly)

Friday 8 October
　A Cure for the Heartache
　A Hard Struggle
　Jessy Vere
Saturday 9 October
　The Prophet of the Moor (D 3a George Almar)
Also this week: *The Sea, The Sea* (twice), *Masks and Faces, Love's Telegraph*
Monday 11 October
　Money
　The Miller and His Men (D 2a Pocock)
Tuesday 12 October
　Ingomar
　Plot and Passion
Wednesday 13 October
　The Miller and His Men
Thursday 14 October
　Leap Year (C 3a Buckstone) **(SEYTON PLAYED MRS. CRISPE)**
　The Flying Dutchman
　ballet by the corp.
Friday 15 October
　Leap Year
　Plot and Passion
Saturday 16 October
　Leap Year
　Raymond and Agnes
Monday 18 October
　Leap Year
　Flowers of the Forest: A Gypsy Story
Tuesday 19 October
　Leap Year **(SEYTON PLAYED MRS. CRISPE)**
　ballet
　Robinson Crusoe **(SEYTON PLAYED INES)**
Wednesday 20 October
　Leap Year
　The Rivals

Thursday 21 October
>   *Leap Year*
>   *Comedy of Errors*

Friday 22 October
>   Benefit of Cicely Nott
>   Patrons: Colonel Douglas and officers of 11th Hussars
>   *Time Works Wonders* (C 5a Jerrold) **(SEYTON PLAYED MRS. GOLDTHUMB)**
>   *The Gentleman in Difficulties* **(SEYTON PLAYED MRS. SEDLEY)**
>   ballet
>   *Family Jars* (F 1a Joseph Lunn)

Also this week: *The Queensbury Fete*

Monday 25 October
>   Guest star for week Charles Pitt
>   *King Lear* **(SEYTON PLAYED REGAN)**

Tuesday 26 October
>   *Othello*
>   ballet
>   *Robinson Crusoe*

Wednesday 27 October
>   *Hamlet* **(SEYTON PLAYED OSRIC)**
>   ballet
>   *The Forty Thieves* (D George Conquest) **(SEYTON PLAYED ZADIN)**

Thursday 28 October
>   *The Robbers* (D 5a)

Friday 29 October
>   *The Robbers*
>   *The Corsican Brothers* **(SEYTON PLAYED ESTELLE)**

Saturday 30 October
>   *Richard III*
>   *The Honeymoon*

Also this week: *Ingomar, Raymond and Agnes, Flowers of the Forest*

Monday 1 November
>   *The Comedy of Errors*
>   *The Heart of Mid-Lothian* **(SEYTON PLAYED THE QUEEN OF ENGLAND)**

Tuesday 2 November
>   As Monday

Wednesday 3 November
>   *Leap Year* **(SEYTON PLAYED MRS. CRISPE)**
>   *The Gentleman in Difficulties* **(SEYTON PLAYED MRS.**

SMEDLEY)
The Miller and His Men **(SEYTON PLAYED RAVINA)**
Thursday 4 November
   Comedy of Errors **(SEYTON PLAYED LESBIA)**
   Flowers in the Forest **(SEYTON PLAYED LEMUEL)**
Friday 5 November
   Leap Year
   Comedy of Errors
Saturday 6 November
   Hamlet **(SEYTON PLAYED OSRIC)**
   Guido Faux **(SEYTON PLAYED LADY ALICE)**
Monday 8 November
   Guest star Alfred and Mrs. Wigan, return to stage after his serious
   illness
   Still Waters Run Deep
   Bengal Tiger (F 1a Dance)
Tuesday 9 November
   Still Waters Run Deep
   ballet
   Bengal Tiger
   Jenny Forster
Wednesday 10 November
   A Sheep in Wolfs Clothing (C 1a Taylor)
   The First Night (C 1a Alfred Wigan)
   An Object of Interest
Thursday 11 November
   as Wednesday
Friday 12 November
   School for Scandal
   A Model of a Wife (F 1a Wigan)
   Love and War (F 1a R. Jephson)
Saturday 13 November
   The Bengal Tiger
   A Sheep in Wolfs Clothing
   First Night
Monday 15 November
   John Bull
   Esmerelda
Tuesday 16 November
   Green Bushes
   Comedy of Errors
Wednesday 17 November
   Annual Military Bespeak

Charles XII (Planché)
Tit for Tat (Captain Horton Rhys)
Leap-Year **(SEYTON PLAYED MRS. CRISPE)**
Thursday 18 November
　Tit for Tat
Friday 19 November
　Amateurs and ladies of the company for Histrionic Society
　Patron Mayor J. Cordy Burrows
　Merchant of Venice
　Urgent Private Affairs (F 1a Stirling Coyne)
　Whitebait at Greenwich
Saturday 20 November
　The Stranger **(SEYTON APPEARED)**
　Pas Seul
　My Poll and My Partner Joe
Monday 22 November
　Hamlet **(SEYTON PLAYED OSRIC)**
　The Wife (D 5a Knowles)
　Jonathan Bradford (D Fitzball)
Tuesday 23 November
　Leap Year **(SEYTON PLAYED MRS. CRISPE)**
　ballet
　Jonathon Bradford
Wednesday 24 November
　The Wife
　ballet
　Jonathon Bradford
Thursday 25 November
　Under the Patronage of the Earl of Yarborough and Masons of the
　Royal York Lodge
　The Secret (F 1a)
　Comedy of Errors
　The Last of the Pigtails (F 1a Selby)
Friday 26 November
　The Wife
　The Last of the Pigtails
　An Object of Interest
Saturday 27 November
　Charles XII
　Green Bushes
Monday 29 November
　Catherine Howard (D3a Suter)
　Victorine

Tuesday 30 November
>   *The Waterman*
>   *Raising the Wind*
>   *Catherine Howard*
>   ballet

Wednesday 1 December
>   *The Last of the Pigtails* **(SEYTON PLAYED LADY STARCHINGTON)**
>   *Faint Heart Never Won Fair Lady*
>   *A Loan of a Lover* **(SEYTON PLAYED ERNESTINE ROSENDALE)**
>   *Perfection; or, The Lady of Munster* (F 1a Bayly)

Thursday 2 December
>   Benefit of Mr. Wheeler, box office
>   *The Soldier's Daughter* (C 3a Andrew Cherry)
>   *Rough Diamond*
>   *The Mistletoe Bough*

Friday 3 December
>   *Catherine Howard*
>   *Leap Year*

Saturday 4 December
>   *The Wife*
>   *Mistletoe Bough*

Also this week: *The Green Bushes, An Object of Interest*

Monday 6 December
>   *Othello*
>   *The Evil Eye* (D 3a Bayle Bernard) **(SEYTON PLAYED MARION)**

Tuesday 7 December
>   *Faint Heart Never Won Fair Lady*
>   *The Last of the Pigtails*
>   *The Comedy of Errors*

Wednesday 8 December
>   *Still Waters Run Deep*
>   ballet
>   *Victorine*

Thursday 9 December
>   Grand Fashionable Box Night
>   *A Hard Struggle*
>   *Home Truths, a rapid sketch faithfully taken in Brighton in one sitting by an invisible hand* (Capt. Horton Rhys)
>   *She Stoops to Conquer*
>   *Slasher and Crasher*

Friday 10 December
> *Charles XII*
> *Catherine Howard* **(SEYTON PLAYED DAME KENNEDY)**

Saturday 11 December
> *Othello*

Monday 13 December
> *Perdita*

Tuesday 14 December
> *Perdita*
> *Home Truths*

Wednesday 15 December
> *Faint Heart Never Won Fair*
> *Lady Perdita*
> *Home Truths*

Thursday 16 December
> Grand Special Night Benefit of Henry Nye Chart
> *The Housekeeper* (C 2a Jerrold)
> *The Bonnie Fishwife* (C 1a Selby)
> *The Bear Hunters* (D Buckstone)

Friday 17 December
> As Thursday. Closed until Boxing night, except 24 December

CORN EXHANGE, LEWES

Monday 20 December
> *Comedy of Errors*
> *Sweethearts and Wives*

Tuesday 21 December
> *Still Waters Run Deep*
> *Slasher and Crasher*

THEATRE ROYAL, BRIGHTON

Friday 24 December
> amateurs with company
> *Married Life*
> *The Waterman*

Monday 27 December
> *Little Red Riding Hood and Baron Von Wolf; or, Harlequin Little
> Boy Blue, Dame Durdenn, and Old Gammer Gurton* (Miss
> Keating) **(SEYTON PLAYED INDUSTRIA)**

Tuesday 28 December
> *The Hunter of the Alps*
> *Red Riding Hood*

Wednesday 29 December

Love and War
Red Riding Hood
Faint Heart Never Won Fair Lady
Thursday 30 December
As Wednesday
Friday 31 December
The Last of the Pigtails
Little Red Riding Hood
Young England

1859

Saturday 1 January
My Wife's Dentist
Little Red Riding Hood and Baron Von Wolf etc. **(SEYTON PLAYED INDUSTRIA)**
The Midnight Watch
Monday 3 January
Little Red Riding Hood
Where There's a Will There's a Way
Tuesday 4 January
As Monday
Wednesday 5 January
The Bonnie Fishwife
Little Red Riding Hood
The Sailor of France
Thursday 6 January
As Wednesday
Friday 7 January
Home Truths
Little Red Riding Hood
Where There's a Will There's a Way
Saturday 8 January
Home Truths
Little Red Riding Hood
Momentous Question
Afterpiece this week: *Lord Darnley* (D 2a Thomas Wilks)
Monday 10 January
Little Red Riding Hood
Samuel in Search of Himself (F 1a Stirling Coyne) **(SEYTON APPEARED)**
Michael Erie, The Maniac Lover; or, The Fair Lass of Lichfield (D 2a T.E. Wilks)

Tuesday 11 January
    As Monday
Wednesday 12 January
    The Morning Call (C 1a Dance)
    Little Red Riding Hood
    Samuel in Search of Himself
Thursday 13 January
    First juvenile night
    Little Red Riding Hood
    The Wandering Boys **(SEYTON APPEARED)**
Friday 14 January
    A Morning Call
    Little Red Riding Hood
    Samuel in Search of Himself
Saturday 15 January
    The Housekeeper
    Little Red Riding Hood
Monday 17 January
    Little Red Riding Hood **(SEYTON PLAYED INDUSTRIA)**
    Samuel in Search of Himself
Tuesday 18 January
    Little Red Riding Hood
    The Prisoner of Rochelle (D G.D. Pitt)
Wednesday 19 January
    Little Red Riding Hood
    The Prisoner of Rochelle
    Warlock of the Glen (D 2a)
Thursday 20 January
    Second juvenile night
    Little Red Riding Hood
    Babes in the Wood
Friday 21 January
    The Prisoner of Rochelle
    Little Red Riding Hood
    Warlock of the Glen
Saturday 22 January
    The Prisoner of Rochelle
    Little Red Riding Hood
    Presumptive Evidence (D 2a Buckstone)
Monday 24 January
    Never Too Late To Mend (Surrey version after Reade novel)
    Little Red Riding Hood
Wednesday 26 January

Benefit for Allano the clown
As Monday
Thursday 27 January
Fourth juvenile night
Little Red Riding Hood
Who's Your Friend (C 2a Planché)
Friday 28 January
Never Too Late to Mend
Little Red Riding Hood
Warlock of the Glen
Saturday 29 January
Never Too Late to Mend
Little Red Riding Hood
Wednesday 2 February
Miss Sanger's benefit.
Patron: Mayor J.C. Burrows
The Babes in the Wood
Little Red Riding Hood
Thursday 3 February
benefit for Messrs. W. Driver, W. English, Mons. Presini
The Children in the Wood
Never Too Late to Mend
Little Red Riding Hood
Friday 4 February
Benefit for Mr. W. Wilson, scene artist
Little Red Riding Hood
Never Too Late to Mend
Saturday 5 February
As Friday
Monday 7 February
Never Too Late to Mend
Tuesday 8 February
Victorine
Wednesday 9 February
Little Red Riding Hood
Michael Erie
Thursday 10 February
Love and War
Little Red Riding Hood
An Unprotected Female (F 1a Stirling Coyne)
Friday 11 February
Benefit for Cicely Nott
Patrons Colonel Douglas and Officers of 11th Hussars

The Child of the Regiment
Ganem, the Slave of Love **(SEYTON PLAYED ALKALOMB)**
The Morning Call
Saturday 12 February
    Where's Brown (Harry Legge)
Monday 14 February
    Benefit of John Chart, treasurer
    Richard III
    Where's Brown
    Conrad and Medora **(SEYTON PLAYED GULNARE)**
Tuesday 15 February
    Benefit for Mr. Charles Verner
    Mind Their Own Business (C 3a Lemon)
    The Corsican Brothers
    Rory O'More
Wednesday 16 February
    Still Waters Run Deep
    Never Too Late to Mend
Thursday 17 February
    Benefit for Miss Ellen Thirwell
    Lady of the Camelias **(SEYTON PLAYED PRUDENCE)**
    Where's Brown?
    ballet
    Jack Sheppard **(SEYTON PLAYED THAMES DARRELL)**
Friday 18 February
    Grand Benefit for Mr. Wheeler, box office. Patrons: Mayor, others
    and 11th Hussars
    The Follies of a Night
    Where's Brown?
    ballet
    Ganem

Monday 21 February
    Benefit of Miss Adelaide Bowering
    All is Not Gold That Glitters
    A Thumping Legacy
    Susan Hopley
Tuesday 22 February
    Benefit for Mr. Dewar
    Victims
    Wanted, 1000 Milliners
    Ruby Ratter
Wednesday 23 February

Benefit for Mr. W. Cooper, 1st old man
Comedy of Errors
ballet
A Phenomenon in a Frock Coat (C 1a William Brough)
Therese **(SEYTON PLAYED COUNTESS DE MORVILLE)**
Thursday 24 February
Victims
ballet
Never Too Late to Mend
Friday 25 February
Benefit of Roberts Tindell
The Little Treasure (C 2a Augustus Harris) **(SEYTON PLAYED FLORENCE)**
Marguerite's Colours; or, The Love Knot **(SEYTON PLAYED HELEN DE MONTBRUN)**
The Charcoal Burners
Saturday 26 February
Benefit of T. Philipps, box office taker
Life's Telegraph
The Forest of Bondy; or, The Dog Montargis (D 3a William Barrymore)
Monday 28 February
Henry Nye Chart's benefit
The Porter's Knot (C 2a Oxenford)
Maid and Milking Pail
Ten Thousand Top Sail Sheet Blocks (C. J. Bosworth)
Monday 7 March - 12 March Charles and Mrs. Mathews appeared, some of the Chart company stayed on to support.

THEATRE ROYAL, COVENTRY
Monday 14 March
Red Riding Hood

Wednesday 16 March
Red Riding Hood
The Housekeeper
Thursday 17 March
Red Riding Hood
The Hard Struggle
Friday 18 March
Red Riding Hood
The Little Treasure **(SEYTON PLAYED LADY FLORENCE)**

Monday 21 March
> *Comedy of Errors*
> *Red Riding Hood*

Wednesday 23 March
> *Red Riding Hood*
> *The Children in the Wood*

Thursday 24 March
> *Red Riding Hood*
> *The Sailor of France*

Friday 25 March
> *Comedy of Errors*
> *Red Riding Hood*

Saturday 26 March
> *My Poll and My Partner Tom*
> *Red Riding Hood*

Tuesday 29 March
> 'Special Night' for Mayor William Wilmot
> *Leap Year*
> *Children in the Wood*

Wednesday 30 March
> *The Hunter of The Alps* **(SEYTON APPEARED)**
> *Red Riding Hood*

Thursday 31 March
> *Charles XII*
> *Merry Clown*

Friday 1 April
> *Comedy of Errors*
> *Leap Year* **(SEYTON PLAYED MRS. CRISPE)**

Also this week: *Rory O'More, Sweethearts and Wives, The Housekeeper*

Wednesday 6 April
> *The Bonnie Fishwife*

Thursday 7 April
> *Never Too Late to Mend*
> *Susan Hopley*

Friday 8 April
> For the Officers of the 4th Light Dragoons
> *Plot and Passion*
> *Single Life*

Also this week: Jack *Sheppard, The Woman of the World, Romeo and Juliet, Rural Felicity*

Friday 15 April
>   *Othello*
>   *The Flying Dutchman*
>   *The Woman of the World*
>   *Jack Sheppard*

Monday 25 April
>   *Jessie Brown; or, The Siege of Lucknow* (Boucicault)
>   *Perdita, or the Royal Milkmaid* (William Brough)

Wednesday 27 April
>   As Monday

Friday 6 May
>   Benefit for Ellen Thirwall and Frank Hall
>   *Life of a Birmingham Policeman*
>   *That Rascal Jack*
>   *The Bottle* (D 2a T.P. Taylor)

Monday 9 May
>   last night, benefit for Henry Nye Chart
>   *Porter's Knot*
>   *The Married Rake*
>   *Othello Travestie* **(SEYTON APPEARED IN THESE)**

THEATRE ROYAL, DONCASTER

Henry Nye Chart company for 12 nights.
>   Lessee of theatre, Mr. Addison
>   Spring Meeting Week of Races

Monday 16 May
>   *Man of Many Friends* **(SEYTON PLAYED MRS. POPPLES)**
>   *Grimshaw, Bagshaw and Bradshaw* (Maddison Morton F 1a)
>   *The Prisoner of Rochelle* **(SEYTON PLAYED BELINDA)**

Tuesday 17 May
>   Race night
>   *The Handsome Father* (C 1a Mrs. Planché)
>   *The Queensbury Fete*
>   *Slasher and Crasher*

Wednesday 18 May
>   Patrons race stewards (Lord Londesborough and J. Merry M.P.)
>   *Porter's Knot*
>   *Crinoline*

The Maid and the Milking Pail
Thursday 19 May
   Single Life
   Young England
   Samuel in Search of Himself
Friday 20 May
   The Last of the Pigtails **(SEYTON A PRINCIPAL)**
   The Bonnie Fishwife
   My Wife's Second Floor **(SEYTON APPEARED)**
This week saw the assembly of the First West Yorkshire Yeomanry
Cavalry in Doncaster.
Monday 23 May
   Never Too Late to Mend **(SEYTON PLAYED NAN)**

Wednesday 25 May
   Patron Earl Fitzwilliam and officers of the West Yorkshire
   Yeomanry Cavalry
   Leap Year **(SEYTON PLAYED MRS. CRISPE)**
   Lend Me Five Shillings
   An Object of Interest
   Regiment band music
Thursday 26 May
   Benefit of Ellen Thirwall
Friday 27 May
   Benefit of Henry Nye Chart
   Weak Points **(SEYTON A PRINCIPAL)**
   Why Don't She Marry (Bayly)
   Urgent Private Affairs
Saturday 28 May
   The Momentous Question
   That Rascal Jack
   Black-Eyed Susan

THEATRE ROYAL, HULL
BRIGHTON COMPANY.
LESSEE JOHN PRITCHARD
Wednesday 1 June
   Rory O'More **(SEYTON PLAYED MARY O'MORE)**
   The Man of Many Friends **(SEYTON PLAYED MRS.**
   POPPLES)

Monday 6 June
   Still Waters Run Deep **(SEYTON PLAYED MRS.**

STERNHOLD)
Rural Felicity **(SEYTON PLAYED HARRIET)**
Tuesday 7 June
The Last of the Pigtails **(SEYTON PLAYED LADY STARCHINGTON)**
An Object of Interest **(SEYTON PLAYED MRS. VERNON)**
Victims **(SEYTON PLAYED MRS. MERRYWEATHER)**
Wednesday 8 June
Lend Me Five Shillings **(SEYTON PLAYED MRS. MAJOR PHOBBS)**
Thursday 9 June
Rory O'More **(SEYTON PLAYED MARY O'MORE)**
The Man of Many Friends **(SEYTON PLAYED MRS. POPPLES)**
Friday 10 June
The Porters Knot
His Last Legs (F 2a Bayle Bernard)
Slasher and Crasher **(SEYTON PLAYED DINAH BLOWHARD)**

PRINCESS THEATRE, LEEDS
Monday 13 June
Leap Year
Young England
Green Bushes **(SEYTON PLAYED MIAMI)**
Tuesday 14 June
Victims
Wednesday 15 June
The Porter's Knot
Crinoline
Last Legs

Saturday 18 June
Othello

Wednesday 23 June
Perdita **(SEYTON PLAYED FLORIZEL)**

Also this week: *Victims, Porter's Knot*
Monday 27 June
Romeo and Juliet
Courier of Lyons

Wednesday 29 June
Courier of Lyons

Also alternately this week: *The Porter's Knot, Leap Year, The Man of Many Friends, The Last of the Pigtails, The Serious Family*

Tuesday 5 July
Closed for short recess before fair, company now divided. Before this: *Macbeth, Richard III, Raby Rattler, The Road to Ruin* (C 5a Thomas Holcroft)
Monday 11 May
Fair Week. Guest star Rebecca Issacs
This week: *Daughter of the Regiment, Kate O'Brien, The Pet of the Public, T'was I*

Monday 18 May
Rebecca Issacs still guest starring this week.
The Daughter of the Regiment

Thursday 21 May
The Black Doctor

Saturday 23 July
Benefit of manager, Mr. Thorpe
Last night of Miss Issacs and Brighton Company
The Heart of Mid-Lothian
Argyll and Dumbedlike
The Married Rake (**SEYTON PLAYED MRS. TRICTRAC**)
Alonzo the Brave and the Fair Imogene (D 2a Dibdin)

THEATRE ROYAL BRIGHTON
LESSEE AND MANAGER, HENRY NYE CHART
Saturday 30 July
Love Chase
Midas
Monday 1 August
Much Ado About Nothing
My Little Adopted (C Bayly)
Midas
Tuesday 2 August
As You Like It
The Maid and the Milking Pail
Midas

Wednesday 3 August
   His Last Legs
   The Porter's Knot
   ballet
   Midas
Thursday 4 August
   Patrons: Stewards of the Races
   The Ladies' Battle (C 3a Charles Reade)
   Tom Noddy's Secret
   ballet
   Midas
Friday 5 August
   Patrons: Jockeys and Trainers of the Brighton Races
   All in the Wrong **(SEYTON PLAYED CLARISSA)**
   Perfection
   ballet
   The Thimble Ring (F Buckstone)
Saturday 6 August
   Othello (burlesque)
   As You Like It **(SEYTON PLAYED CELIA)**
Monday 8 August
   The Ladies' Battle
   Kenilworth; or, Ye Queene, ye Earle and ye Maydenne (burlesque
   by Frederick Laurence and Andrew Halliday)
   Michael Earle **(SEYTON PLAYED MARY WOODWARD)**
Tuesday 9 August
   All in the Wrong **(SEYTON PLAYED CLARISSA)**
   Kenilworth
   Ici on Parle Francais **(SEYTON PLAYED JULIA)**
Wednesday 10 August
   Town and Country (3a Morton) **(SEYTON PLAYED MRS.
   GLENROY)**
   Kenilworth
Thursday 11 August
   The Ladies' Battle
   Kenilworth
Friday 12 August
   Town and County **(SEYTON PLAYED MRS. GLENROY)**
   Kenilworth
Saturday 13 August
   The Lady of Lyons **(SEYTON PLAYED WIDOW MELNOTTE)**
   Kenilworth
Monday 15 August

Nine Points of the Law (C 1a Taylor)
Kenilworth
Ici on Parle Francais **(SEYTON PLAYED JULIA)**
Tuesday 16 August
As Monday
Wednesday 17 August
Nine Points of the Law
Kenilworth
Ici on Parle Francais
Thursday 18 August
Grand Fashionable Night
If the Cap Fits (C 1a N. Harrington and Edmund Yates)
Where's Brown
Kenilworth
Friday 19 August
Nine Points of the Law
Kenilworth
Where's Brown
Saturday 20 August
Faint Heart Won Fair Lady
Nine Points of the Law
Kenilworth
His Last Legs
Monday 22 August
The Marble Heart **(SEYTON PLAYED CLEMENTINE)**
Kenilworth
Tuesday 23 August
As Monday
Wednesday 24 August
Nine Points of the Law
Kenilworth
If the Cap Fits
Thursday 25 August
Faint Heart Never Won Fair Lady
Kenilworth
Harold Hawk; or, The Convict's Vengeance (D 2a Selby)
Friday 26 August
Delicate Ground
Kenilworth
Jack Long of Texas (D) **(SEYTON PLAYED MAY GIBBS)**
Saturday 27 August
The Morning Call
The Marble Heart **(SEYTON PLAYED CLEMENTINE)**

Jack Long of Texas **(SEYTON PLAYED MAY GIBBS)**

Monday 29 August

George Vining guest star for 6 nights

Not a Bad Judge (C 2a J.R. Planché)

Little Toddlekins (C 1a Charles Mathews)

Tuesday 30 August

The Sheriff of the County (C 3a R.B. Peake)

The Captain of the Watch (F 1a J.R. Planché)

Wednesday 31 August

The Morning Call

A Bachelor of Arts (C 2a Pelham Hardwick)

Kenilworth

Thursday 1 September

The Sheriff of the County **(SEYTON PLAYED MARION)**

The Young Widow

Kenilworth

Friday 2 September

A Bachelor of Art

The Young Widow

Kenilworth

Saturday 3 September

Benefit George Vining

Naval Engagements (C 2a Dance)

School for Scandal (a scene)

Victorine

Monday 5 September

Madame Celeste guest star for two weeks.

Green Bushes

Tuesday 6 September

The Mysterious Stranger (D 2a Selby) **(SEYTON PLAYED MADAME DE SCRICOURT)**

Nine Points of the Law

Ici on Parle Francais **(SEYTON PLAYED JULIA)**

Wednesday 7 September

Green Bushes

ballet

Asmodeus; or, The Little Devil's Share (C 2a Archer) **(SEYTON PLAYED ISABEL, QUEEN OF SPAIN)**

Thursday 8 September

If the Cap Fits

The Sister's Sacrifice **(SEYTON PLAYED MADAME BELAN)**

The Ladies' Battle

Friday 9 September

If the Cap Fits
The Mysterious Stranger **(SEYTON PLAYED MADAME DE SCRICOURT)**
an extract from *Kenilworth*
Nine Points of the Law
Saturday 10 September
 The Sister's Sacrifice **(SEYTON PLAYED MADAME BELAN)**
 The Child of the Wreck (D 2a Planché)
Also this week: *Ici on Parle Francais* (F 1a T.J. Williams)
Monday 12 September
 The French Spy; or, The Siege of Constantina (D 3a Haines)
 The Mysterious Stranger **(SEYTON PLAYED SCRICOURT)**
Wednesday 14 September
 The Green Bushes
 ballet
 The Child of the Wreck
Thursday 15 September
 The Mysterious Stranger
 The French Spy
Friday 16 September
 Madame Celeste's benefit
 The Last Hope (D 3a Oxenford)
 The Child of the Wreck
 Green Bushes
Saturday 17 September
 The Last Hope
 The French Spy
Monday 19 September
 Guest star this week was James Bennett
 Hamlet **(SEYTON PLAYED GEUTRUDE)**
 Jessy Vere
Tuesday 20 September
 Virginius; or, The Roman Father (T Sheridan Knowles) **(SEYTON PLAYED SERVIA)**
 Kenilworth
Wednesday 21 September
 Virginius **(SEYTON PLAYED SERVIA)**
 Kenilworth
Thursday 22 September
 Benefit of Esther Jacobs
 King John **(SEYTON PLAYED QUEEN ELEANOR)**
 Kenilworth
Friday 23 September

Evadne
Leon of Arragon; or, Rule a Wife and Have a Wife
Kenilworth
Saturday 24 September
Richard III
Susan Hopley
Monday 26 September
Ira Aldridge guest star for week.
Othello
Tuesday 27 September
The Slave **(SEYTON PLAYED ZELINDA)**
The Mummy
Wednesday 28 September
Macbeth
ballet
The Padlock
Thursday 29 September
Othello
ballet
The Padlock
Friday 30 September
Ira Aldridge's benefit
The Maid and the Magpie; or, The Fatal Spoon (D 3a S.J. Arnold)
The Black Doctor
ballet
The Mummy
Saturday 1 October
Stage Mad
OBI; or, Three Fingered Jack (D)
Monday 3 October
Ingomar
Mary the Maid of the Inn **(SEYTON PLAYED MARY)**
Kenilworth
Tuesday 4 October
The Maid and the Magpie
Samuel in Search of Himself
Wednesday 5 October
The Porter's Knot
The Maid and the Magpie
French Before Breakfast **(SEYTON PLAYED JULIA)**
Thursday 6 October
With amateurs, officers from 4th Dragoon Guards
Helping Hands (D 2a Taylor)

To Paris and Back for Five Pounds
Friday 7 October
  The Maid and the Magpie
  Richlieu **(SEYTON PLAYED FRANCOIS)**
Saturday 8 October
  Nine Points of the Law
  The Maid and the Magpie
  Jessie Vere

Monday 10 October
  The Yew Tree Ruins (D J.T. Haines) **(SEYTON PLAYED ROSE KYNON)**
  The Maid and the Magpie
Tuesday 11 October
  As Monday
Wednesday 12 October
  The Porter's Knot
  The Maid and the Magpie
  Which of the Two
Thursday 13 October
  Fashionable Night
  Nine Points of the Law
  Porter's Knot
  The Maid and the Magpie
Friday 14 October
  As Thursday
Saturday 15 October
  The Yew Tree **(SEYTON APPEARED)**
  The Chevalier of the Maison Rouge (Hazlewood) **(SEYTON PLAYED MARIE ANTOINETTE)**
Monday 17 October
  Mr. and Mrs. Alfred Wigan guest stars for 2 weeks
  The House and Home (C 2a Taylor)
  A Model for a Wife **(SEYTON PLAYED MRS. STUMP)**
Tuesday 18 October
  Still Waters Run Deep
  The First Night
Wednesday 19 October
  The House and Home
  Bengal Tiger **(SEYTON PLAYED CHARLOTTE HENDERSON)**
  A Model of a Wife **(SEYTON PLAYED MRS. STUMP)**
Thursday 20 October

The Sheep in Wolfs Clothing
The First Night
The Prisoner of Rochelle **(SEYTON PLAYED BELINDA BELMONT)**
Friday 21 October
Still Waters Run Deep
ballet
A Model Wife **(SEYTON PLAYED MRS. STUMP)**
Perfection
Saturday 22 October
Jenny Foster
Monday 24 October
Still Waters Run Deep **(SEYTON PLAYED MRS. STERNHOLD)**
The Wandering Boys **(SEYTON PLAYED THE BARONESS)**
Tuesday 25 October
Lucky Friday (F 1a Wigan) **(SEYTON PLAYED BESSIE)**
The Jealous Wife
Which of the Two
Wednesday 26 October
The House or the Home
The Bengal Tiger **(SEYTON PLAYED CHARLOTTE)**
ballet
A Lucky Friday **(SEYTON PLAYED BESSIE)**
Young England **(SEYTON PLAYED MRS. DASHALONG)**
Thursday 27 October
Monsieur Jacques
The House or the Home
A Lucky Friday **(SEYTON PLAYED BESSIE)**
Friday 28 October
Benefit of Mr. and Mrs. Wigan
The Jealous Wife
ballet
The Bengal Tiger
Monsieur Jacques
Saturday 29 October
The Jealous Wife
The Bengal Tiger **(SEYTON PLAYED CHARLOTTE)**
The First Night
Also this week: *A Sheep in Wolf's Clothing, The Wandering Boys*
Monday 31 October
The Hunchback
Jessie Brown; or, The Relief of Lucknow **(SEYTON PLAYED**

MRS. CAMPBELL)
Tuesday 1 November
    As Monday
Wednesday 2 November
    Mdme. Celeste guest star for 3 nights
    Green Bushes **(SEYTON PLAYED GERALDINE)**
    The Power of Love
Thursday 3 November
    The Mysterious Stranger **(SEYTON PLAYED**
    MADEMOISELLE DE NANTELLE)
    The French Spy
Friday 4 November
    A Sister's Sacrifice **(SEYTON PLAYED MADAME BELAN)**
    ballet
    The Mysterious Stranger **(SEYTON PLAYED NANTELLE)**

Monday 7 November
    Guest stars for week Mr. and Mrs. Charles Kean for 7 shows
    Day After the Wedding
    The Wife's Secret (D 5a George Lovell)
Tuesday 8 November
    Louis XI
Wednesday 9 November
    Samuel in Search of Himself
    Hamlet
    French Before Breakfast **(SEYTON PLAYED JULIA)**
Thursday 10 November
    The Spitalfields Weaver
    The Wife's Secret
    The Married Rake **(SEYTON PLAYED MRS. TRICTRAC AND**
    CORNET FITZHERBERT)
Friday 11 November
    Perfection
    Macbeth
    Samuel in Search of Himself
Saturday 12 November
    The Flowers of the Forest **(SEYTON PLAYED LEMUEL)**
    Jessie Brown **(SEYTON PLAYED MRS. CAMPBELL)**
    Pauline; or, The Lone Chateaux
Monday 14 November
    Louis XI
Tuesday 15 November
    Benefit of the Keans

    Much Ado About Nothing
    Pauline
Wednesday 16 November
    The Rivals **(SEYTON PLAYED JULIA)**
    ballet
    The Porter's Knot
Thursday 17 November
    The School for Scandal **(SEYTON PLAYED LADY SNEERWELL)**
    ballet
    The Wandering Boys
Friday 18 November
    Amateurs from Royal Irish Dragoon Guards
    Where There's a Will There's a Way
    Uncle John (F Buckstone) **(SEYTON PLAYED MISS HAWK)**
    The Bonnycastles **(SEYTON PLAYED HELEN)**
Saturday 19 November
    Rebecca Issacs guest star for 2 weeks
    The Daughter of the Regiment
    The Very Latest Edition of the Lady of Lyons (H.Byron)
Monday 21 November
    The Daughter of the Regiment
    The Lady of Lyons
    The Married Rake **(SEYTON PLAYED MRS. TRICTRAC AND CORNET)**
Tuesday 22 November
    Delicate Ground
    The Very Latest Edition of the Lady of Lyons
    Black Eyed Susan
Wednesday 23 November
    Our Nelly (D 2a H.T. Craven) **(SEYTON PLAYED MISS THURLOW)**
    The Very Latest Edition of the Lady of Lyons
    Never Taste Wine at the Docks (Robert Soutar)
Thursday 24 November
    The Heart of Mid-Lothian **(SEYTON PLAYED QUEEN ANNE)**
    The Very Latest Edition of the Lady of Lyons
    A Thumping Legacy
Friday 25 November
    Many Happy Returns
    The Very Latest Edition of the Lady of Lyons
    The Prisoner of Rochelle
Saturday 26 November

The Very Latest Edition of the Lady of Lyons
Harold Hawk **(SEYTON PLAYED MRS. LINCOLN)**
Also this week: *Delicate Ground, The Flying Dutchman*
Monday 28 November
    Lucretia Borgia **(SEYTON PLAYED JEPPO LIVERETTO)**
Tuesday 29 November
    Masonic Bequest of Royal York Lodge
    The Daughter of the Regiment
    My Son Diana (F 1a Augustus Harris)
    The Very Latest Edition of the Lady of Lyons
    Lucretia Borgia **(SEYTON APPEARED)**
Wednesday 30 November
    Many Happy Returns of the Day
    My Son Diana
    The Very Latest Edition of the Lady of Lyons
Thursday 1 December
    Our Nelly
    The Very Latest Edition of the Lady of Lyons
    The Prisoner of Rochelle
Friday 2 December
    Patrons Earl and Countess of Yarborough
    Rebecca Issacs's benefit
    Lucretia Borgia **(SEYTON PLAYED JEPPO)**
    The Daughter of the Regiment
    The Very Latest Edition of the Lady of Lyons
Saturday 3 December
    Plot and Passion
    Raby Rattler **(SEYTON PLAYED MISS LANDROSE)**
Monday 5 December
    Romeo and Juliet **(SEYTON PLAYED THE NURSE)**
    Dumb Girl of Genoa
Tuesday 6 December
    Money **(SEYTON PLAYED LADY FRANKLIN)**
    ballet
    The Porter's Knot
Wednesday 7 December
    As Tuesday
Thursday 8 December
    Grand night. Benefit for Mr. Wheeler, box office and book keeper.
    My Wife's Daughter (C 2a Stirling Coyne)
    ballet: Grand Special Fate. bolero, corp and Marion Lees
    Done on Both Sides **(SEYTON PLAYED MRS. WHIFFLES)**
    The Vampire; or, The Bride of the Isles (Planché) **(SEYTON**

PLAYED EFFIE)
Friday 9 December
    As Thursday
Saturday 10 December
    Romeo and Juliet **(SEYTON PLAYED THE NURSE)**
    The Vampire **(SEYTON PLAYED EFFIE)**
Monday 12 December
    Benefit of Mr. J. Chart, treasurer.
    The Fool's Revenge **(SEYTON PLAYED FRANCESCA)**
    The Dead Shot (F 1a Buckstone)
    Dick Turpin
Tuesday 13 December
    As Monday
Wednesday 14 December
    Benefit of Frank Hall and Ellen Thirwall
    The Cricket on the Hearth (duologue by Sawyer)
    The Spitalfield's Weaver
    Black-Eyed Susan
Thursday 15 December
    The Fool's Revenge **(SEYTON PLAYED FRANCESCA)**
    The Married Rake **(SEYTON PLAYED MRS. TRICTRAC AND CORNET)**
    Never Taste Wine at the Docks
Friday 16 December
    benefit of Charles Vernar
    Secret Service
    The Rifle Brigade; or, Our National Defences
    Luke the Labourer
Saturday 17 December
    The Fool's Revenge **(SEYTON PLAYED FRANCESCA)**
    The Dumb Girl of Genoa
Monday 19 December
    Patrons Marquis and Marchioness of Normandy.
    Benefit of Henry Nye Chart
    A Husband to Order (C 2a Maddison Morton)
    The Rifle and How to Use It (F 1a J.V. Bridgeman) **(SEYTON PLAYED MRS. FLOFF)**
    Margaret Catchpole (D 3a Stirling)
Brighton Theatre Royal closed until the pantomime.

CORN EXCHANGE, LEWES
Tuesday 20 December
    Leap Year

Done on Both Sides
Wednesday 21 December
   The Wonderful Woman
   The Rifle and How to Use It

THEATRE ROYAL, BRIGHTON
Monday 26 December
   The Scapegoat; or, The Rake and His Tutor (F 1a J. Poole)
   Harlequin House That Jack Built, Ye Lorde Lovelle and Nancye
   Belle; or, Old Mother, Humpty Dumpty, and the Fairies of the
   Silver Grotto (Miss Keating)

Wednesday 28 December
   The Scapegoat **(SEYTON APPEARED)**
   Harlequin House
   The Married Rake

Friday 30 December
   A Day After the Wedding (F 1a M.T. Kemble)
   Harlequin House
   Rough Diamond
Saturday 31 December
   As Friday

1860

Wednesday 4 January
   A Pretty Piece of Business **(SEYTON A PRINCIPAL)**
   Harlequin House
   The Rifle and How to Use It
Thursday 5 January
   As Wednesday
Friday 6 January
   The Bonnie Fishwife
   Harlequin House
   Warlock of the Glen
Saturday 7 January
   The Bonnie Fishwife
   Harlequin House
   Warlock of the Glen **(SEYTON APPEARED)**
Monday 9 January
   The Idiot Witness

Wednesday 11 January
Bamboozling
Harlequin House
The Rifle and How to Use It
Thursday 12 January
First 2 as Wednesday
Fish Out of Water (F 1a Joseph Lunn)
Friday 13 January
First juvenile night
A Kiss in the Dark (**SEYTON APPEARED**)
Harlequin House
The Children in the Wood (**SEYTON A PRINCIPAL**)
Saturday 14 January
A Kiss in the Dark (**SEYTON APPEARED**)
Harlequin House
The Idiot Witness

Wednesday 18 January
Harlequin House
Bamboozling
A Pretty Piece of Business
Thursday 19 January
Has Anybody Seen Brown? Or Brown, Jones, and Robinson
Married and Settled?
Harlequin House
Bamboozling
Friday 20 January
A Kiss in the Dark (**SEYTON APPEARED**)
Harlequin House
Has Anybody Seen Brown
Saturday 21 January
A Kiss in the Dark (**SEYTON APPEARED**)
Harlequin House
Jesse Vere
Monday 23 January
The Loan of a Lover (**SEYTON APPEARED**)

Wednesday 25 January
Harlequin House
A Kiss in the Dark
The Hunter of the Alps
Thursday 26 January
Benefit for Allano the clown

Time Tries All
Harlequin House
Wilful Murder **(SEYTON A PRINCIPAL)**
Saturday 28 January
Pretty Piece of Business **(SEYTON APPEARED)**
Loan of a Lover
Harlequin House That Jack Built
Also this week: *The Floating Beacon*
Monday 30 January
Quicksands and Whirlpools (Robert Soutar) **(SEYTON PLAYED ADELAIDE LACY)**
Tuesday 31 January
Quicksands and Whirlpools
Wednesday 1 February
Quicksands and Whirlpools
Last juvenile night of panto
Thursday 2 February
Last juvenile Night
Harlequin House
Wilful Murder **(SEYTON APPEARED)**
Friday 3 February
Quicksands and Whirlpools
Harlequin House
Saturday 4 February
As Friday
Monday 6 February
Grand extra juvenile night and last but three of pantomime
Tuesday 7 February
Benefit of Alfred Sanger, stage manager, and Miss Rachel Sanger.
The Climbing Boy (D R.B. Peake) **(SEYTON PLAYED ROSALIE DE MONNEVILLE)**
Harlequin House
Wednesday 8 February
Benefit of Miss Marian Taylor
My Wife's Dentist
A Kiss in the Dark
Thursday 9 February
Benefit of Mr. English Wilsone and Mr. Russelle
My Wife's Daughter **(SEYTON PLAYED MRS. IVYLEAF)**
A Kiss in the Dark
Harlequin House
Friday 10 February
The Climbing Boy **(SEYTON PLAYED ROSALIE)**

Harlequin House
Saturday 11 February
    Harlequin House (last night)
    Quicksands and Whirlpools **(SEYTON PLAYED ADELAIDE)**

Tuesday 14 February
    Benefit for Frederick Dewar
    Perourou, or, The Bellows Mender (D.W. Moncreiff)
    Tom Noddy's Secret
    Don Juan; or, The Spectre on Horseback **(SEYTON PLAYED OCTAVIA)**
Wednesday 15 February
    Ticket night for 3 ladies of the Company, one of whom was **SEYTON.**
    Time Tries All
    The Rifle and How to use It
    Quicksands and Whirlpools
Thursday 16 February
    Patron: Mayor J. Cordy Burrows.
    Benefit for Robert Soutar by Amateur gentlemen
    A Wonderful Woman
    John Dobbs **(SEYTON PLAYED MRS. CHESTERTON)**
    Eustache **(SEYTON PLAYED COUNTESS D'ALBERTE)**
Friday 17 February
    Benefit of Mr. Wheeler, Box office Book-keeper
    Sweethearts and Wives
    ballet from *Conrad and Medora*
    A Day at Boulogne, or Run to Earth (Marshall Hall)
    Ethiopian Minstrel Troupe
    Robert Macaire
Saturday 18 February
    A Kiss in the Dark **(SEYTON PLAYED MRS. SELIM PETTIBONE)**
    Sweethearts and Wives
    The Ocean Child
Monday 20 February
    Benefit for Mr. Cooper
    Paul Pry
    A Day at Boulogne
    Alice Gray
Tuesday 21 February
    Benefit for Mr. G.K. Maskell
    St. Mary's Eve

Sarah's Young Man **(SEYTON PLAYED ARAMINTA)**
Hearts are Trumps
Thursday 23 February
Benefit for Miss Margaret Eburne
The Pride of the Market (C 3a Planché)
The Silent Woman (F 1a T.H. Lacy)
ballet by corp
Phoebe Hessell (D 3a Johnstone) **(SEYTON PLAYED LYDIA)**
Friday 24 February
Benefit for Mrs. Woollidge
The Ladies' Club (C 2a Lemon) **(SEYTON PLAYED MRS. MORTAR)**
The Star of the Rhine (ballet Marian Lees)
Popping the Question (F 1a Buckstone)
The Dumb Man of Manchester (D 3a B.F. Rayner)
Saturday 25 February
Paul Pry (F 1a Charles Mathews)
The Silent Woman
Phoebe Hessell **(SEYTON PLAYED LYDIA)**
Monday 27 February
The Pride of the Market
Sarah's Young Man **(SEYTON PLAYED ARAMINTA)**
The Sea
Tuesday 28 February
Benefit of Henry Nye Chart
Last night of the season under the patronage of Major Jones and the Officers of the 4th Dragoon Guards and several other persons of distinction, after which Henry Nye Chart and company went to Cheltenham and Braddon retired from the stage.
Old Offenders (C 2a Planché)
The Head of the Family (C 1a W.S. Emden)
Anchor of Hope
Miss Marian Lees and corp de ballet, 4th Dragoon band

Appendix Two
A Bibliography of Braddon's Writing

A writer as prolific as Braddon causes a number of problems for the bibliographer. Not only was her output vast, but a good deal of it was also anonymous, meaning that some is difficult or impossible to trace. From the beginning of her literary career, when she was contributing poems to provincial newspapers, she was also writing 'political squibs' and parodies for, probably, the *Brighton Herald*.[1] If this is the case, like most pieces in newspapers of the period, they are unsigned and unidentifiable.

Anyone writing about Braddon owes a debt to Robert Lee Wolff's bibliographical skills in his biography of Braddon and in his catalogue. Despite Wolff's work there was much that remained untraced, particularly from the earliest part of her career, and uncollected essays and fiction from the 1890s onwards. This appendix is intended to fill in some of the gaps in Wolff's bibliography.

Even now there are occasional errors, such as works by Ada Buisson which have been mistakenly credited to Braddon (see section D.) and the novel *For Better For Worse* which appeared anonymously in the first three volumes of *Temple Bar* between December 1860 to September 1861.[2] The *Temple Bar* index, which formed volume one hundred of that magazine, attributes this serial to Braddon.[3]

Coincidentally Braddon later used the title *For Better, For Worse* for a play adapted from her novel *Like and Unlike* (1887), which was performed in several provincial towns in 1890 and 1891, starring her son Gerald. However, it is highly unlikely that Braddon was responsible for the serial. Edmund Yates, who did much of the commissioning and editing for the magazine recalled that for the very first issue of *Temple Bar*:

> I had some difficulty in getting a serial story, for the leading lights of those days were most of them engaged, (...) At last I obtained from a lady who had never written previously for the press, and who was the wife of a provincial clergyman, a by no means brilliant, but quite sufficiently interesting "makeweight," story, without much incident, but remarkably well written, and giving a curious insight into Quaker life, the author having in her youth belonged to that community. It was called "For Better, For Worse," and perhaps may be best described as Trollope-and-milk.[4]

The subject matter of Quakerism and the lack of exciting incident, which so characterised her serial fiction at this time, seems to count against the novel being by Braddon. It is not written in any recognisable style, although Braddon was capable of writing quite differently in different genres. The fact that when *For Better For Worse* was published in two volumes in 1864 it said on its title page that it was edited by Edmund Yates does, I believe, count against it being by Braddon, as by that date there would be no reason for her not to have acknowledged the novel and no need for it to be edited by Edmund Yates. When Yates came to write his autobiography there would have been even less reason to invent the story of the Quaker lady. When the *Temple Bar* index was published the magazine had different owners to when Braddon wrote for it, so the most likely explanation is that the attribution was an error, as the index makes no claim to identify the authors of other anonymous short stories and essays.

Yates went on to write that Braddon's first piece to appear in *Temple Bar* was the short story 'The Mystery of Fernwood' which appeared in November and December 1861.

> Towards the end of the same year appeared in *Temple Bar* a story called "The Mystery of Fernwood," the first contribution of one whose work perhaps was more useful than that of any writer in it – Miss M.E. Braddon.[5]

However, it does seem strange that Braddon would have made no contribution to her lover's most prestigious and ambitious journal, the only one to aim truly at the core middle class readership, until the very end of the third volume. There may have been others which were not shown to Yates for selection. There are three stories which appear in *Temple Bar* before 'The Mystery of Fernwood' which could tentatively be attributed to Braddon. Moreover they are signed 'M.B.', and there does not seem to have been another *Temple Bar* contributor at this time with the same initials.[6] Braddon used these initials at times in later years to denote some of her contributions to the *World*. Even Braddon's first serial novel for *Temple Bar*, *Aurora Floyd*, was completely anonymous. This trend continued with her own magazine, *Belgravia*, when the main serial was acknowledged by her, but many of the short stories were anonymous until she collected them in volume form. I have not attempted to attribute any other anonymous stories or essays as works uncollected by Braddon, but, as will be seen, I have attributed those signed 'M'. The initial 'M' was used by Braddon for a few of her *World* contributions, and it seems unlikely that any other contributor to *Belgravia* would have used it.

There can be little doubt that Braddon did write novels which were not published under her name. Those which are known about are *Circe,*

The Good Hermione, and her serials for the *Halfpenny Journal*. There may have been others. Clive Holland wrote:

> To the long list of her many novels must be added also a considerable number which have been published anonymously and never acknowledged as being from her pen. One or two were so "Braddonesque," however, if one may coin the term, that keen admirers and constant readers of hers must have more than a suspicion regarding the identity of the anonymous author.[7]

Braddon also told Clive Holland that she had 'contributed innumerable essays and articles to various newspapers under her own name and anonymously.'[8] Braddon became a regular contributor to her friend Edmund Yates's newspaper the *World*, and seems to have written dozens of essays from the 1880s to early 1900s, but nearly all of these were anonymous. A few can be identified from clues in her diaries, and where, in a few rare cases, they are initialled and written from the place she was staying at. These essays would have brought her neither fame nor further fortune, and represent, like her historical fiction, her attempts at 'serious' work, and it seems as if she worked extremely hard on these anonymous works of journalism:

> I hope you & Mr. Yates may like it – The writing has cost me more time & trouble than twice the pages of my current novel – & yet I fear it contains very little that has not been said before in some form or other.[9]

For the first part of her career John Maxwell handled the sales and rights of his wife's fiction, effectively acting as her agent in negotiating with overseas publishers and with British newspapers syndicates. In later years, after the demise of the Maxwell publishing company, and when Maxwell was in declining health, she enlisted the services of the first literary agent, A.P. Watt. Despite becoming his client, Braddon seems to have continued to make her own arrangements with the *World* and for essays written for the magazine *Theatre*. Fortunately many of the Watt papers dealing with Braddon's later works and copyright arrangements after her death still exist at the University of South Carolina, and although there are clear gaps in the papers, they provide some indication as to where some of her later work may have appeared, even if it does not provide comprehensive details. Two files have been mistakenly filed as Braddon's.[10]

This appendix is intended to serve as a bibliographical addenda to that provided in Wolff's biography and catalogue. It provides information on a number of previously unrecorded poems, essays, and short stories. Much of Braddon's fiction was serialised in weekly or monthly parts from *Three Times Dead* in 1860 to *The Rose of Life* in 1906, and where known I have given brief details of the original serialisation or appearance before book form. Information on her newspaper fiction and its serialisation was jointly acquired with Professor Graham Law for the essay 'Our Author', in which the information appears in far greater detail.[11] I am also indebted to Professor Law for showing me the Watt papers.

I have put the bibliographical information in the following sections: novels, short stories, books edited by Braddon, plays, poetry, lyrics and libretto, and parodies and non fiction.

Footnotes

1. The mention of 'political squibs' and parodies appears in a number of the obituaries of Braddon, including 'Death of Miss Braddon', *Morning Post*, 5 February 1915, p.4.
2. *For Better For Worse*, *Temple Bar*, vols. I-III, December 1860 – September 1861, published anonymously. Attributed to M.E. Braddon in the index to *Temple Bar*, vol. C. Published in two volumes in 1864, edited by Edmund Yates.
3. *Temple Bar*, vol. C, p.14, p.43, p.151.
4. Edmund Yates, *Edmund Yates: His Recollections and Experiences* 2 vols (London: Richard Bentley, 1884), II, pp.58-59.
5. Yates, p. 63.
6. The short stories signed 'M.B.' were: 'John's Wife', *Temple Bar*, vol. II, May 1861, pp.254-267; 'Told at Frascati', *Temple Bar*, vol. II, July 1861, pp.547-556; 'The Corporal's Story', *Temple Bar*, vol. III, September 1861, pp.273-282. Interestingly, after Braddon became an acknowledged contributor, there are no more stories 'By the Author of John's Wife', but there is an essay about Cornwall signed M.B., 'Trontlemouth', *Temple Bar*, vol. XVI, January 1866, pp.198-205. Although Braddon was the only *Temple Bar* contributor to have the initials M.B., Maxwell authors working on his other magazines were Mary Bennett and Mary Bird.
7. Clive Holland, 'Fifty Years of Novel Writing', *Pall Mall Magazine*, vol. XIV, November 1911, p.700.
8. Holland, p.700.
9. M.E. Braddon to Mr. Thomas (? Braddon's other letters about essays are addressed to Mr. Thomas) of the *World*, 2 March 1892, Wolff collection. Holland stated she also wrote verses and sketches for the *World*.

10. The first of these is 'Dick's Diamonds', file 19.11. The file title reads 'Miss Maxwell'. Sybil Maxwell's (no relation) short story was published in *The Leisure Hour*, 1894, pp.615-622.

The second is the file 'Mrs. Maxwell 85.13' (confusingly the Watt papers varyingly describe Braddon as 'Miss Braddon' and 'Mrs. Maxwell'), and deals with a novel promoting Jewish conversion written for the Religious Tract Society, *Carpenter and King* (1907). This Mrs. Maxwell was Anna Maxwell, who later wrote *Hampstead: Its Historic Houses – Its Literary Associations* (London: James Clarke & co, 1912) and *Pietro the Garibaldean* (London: Leonard Parsons, 1925).

11. Jennifer Carnell and Graham Law '"Our Author": Braddon in the Provincial Weeklies'. Essay in book *Beyond Sensation: Mary Braddon in Context* edited by Marlene Tromp, Pamela Gilbert and Aeron Haynie, (New York: State University of New York Press, 2000).

(A.) NOVELS BY M.E. BRADDON

Three Times Dead (London: W. & M. Clark; Beverley: Empson, 1860). Sold in weekly parts starting in February 1860. Wolff's copy was a yellowback, but, as shown by the British Library copy, it was also published as a paperback in red wrappers. Maxwell reprinted it as *The Trail of the Serpent* in March 1861. It was also serialised as *The Trail of the Serpent* in the *Halfpenny Journal*, vol. IV, in 28 weekly parts from 1 August 1864 to 6 February 1865.

The Lady Lisle (London: Ward & Lock, 1862). Published as the third volume in the Ward & Lock Shilling Library, the volume was advertised as available for sale on 1 December 1861. Serialised in the *Welcome Guest*, vol. IV, in 21 weekly parts, May to September 1861.

The Black Band; or, The Mysteries of Midnight, serialised in the *Halfpenny Journal*, vol. I, in 52 weekly parts from 1 July 1861 to 23 June 1862. The first eleven numbers by Lady Caroline Lascelles, thereafter anonymous. A heavily abridged book version was published as a yellowback and in seventeen penny parts (London: George Vickers, 1877).

The Octoroon; or, The Lily of Louisiana, serialised in the *Halfpenny Journal*, vol. I, in 18 weekly instalments from 18 November 1861 to 17 March 1862 'by the author of "The Black Band"'.

Captain of the Vulture (London: Ward & Lock, 1862). Published as the fourteenth volume in the Ward and Lock Shilling Library in April 1862. Serialised in the *Sixpenny Magazine*, vols. I-II, September 1861 to March 1862.

Ralph the Bailiff (London: Ward & Lock, 1862). Published as the eighteenth volume in the Ward & Lock Shilling Library in June 1862. Serialised in the *St. James's Magazine*, vol. I, April to June 1861. The 1867 edition contained four stories not in the first.

Woman's Revenge; or, The Captain of the Guard, serialised anonymously in the *Halfpenny Journal*, vol. I, 24 March 1862 to 4 August 1862. Wolff suggests in *Sensational Victorian* (p.119) that Braddon may have written this anonymous novel on account of her interest in Restoration England settings. Braddon's penny blood novels were published as paperbacks in America under her name, one of which was called *The Blue Band; or, A Story of Woman's Vengeance* (New

York, DeWitt). If these two novels are the same it would add credence to Wolff's assertion.

Lady Audley's Secret (London: Tinsley, 1862), serialised in *Robin Goodfellow* for 13 weeks from 6 July to 28 September 1861. This magazine folded with the serial incomplete, and reran from the beginning in the *Sixpenny Magazine*, vols. II-IV, January 1862 to December 1862. Reserialised in the *London Journal*, vols. XXXVII -XXXVIII, in 22 weekly parts from 21 March to 15 August 1863.

The White Phantom, serialised in the *Halfpenny Journal*, vols. I-II in 34 weekly instalments from 26 May 1862 to 12 January 1863 'by the author of "The Black Band".'

The Factory Girl; or, All is Not Gold That Glitters serialised in the *Halfpenny Journal* vols. II-III, in 40 weekly parts from 12 January 1863 to 26 October 1863 'by "The Author of "The Black Band".'

Oscar Bertrand; or, The Idiot of the Mountain, serialised in the *Halfpenny Journal*, vol. III, in 33 weekly parts from 2 November 1863 to 13 June 1864 'by "The Author of "The Black Band".'

Aurora Floyd (London: Tinsley, 1863). Serialised in *Temple Bar*, vols. IV-VII, in 13 monthly parts from January 1862 to January 1863.

Eleanor's Victory (London: Tinsley, 1863). Serialised in *Once a Week,* vols. VIII-IX, 7 March to 3 October 1863.

John Marchmont's Legacy (London: Tinsley, 1863). Serialised in *Temple Bar*, vols. VII-IX, in 14 monthly parts from December 1862 to January 1864.

Henry Dunbar (London: Maxwell, 1864). Serialised as *The Outcasts* in the *London Journal*, vols. XXXVIII-XXIX, 12 September 1863 to 26 March 1864.

The Doctor's Wife (London: Maxwell, 1864). Serialised in *Temple Bar*, vols. X-XIII, in 12 monthly parts from January to December 1864.

Only a Clod (London: Maxwell, 1865). Serialised in the *St. James's Magazine*, vols. XI-XIV, August 1864 to August 1865.

Sir Jasper's Tenant (London: Maxwell, 1865). Serialised in *Temple Bar*, vols. XIII-XVI, in 11 monthly parts from February to December 1865.

The Lady's Mile (London: Ward, Lock & Tyler, 1866). Serialised in the *St. James's Magazine*, beginning in vol. IV, September 1865.

Circe (as Babington White) (London: Ward, Lock & Tyler, 1867). Serialised in *Belgravia*, vols. II-III, in 6 monthly parts from April 1867 to September 1867.

Rupert Godwin (London: Ward, Lock & Tyler, 1867). Serialised as *The Banker's Secret* in the last issue of the *Welcome Guest* (see p.186) and in the *Halfpenny Journal*, vol. IV, in 29 weekly parts from 21 November 1864 to 5 June 1864.

Birds of Prey (London: Ward, Lock & Tyler, 1867). Serialised in *Belgravia*, vols. I-III, in 12 monthly instalments from November 1866 to October 1867.

Dead Sea Fruit (London: Ward, Lock & Tyler, 1868). Serialised in *Belgravia*, vols. III-VI, in 14 monthly instalments from August 1867 to September 1868.

Charlotte's Inheritance (London: Ward, Lock Tyler, 1868). Serialised in *Belgravia*, vols. V-VII, in 11 monthly instalments from April 1868 to February 1869.

Run to Earth (London: Ward, Lock & Tyler, 1868). Serialised as *Diavola: or the Woman's Battle* in the *London Journal*, vols. XLIV-XLIV, in 39 weekly parts from 27 October 1866 to 20 July 1867 'by the author of the Black Band.'

Fenton's Quest (London: Ward, Lock & Tyler, 1871). Serialised in *Belgravia*, vols. XI-XIV, in 13 monthly instalments from April 1870 to April 1871.

The Lovels of Arden (London: Maxwell, 1871). Serialised in *Belgravia*, vols. XIII-XVI, in 13 monthly instalments from February 1871 to February 1872.

Robert Ainsleigh (London: Maxwell, 1872). Serialised as *Bound to John Company; or the Adventures and Misadventures of Robert Ainsleigh* in

Belgravia, vols. VI-IX, in 16 monthly instalments from July 1868 to October 1869. Braddon fell ill after the first five instalments and the serial was continued by another writer, whose instalments she replaced for the book edition.

To the Bitter End (London: Maxwell, 1872). Serialised in *Belgravia*, vols. XVI-IXX, in 11 monthly instalments from February 1872 to December 1872.

Milly Darrell (London: Maxwell, 1873). Serialised in *Belgravia*, vol. XIII, in 3 monthly instalments from November 1870 to January 1871.

Strangers and Pilgrims (London: Maxwell, 1873). Serialised in *Belgravia*, vols. IXX-XXI, in 12 monthly instalments from November 1872 to October 1873.

Lucius Davoren (London: Maxwell, 1873). Serialised as *Publicans and Sinners! A Life Picture* in the *Home Journal*, vols.I-II, in 36 weekly instalments 9 August 1873 to 3 January 1874.

Taken at the Flood (London: Maxwell, 1874). Syndicated by Tillotson in various newspapers including the *Bolton Weekly Journal*, in 34 weekly parts from 30 August 1873 to 18 April 1874

Lost for Love (London: Chatto & Windus, 1874). Serialised in *Belgravia*, vols. XXII-XXV, in 13 instalments from November 1873 to November 1874.

A Strange World (London: Maxwell, 1875). Syndicated by Tillotson in various newspapers including *Bolton Weekly Journal*, in 33 weekly parts from 18 April to 5 December 1874.

Hostages to Fortune (London: Maxwell, 1875). Serialised in *Belgravia*, vols. XXV-XXVIII, in 13 monthly instalments from November 1874 to November 1875.

Dead Men's Shoes (London: Maxwell, 1876). Syndicated by Tillotson in various newspapers including *Bolton Weekly Journal*, in 33 weekly parts from 31 July 1875 to 11 March 1876.

Joshua Haggard's Daughter (London: Maxwell, 1876). Serialised in Belgravia, vols. XXVIII-XXXI, in 13 monthly instalments from December 1875 to December 1876.

Weavers and Weft (London: Maxwell, 1877). Syndicated by Tillotson in various newspapers including *Bolton Weekly Journal*, in 16 weekly parts from 26 August to 9 December 1876.

An Open Verdict (London: Maxwell, 1878). Syndicated by Tillotson in various newspapers including *Bolton Weekly Journal*, in 33 weekly parts from 5 May to 15 December 1877.

Vixen (London: Maxwell, 1879). Serialised in *All the Year Round*, vols. XXI-XXII (New Series), in 37 weekly parts from 5 October 1878 to 14 June 1879.

The Cloven Foot (London: Maxwell, 1879). Syndicated by Tillotson in various newspapers including *Newcastle Weekly Chronicle*, in 24 weekly parts from 5 October 1878 to 15 March 1879.

The Story of Barbara (London: Maxwell, 1880). Serialised in the *World* as *Her Splendid Misery* in weekly parts from 30 July 1879 to June 1880.

Just As I Am (London: Maxwell, 1880). Syndicated by Tillotson in various newspapers including *Bolton Weekly Journal*, in 33 weekly parts from 7 February to 18 September 1880.

Asphodel (London: Maxwell, 1881). Serialised in *All the Year Round*, vols. XXV-XXVI (New Series), in 34 weekly parts from 31 July 1880 to 19 March 1881.

Le Pasteur de Marston, serialised in *Le Figaro*, in 8 daily instalments from 26 to 30 November, 3 to 5 December 1881, p.2 of each issue.

Mount Royal (London: Maxwell, 1882).

The Golden Calf (London: Maxwell, 1883).

Phantom Fortune (London: Maxwell, 1883). Syndicated by Tillotson in various newspapers including *Leigh Journal & Times*, in 27 weekly parts, 9 March to 7 September 1883.

Flower and Weed (London: Maxwell, 1884). (*Mistletoe Bough* 1884).

Ishmael (London: Maxwell, 1884). Serialised in the *Whitehall Review*, new Series no. 59-94, 36 weekly parts from 17 January to 18 September 1884.

Wyllard's Weird (London: Maxwell, 1885). Syndicated by Tillotson in various newspapers including *Leigh Journal & Times,* in 27 weekly parts from 19 September 1884 to 20 March 1885.

The Good Hermione (London: Maxwell, 1886). (Pseudonym, Aunt Belinda)

Under the Red Flag (London: Maxwell, 1886) (*Mistletoe Bough* 1883).

One Thing Needful (London: Maxwell, 1886). Syndicated by Tillotson in various newspapers including *Sheffield & Rotherham Weekly Independent Budget*, in 20 weekly parts from 27 March to 7 August 1886.

Cut By the County (London: Maxwell, 1886). Syndicated by Tillotson in various newspapers including *Bolton Weekly Journal*, in 6 weekly parts from 3 July to 7 August 1885.

Mohawks (London: Maxwell, 1886). Serialised in Belgravia, vols. LVIII-LXI, in 13 monthly instalments from January 1886 to January 1887.

Like and Unlike (London: Spencer Blackett, 1887). Syndicated by Tillotson in various newspapers including *Bolton Weekly Journal*, in 27 weekly parts from 26 March to 24 September 1887.

The Fatal Three (London: Simpkin, Marshall, 1888). Syndicated by Lengs in various newspapers including *Sheffield Weekly Telegraph*, in 24 weekly parts from 14 January to 23 June 1888.

The Day Will Come (London: Simpkin, Marshall, 1889). Syndicated by Lengs in various newspapers including *Sheffield Weekly Telegraph*, in 25 weekly parts from 12 January to 29 June 1889.

One Life, One Love (London: Simpkin, Marshall, 1890). Syndicated by Lengs as *Whose Was the Hand* in various newspapers including *Sheffield Weekly Telegraph*, in 23 weekly parts from 11 January to 14 June 1890.

Gerard (London: Simpkin, Marshall, 1891). Syndicated by Lengs as *The World the Flesh & the Devil and The Fate Reader* in various newspapers including *Sheffield Weekly Telegraph*, in 22 weekly parts from 10 January to 6 June 1891.

The Venetians (London: Simpkin, Marshall, 1892). Syndicated by Lengs as *The Venetians; or, All in Honour* in various newspapers including *Sheffield Weekly Telegraph*, in 23 parts from 9 January to 11 June 1892.

All Along the River (London: Simpkin, Marshall, 1893). Syndicated by Tillotson in various newspapers including *Newcastle Weekly Chronicle*, in 20 weekly parts from 21 January to 3 June 1893.

The Christmas Hirelings (London: Simpkin, Marshall, 1894). Appeared in 1893 Christmas edition of *Lady's Pictorial*.

Thou Art the Man (London: Simpkin, Marshall, 1894). Syndicated by Lengs in *Sheffield Weekly Telegraph*, in 23 weekly parts from 6 January to 9 June 1894.

Sons of Fire (London: Simpkin. Marshall, 1895). Syndicated by Lengs in *Sheffield Weekly Telegraph*, in 23 weekly parts from 5 January to 8 June 1895.

London Pride (London: Simpkin, Marshall, 1896). Syndicated by Tillotson in *Birmingham Weekly Mercury*, in 26 weekly parts from 5 October 1895 to 28 March 1896.

Under Love's Rule (London: Simpkin, Marshall, 1897). Syndicated by Tillotson as *The Little Auntie* in *Newcastle Weekly Chronicle*, in 10 weekly parts from 10 October to 12 December 1896.

In High Places (London: Simpkin, Marshall, 1898). Syndicated by Hutchinson, it was serialised in the *Lady's Realm* vols. III-IV, in 12 monthly parts from November 1897 to October 1898, and in the newspaper *Sheffield Weekly Telegraph* 29 October 1898 to 1 April 1899.

Rough Justice (London: Simpkin, Marshall, 1898). Syndicated by Lengs as *A Shadowed Life* in *Sheffield Weekly Telegraph*, in 19 weekly parts from 16 January to 22 May 1897.

His Darling Sin (London: Simpkin, Marshall, 1899). Serialisation untraced.

The Infidel (London: Simpkin, Marshall, 1900)

The Conflict (London: Simpkin, Marshall, 1903). Serialised in *The People*, in 29 weekly parts from 7 September 1902 to 22 March 1903.

A Lost Eden (London: Hutchinson, 1904)

The Rose of Life (London: Hutchinson, 1905). Serialised in *Tit-Bits*, vols. XLVI and XLVII in 18 weekly parts from 18 June to 15 October 1904.

The White House (London: Hurst & Blackett, 1906)

Dead Love Has Chains (London: Hurst & Blackett, 1907). Serialised as *Alias Jane Brown* by the Northern Newspaper Syndicate, c. January to June 1906.

Her Convict (London: Hurst & Blackett, 1907)

During Her Majesty's Pleasure (London: Hurst & Blackett, 1908). Syndicated by Lengs in *Sheffield Weekly Telegraph*, in 11 weekly parts from 12 January to 23 March 1901.

Our Adversary (London: Hutchinson, 1909).

Beyond These Voices (London: Hutchinson, 1910).

The Green Curtain (London: Hutchinson, 1911).

Miranda (London: Hutchinson. 1913)

Mary (London: Hutchinson, 1916).

(B.) Short stories

The stories listed 'untraced' may well have appeared in Edwardian magazines and newspapers under different titles, as Braddon often wrote them years before they appeased in print; for example she wrote several of her single volume novels a few years before the demise of the three volume format. Those short stories which appeared in books usually first appeared in *Belgravia* or *Mistletoe Bough*

The Wolff collection also contains two unfinished manuscript drafts of short stories, 'Tom Pearson's Last Party' (c.1870) and a theatrical story 'Maria Jones, Her Book' (c.1900), which may or may not have been published. I have also made reference to those stories not yet located.

Ralph the Bailiff and Other Tales (1867). See under novels for earlier edition. The short stories in the volume were:
'Captain Thomas' (*Welcome Guest*, vol. II, 1860)
'The Cold Embrace' (*Welcome Guest*, vol. III, 1860)
'My Daughters' (*Welcome Guest*, vol. III, 1860)
'The Mystery of Fernwood' (*Temple Bar*, vols. III-IV, November to December 1861)
'Samuel Lowgood's Revenge' (*Welcome Guest*, vol. III, 1861)
'The Lawyer's Secret' (*Welcome Guest*, vol. III, 1861)
'My First Happy Christmas' (*Welcome Guest*, vol. III, 1861; reprinted, *Halfpenny Journal*, 29 December 1862)
'Lost and Found' (part of *The Outcasts*, London *Journal*, 1864)
'Eveline's Visitant: A Ghost Story' (*Belgravia*, vol. I, January 1867)
'Found in the Muniment Chest' (*Belgravia* Annual 1867)
'How I Heard My Own Will Read' (*Belgravia*, vol. I, 1867)
'The Scene Painter's Wife' (*Belgravia* Annual 1869, reprinted in *Weavers and Weft* 1877)

'The Mudie Classics, No. I, Sir Alk Meyonn, or the Seven Against the Elector', *Belgravia*, vol. V, March-April 1868, pp.41-50, 162-175. Written as Babington White.

'The True Story of Don Juan', *Belgravia* Christmas Annual 1869 (by Babington White).

The Summer Tourist. A Book for Long or Short Journeys by Rail, Road, or River (London: Ward, Lock & Tyler, 1871). The title page describes this book as 'edited by M.E. Braddon'. It consisted of the short story 'The Zoophyte's Revenge', acknowledged by Braddon, and thirteen anonymous short travel essays. Wolff surmised in his catalogue (no. 754) that Braddon may have written the essays too.

Milly Darrell and Other Tales (1873) The other short stories were:
'Old Rudderford Hall' (*Belgravia* Christmas Annual 1871)
'The Splendid Stranger' (*Belgravia*, vol. XI, March, 1870)
'Hugh Damer's Last Leger'
'The Sins of the Fathers' (*Belgravia*, vol. XII, October 1870)
'Mr. and Mrs. de Fontenoy' (*Belgravia*, vol. X, February 1870)
'A Good Hater' (*Belgravia* Christmas annual 1872)
'The Dreaded Guest' (*Belgravia* Christmas Annual 1871)
'Colonel Benyon's Entanglement' (*Belgravia*, vol. XVI, July 1872)
'The Zoophyte's Revenge' (see above)
'At Chrighton Abbey' (*Belgravia* vol. XIV, May 1871)
'Three Times' (*Belgravia* Christmas Annual 1872)
'On the Brink' (*Belgravia*, vol. VII, September 1870).

Weavers and Weft (1877) The stories which form the second and third volume were:
'In Great Waters' (*Belgravia*, vol. XV, August 1871)
'Sebastian' (*Belgravia* Holiday No., 1876)
'Levison's Victim' (*Belgravia*, vol. X, January 1870)
'Christmas in Possession' (*Belgravia* Annual for 1868)
'John Granger' (*Belgravia* Christmas Annual 1870)
'Prince Ramji Rowdedow' (*Belgravia* Christmas Annual 1874)
'Too Bright to Last' (*Belgravia* Christmas Annual 1870)
'The Scene-Painter's Wife' (see details under *Ralph the Bailiff*)
'Sir Luke's Return' (*Belgravia* Christmas Annual 1875)
'Her Last Appearance' (*Belgravia* Christmas Annual 1876)
'Sir Hanbury's Bequest' (*Belgravia* Christmas Annual 1874)
'A Very Narrow Escape' (*Belgravia*, vol. X, 1869)
'My Unlucky Friend' (*Belgravia*, vol. X, 1869).

Flower and Weed and Other Tales (1884) The short stories were:
'George Caulfield's Journey' (*Mistletoe Bough* 1879)
'The Clown's Quest'
'Dr. Carrick' (*All the Year Round*, Extra Summer Number 1878)
'If She Be Not Fair to Me' (*Mistletoe Bough*, 1880)
'The Shadow in the Corner' (*All the Year Round*, Extra Summer Number 1879)
'His Secret' (*Mistletoe Bough*, 1881)
'Thou Art the Man'

'The Fatal Marriage', c. 1885. Place of publication unknown, see under American editions.

Under the Red Flag and Other Tales (1886) The short stories were:
'Sir Philip's Wooing' (*Belgravia* Christmas Annual, 1869)
'Dorothy's Rival' (*Belgravia* Annual, 1867)
'At Daggers Drawn' (as Babington White, *Belgravia*, vol. I, January 1867)
'A Great Ball and a Great Bear' (as Babington White, *Belgravia*, vol. IV, 1868)
'The Little Woman in Black' (*Mistletoe Bough*, 1885)
'Across the Footlights' (*Mistletoe Bough*, 1884)
'My Wife's Promise' (*Belgravia* Annual, 1868),

Wolff, in his catalogue, attributes the following anonymous short stories in *Mistletoe Bough* to Braddon. For some of those I have read (*Mistletoe Bough* 1886-1889), I have added comments which strengthen the case for attribution to several of them.
'Sidonie's Birthday Presents' (1878)
'The Little Black Bag' (1879)
'Ceres: Miss Flossie Burgoyne' (1879)
'Catherine Carew' (1880)
'Thrapstow Bank' (1881)
'The Sergeant's Wife' (1881)
'Wooing an Heiress' (1881)
'Lorenzo' (1881)
'The Cost of a Kiss' (1881)
'Only a Girl' (1884)
'The Longmoney Conspiracy' (1884)
'The Painted Warning' (1884)
'How We Marry' (1884)
'Mrs. Barter's Request' (1884)
'A Christmas Tragedy' (1884)
'For Love or Gold' (1884)
'Out of the Depths' (1884)
'A Night's Lodging' (1886)
'Dolly Danver's Dilemma' (1886). Set in a garrison town on the South Downs, obviously Brighton; Braddon had used the surname of Danvers before.
'Peradventure' (1886) The style seems, perhaps, a little different to Braddon's, but Braddon often used Cornish surname's like Tredethlyn.
'The Flight from Wealdon Hall'. This is almost certainly by Braddon, with its echoes of *Jane Eyre* and Braddon's earlier story 'The Mystery

of Fernwood'. It offers a twist on *Jane Eyre*: the governess helps the 'mad' wife escape.

'The Secret of Sophia' (1886)

'Susan Eliza' (1886)

'Not in Debrett' (1888) The plot has marked similarities to Braddon's later novel *Gerard* (1891), when an unmarried dressmaker commits infanticide.

'The Ninth Widow' (1888) Written in a similar manner to other ghost stories by Braddon.

'My Cousin Fay' (1888)

'A Terrible Experience' (1889). An excellent detective story.

'Poverty and the Peer' (1889). Again partly set in Brighton, use of actresses, living in sin and divorce. There is also a resemblance to *Beyond These Voices* (1910).

'The Black Boy's Room' (1889)

'My First Living' (1889). There are definite echoes of Wilkie Collins and *The Woman in White* with its use of church marriage registers. The village of Seaton is mentioned and a baby is christened at St. Anne's Church, Soho, as Braddon was.

'Miss Bristow's Benefit' (1890)

'Her Fatal Beauty' (1890)

'From Another World' (1891)

'Venetian Glass' mentioned in Braddon's diary 27 December 1892. See 'Herself' (1894).

'The Fly From the George' Mentioned by Braddon in her diaries on 17 & 21 January 1893. Location untraced, but Tillotson paid £50 for the serial copyright, Tillotson Notebooks A/B, Bodleian (information on the Bodleian notebook from Graham Law).

'Does Anything Matter' location untraced. Mentioned in Braddon's diary 7 February 1893.

All Along the River (1893) The short stories in the third volume were:

'One Fatal Moment' (*Mistletoe Bough*, 1889)

'It Is Easier for a Camel' (*Mistletoe Bough*, 1888)

'The Ghost's Name' (*Mistletoe Bough*, 1891)

'Stapylton's Plot' (*Mistletoe Bough*, 1887)

'His Oldest Friends' (*Mistletoe Bough*, 1890 Reprinted in *Sheffield Weekly Telegraph*, 16 & 23 June 1894), the latter unrecorded by Wolff.

'If There Be Any of You' (*Mistletoe Bough*, 1889)

'The Island of Old Faces' (*Mistletoe Bough*, 1892; reprinted in *Printer's Pie. A Festival Souvenir of the Printers' Pension Corporation* 1903)
'My Dream' (*Mistletoe Bough*, 1899)

'A Modern Confessor', *Pall Mall Magazine*, vol. I, June 1893, pp.140-146.

'The Dulminster Dynamiter', *Pall Mall Magazine*, vol. I, August 1893, pp.469-482.

'Drifting', *To-Day A Weekly Magazine-Journal*, 23 December 1893, pp.1-4. This must be the 'Dramatic Sketch "Drifting" ' mentioned in Braddon's diary, 18 April 1893. I am indebted to Dr. Richard Beaton for providing me with details of this publication. Unrecorded by Wolff.

'The Higher Life' 1894 location untraced, but the proofs are in the Wolff collection. Braddon's diary for the week of 21 February 1894 says 'Revised the Higher Life'.

'Sweet Simplicity', *Today A Weekly Magazine-Journal*, vol. II, 24 March 1894, pp.193-200. Unrecorded by Wolff.

'Herself', (Sheffield) *Weekly Telegraph*, 17 November 1894, pp.1-10. Mentioned in Braddon's diary 3 January 1893, 'Herself' is the 'Venetian Glass' she had worked on the previous month. Untraced by Wolff.

'His Good Fairy', *Illustrated London News*, Summer Holiday number, 28 May 1894, pp.2-7. Mentioned in Braddon's diary 21 February 1894. I am grateful to Graham Law for providing me with the place of publication. Location unrecorded by Wolff.

'Where Many Footsteps Pass', location untraced, mentioned in Braddon's diary 22 August 1895.

'The Honourable Jack', c.1895. Location untraced.

'Jane', c.1895. Braddon's diary, 21 November 1895, reads, 'Began Jane novelette'. One of Braddon's note books shows it was about a murderess killed by her conscience. In *Sensational Victorian* (p.504) Wolff surmised that 'Jane' and, 'Naomi', were one and the same. They were and the story was published as 'The Heart Knoweth' (see below).

'Poor Uncle Jacob', *Bolton Journal and Guardian*, 25 April 1896, p.11. Untraced by Wolff, this must be the 'Uncle Jacob' mentioned in her diary 11 December 1893. Reprinted in the *Englishwoman*, vol. V, August 1897, pp.490-502.

'Wild Justice', *Bolton Journal and Guardian*, 8 August 1896, p.11. Unrecorded by Wolff.

'Theodora's Temptation', *Englishwoman*, vol. IV, October-November 1896, pp.99-107 and pp.205-214. Reprinted as 'The Doll's Tragedy', *Leigh Journal and Times*, 10 June 1898, p.3. Location unrecorded by Wolff, mentioned in her diary, 19 March 1894.

'The Winning Sequence', *Englishwoman*, vol. VI, September 1897, pp.46-55. 'The Winning Card' was mentioned by Braddon in her diary for 17 October 1895, and Tillotsons paid Lengs for the serial copyright of 'The Winning Sequence', so the *Englishwoman* publication was probably its second appearance. Location unrecorded by Wolff.

'The Good Lady Ducayne', *Strand Magazine*, vol.XI, February 1896, pp.185-199 and (Sheffield) *Weekly Telegraph* in 2 parts, 21 and 28 March 1896, the latter appearance unrecorded by Wolff.

'In the Nick of Time', c.1897, location untraced. Mentioned in Braddon's diary as being twenty pages in length, 25 February 1897.

The Christmas Tree. Downey's annual for 1898, contains a story by Braddon. Unfortunately the British Library copy has been lost, so I been able to see what the story was. An advert in the *World*, 7 December 1898, p.38, describes it as a shilling Xmas annual 'Containing Original stories by Miss Braddon, Barry Pain, Christie Murray, Mrs. Riddell, Tighe Hopkins, S. Baring Gould, J. Newnham Davis, F. Frankfort Moore, Katharine Macquoid, Emily Soldene, George Manville Fenn, Morley Roberts and James Payn.' Unrecorded by Wolff.

'As the Heart Knoweth' *T.P.'s Weekly*, vol. II, 24 July 1903, pp.206-210, 212-214, 217-218. 221-222, 225-227. It was probably published in the late 1890s as 'Naomi'. Unrecorded by Wolff.

'For His Son's Sake', *Cassell's Magazine*, December 1905, pp.72-79.

'The Cock of Bowkers', *London Magazine*, vol. XVI, April-May 1906, pp.287-295.

(C) American Editions of Braddon's Novels

Nearly all of Braddon's novels were published in America, some authorised, some pirate editions. Her penny dreadful fiction was published under her own name in America. Usually they were cheap paperbacks. Short stories often had their titles altered; for example, 'His Secret' was published as a book by Peterson in America as *Jasper Dane's Secret*. Most of the time they retained the British title, or if changed can easily be identified. Others were published in Britain as edited by Braddon, and in America as being by Braddon: for example Braddon edited 'My Sister Caroline' for *Belgravia* in 1870, and in America it was published as a Braddon under the title 'My Sister's Confession.' Sometimes a Braddon novel was split to form two books in America; for example, Munro published the second half of *John Marchmont's Legacy* as *Risen From the Grave* and *Bohemia* as the 'sequel' to *Mohawks*. However, there are a number of American Braddon titles I have not been able to tie to their British counterparts. It is of course possible they are not by Braddon, and just assigned to her to make good sales. Maxwell complained that the publisher Mr. Cauldwell, owner of the *New York Mercury* and the *Sunday Mercury*, who bought genuine Braddon's for serialisation, was a 'scoundrel' who had also 'used Miss Braddon's good name as Author of literary rubbish that she never saw.' (Maxwell to Tillotson, 16 September 1884, *Bolton Evening News* Archive, Bolton Central Library, Greater Manchester.) Presumably those published by George Munro were genuine, as Maxwell praised him as paying for titles and for helping his son Gerald when he fell ill in America. It is possible that some of these titles could be British short stories which have never been located in newspapers.

The Blue Band; or, A Story of a Woman's Vengeance (DeWitt)
Wages of Sin (Ogilvie, 1881)
Meeting Her Fate (Carleton, 1881) This contained all of the stories from *Milly Darrell*, with the anomalous title story.
Great Journal and Other Stories (Ogilvie, 1882)
Leighton Grange; or, Who Killed Edith Woodville (DeWitt) Also published as *The Mystery of Leighton Grange* (New York: G. Munro, 1878) The NUC catalogue lists this as being 31 pages in length.
His Second Wife (possibly the same story as 'The Fatal Marriage'.
The Fatal Marriage (Munro, 1885). First published with 'The Shadow in the Corner' from *Flower and Weed and Other Stories*, 'The Fatal Marriage' is about a woman who discovers her husband is a bigamist.

396

(D.) Books Edited by M.E. Braddon

Braddon was invaluable to her husband and step-sons, not only as his most successful author, but as an editor and reviser of some of his cheap fiction. In the main those works which are known to have been worked on by Braddon, are works where the authors had died or works originally published in America.

Buisson, Ada, *Put to the Test* (London: Maxwell, 1865). It was first published anonymously in three volumes in 1865. When published in one volume in 1876 the title page read, 'Edited by the author of "Lady Audley's Secret".' Consistently, to the present day, this novel and Buisson stories in *Belgravia* have been attributed to Braddon. This error came about when the bibliophile Montague Summers claimed Ada Buisson was a pseudonym used by Braddon to avoid having her earnings sequestered by Maxwell's creditors (see *Times Literary Supplement*, 29 August 1942, p.432; 24 April 1943, p.204; and 18 September 1944). To begin with this is erroneous, since as Braddon was not Maxwell's wife her earnings could not be taken to pay his debts. Summers's theory was overthrown when Buisson's nephew proved through family letters that she was a real person and the author of *Put to the Test* (See *Times Literary Supplement*, October 21 1944, and December 23 1944). Braddon probably abridged the reprint because Buisson was dead by that date.

The Summer Tourist. A Book for Long or Short Journeys by Rail, Road, or River edited by M.E. Braddon (London: Ward, Lock and Tyler, 1871). Wolff surmised that Braddon may have written all of the sketches.

Only a Woman edited by Braddon 1878.

Miss Braddon's Revised Edition of Aladdin or the Wonderful Lamp. Sinbad The Sailor; or The Old Man of the Sea. Ali Baba; or, The Forty Thieves (London: Maxwell, 1880). Illustrated by Gustave Doré and other artists. This seems to be a selective abridgement of the lavish productions of *The Arabian Nights* brought out by other publishers in the 1860s. However, I believe the page long preface is by Braddon.

Married in Haste (London: Maxwell c.1883) 'Edited by Miss M.E Braddon'. This edition is not in the British Library, but it could have been an edition of Sir Frederick Charles Lascelles's novel of the same name, first published in three volumes in 1863. Lascelles was one of

Maxwell's editors in the early 1860s. The fact that her diary notes editing a novel by the long dead Lascelles Wraxall on 25 October 1882 adds to the theory that the two books are one and the same.

My Sister Caroline. Anonymous novel edited by Braddon in *Belgravia* vol. X, February-March 1870, and published in America with Braddon short stories (Chicago: C.H. Shaver, 1880). See Wolff Catalogue 749a

On Her Majesty's Service revised by Braddon c.1884. No copy in British Library.

Madeline's Mystery. One volume reprint published by Maxwell in 1882 'edited by the "Author of Lady Audley's Secret" ' The three volume edition was published by Maxwell in 1881 as *A Modern Spinx* carrying the author's name, Major E. Rogers.

Miss Braddon's Penny Edition of Sir Walter Scott 16 penny paperbacks (London: Maxwell, 1881-1882). The novels were abridged and were criticised by, amongst others, Robert Louis Stevenson.

Wolff, in *Sensational Victorian* (p.496), mentions Braddon working on an edition of Victorien Sardou's play *Fédora* in 1883. This must have been *Feodora* adapted as a tale by H.L.W. (i.e. Henry Llewellyn Williams) (London: Maxwell, 1883).

Wolff also lists (p.496) a novel by Williams in 1882, Irish novel 1883, Tales of the English Peasantry 1883.

(E.) Plays by M.E. Braddon

Throughout Braddon's literary career she longed for success as a playwright, and she continued to write plays until almost the end of her life. Although her novels were frequently adapted for the stage (*The Trail of the Serpent* was adapted by May Holt as *Dark Deeds*, and *Joshua Haggard* by J. Wilton Jones as *Recommended to Mercy* as late as 1882), her own plays were not successful. Despite her great fame and ability to interest as a novelist, it seems that her talents were limited as a playwright. It may well be that she wrote other plays which were not acknowledged, as in her interview with Clive Holland ('Fifty Years of Novel Writing', *Pall Mall Magazine*, 1911) he described her as having written in addition to her known plays 'many unacknowledged farces.' (p.700), adding in a further article that these were performed in the 1860s and 1870s. Even if this is so, she hoped that the plays she wrote under her own name would win her acclaim as a major playwright. Those plays which were produced did not have long runs, and nor did they become a part of the repertoire of provincial managers. Part of Braddon's anger at the unauthorised versions of her most popular novels must have stemmed from the fact that they were enormously popular, while her own plays were not. *Griselda*, an updating of Chaucer's 'Patient Griselda', at the Princess's theatre in London, was distinctly old fashioned in subject matter, far away from the controversial plots which had made her famous; Percy Fitzgerald described it as a Tennyson styled 'poetical drama', which was 'an attractive, interesting thing, but too delicate and finely spun' for modern tastes. (Fitzgerald, Percy, *Memoirs of An Author* 2 vols (London: Richard Bentley, 1895), I, p.278.) When her play *Genevieve; or, The Missing Witness* was performed at the Royal Alexandra Theatre, the *Porcupine* observed, 'Miss Braddon's enthusiastic reception, on Monday evening, was a tribute paid rather to her popularity as a novel-writer than her success as a dramatist.' ('Miss Braddon in Liverpool', *Porcupine*, 11 April 1874, p.26). It went on to accuse the play of being too old fashioned, and in the style of Dion Boucicault's plays of ten years earlier, 'It is a melodrama of pronounced style, loose in its construction, and weak and improbable to the last degree in action and motive.' ('Genevieve,' *Porcupine*, 11 April 1874, p.28). The staging and scenery was elaborate, there were new and expensive costumes, and further spectacle was provided when the heroine was buried alive by an avalanche. It seems Braddon was persisting with a style of play that was already out of date, and the criticism of her unrealistic dialogue was to persist. Nor did she give up on *Genevieve*: the printed copy in the Wolff collection (no.723) shows extensive hand-written revision and insertions, adding, in my opinion, at the very end a more melodramatic piece of dialogue than in the original. Perhaps as a result of the accusation that *Genevieve* was of the old school, Braddon seems to have tried to write a more modern society comedy. *Married Beneath Him* (1882), which was not read by Wolff, is a light four act comedy of class, adoption, and mistaken identity.

When Braddon died, her son, W.B. Maxwell, found seven unpublished plays in her desk (*Time Gathered*, p.281), written in the 1890s and early 1900s. Although their present location (apart from *A Life Interest*, 1892) is unknown I have included them in this bibliography, as they may yet turn up.

These late plays were shown by Braddon to a number of writers and producers, including Arthur Wing Pinero who read two of them (Pinero to Braddon, 24 December 1895, Wolff Collection), the producer Edward Terry (Braddon to Edward Terry, 8 December 1896; Edward Terry to Braddon, 11 December 1896, Wolff Collection), Herbert Beerbohm Tree (Beerbohm Tree to Braddon, 29 December 1897, Wolff Collection), Lionel Brough (Brough to Braddon, 13 March and 24 May, 1902, Wolff Collection), and Bram Stoker (believing the role of a parson would be suitable for Henry Irving, 5 July and 26 July 1898, Brotherton Library, Leeds). All of these people were of the opinion that the plays were not suitable for performance: Terry said the characters:

> are so uncongenial they leave a most unpleasant taste in the mouth (...) The piece is a domestic Tragedy – very true, but I don't think the public like these sort of things in their amusements.

and Brough felt they needed a great deal of work, 'as they are at present they are not presentable – there are many faults in construction and too much talk'. As late as 1912 Braddon wrote in her diary that Arthur Conan Doyle was 'to read acts 4 & 5.' She may have asked Elizabeth Robins for advice, as they arranged a meeting in January 1912. Her lack of success was not for want of trying, and she tried to learn from new schools of writing. In 1893 she wrote in her diary on the fourth of March that she was reading *Hedda Gabler* for the second time, and a few days later: 'Finished Hedda. Carefully read.'

The Loves of Arcadia (1860), unpublished, performed at the Strand Theatre. L.C.

The Model Husband (1868), performed at the Surrey 28 September to 17 October 1868. The play had a French setting, and starred W. Crosby as Claude de Mauprat, Miss E. Webster as Marie de Mauprat and Mat Robson as Chevalier de Mericourt. Unrecorded by Wolff.

Griselda; or, The Patient Wife (1873), performed at the Princess Theatre, November 11. L.C.

The Missing Witness (London: Maxwell, 1880), performed in Liverpool as *Genevieve* 6 April to 18 April 1874.

Margery Daw (1881), later published in *Under the Red Flag* (1886).

Married Beneath Him A Comedy in Four Acts (London: Maxwell, 1882), never produced.

Dross; or, the Root of Evil (London: Maxwell, 1882), never produced, but republished by Maxwell in *Under the Red Flag*.

For Better for Worse (1890), unpublished but performed at Whitby and Brighton. Based on her novel *Like and Unlike*.

Nero (1890), unpublished and never produced. Location unknown.

A Life Interest (1892), written for her friend, the actress Madge Kendal, it was never produced or published and she reused the plot for *The White House* (1906). The typed manuscript is in the Wolff collection. The typescript has the authorial name of Mrs. Maxwell, meaning the lost plays, if they still exist, may also have the name of Maxwell on them.

Worldlings (1893), unpublished and never produced. Location unknown.

Free Lances (1893), unpublished and never produced. Location unknown.

The Garreteers (1894), unpublished and never produced. Location unknown.

The Breadwinner (1895), unpublished and never produced. In her diary for 21 October 1895 Braddon described this as a 'sketch & experiment in Robertsonian comedy.' Location unknown.

Sigismund (1904), unpublished and never produced. Location unknown.

(F.) Poetry

I have included the texts of Braddon's newspaper poetry in full because I have discussed them in the main body of the book, and because they are not easily accessible. None of the poems quoted in full were recorded by her biographer Robert Lee Wolff, nor did he know that many of the poems in *Garibaldi* had been previously published.

Mary Seyton, 'Rest,' *Beverley Recorder and General Advertiser*, 9 May 1857, p.4.

Rest

All joys on earth have we,
All fears on earth we see,
All cares on earth there be,
    But never rest.
Youth comes the all believing,
Hope comes the all deceiving,
Death comes sad hearts bereaving,
    Yet comes not rest.

Beloved, ah joy and gladness!
Deceived, what bitter madness!
Death robs us – oh! what sadness
    Never comes rest,
Tho' we invoke her power
In dark life's darkest hour,
When sorrows round us lower,
    We to her rest.

Fain, fain would fly that sleep,
She who doth ever keep
Sweet dews for eyes which weep,
    Might on her breast
Lull the tired heart awhile
With her serenest smile,
Pain and grief to beguile,
    Yet comes not rest.

Unknown on earth is she,
Ne'er upon earth will be
For mortal eyes to see

The spirit – rest.
But in the heaven above,
Where dwelleth hope and love,
Where purest spirits rove,
    Makes she her rest.

Mary Seyton, 'Song', *Beverley Recorder and General Advertiser*, 6 June 1857, p.4.

Song (Original)

Who would pearls and diamonds wear,
When flowers braided in the hair,
Are far more sweet, and thrice as fair,
And bear a brighter hue?
Or who would court the rich and great,
Or eager sigh for high estate,
Or murmur 'gainst a lowly fate.
    If blessed with love that's true?

Give me the heart that's all my own,
That beats for me, and me alone,
And let the monarch on his throne
    Be happier than I.
And tho' the maiden lowly be,
She stoops who gives her heart to me,
If it be true, and pure, and free,
    How high so e'er am I.

And let the haughty lady learn
Who for my rank and wealth doth yearn,
That I her grace and beauty spurn,
    How fair so e'er she be;
For honest faith and simple worth,
Are all I seek. The violet's birth
Is lowly; yet no gem of earth
    Is half so fair to me.

M.S., 'Delhi', *Beverley Recorder*, 26 September 1857, p.4. This poem must be by Braddon, in view of the initials, the subject matter of this and succeeding poems, and because there was no other original poetry in the *Beverley Recorder* since 'Song' three months earlier.

Delhi

Down to the Ground! Scattered be every stone!
Annihilation be thy mildest fate;
And be thine epitaph, these words alone:
"Here lie the bones of fiends infuriate –
"Here rot the carcasses of a million slaves;
"And here, *free* Britain's unstained banner waves!"

Gone be thy palaces, and razed thy towers!
Thy gorgeous beauty in the dust low lying;
From thy polluted soil Spring keep her flowers,
Thou "Whited Sepulchre!" and let the dying
With the black torrent of their traitor blood –
Poison the earth on which proud Delhi stood!

Thou shalt to future ages be a name
Synonymous with all things vile and base.
Thou *monument* of murder, death, and shame!
From India's map thy title we erase;
But in men's minds for ever it shall be
The darkest term for darkest treachery!

Down to the ground! loud curses sing thy fall!
Down to the ground! each Briton's hatred taking;
Down to the ground! deserted, fled by all, –
The vulture e'en thy tainted air forsaking!
Ravaged by fire, famine, flood, and sword!
Down to the ground! thou *Home of the Abhorred*!

Mary Seyton, 'On the Queen's Health Being Drunk Within the Walls of Delhi, After the Battle,' *Beverley Recorder*, 21 November 1857, p.4.

On the Queen's Health Being Drunk Within the Walls of Delhi, After the Battle

Here's a health to our Queen! in the lair of the foe
Whilest their howl fiercely blend with the night winds that blow;
Whilest their blood steeps the soil which their deeds have defiled,
Whilest they lie like slain tigers in ghastly heaps piled,
Where the watch fires flame red on the ruinous scene,
Let us raise a full glass to the health of our Queen.

We have conquered! for He, who long ages ago,
Held the sword when th' Assyrian lay vanquished and low,
Has gone out with our armies such foul fiends to slay,
As ne'er before darkened the face of the day:
And while we remember whose servants we've been,
We'll mingle a prayer with the health of our Queen.
Victoria! We've conquered! for Him and for thee,
With hearts wild for vengeance we've crossed the broad sea,
For our sons, for our daughters, for justice, for right,
We've been the glad instruments of His dread might;
And as we thank God that we've conquers been,
We'll drain a deep glass to the health of our Queen.

Mary Seyton, 'Captain Skene', *Beverley Recorder*, 17 October 1857, p.4; Mary Seyton, Theatre Royal, Brighton, *Brighton Herald*, 2 January 1858, p.4.

Captain Skene

Who shall say Virginius lives not – when, across the boundless wave,
Comes the story of the Saxon, battling 'gainst the coward slave –
Who, opprest with countless numbers, with his wife upon his breast,
Fell with murderers around him, like a tranquil child to rest!

Who shall say the Roman glory only lives in classic story:
Or that heathen heroes only brave death's river dark and lonely,
When they read the Saxon's story – passage bright of British glory:
How, so friendless, lost, and lonely, with his wife beside him only,
He, in her pale face first gazing – her heroic smile first tracing –
Her cold lips his last kiss pressing; murmuring one parting blessing,
Placed the pistol 'gainst her bold heart, with a shiver in his cold heart,
Cold with anguish! clasped her stronger, lingered not for struggle longer,
Fired! – turned his pistol – fired! and, without a groan, expired!
So that they, who had beheld them, would have said one blow had felled them!
As, his wife upon his breast, calm the soldier sank to his rest!

Who shall say from what pollution his fair bride the Saxon saved?
Who shall coldly paint them, lying, with their mingling tresses waved –
Who shall ever think, not weeping, of this wife and husband sleeping,
Midst the carnage and the dying, coward slaves around them lying, –
Winds of heaven on them blowing, traitor soldiers coming, going,–

Ruin round them, ruin near them, none approaching but to fear them:
None to pity or deplore them – all their friends gone long before them –
Yet with such heroic glory, lighting up their saddest story,–
That, while England lives victorious, evermore 'midst her most glorious
Of memories shall be the scene, the dying hour of – Captain Skene!

Mary Seyton of Theatre Royal, Brighton, 'Our Heroes', *Brighton Herald*, 12 December 1857, p.4.

Our Heroes

Oh! tell us not of Marathon, or the heroic days,
When, in the Pass, Leonidas won his immortal bays;
Say not the spirit of the Bruce (in Scotland's heart no more)
Departed with the Wallace and the Douglases of yore;
But say, how in our modern day of luxury and ease,
A crowd of heroes bear our fame across the boundless seas;
And tell them, who miscall our times "degenerate", that they
Are liars! and are proved so by our deeds of yesterday!
Go, bid them ransack history, from the first page to the last,
And, if they can, find *Havelock* eclipsed in all the past!
And let them tell of men in mail, who fought in "auld lang syne",
Whose deeds could shame our modern Alexanders of the line;
Who, day by day, and mile by mile, beneath a burning sun,
Have stole through heat, and dust and toil, to the battles they have won.
We'll hear no more regretful strains, in praise of long ago:
No! our part be it to adore the heroes whom we know,
O'er whom Time sheds no golden light, nor History flings her veil;
But whom we've known and tried, and proved as souls that could not fail
In any enterprise to which the high heart could aspire,
In any deed how great so'eer which the high soul could fire;
And who afar, in tropic climes, beneath a tropic sky,
Have proved themselves the shining lights of modern chivalry.
Oh! lived the poet who, "of the three hundred" asked "but three",
We'd say we've found them, and have made our New Thermopyæ!

Mary Seyton, 'The Old Year', *Beverley Recorder*, 2 January 1858, p.4.
printed with the note, 'Received too late for insertion in our last week's paper.'

The Old Year

Farewell to the Old Year! – the joys and the woes
That have chequered its course shall not chequer its close;
For, with light hearts, we'll drink its farewell as it goes
Since we know that its course has borne death to our foes!
Since we honour the deeds that have marked it with glory,
And the conquering sword that's enrolled it in story,
We forget, for the moment, its dark list of woes,
And drink a farewell to the year as it goes.
And yet, while the Old Year in darkness is dying,
Can we fail to remember the heroes low lying –
The soldier who fired the death dealing train,
Or high hearts we count in the lists of the slain?
Oh! sad be thy farewell, dark year of our sorrow!
From thy glories our nation its brightness may borrow:
But when we reflect what those glories have cost,
We water thy grave with our tears for the lost.
But one God be our help, and our faith be our rock,
And dark tho' the troubles and ruthless the shock –
That have marked the past year with its story of woes
We know whose Will guided it on to its close.
May He wipe off all tears for all dear ones departed –
May He give His peace unto all broken-hearted –
And may He who has helped us to conquer our foes
The New Year watch o'er from its birth to its close!

Mary Seyton, 'Havelock', *Brighton Herald*, 2 January 1858, p.2; *Beverley Recorder*, 16 January 1858, p.4.

Havelock

In the flood-tide of glory he sinks to his rest,
The bravest, the boldest, the truest, the best;
And while England is praising the deeds of her son,
Come the tidings that tell her his glories are done.

When she trusted him Firmest, and hoped in him most,
When she owned him her champion, her saviour, her boast,
When she watched his career with a fond mother's pride,
And sent forth her brave children to fight by his side!

When his name was the watchword of conquest and glory,

When his deeds shamed the pages of old Roman story,
When his arm was our hope in the day of despair,
And we felt India saved, for brave Havelock was there.

And the heart is not English which shall not deplore
The hero! whose bright path of glory is o'er;
And that voice is not English which shall not be loud
In its sorrow for him of whom England was proud.

And those he has left we will honour and love,
The truth of our grief and our rev'rence to prove;
And his widow and children shall find so the last,
That England forgets not the glorious past!

In the flood-tide of glory he sinks to his rest,
But we know he was bravest, and truest and best,
And we know from the red fields of glory he trod,
That his soul has gone forth at the call of his God!

Mary Seyton, 'Lines to the Princess Royal on Her Wedding Day,' *Brighton Herald*, 23 January 1858, p.3; *Beverley Recorder*, 30 January 1858, p.4. The latter printed with the note, 'Too late for last week's impression.'

Lines to the Princess Royal on her Wedding Day

Go forth in thy beauty, fair rose of the land,
And proud be the wooer whose pride is thy hand;
May thy heart still be English, though far thou mayest be,
While old England is loved, represented by thee!

May thy graces and virtues, wherever thou art,
Be the pride of each nation, the loved of each heart;
As to spread far abroad England's fame and renown,
We part the first gem from the light of our Crown.

Be its lustre our pride, and its brightness our boast –
Tis not pomp, wealth, or power that honours us most;
But our glory is this, that the Court of our Queen
Is the first spot where pure English virtues are seen.

Then ring out loud joy-bells, to welcome the dawn:
Fair sun, shed your light on the glad wedding morn,

While the first flowers of Spring open their dew-spangled eyes,
To take a last peep at the Princess we prize.

Go forth England's daughter! not long shall we part;
Still fondly thou'rt shrined in the Nation's true heart.
We shall see thee again, and thy welcome shall be
Such a welcome as bursts from the hearts of the free.

Mary Seyton, 'Robespierre at the Guillotine,' *Brighton Herald*, 13
February 1858, p.4.

Robespierre at the Guillotine

On rolls the tumbrill, – dark and high,
Frowning against the outraged sky,
With dripping mouth and glittering blade,
In its worst ghastliness arrayed
It stands, the guillotine! From far,
With deafening about and wild hurrah,
They flock, surround him on his way,
Their king, their idol, yesterday.
A mother with a silvered head,
Mad with the memory of the dead,
Frenzied with brooding on her woes,
Shrieks her loud curses as he goes.
The headsman – creature of *his* law,
Wrenches from off the shattered jaw
The blood-stained bandage. One last look
On life and light; and can he brook
The infinite joy of every face,
The laugh that mocks the dismal place?
Oh! but one sad glance to trace,
One pitying eye, one friendly tear!
So brief the moment, death so near,
And o'er his soul, so wild and drear,
Rushing the blackness of his fear.
Yet has he time, in that short space,
To note that in no single face
Is grief or love, but, hewn in stone,
Reigns on each visage hate alone;
For woman's eye, with weeping dim,
Looks not with pity upon him.
All this he knows, all this can mark,

And in that hour so dread and dark,
The God his policy had raised,
The power his specious lips had praised,
The mockery of faith that he
Had linked into his tyranny,
In impotence to shield or save,
Laugh as they hurl him to his grave.

Miss Seyton, 'We May Roam Through This World,' *Beverley Recorder*, 20 February 1858, p.4.

We May Roam Through This World (Altered from Moore)

We may float through this world like a Phipps at the Court,
Who attends to his sovereign and never knows rest,
And the honours brave heroes with high deeds have bought.
We may get without earning, and wear with the best.
 For if orders from a sov'reign's hand
 Are the best rewards that Fate bestows,
 We never need leave our native land,
 Or bleed, or fight, to merit those.

We may pass through such perils as never were told,
And our fame may be spread from the East to the West
While our courage is proved of such standard gold
As survives every trial, outlives every test; –
 But the honours our grateful nation gives,
 Will not be better, and may be worse
 Than the Phipps of the day who in comfort lives,
 Will get for minding the royal purse.

So, who'd be heroic, victorious, or great,
Or win laurels and fame at the point of the sword?
When some Phipps, who eats daily his dinner in State,
Will receive the same smiles and the same reward.
 But the deeds of the brave, this charm shall bear,
 They shall live in men's hearts till the world grows old;
 While the honours *Court* favour would scatter there,
 Will serve only to "gild refined gold."

Mary Seyton, 'Queen Guinevere,' *Brighton Herald*, 10 September 1859, p.4. Dated 'Brighton, Sept. 3rd'. Reprinted in *Garibaldi and other Poems* (London: Bosworth & Harrison, 1861), pp.269-271.

Mary Seyton, 'Tired of Life', *Brighton Herald*, 5 November 1859, p.4. The byline indicates that it also appeared in the November edition of the magazine *Titan*. I was unable to check this as *Titan* is missing from the British Library. Braddon probably had at least one other poem printed in *Titan* because John Gilby wrote to her to get 'the two last nos of Titan, (wh. you so provokingly lost) – I want them for the printers.' (Gilby to Braddon, 5 November 1860, Wolff Collection). Reprinted in *Garibaldi*, pp.284-287.

Mary Seyton, 'Among the Hyacinths', *Brighton Herald*, 12 November 1859, p.4. Dated 'Brighton, November 7th, 1859'. Reprinted in *Garibaldi*, p.315.

Mary Seyton, 'Islam', *Brighton Herald*, 26 November 1859, p.4. Dated 'Brighton, Nov. 21'. *Beverley Recorder*, 25 August 1860, p.4. Wolff reprints this poem on p.422 of *Sensational Victorian* as a clipping is pasted into one of her notebooks owned by the Houghton Library, Harvard University. He did not know which newspaper it was from.

Mary Seyton, 'The Peril of Christmas Eve,' *Brighton Guardian*, 23 December 1859, p.4.

The Peril of Christmas Eve

Why comes he at the close of day,
When lights from tower and hall gleam gay,–
Why comes he by the lonely stair?
    And up the secret stair?
Why comes he softly through the snow,
By paths no other footsteps know, –
Though Christmas lords it high and low,
    And wild the mirth elsewhere?

Loud in the hall and in the tower
Rings out the glad and festal hour;
But lonely in my lady's bower,
    Silent, and dark, and dim,
The shadows on the curtain'd wall
On ghastly subjects darkly fall,
But blacker shadows than them all
    Surround and circle *him*.

Shadows of evil deeds long done, –
Shadows of crimes that fear the sun,
Bad thoughts, dark fights unfairly won,
 Murder, and death, and sin,
And yet unto my Lady Clare,
None other half so brave or fair,
She scarce could pray that Heaven to share
 Would it allot to him.

"And better this, and better so,
Better in this world below;
None others know, or e'er can know,
 How brave, how true, how great
Thou art my exil'd, traduc'd knight,
Whose shield for me is still more bright,
Since men's hard words have dimmed its light,
 And sorrow seal'd thy fate.

Proud am I of thy branded name,
Proud that I'm thine in grief or shame,
Proud even of thy tarnished fame,
 And of thine evil deed.
Thinking the worst men tell of thee
Better than other's courtesy,
Since life has this alone for me,
 Thy path, thy doom, thy creed."

So speaks the wealthy Lady Clare,
Sweet simple maid, with flaxen hair
Mild eyes, and brow so mildly fair,
 But heart, – brave, bold, and high.
Oh better she were lying low,
Fair head down-trodden in the snow,
Where passing footsteps come and go
 Under the winter sky.

Better e'en death than such a life,
Praying to be a bad man's wife,
Daring all danger, crime, or strife,
 For dark Sir Roland's sake;
Better than on that haughty breast
Her gentle head should seek to rest,
Being accurs'd in being blest,

  The gentle heart should break.

So spake she in her lonely bower,
While from high tower unto high tower
Peal the rejoicings of the hour,
  And the loud Christmas cheer;
Knights at the board, knights in the hall,
Pages and grooms in turrets tall,
And joy for each, and joy for all,
  But only sorrow here.

Bitter love that knows not change,
And constant faith that cannot range,
Though life be cold and friends are strange,
  And deaf to cry or prayer.
Well wots she were this meeting known,
Her father's heart would turn to stone,
She knows he would his child disown,
  This helpless Lady Clare.

"But come the worst while thou art near,
Or lay me lowly on my bier;
So thou lett'st fall one pitying tear
  How little do I care!
And let them, when that I am gone,
To prove I loved for thee alone,
Carve thus my name upon the stone,
  'Sir Roland's Lady Clare!'

"So that whatever guilt no, or shame,
Whatever of a fallen name,
May hang around thy banish'd name,
  May still be shared by me.
So that in death I yet may know
Half thy disgrace and half thy woe,
Even when lying still and low,
  Sharing thy misery."

And as she speaks, with slender hand
Tuin'd round the head, men'd curses brand,
And binding him, her arm the band,
  That roots him to the spot, –
Even as she speaks, upon her ear

There breaks the sound of footsteps near,
Half lost in wonder, doubt, and fear,
    Whose step she knoweth not;

Till a harsh voice without the door
Clamours for entry, and before
She can answer or implore,
    Her father strikes his sword; –
Strikes heavy on the solid wood;
Brave door! resistance brave and good!
If he should enter, – if he should,
    Behold the knight abhorr'd!

Then death for her and death for him, –
Her sight grows clouded, thick and dim,
She totters, shivering in each limb, –
    "Roland! that sound is fate!
There is no issue from this room,
My father's sword brings death and doom,
Honour now points unto our tomb, –
    Roland! ere 'tis too late,

"I pray thee that when I am dead,
Thou wilt not harm that silver'd head, –
Better thy blood by him be shed,
    Than he be slain by thee.
Better" – but stay, the dark eyes gleam,
Bright as the eyes that haunt a dream,
With not all sadness in their beam, –
    "My lady list to me,

"I know that thou art brave and true,
And bold to speak, and dare to do;
For such, death sometimes yiels his due:
    Wilt thou be ruled by me?
Then twine thine arms around my neck,
We yet may 'scape our young hope's wreck,
So thou wilt follow at my beck,
    As I would follow thee.

"Thou knowest that 'neath this lattice high
The deep blue lake gives back the sky,
Where wraiths of pale stars palely lie,

Three hundred feet below.
One desperate leap, and I with thee,
Twin'd in my arms, perchance may be
Or lost and drowned, or saved and free, –
    Say, wilt thou with me go?

"If not, to save thy maiden name,
And add unto my own dark fame
Another deed for men to blame,
    Alone I take the leap."
(And all this while without the door,
Her father's voice in long loud roar,
Clamours for entry as before,)
    The lake is wide and deep.

"And nothing but the stars will see
Love's hazzard. Wilt thou trust to me, –
So trusting as I trust in thee, –
    Wilt come my Lady Clare?"
She twines her white arms round his breast,
Lays her fair head on his broad chest,
"I know no sweeter place of rest,
    What death thou dar'st, I dare."

Some say that in the deep dark stream
They both were lost; some call a dream
This story of the Past; some deem
    That in a strange wild land,
A dark knight and a lovely dame
Won for themselves a golden name,
And linked in an heroic fame,
    To death went hand in hand,

But shunned by all the lonely way,
And shunned by all the secret stair, –
For as men say, by night and day,
    Strange footfalls echo there, –
And when the Christmas mirth is loud,
Louder than the echoes sound,
When footsteps of the merry crowd
    Fall soft on snow-clad ground.

Mary Seyton, 'Shadows', *Brighton Herald*, 31 December 1859, p.4. Dated 'Brighton, December 20th, 1859'. Reprinted in *Garibaldi* as 'A Shadow', pp.304-305.

Mary Seyton, 'Louise de la Valliere', *Brighton Herald*, 21 January 1860, p.4. Dated 'January 14, 1860', Reprinted in *Garibaldi*, pp. 266-268.

Mary Seyton, 'The Marquis', *Brighton Herald*, 25 February 1860, p.4.

The Marquis

He rides through the sunset, impassive and cold,
    The rein falling loose from his listless hand;
Through shadows of purple and lights of red gold,
    Rides this lord of title and land.

The deepening flush on his pale, dark face,
    Is a ray that glints from the crimson west;
Does he, under his haughty patrician grace,
    Hide as warm a light in his breast?

No thought of his soul looks out in his eyes,
    Brown over blue, or now, blue over brown,
You might watch him for ever, and never surprise –
    Himself in a smile or a frown.

You may read his pedigree, if you will,
    Knights under Charlemagne – Barons of France;
But his face is a mystery – shrouded and still,
    With a passionless far-off glance.

Has he loved or lost? can he suffer or weep?
    Has he one wild hope, or one daring dream?
Has his soul known no shipwreck in life's wide deep,
    Nor peril on Time's dark stream?

How shall he to future years be known?
    As a scoffer at every sacred creed,
For a classical profile and heart of stone,
    Or, for a great and heroic deed?

Oh, cast him forth in some wild, now world –

In a nation strong in primaeval youth,
That the cynical lip, now so proudly curled,
   May be loud in the cause of Truth!

Or put a broad sword in that idle hand,
   In the thickest press of a battle field –
Let him prove that the ancient blood of his land
   Can be wasted – but cannot yield.

Give his soul a faith and his life an aim;
   Give him wrongs to right and the weak to save;
Let hearts, in long ages, beat high at his name,
   And proud knees kneel at his grave!

Mary Seyton, 'Footsteps', *Brighton Herald*, 14 April 1860, p.4.

Footsteps

She cannot hear my footsteps in the night:
Calmly she sleeps beneath the breaking light
   And cannot hear my tread:
She cannot hear the footsteps on the stone,
Whose echoes cry with an unvarying tone
   "Oh, better to be dead!"

Oh, better than to drag out days of pain,
Mocked by false dreams and hopes as wild as vain,
   Far better to be dead:
E'en though no gentle hand should close my eyes,
Or o'er the last home of my miseries
   No friendly tear be shed.

My weary footfall through the long, dark night,
My tired wanderings under morn's chill light,
   Break not her tranquil rest.
So no less calmly hath she slept
For the unquiet watches nightly kept
   By him who loves her best.

Having, in one wild moment, fondly dreamed
By her a wasted youth might be redeemed
   And the dark Past erased –
By her a soul, long dim with many a stain,

Might some old glimpses of lost light regain,
    Ere utterly debased –

So, having wakened from this cherished dream,
So, having passed from out this wandering beam,
    Better to bow the head
To the stern hand that shuts the shining gate
Of a fair region on the desolate –
    Yes, better dead!

So may my unrest never break her peace;
And when the echoes of my footfall cease,
    With life's wild fever fled,
May she not know the passion and the pain
Of this poor breaking heart, that breaks in vein,
    Even when I am dead!

Mary Seyton, 'Vale', *Brighton Herald*, 2 June 1860, p.4. Reprinted in *Garibaldi*, pp.294-296.

Mary Seyton, 'The Last Hours of the Girondists', *Brighton Herald*, 16 June 1860, p.4. Reprinted in *Garibaldi,* pp.255-259.

Mary Elizabeth Braddon, 'Sophia Dorothea', *Brighton Herald*, 15 September 1860, p.4. With the note, 'See the lectures on the "Four Georges" in the *Cornhill Magazine*, for concise information concerning the hapless Sophia Dorothea.'

Sophia Dorothea

Only this record left when all is o'er,
    A few old letters with the ink gone pale:
    And they who wrote them, were they false or frail?
Dare we have pity – must we but deplore?

They loved, and they were luckless – loved amiss.
    Poor shivering Cupid with the draggled wings,
    What hadst thou, feeble one, with courts and kings,
Thou painted god of transitory bliss?

Oh, the poor letters! foolish, it may be –
    Ill spelt – ill written – only, only true.
    How earnestly she wrote – how little knew

What cold, hard eyes those loving words should see.

Think of her, trembling o'er the secret page;
    Think of the tearful eyes that fondly dwelt
    Above the leaf where all she thought and felt
Was written! Did her desolate old age

Rise, a pale phantom of the dread to come,
    Shadowing that future, terrible as dim?
    How should she think of this? She thought of him,
And every earthly voice save his was dumb.

If you had in a picture made her see
    Ahlden's forgotten Princess, and had said,
    "This is yourself, and he you love is dead;
You live, and he is not. This is to be!"

Had she believed you? She had smiled at you,
    As one who spoke a language wild and strange.
    How should she know Earth's hardest truth, – We change,
And live to wonder at the hearts we knew.

She did outlive him – through the weary years,
    Whose very silence makes their story sad,
    She lived. If mad, she was not loudly mad.
She lived, we have no record of her tears.

The peasants met her riding o'er the plain,
    And saw but this: a woman, with white hair.
    How should they guess her lingering despair,
Her long unpitied days of speechless pain?

How should they see as she saw? Had she not
    The memory of one terrific night,
    To haunt her through the day, the dark, the light?
The unavenged, unshriven, unforgot!

Each detail of a death she did not see –
    The four armed guards – the darkness of the place –
    A woman trampling on that perfect face –
Must not these be with her eternally?

Those two-and-thirty melancholy years,

They may have been her penance – may have gone
Even for him they murdered to atone,
Washing his soul in her repentant tears.

But the poor letters. How shall they be read
Now the frail hearts recorded thus are dust?
Weep o'er the words that tell her love, her trust;
And think but this, – They suffered, they are dead.

Mary Elizabeth Braddon, 'Stanzas', *Brighton Herald*, 24 November 1860, p.4. Reprinted in *Garibaldi* as 'Life Is a Child', pp.306-307.

M.E. Braddon, 'Waking', *Brighton Herald*, 2 February 1861, p.4. 'From "Garibaldi and other Poems", by M.E. Braddon.' pp.302-303 in *Garibaldi*.

Garibaldi and Other Poems (London: Bosworth and Harrison, 1861). The other poems in the book were: 'Garibaldi', 'Olivia', 'Under the Sycamores', 'The Secretary', 'Joanna of Naples', 'Si and No', 'By the Sea-Shore', 'At Last', 'Waiting', 'Under Ground', 'Going Down', 'Gabriel', 'Farewell, To a Coquette', 'The Loft Pleiad', and 'After the Armistice'.

'In Memoriam', *Temple Bar*, vol. IV, January 1862, p. 180. Poem on the death of Prince Albert. Signed M.E.B.

'Sweet Violets', *Belgravia*, vol. II, April 1867, pp.223-224. Signed M. Unrecorded by Wolff.

'May', *Belgravia*, vol. II, May 1867, p.287. Signed M. Unrecorded by Wolff.

'The Dinner at Richmond', *Belgravia*, vol. II, June 1867, pp.409-410. Signed M. Unrecorded by Wolff.

'Lunch on the Hill', *Belgravia*, vol. III, September 1867, p.302. Signed M. Unrecorded by Wolff.

'After the Battle', *Belgravia*, vol. IV, February 1868, p.506. Signed M.E. Braddon. Unrecorded by Wolff.

'The Hawking Party', *Belgravia*, vol. V, March 1868, p.77. Signed M.E. Braddon. Unrecorded by Wolff.

'The Lady of the Land', *Belgravia*, vol. VI, July 1868, p.81-85. Signed M.E. Braddon. Unrecorded by Wolff.

'In the Firelight', *Belgravia*, vol. VII, January 1869, p.369. Signed M. Unrecorded by Wolff.

'Violets', *Belgravia*, vol. XI, April 1870, p.260. Written as Babington White.

'In Memoriam', *Belgravia*, vol. XX, June 1873, pp.542-543. Poem in memory of Bulwer Lytton, Braddon's mentor, signed M.M. Almost certainly standing for Mary Maxwell. The poet relates a visit to Torquay to see where he died. Unrecorded by Wolff.

'An East End Andromeda', *World*, 19 September 1888, p.21. Braddon may have written this poem, which is signed M.M.

'Strawberries. A Lament', *World*, 10 August 1892, p.945. Signed M.E.B. Unrecorded by Wolff.

Braddon wrote in her diary on 22 October 1892, 'Wrote page verses for MB'. There were only two poems in *Mistletoe Bough* for 1892, so this poem must have either been 'Lady St. James is at Home To-night' or 'In a Philistine Garden'. Unrecorded by Wolff.

'Ã Mon Maître', *World*, 17 October 1894, p.13. Signed M. Unrecorded by Wolff.

(G.) Lyrics and Libretto

Duchess De La Vallierre, c.1856-1857. An opera by the Hull composer Henry Deval, for which Braddon wrote the libretto. Unrecorded by Wolff.

'My Heart is Thine: A New Musical Valentine', *Belgravia*, February 1876, p.576. The lyrics of a song written by M.E. Braddon for the composer Elizabeth Philip. Both music and lyrics were published by E. Rimmel. Unrecorded by Wolff.

In 1884, according to the *World*, 21 May 1884, p.15, Elizabeth Philip gave a concert at the St. James's Hall, for which 'Miss Braddon has written words for two of Miss Philip's new songs.'

(H.) Parodies and Non-Fiction

Wolff writes that his catalogue is 'almost surely incomplete. I have not, for example, been able to consult a file of Edmund Yates's weekly newspaper, the *World*, which began publication on July 8, 1874, and to which she made many contributions.' Braddon did indeed make many contributions to the *World*, but unfortunately many were anonymous and cannot be identified. I have identified some from her diaries, and from this find that some carried the byline 'M', or more obviously 'M.E.B.' The travel pieces match her own holiday destinations.

'London on Four Feet', *Welcome Guest*, January 1861, pp.277-288. An article highlighting the cruel treatment of horses in London, compared to those in Yorkshire.

'How the Romans Supped', *Welcome Guest*, January 1861, pp.376-378. Historical essay. Unrecorded by Wolff. The conclusion of the essay promises a sequel on Roman eating habits, but this never appeared. Doubtless Braddon contributed more essays and short stories to the fourth volume of the *Welcome Guest* in this format, but unfortunately Maxwell decided that all contributions would be anonymous.

'Address given by Miss Braddon, Delivered by Miss Woolgar at the St. James's Hall Concert for the Benefit of the Widow and Children of the late Mr. Sam Cowell June 1864', 4pp. leaflet.

'Trontlemouth', *Temple Bar*, vol. XVI, January 1866, pp.198-205. Signed M.B. An essay about Cornwall, possibly by Braddon.

'French Novels', *Belgravia*, vol. III, July 1867, pp.78-82. Signed M. Unrecorded by Wolff.

'A Remonstrance', *Belgravia*, vol. IV, pp.80-86. Anonymous.

'Glimpses at Foreign Literature', *Belgravia*, vol. V, pp.156-160. Signed M. An essay on George Sand. Unrecorded by Wolff.

'Whose Fault is It?', *Belgravia*, vol. IX, August 1869, pp.214-216. M.E. Braddon.

'Lord Lytton', *Belgravia*, vol. XX, March 1873, pp.73-88. A memorial tribute.

'Ireland for Tourists. A Reminiscence of a Recent Excursion', *Belgravia*, vol. XXIV, July-August 1874, pp.76-88 and pp.177-190.

'Macbeth at the Lyceum Theatre', *Belgravia*, November 1875, pp.69-79. Signed M.E.B.

One of her notebooks in the Wolff collection (with the title on the spine 'M.S.S. Vol. V.') has a schedule for work, and states that between 1 September and 10 September 1876 Braddon was working on a 'Brittany article'. This may have appeared in the *World*.

'The Steam Roller', *The Times*, 28 November 1877, p.11. Letter from M.E. Braddon-Maxwell defending her side of the court case in which she and Maxwell had unsuccessfully sued a steam roller company for damages, after a dangerous accident she had been involved in with her carriage in Kensington. The case was reported in the same paper, 23 November 1877, p.11. Unrecorded by Wolff.

'Dinners at Elementary Schools', *The Times*, 30 April 1880, p.10. Letter to the editor about the importance of school dinners . Signed M.E. Braddon, and dated 27 April, and written from Lyndhurst. Unrecorded by Wolff.

'Boscastle, Cornwall, an English Engladine'. A tourist pamphlet listed in British Library catalogue for 1881. The essay appeared anonymously in the *World*, September 1880, pp.16-17.

'The Observant', mentioned by Wolff as listed in Braddon's diary for the *World*. It was probably the anonymous 'The Observant Child', 28 September 1881, pp.322-323.

'A Little Hunting', mentioned by Wolff as listed in Braddon's diary. It appeared anonymously in the *World*, 5 October 1881, pp.344-345.

'The Children', mentioned by Wolff as listed in Braddon's diary for the *World*. It was probably the anonymous 'The Children at Christmas', 21 December 1881, pp.606-607.

'People Who Write to the Times', *Whitehall Review*, new Series no. 60, 24 January 1884, p.8. Published anonymously. Publication date unrecorded by Wolff.

'Emile Zola and the Naturalistic School, or Realism in French Literature', 1885. 22pp. essay of literary criticism. An essay which was intended for the *Fortnightly Review*. The manuscript in Wolff's collection was not a completed article. It is in fact two rough drafts put together, being neither complete nor consecutive. At the end of the manuscript, heavily crossed out, can just be seen the name Babington White.

'A Friendly Mount', *World*, 30 June 1886, pp.27-28. Published anonymously, but the essay matches proofs in the Wolff collection. Location unrecorded by Wolff.

'St. Ives', *World*, 18 August 1886, pp.18-19. Signed M.E.B. Unrecorded by Wolff.

'The Queen of the West', *World*, 25 August 1886, pp.18-19. Signed M.E.B. An article about Bath. Braddon quoted a passage of this essay in a letter to the *World*, asking for changes, although she did not name it. Unrecorded by Wolff.

'Clovelly-Falmouth-Fowey', *World*, 15 September 1886, pp.17-18. Signed M.E.B. Unrecorded by Wolff.

'Paremé, St. Malo', *World*, 22 September 1886, pp.19-20. Signed M.E.B. Unrecorded by Wolff.

'In the Olive Grove', *World*, 21 December 1887, p.20. Signed M.E.B. An essay about San Remo, dated 15 December. Unrecorded by Wolff.

'In Southern Latitudes', *World*, 22 February 1888, pp.19-20. Signed M.E.B, where Braddon was staying at the Villa de la Madeleine, Cannes. Braddon also filed reports to 'What the World Says' from San Remo, published 15 February p.19, from Cannes 18 April p.12, and from Rome 25 April p.13. Unrecorded by Wolff.

'The Ubiquitous Man. British Individualists no. 1'. Location untraced, mentioned in Braddon's diary on 26 April 1890. Typescript in the Wolff collection, but unrecorded by Wolff.

'Jonnie', by 'Alphone Daudet', Mr. Punch's Prize Novels, no. 8, *Punch*, 29 November 1890, p.253.

'Le Pétrolium; ou les Saloperies Parisiennes' by 'Zorgon-Gola', Mr. Punch's Prize Novels, no. 14, *Punch*, 28 February 1891, pp.100-101.

'From Forest Depths', *World*, 9 March 1892, pp. 20-21. Signed M.E.B. This must be the 'N.F. article' Braddon mentions in her diary as posting on 2 March 1892, as it is about the New Forest. Unrecorded by Wolff.

Wolff notes that Braddon's diary for July 1892 records a "squib" for *Punch*. Wolff suggests this may have been 'Racine With the Chill Off', *Punch*, 16 July 1892.

'On Cranbourne Chase', *World*, 21 September 1892, pp.24-25. Signed M. F. B, (sic). Surely by Braddon, being about hunting and the New Forest.

'Switzerland in Eight Hours', *World*, 28 September 1892, pp.14-15. Signed M.E.B. This must be the 'tourist article' Braddons diary for 23 September 1892 mentions posting to the *World*. Unrecorded by Wolff.

'A Lost Pleid', *World*, 23 November 1892, p.24. Signed M.E.B. This is the 'paper on Byron' Braddon's diary for 20 November 1892 mentions as being for the *World*. Unrecorded by Wolff

'Furniture in Fiction', *Sala's Journal*, vol. III, 15 July 1893, pp.25-26. Signed M.E. Braddon. Unrecorded by Wolff.

'Herman Sudermann', *National Review*, 21 August 1893, pp.751-770.

'My First Novel, *The Trail of the Serpent*', *Idler*, vol. III, 1893, pp. 19-30.

'Time Was', *World*, 18 July 1894, pp.12-13. Signed M.E.B. (about Tintagel). Braddon's diary for 17 June recorded finishing a 'tourist article', presumably this one. Unrecorded by Wolff.

'Holiday Island', *World*, 22 August 1894, pp.24-25. Signed M. Braddon's diary states she wrote 'Holiday Island' on 1 August 1894. Unrecorded by Wolff.

'In the Days of My Youth', *The Theatre*, vol. XXIV, September 1894, pp.120-125. Unrecorded by Wolff.

'In a Van in Wharfedale', *World*, 5 September 1894, pp.26-27. Signed M. (about the painter Bernard Evans). Unrecorded by Wolff.

'A Voice from Marienbad', *World*, 19 September 1894, pp.24-25. Signed M.B. Braddon wrote in her diary that she was writing a 'tourist paper' on 10 September 1894, which must have been this one. Unrecorded by Wolff.

'Honeymoon Land', *World*, 3 October 1894, pp.22-23. Signed M.E.B. Unrecorded by Wolff.

'The German Play of the Hour', *Theatre*, vol. XXV, March 1895, p.131. About Sudermann's play *Die Ehre*. Unrecorded by Wolff.

'Cornubia Felix', *World*, 5 June 1895, p.28. Signed M.E.B. Braddon's diary records writing '3 small paras for World' on 19 May 1895 which may have been this. Unrecorded by Wolff.

'Mudie's Library', *The Times*, 23 September 1895, p.4. Criticising Mudie's Library for refusing to take her three decker novel *Sons of Fire*. Unrecorded by Wolff.

Braddon wrote a short piece c.1895 on which of her novels she liked best for the *Ludgate Magazine*. Manuscript in Wolff collection.

Braddon's diary for 12 December 1895 records writing 'Trilby sketch'. Location unknown, unrecorded by Wolff.

'Homburg Versus Marienbad', *World*, 22 September 1897, p.30. Signed M. Unrecorded by Wolff.

'Pallanza', *World*, 29 September 1897, pp.28-29. Signed M and dated 22 September. About the Italian lakes. Unrecorded by Wolff.

'Zinal (Valais)', *World*, 24 August 1898, pp.31-32. Signed M and dated 17 August. Unrecorded by Wolff.

'Saas Fee (Valais)', *World*, 31 August 1898, p.25. Signed M and dated 25 August. Unrecorded by Wolff.

'North Cornwall', *World*, 31 August 1898, p.26. Signed M.B. Recalling Braddon's holiday in February. Unrecorded by Wolff.

'Zermatt', *World*, 7 September 1898, pp.26-27. Signed M and dated 2 September. Unrecorded by Wolff.

'Cadenabbia, Lago Di Como', *World*, 14 September 1898, pp.26. Signed M.M. and dated 9 September, when she was staying there. Unrecorded by Wolff.

'Beaulieu', *World*, 28 December 1898, pp.25-26. Signed M.B. Unrecorded by Wolff.

'Fifty Years of the Lyceum Theatre', *Strand Magazine*, vol. XXIV, January 1903, pp.36-40.

An introduction for *Little Dorrit*. Braddon wrote this for F.G. Kitton, writing to him about it in January 1903, when he told her it was not needed for another six months. This must have been Frederick Kitton's Autograph Edition published by the American publisher George D. Sproul in 1904. Kitton died in 1904 and the edition left incomplete. Unrecorded by Wolff.

'I Remember, I Remember', *Daily Mail*, c.December 1903. Watt posted the manuscript on 22 December. It may have been published as the anonymous, 'Changing Christmas', *Daily Mail*, 25 December 1903, p.4. Unrecorded by Wolff.

'Little Books', *Black and White*, vol. XXIX, 7 January 1905, p.34. About the availability of classic books in convenient little volumes. Unrecorded by Wolff.

'My Best Story and Why I Think So', *Grand Magazine*, vol. I, July 1905, p.881. Preface note to reprint of her story 'His Oldest Friends'. Unrecorded by Wolff.

'The Life Beautiful', *Chambers Journal*, no. 467, 6th series, December 1905-November 1906, 10 November 1906, pp.785-787. Unrecorded by Wolff.

'At the Shrine of "Jane Eyre"', *Pall Mall Magazine*, new series vol. XXXVII, 1906, pp.174-176. Unrecorded by Wolff.

'The Woman I Remember', *Press Album* (London: John Murray, 1909), pp.3-6.

'The Smart Sets in History', *Strand Magazine*, vol. XXXIX, 1910. Unrecorded by Wolff.

King Albert's Book (1914). p.112. The book contains a short tribute to King Albert of Belgium by Braddon.

Before the Knowledge of Evil (1914). Unpublished manuscript of 185pp. of typescript. A memoir of her childhood and early life. I have included this unpublished work because of its length and its importance.

Braddon's diary for 28 October 1914 indicates she 'Wrote par for Hall Caine's book.'

There are a number of essays which I have not traced. One of her notebooks has notes for the following essays: 'The New Parvenu', 'The Great Lady', 'The Stylist', and 'The Babymanager. There are also notes which may have been for possible essays on Sandwich and Ramsgate, The Derby, Shelley's Grave and Rome, and in September 1905 Robin Hood's Bay.

Bibliography

Altick, Richard D., *Victorian Studies in Scarlet* (New York: Norton, 1970).

Baker, Michael J.N., *The Rise of the Victorian Actor* (London: Croom Helm, 1978).

Boase, Frederick, *Modern English Biography* (1921; repr. London: Frank Cass, 1965).

Booth, Michael, *English Melodrama* (London: Herbert Jenkins, 1965).

Boyle, Thomas, *Black Swine in the Sewers of Hampstead: Beneath the Surface of Victorian Sensationalism* (London: Hodder and Stoughton, 1990).

Boucicault, Dion, *Jessie Brown; or, The Relief of Lucknow* (London: Dick's Standard Plays, c.1880).

Braddon, M.E., *Garibaldi and Other Poems* (London: Bosworth & Harrison, 1861).

Braddon, M.E., *The Black Band; or, The Mysteries of Midnight* (*Halfpenny Journal* 1861-1862; repr. Hastings: The Sensation Press, 1998).

Braddon, M.E., *The Trail of the Serpent* (London: Ward, Lock & Tyler, 1861; repr. London: Simpkin, Marshall, c.1905).

Braddon, M.E. *The Octoroon; or, The Lily of Louisiana* (Halfpenny Journal 1861-1862; repr. Hastings: The Sensation Press, 1999).

Braddon, M.E., *Lady Audley's Secret* (Oxford: Oxford University Press, 1987).

Braddon, M.E., *Lady Audley's Secret* (New York: Dover, 1974).

Braddon, M.E., *The Lady Lisle* (London: Ward, Lock & Tyler, 1862; repr. London: Ward, Lock & Tyler, c. 1867).

Braddon, M.E., *Aurora Floyd* (London: Tinsley, 1863; repr. London: Virago, 1984).

Braddon, M.E., *Eleanor's Victory* (London: Tinsley, 1863; repr. Far Thrupp, Stroud: Alan Sutton, 1996).

Braddon, M.E., *John Marchmont's Legacy* (London: Tinsley, 1863; repr. London: Simpkin, Marshall, 1892).

Braddon, M.E., *Henry Dunbar*, 2 vols. (Leipzig: Tauchnitz, 1864).

Braddon, M.E., *The Doctor's Wife* (London: Maxwell, 1864; repr. London: Ward, Lock & Tyler, c.1866).

Braddon, M.E., *Only a Clod*, 2 vols. (Leipzig: Tauchnitz, 1865).

Braddon, M.E., *The Lady's Mile* (London: Ward, Lock & Tyler, 1866; repr. London: Maxwell, c.1885).

Braddon, M.E., *Circe* 2 vols. (London: Ward, Lock & Tyler, 1867).

Braddon, M.E., *Birds of Prey* 3 vols. (London: Ward, Lock & Tyler, 1867).

Braddon, M.E., *Charlotte's Inheritance* (London: Ward, Lock & Tyler, 1867; repr. London: Simpkin, Marshall, 1892).

Braddon, M.E., *Dead Sea Fruit* (London: Ward, Lock & Tyler, 1868; repr. Ward, Lock & Tyler, c.1869).

Braddon, M.E., *The Lovels of Arden* (London: Maxwell, 1871; repr. Ward, Lock & Tyler, 1872).

Braddon, M.E., *To the Bitter End* (1872; repr. London: Ward, Lock & Tyler, c.1874).

Braddon, M.E., *Strangers and Pilgrims* (London: Maxwell, 1873; repr. Maxwell, 1885).

Braddon, M.E., *Lucius Davoren* 3 vols. (Leipzig: Tauchnitz, 1873).

Braddon, M.E., *Taken at the Flood* 3 vols. (London: Maxwell, 1874).

Braddon, M.E., *A Strange World* (London: Maxwell, 1875; repr. Ward, Lock & Tyler, c.1877).

Braddon, M.E., *Hostages to Fortune* (London: Maxwell, 1875; repr. Ward, Lock & Tyler. c.1877).

Braddon, M.E., *Dead Men's Shoes* (London: Maxwell, 1876; repr. London: Simpkin, Marshall, c.1905).

Braddon, M.E., *Joshua Haggard's Daughter* 3 vols. (London: Maxwell. 1876).

Braddon, M.E., *The Story of Barbara* (London: Maxwell, 1880; repr. London: Maxwell, c.1881).

Braddon, M.E., *Just As I Am* (London: Maxwell, 1880; repr. Maxwell, c.1885).

Braddon, M.E., *The Golden Calf* (London: Maxwell, 1883; repr. Maxwell, c.1885).

Braddon, M.E., *Ishmael* (London: Maxwell, 1884; repr . Maxwell, c.1885).

Braddon, M.E., *Wyllard's Weird* (London: Maxwell, 1885; repr. London: Simpkin, Marshall, c.1905).

Braddon, M.E., *Cut By the County* (London: Maxwell, 1886).

Braddon, M.E., *Under the Red Flag* (London: Maxwell, 1886; repr. London: Simpkin, Marshall, 1890).

Braddon, M.E., Like and Unlike (London: Spencer Blackett, 1887; repr. London: Simpkin, Marshall, c. 1890).

Braddon, M.E., *The Day will Come* (London: Simpkin, Marshall, 1889; repr. London: Simpkin, Marshall, c.1890).

Braddon, M.E., *One Life, One Love* 3 vols. (London: Simpkin, Marshall, 1890).

Braddon, M.E., *Gerard, or, The World, The Flesh, and the Devil* 3 vols. (London: Simpkin, Marshall, 1891).

Braddon, M.E., *Rough Justice* (London: Simpkin, Marshall, 1898).

Braddon, M.E., *His Darling Sin* (London: Simpkin, Marshall, 1899).

Braddon, M.E., *A Lost Eden* (London: Hutchinson, 1904).

Braddon, M.E., *Dead Love Has Chains* (London: Hurst & Blackett, 1907).

Braddon, M.E., *Our Adversary* (London: Hutchinson, 1909).

Braddon, M.E., *Beyond These Voices* (London: Hutchinson, 1910).

Braddon, M.E., *The Green Curtain* (London: Hutchinson, 1911).

Braddon, M.E., *Mary* (London: Hutchinson, 1916).

Bridges, Yseult, *The Tragedy at Road-Hill House* (New York: Rhinehart, 1955).

Burstyn, Joan N., *Victorian Education and the Ideal of Womanhood* (London: Croom Helm, 1980).

Calvert, Mrs. Adelaide, *Sixty-Eight Years on the Stage* (London: Mills and Boon, 1911).

Carder, Timothy, *The Encyclopedia of Brighton* (Lewes: East Sussex County Libraries, 1990).

Collins, Wilkie, *The Woman in White* (1860; repr. London: Penguin, 1882).

Collins, Wilkie, *Armadale* (1866; repr. London: Penguin, 1995).

Craig, Patricia, and Cadogan, Mary, *The Lady Investigates: Women Detectives and Spies in Fiction* (Oxford: Oxford University Press, 1986).

Cross, Gilbert B., *Next Week East Lynne: Domestic Drama In Performance 1820-1874* (London: Associated University Presses, 1977).

Cruise, Amy, *The Victorians and Their Books* (London: George Allen and Unwin, 1935).

Dale, Antony, *The Theatre Royal Brighton* (Stocksfield: Oriel Press, 1980).

Dance, Charles, *Delicate Ground* (London: Dick's Standard plays, c.1880)

Davis, Tracy C., *Actresses as Working Women: Their Social Identity in Victorian Culture* (London: Routledge, 1991).

Dickens, Charles and Collins, Wilkie, *No Thoroughfare and Other Stories* (Far Thrupp, Stroud: Alan Sutton, 1990).

Edwardes, Annie, *Miss Forrester* (1866; repr. London: Tinsley, c.1867)

Edwardes, Michael, *Red Year The Indian Rebellion of 1857* (London: Hamish Hamilton, 1973; repr. London: Cardinal, 1975).

Edwards, P.D., *Some Mid-Victorian Thrillers: The Sensation Novel, Its Friends and Foes* (Queensland: University of Queensland Press, 1971).

Edwards, P.D., I.G. Sibley and Margaret Versteeg, *Indexes to Fictions in Belgravia* (Queensland: Victorian Fiction Research Guide 14, Department of English, University of Queensland, 1990).

Edwards, P.D., *Dickens's 'Young Men': George Augustus Sala, Edmund Yates and the World of Victorian Journalism* (Aldershot: Ashgate, 1997).

Escott, T.H.S., *Platform, Press, Politics and Play* (Bristol: Arrowsmith, 1895).

Falk, Bernard, *The Naughty Seymours* (London: Hutchinson, 1940).

Fitzgerald, Percy, *Memoirs of an Author* 2 vols. (London: Richard Bentley, 1895).

Frith, W.P., *Further Reminiscences* (London: Bentley, 1888).

Fryckstedt, Monica Correa, *On the Brink: English Novels of 1866* (Uppsala, Sweden: University of Uppsala, 1989).

Gascoyne, Somers T. *Recollections of Richmond Its Institutions and Their Development* (Richmond: Frederick W. Dimbleby, 1898).

Griest, Guinevere L., *Mudie's Circulating Library and the Victorian Novel* (Newton Abbot: David and Charles, 1970).

Harris, A., *The Little Treasure* (London: Samuel French, c.1880).

Hartman, Mary S., *Victorian Murderesses* (London: Robson Books, 1977; repr. 1985).

Hubin, Alan J., *Crime Fiction: A Comprehensive Bibliography 1749-1990* 2 vols. (New York: Garland, 1994).

Hughs, Winifred, *The Maniac in the Cellar: Sensation Novels of the 1860s* (Princeton, New Jersey: Princeton University Press, 1980).

Jackson, Russell, ed., *Victorian Theatre* (London: A. C. Black, 1989).

James, Louis, *Fiction for the Working Man 1830-1850* (Oxford: Oxford University Press, 1963).

Jay, Harriet, *Robert Buchanan: Some Account of His Life, His Life's Work and His Literary Friendships* (London: T. Fisher Unwin, 1903).

Kalikoff, Beth, *Murder and Moral Decay in Victorian Popular Literature* (Michigan: University of Michigan Research Press, 1986).

Karl, Frederick, *George Eliot* (1995; repr. London: Flamingo, 1996).

Keith, Angus J., *A Scotch Play-House: being the historical records of the Old Theatre Royal, Marishal Street, Aberdeen* (Aberdeen: D. Wyllie & Son, 1878).

Knight, W.G., *A Major London 'Minor': the Surrey Theatre 1805-1865* (London: Society for Theatre Research, 1997).

Lonoff, Sue, *Wilkie Collins and His Victorian Readers* (New York: AMS Press, 1982).

Mckenzie, Judy, ed., *Letters of George Augustus Sala to Edmund Yates* (Queensland: Victorian Fiction Research Guides 19-20, Department of English, University of Southern Queensland, 1993).

Maxwell, W.B., *Time Gathered* (London: Hutchinson, 1937).

Mathews, Charles, *Little Toddlekins* (London: Thomas Hailes, c.1880).

Morland, Nigel, *That Nice Miss Smith* (1957; repr. London: Souvenir Press, 1988).

Mullin, Donald, *Victorian Plays: A Record of Significant Productions on the London Stage, 1837-1901* (New York: Greenwood Press, 1987).

Murch, A.E., *The Development of the Detective Novel* (London: Owen, 1958).

Nicoll, Allardyce, *A History of Late Nineteenth Century Drama 1850-1900* Handlist of plays produced between 1850-1900 vol. II (Cambridge: Cambridge University Press, 1946.

Paget, Francis E., *Lucretia, the Heroine of the Nineteenth Century* (London: Joseph Masters, 1868).

Panton, Mrs. J.E., *Leaves From A Life* (London: Eveleigh Nash, 1908).

Parker, Willis N., *Hurry-Graphs; or, Sketches of Scenery, Celebrities, and Society, Taken From Life* (London: Ward, Lock, 1851).

Peterson, Audrey, *Victorian Masters of Mystery* (New York: Frederick Ungar, 1984).

Porter, H.C., *The History of the Theatres of Brighton from 1774 to 1886* (Brighton: King & Thorne, 1886).

Pykett, Lyn, *The Improper Feminine: The Women's Sensation Novel and the New Woman Writing* (London: Routledge, 1992).

Pykett, Lyn, *The Sensation Novel from The Woman In White to The Moonstone* (Plymouth: Northcote House, 1994).

Rance, Nicholas, *Wilkie Collins and Other Sensation Novelists: Walking the Moral Hospital* (London: Macmillan, 1991).

Redmond, James, Melodrama (Cambridge: Cambridge University Press, 1992).

Rita (Mrs. Desmond Humphries), *Recollections of a Literary Life* (London: Andrew Melrose, 1936).

Robinson, Emma, *Madeline Graham* (1864; repr. London: Maxwell, 1865)

Rowell, George, ed., *Nineteenth century Plays* (1953; repr. Oxford: Oxford University Press, 1987).

Sadleir, Michael, *Things Past* (London: Constable, 1944).

Sadleir, Michael, *XIX Century Fiction. A Bibliographical Record Based on His Own Collection*, 2 vols. (London: Constable, 1951).

Sheahan, James Joseph, *General and Concise History and Description of the Town and Port of Kingston-Upon-Hull* (London: Simpkin Marshall, 1864).

Showalter, Elaine, *A Literature of Their Own: British Women Novelists from Bronte to Lessing* (1977, revised 1982 London: Virago).

Sladen, Douglas, *Twenty Years of My Life* (London: Constable, 1915).

Sladen, Douglas, *My Long Life* (London: Hutchinson, 1939).

432

Slung, Michele, ed., *Crimes on Her Mind: Fifteen Stories of Female Sleuths from the Victorian Era to the Forties* (London: Penguin, 1977).

Stewart, R.F., *...And Always a Detective: Chapters on the History of Detective Fiction* (Newton Abbot: David and Charles, 1980).

Storey, Graham, and Tillotson, Kathleen, ed., *The Letters of Charles Dickens 1856 - 1858*, vol. 8 (Oxford: Clarendon Press, 1995).

Straus, Ralph, *Sala The Portrait of an Eminent Victorian* (London: Constable, 1942).

Summers, Montague, *A Gothic Bibliography* (London: Fortune Press, 1940).

Surtees, Virginia, *The Actress and the Brewer's Wife* (Wilby, Norwich: Michael Russell, 1997).

Sutherland, John, *The Longman Companion to Victorian Fiction* (Harlow, Essex: Longman, 1988).

Symons, Julian, *Bloody Murder* (1972; revised, London: Penguin, 1985).

Taylor, George, ed., *Trilby and Other Plays* (Oxford: Oxford University Press, 1996).

Taylor, Jenny Bourne, *In the Secret Theatre of Home: Wilkie Collins, sensation narrative, and nineteenth century psychology* (London: Routledge, 1988).

Taylor, Tom, *Still Waters Run Deep* (London: Samuel French, c.1880).

Terry, R.C., *Victorian Popular Fiction 1860-1880* (London: Macmillan, 1983).

Thomas, Donald, *Swinburne The Poet in His World* (Oxford: Oxford University Press, 1979).

Tinsley, William, *Random Recollections of a Publisher* 2 vols. (London, Simpkin, Marshall & Co, 1900).

Tomalin, Claire, *The Invisible Woman: The Story of Nelly Ternan and Charles Dickens* (London: Viking, 1990).

Trodd, Anthea, *Domestic Crime in the Victorian Novel* (London: Macmillan, 1989).

Tromp, Marlene, Gilbert, Pamela K., and Haynie, Aeron, ed., *Beyond Sensation: Mary Elizabeth Braddon in Context* (New York: State University of New York Press, 2000).

Underwood, Eric, *Brighton* (London: Batsford, 1978).

Vizetelly, Henry, *Glances Back Through Seventy Years: Autobiographical and Other Reminiscences* 2 vols. (London: Kegan Paul, 1893).

Walbank, Alan, *Queens of the Circulating Library* (London: Evans Brothers, 1950).

Walvin, James, *Victorian Values* (London: Sphere, 1987).

Watson, Colin, *Snobbery With Violence* (London: Methuen, 1971; repr. 1987).

Wilde, E.E., *Ingatestone and the Essex Great Road* (Oxford: Humphrey Milford, 1913).

Wohl, Anthony S., ed., *The Victorian Family* (London: Croom Helm, 1978).

Wolff, Robert Lee, *Sensational Victorian: The Life and Fiction of Mary Elizabeth Braddon* (New York: Garland, 1979).

Wolff, Robert Lee, *Nineteenth-Century Fiction: A Bibliographical Catalogue* 5 vols. (New York: Garland, 1981).

Wood, Marilyn, *Rhoda Broughton* (Stamford: Paul Watkins, 1993).

Yates, Edmund, ed., *Celebrities at Home* 1st series (London: World, 1877)

Yates, Edmund, *Edmund Yates: His Recollections and Experiences*, 2 vols. (London: Richard Bentley, 1884).

Modern Articles and Criticism in Journals

Brantlinger, Patrick, 'What is Sensational about the sensation novel?', *Nineteenth Century Fiction*, vol. 37, 1982, pp.1-28.

Edwards, P.D., 'M.E. Braddon Manuscripts in Australia', *Notes and Queries*, vol. 35, 1988, pp.326-328.

Fahnestock, Jeanne, 'Bigamy: The Rise and Fall of a Convention', *Nineteenth Century Fiction*, vol. 136, 1981, pp.47-71.

Hartman, Mary S., 'Madeline Smith: Murder for Respectability', *Victorian Studies*, vol. 16, June 1973, pp.381-400.

Helfield, Randa, 'Poisonous Plots: Women Sensation Novelists and Murderesses of the Victorian Period', *Victorian Review*, vol. 21, Winter 1995, pp.161-190.

Loftes, W.O.G., and Adley, D. 'A History of "Penny Bloods"', *Book and Magazine Collector*, no. 32, November 1986, pp.48-55.

Robinson, Solveig, 'Editing *Belgravia*: M.E. Braddon's Defense of "Light Literature" ', *Victorian Periodicals Review*, vol. 28, 1995, pp.108-122.

Springhall, John, ' "A Life Story for the People" Edwin J. Brett and the "Low-Life" Penny Dreadfuls of the 1860s', *Victorian Studies*, vol. 33, Winter 1990, pp.223-246.

Summers, Montague, 'Miss Braddon', *Times Literary Supplement*, vol. 41, 29 August 1942, p.432.

Summers, Montague, 'Miss Braddon's Black Band', *Times Literary Supplement*, vol. 42, 24 April 1943, p.204.

Wolff, Robert Lee, ed., 'Devoted Disciple: The Letters of Mary Elizabeth Braddon to Sir Edward Bulwer Lytton, 1862-1873', vol. 12, *Harvard Library Bulletin*, 1974, pp.5-35 and pp.129-161.

Contemporary Articles and Criticism

Other newspapers and magazines consulted for general information include: *Bath Chronicle, Hampshire Independent, Hampshire Advertiser, Era, The Times, Daily News, Lincolnshire Chronicle, Hull Packet, Brighton Gazette, Brighton Herald, Brighton Examiner, Brighton Guardian, Brighton Observer, Brighton Chronicle, Sussex Mercury and Hampshire Chronicle, Coventry Weekly Times, Coventry Herald and Observer, Coventry Standard, Coventry Weekly Times, Royal Leamington Spa Courier and Warwickshire Standard, Doncaster Chronicle, Doncaster, Nottingham and Lincoln Gazette, Leeds and West Riding Express, Beverley Recorder, Beverley Guardian, Court Journal, Thames Valley Times, Richmond and Twickenham Times, Richmond Herald, Halfpenny Journal, Welcome Guest, Temple Bar*, and *Belgravia*.

'Provincial Theatres and Unprincipled Managers', *Era*, 4 March 1855, p.11.

'The Fate of a Heroine', *Brighton Herald*, 5 September 1857, p.4.

'Elopement of a Lady of Fortune', *Brighton Guardian*, 20 October 1858, p.5.

'Three Times Dead', *Brighton Herald*, 18 February 1860, p.4.

'Our Survey of Literature and Science', *Cornhill Magazine*, vol. VII, 1862, pp.134-137.

'Our Female Sensation Novelists', *Christian Remembrancer*, vol. XLVI, 1863, pp.209-236.

'Eleanor's Victory', *Athenaeum*, 19 September 1863, pp.361-362.

'Eleanor's Victory', *Saturday Review*, vol. XVI, 19 September 1863, pp.396-397.

'Sensation Novels', *Medical Critic and Psychological Journal*, vol. III, 1863, pp.513-519.

'John Marchmont's Legacy', *Athenaeum*, 12 December 1863, pp.792-793.

'Our Weekly Gossip', *Athenaeum*, 28 May 1864, p.743.

'Henry Dunbar', *Sixpenny Magazine*, vol. VIII, 8 June 1864, pp.82-84.

'Detectives in Fiction and in Real Life', *Saturday Review*, vol. XVII, 11 June 1864, pp.712-13.

'Henry Dunbar', *Saturday Review*, vol. XVIII, 9 July 1864, pp.64-65.

'Henry Dunbar', *Athenaeum*, 21 May 1864, p.703.

'The Doctor's Wife', *Athenaeum*, 15 October 1864, pp.494-495.

'The Doctor's Wife', *Saturday Review*, vol. XVIII, 5 November 1864, pp.571-572.

'The Road Murder', *Saturday Review*, vol. XIX, 29 April 1865, pp.495-496.

'Miss Forrester', *Athenaeum*, 7 October 1865, p.466.

'Homicidal Heroines', *Saturday Review*, vol. XXI, 7 April 1866, pp.403-405.

'The Trail of the Serpent', *Spectator*, vol. XIX, 11 August 1866, p.891.

'The Manufacture of Novels', *Athenaeum*, 16 February 1867; 23 February, p.254; 2 March, p.290; 9 March, p.323; 16 March, p.354; 23 March, p.387.

'English Authors in America', *Athenaeum*, 11 May 1867, pp.623-624; 18 May, p.663.

'Miss Braddon: The Illuminated Newgate Calendar', *Eclectic Review*, vol. XIX, January 1868, pp.22-40.

'Miss Braddon', *The Mask*, vol. I, June 1868, pp.137-139.

'Miss Braddon in Liverpool', *Porcupine*, 11 April 1874, p.26.

'Genevieve', *Porcupine*, 11 April 1874, p.28.

'A Conscientious Authoress', *World*, 16 September 1874, pp.13-14.

'Miss Braddon as a Bigamist', *New York Times*, 22 November 1874, p.1.

'A Strange World', *Athenaeum*, 16 February 1875, pp. 225-226.

'Death of Mr. Nye Chart', *Brighton Herald*, 24 June 1876, p.3.

'Miss Braddon at the Theatre Royal', *Jersey Express*, 12 August 1876, p.2.

'Theatre Royal', *Jersey Observer*, 15 August 1876, p.2.

'Miss M.E. Braddon at the Theatre Royal', *Jersey Weekly Express*, 19 August 1876, p.10.

'Death of Mrs. Sawyer', *Brighton Herald*, 7 May 1881, p.3.

'Death of Mr. William Sawyer', *Brighton Herald*, 4 November 1882, p.3.

'William Kingston Sawyer', *South London Press*, 4 November 1882, p.1.

'The Late Mr. Sawyer', *South London Press*, 11 November 1882, p.10.

'Suicide of Mr. John Gilby', *Beverley Recorder*, 17 May 1884, p.5.

'Melancholy Death of Mr. John Gilby of Beverley', *Beverley Guardian*, 17 May 1884, p.8.

Untitled piece on Braddon's connection with John Gilby: *Beverley Recorder*, 24 May 1884, p.4.

'Wyllard's Weird', *Athenaeum*, 21 March 1885, p.371.

'Mudie's Library', *Leisure Hour*, 1886, pp.187-189.

'Death of Mr. John Maxwell', *Richmond and Twickenham Times*, 9 March 1895, p.6.

'Miss Braddon, An Enquiry', *Academy: A Weekly Review of Literature and Life*, vol. LVII, 14 October 1899, pp.431-432.

'His Darling Sin', *Spectator*, 4 November 1899, vol. LXXXIII. p.662.

'Miss Braddon's Birthday. How the Author of "Lady Audley's Secret" Writes Her Novels', *Daily Mail*, 4 October 1901, p.7.

'Death of Sir Edward Braddon', *Tasmanian Mail*, 6 February 1904, p.32.

'My First Time in Print', *Grand Magazine*, vol. I, May 1905, pp.537-538.

'Miss Braddon at Home', *Daily Telegraph*, 4 October 1913, p.9.

'Death of Miss Braddon', *Daily Telegraph*, 5 February 1915, pp.9-10.

'Miss Braddon', *The Times*, 5 February 1915, p.9.

'Death of Miss Braddon: A Typical English Novelist', *The Times*, February 1915, pp.11-12.

'Death of Miss Braddon', *Morning Post*, 5 February 1915, p.4.

'A Famous Novelist: Death of Miss Braddon', *Glasgow Herald*, 5 February 1915, p.11.

'Death of Miss Braddon. Great Victorian Novelist: Tributes by Novelists of To-Day', *Daily Mail*, 5 February 1915, p.3.

'The Late Miss Braddon and Beverley', *Beverley Recorder and Independent*, 6 February 1915, p.5.

'Death of Miss Braddon. The Famous Novelist's Associations With Beverley', *Beverley Guardian*, 6 February 1915, p.2.

'Death of Miss Braddon', *Richmond and Twickenham Times*, 6 February 1915, p.6.

'Death of Miss Braddon', *Richmond Herald*, 6 February 1915, p.5.

'The Late Miss Braddon: funeral at Richmond', *Thames Valley Times*, 10 February 1915, p.2.

'The Late Miss Braddon', *Richmond Herald*, 13 February 1915, p. 12.

Adams, Charles F., 'Miss Braddon's Novels', *Dublin University Magazine*, vol. LXXV, April 1870, pp.436-445.

Braddon, M.E., 'At the Shrine of Jane Eyre', *Pall Mall Magazine*, vol. XXXVII, 1906, pp.174-176.

Braddon, M.E., 'My First Novel. The Trail of the Serpent', *Idler*, vol. III, 1893, pp.19-30.

Braddon, M.E., 'In the Days of My Youth', *Theatre*, vol. XXIV, 24 September 1894, pp.120-125.

Braddon, M.E., 'Fifty Years at the Lyceum', *Strand Magazine*, vol. XXV, January 1903, pp.36-40.

Braddon, M.E., 'The Woman I Remember, *The Press Album* (London: John Murray, 1909), pp.3-6.

Collins, Wilkie, 'The Unknown Public', *Household Words*, vol. VIII, 21 August 1858, pp.217-222.

Dickens, Mary Angela, 'Miss Braddon At Home', *Windsor Magazine*, vol. VI, September 1897, pp.415-418.

Hatton, Joseph, 'Miss Braddon At Home. A Sketch and an Interview', *London Society*, January 1888, pp.22-29.

Hatton, Joseph, 'Miss Braddon. Some Reminiscences of Lichfield House', *The People*, 31 August 1902, p.3.

Hoey, Mrs. Cashel, 'A Glance at Miss Braddon's Work', *World*, 25 April 1905, p.713.

Holland, Clive, 'Fifty Years of Novel Writing. Miss Braddon at Home', *Pall Mall Magazine*, November 1911, pp.697-709.

Holland, Clive, 'Miss Braddon: The Writer and Her Work', *Bookman*, vol. XLII, July 1912, pp.149-157.

Humberstone, F.W., 'Miss Braddon and Coventry', *Coventry Herald*, 12 February 1915, p.5.

Mansel, Henry, 'Sensation Novels', *Quarterly Review*, vol. CXIII, April 1863, pp. 481-514.

Oliphant, Mrs., 'Sensation Novels', *Blackwood's Edinburgh Magazine*, vol. XCI, May 1862, pp.564-584.

Oliphant, Mrs., 'Novels', *Blackwood's Edinburgh Magazine*, vol. CII, September 1867, pp.257-280.

Oliver, David, 'The Late Miss Braddon. An Appreciation', *Hull Times*, 13 February 1915, p.3.

Payn, James, 'Penny Fiction', *Nineteenth Century*, vol. IX, January 1881, pp.245-154.

Rae, W. Fraser, 'Sensation Novelists: Miss Braddon', *North British Review*, vol. XLIII, September 1865, pp.180-204.

Robinson, F.M., 'My First Book', *Idler*, vol. III, 1893, pp.205-212.

Sala, George Augustus, 'On the "Sensational" in Literature and Art', *Belgravia*, vol. IX, 1868, pp.449-458.

Sala. George Augustus, 'The Cant of Modern Criticism', *Belgravia*, vol. IV, November 1867, pp.45-55.

Sala, George Augustus, 'Griselda: A Study at the Princess Theatre', *Belgravia*, vol. XXII, pp.246-256.

Wright, Thomas, 'Concerning the Unknown Public', *Nineteenth Century*, vol. XIII, February 1883, pp.279-296.

Manuscript Material

Robert Lee Wolff Collection of Victorian Fiction, Harry Ransom Humanities Research Center, The University of Texas at Austin.

Letters from M.E. Braddon in the Bram Stoker Correspondence, Brotherton Library, University of Leeds.

T.H.S. Escott papers, British Library, Add.Mss.58786.

Bolton Evening News Archive, Bolton Central Library, Greater Manchester.

A.P. Watt Collection (#11036) General and Literary Manuscripts, Wilson Library, The University of North Carolina at Chapel Hill.

Letters from Braddon to Edward Bulwer Lytton, Hertfordshire Archives and Local Studies Office (D/ELC12/119).

Although I was not able to see them, the Houghton Library at Harvard University has Braddon notebooks and manuscripts (used by Robert Lee Wolff in his biography), and the State Library of Tasmania has the manuscripts of 29 of Braddon's novels (as documented by P.D. Edwards in *Notes and Queries*).